Transition to Capitalism?

Transition to Capitalism?

THE COMMUNIST LEGACY IN EASTERN EUROPE

János Mátyás Kovács
EDITOR

Transaction Publishers
New Brunswick (U.S.A.) and London (U.K.)

Library of Congress Catalog Number: 93–50827
ISBN: 1–56000–167–4 (cloth)
Printed in the United States of America

Library of Congress Cataloging-in-Publication Data

Transition to capitalism? : the communist legacy in Eastern Europe / edited by János Mátyás Kovács.
p. cm.
Includes bibliographical references and index.
ISBN 1–56000–167–4 (cloth)
1. Europe, Eastern—Social conditions. 2. Privatization—Europe, Eastern. 3. Mixed economy—Europe, Eastern. 4. Europe, Eastern—Economic conditions—1989– 5. Post-communism—Europe, Eastern.
I. Kovács, János Mátyás.
HN380.7.A8T74 1994
306'.0947—dc20 93–50827
CIP

Contents

II. Democracy and/or Liberalism: On the Politics of Transformation

III. From Civil Society to Civil Disobedience? On the Sociology of Transformation

IV. Comparative Perspectives

Contributors

PETER L. BERGER, Institute for the Study of Economic Culture, Boston University

IVAN BERNIK, Department of Sociology, Ljubljana University

ANDRÁS BOZÓKI, Department of Political Science, Central European University, Budapest

LÁSZLÓ BRUSZT, Department of Political Science, Central European University, Budapest

MARTIN BÚTORA, Department of Sociology and Social Policy, Faculty of Social Sciences, Charles University, Prague

ZORA BÚTOROVÁ, Center for Social Analysis, Bratislava

GYÖRGY CSEPELI, Institute of Sociology, Eötvös University, Budapest

ISTVÁN R. GÁBOR, Department of Labour Economics, Budapest University of Economics; Visiting Professor, Budapest College

VLADIMIR GLIGOROV, Institute of Economics, Belgrade; Visiting Professor, University of Uppsala

JAN T. GROSS, Department of Politics, New York University

OLGA GYÁRFÁSOVÁ, Center for Social Analysis, Bratislava

JÁNOS MÁTYÁS KOVÁCS, Institute for Human Sciences, Vienna; Institute of Economics, Hungarian Academy of Sciences, Budapest

Marcin Król, Res Publica, Warsaw

Barry B. Levine, Department of Sociology, Florida International University, Miami

Antal Örkény, Institute of Sociology, Eötvös University, Budapest

Jerzy Osiatynski, former Minister of Finance; Institute of the History of Science, Polish Academy of Sciences, Warsaw

George Schöpflin, Department of Government, London School of Economics

Endre Sik, Institute of Political Studies, Budapest

David Stark, Department of Sociology, Cornell University, Ithaca

Robert P. Weller, Institute for the Study of Economic Culture, Boston University

Introduction: Official and Alternative Legacies

János Mátyás Kovács

"Hangover in the Eastern Bloc", "The Revolution Devours Its Own Children", "Wild-East Nationalism", "Balkanization of Eastern Europe", "Civil Society Under State Control"—one rarely opens a newspaper in London or Prague, Tokyo or Budapest without such headlines during the last three years. While 1989 was a euphoric year of political revolutions in Eastern Europe, 1990 and 1991 saw a growing disillusionment with the long-awaited Great Transformation. According to many analysts, the big question of the years 1992 and 1993 was whether anything one might be proud of from among the achievements of 1989 has survived. By now frustration is deep-seated not only in the mass media but also in scholarly and political communities.

Liberals and conservatives are concerned about the collectivist-statist leanings of the new political elites in Eastern Europe and the survival/comeback of the communist nomenklatura. Furthermore, they are apprehensive about the twists and turns of economic deregulation and the sluggish establishment of the rule of law in the new democracies. Social democrats are shocked by the harsh stabilization measures of the first non-communist governments, the lack of welfare guarantees, and the weakness of industrial democracy in the former socialist countries. Christian-Democrats in the West discover that their sister parties in Eastern Europe tend to adopt authoritarian-nationalist-populist policies. Finally, a great number of social scientists all over the world, who had put much faith in one of the unexplored "Third

Roads" the former communist states might take during the 1990s, have been frustrated seeing that those roads may lead back to the 1930s. Weimarization and Balkanization have become fashionable labels in the literature.

Quite a few observers claim that most of the predictions that were made prior to 1989 about the fate of Eastern Europe have proven misleading: the markets are still under state tutelage and being dominated by post-communist mafias; the parliaments are run by the old-new ruling oligarchies; the state replaces civil society, just as chauvinism replaces patriotism, or church bureaucracy religion. Imitation—frequently of outdated patterns—serves as a substitute for social innovation. Invention is suppressed by improvization, spontaneous evolution by social engineering. Many of the anti-communist heroes of yesterday have become anti-heroes of post-communism today.

As paradoxical as it may be, Eastern Europe can provide everyone with a sufficient amount of pessimism, regardless of whether they come from the East or the West, from the left or the right. Of course, the cool-headed analyst might point out how exaggerated the preliminary expectations about the political revolutions were, and why wishful thinking has resulted in general disillusionment and over-anxiety. Unfortunately, pessimism resists such comparisons and implies a blanket characterization of countries, which were considerably different from each other already under communism. The heterogeneity of the countries' pasts notwithstanding, most recent studies of Eastern Europe exclusively focus on *current economic and political details* of the transformation processes. They also tend to overlook the huge gap between the pre-1989 and 1989 transition programs and the post-1989 reality, as well as the lessons drawn by the "transformers" (the agents of the transformation) from the mistaken predictions. Yet, the fact that none of the once celebrated scenarios—neoliberal breakthrough, all-out social-democratization, renaissance of the civil society, etc.—have been implemented so far might suggest that the legacy of the *ancien régime*, i.e., the point of departure for the transition from socialism, was widely misinterpreted.

The greatest calculation errors probably occurred in the estimation of the *unofficial ("alternative," "positive")* rather than the "official" part of the legacy of the Soviet-type systems. Understandably, in order to find the proper agents of the transformation, the scenario writers searched for the embryo of the new order in the womb of the old one. Although the majority of them stressed that the transformation would basically start from scratch—in other words, that the official legacy of the old regime was to be of no use—they entertained hopes about the alternative "heirlooms" of real socialism, optimistically assuming that those would *sui generis* promote the transition processes.

The word "transition" was used in the singular to stress the basic similarities in the direction of change. "The common destination is capitalism", many analysts said, more exactly, a kind of *Western* capitalism somewhere between Margaret Thatcher and Willy Brandt. Communism will disappear for good, and although in the near future there may occur shorter or longer detours in Eastern European history, it is democracy, rule of law, private property and the market that will be the final products of the transformation.

To be sure, the communist heritage was not disregarded under the spell of the 1989 euphoria. It was rather divided into active and inactive parts. The components of the official legacy, i.e., the systemic features of communist economies and polities such as large-scale nationalization, obsolete industrial structures, environmental pollution, huge state bureaucracies and lack of entrepreneurial spirit, were regarded as factors which—due to their inertia—would in the beginning slow down the transition to capitalism. However, it was also assumed rather optimistically that they would not be able to re-invigorate themselves. Essentially, they were seen as the *inactive* (deactivated) trash of the old system, ready for removal. Many observers believed that it would depend only on the capacity of the garbage collector as to when the trash would finally be burnt or recycled.

Ironically, this approach to the remnants of the previous regime reminds the observer of the way in which early communist theorists had expected the "evaporation" of the feudo-capitalist heritage in Eastern Europe after the war. Just as those theorists had been unable to predict the rebirth of liberalism under communist rule, the early post-communist transformers failed to foresee the survival or renaissance of collectivism in our days.

The *active* part of the communist legacy was associated with the non-systemic features of the former regimes, ranging from "peaceful" networks of informal business activity to militant anti-communist political organizations. These factors were supposed to support the transition to capitalism at least as vigorously as they had contributed to the demise of the old system. It was widely presumed that this—unofficial—part of the legacy would not have to be deactivated after 1989. On the contrary, it must be given free room to develop and adjust to the new conditions. Capitalism means markets; why, then, could not the illegal or semi-legal transactions in the planned economy be converted to legal ones in market economies? Capitalism means democracy; why could not the independent trade unions, civic initiatives, patriotic movements find a place in the new political configuration?

The naively optimistic message of these questions was usually based on the umbrella concept of "civil society" (second society) that gained enormous popularity in East and West during the 1980s. There were theorists who trusted in the liberal (entrepreneurial) strength of the *shadow economy*; others believed in the democratic force of the *new social* (national, peace, trade union, etc.) *movements* in Eastern Europe; again others assumed that the *reformist elites* of late socialism would remain important catalysts of change even after the political revolutions; and also there were many who based their optimism on those legal attitudes, moral values, religious beliefs and everyday forms of behaviour which could survive as a kind of counter-culture in the "*niches*" of the old regime. Some of the analysts even predicted that this unofficial heritage—as soon as it came to light—would broaden the institutional and cultural repertoire of advanced industrial societies, too.

While one could easily foresee that most of the surviving systemic features of the Soviet-type economies and polities would hamper the starting moves of the transition, many observers presumed that the alternative (secondary, parallel, informal, shadow) characteristics of planned economy and one-party rule would fit in well with the new world of market economy and parliamentary democracy. Now, recognizing the friction in this adjustment (resistance of the shadow economy to privatization, conflicts between the former opposition movements and the new parties, independent trade unions blocking economic liberalization, national emancipation leading to civil wars, etc.), even the disciples of the "civil society" school begin to admit that—in addition to the official remnants of the Soviet-type system—its alternative legacy may also *inhibit* economic and political liberalization. What was instrumental in undermining the old communist regimes may not always contribute to the integration of new democratic ones.

Why did these theorists overestimate the liberal capacity of the unofficial heirlooms of real socialism? Why did they ignore the expressly collectivist-statist components of the counter-culture? What happened to the alternative legacy in the last couple of years? What kind of transformation programs grew out of it, and how did they work or fail during the first stages of the transition?

What had been used in the singular became plural. Eastern Europe in 1993/94 is witnessing *transitions* instead of one single kind of transition. We may even apply the term "transformations" to express a variety of changes without clear and predetermined directions.

In 1989, no serious analyst believed, of course, that the transition process would turn out to be one-dimensional. Complex societal systems have been undergoing change from Warsaw to Ljubljana, from the Central Planning Office down to the smallest village council, from military doctrines to family behavior. Nevertheless, it was generally expected that the changes in the individual dimensions would point in the same direction and thus reinforce each other.

Synergy was a premise in the logic of transition. In the economy, stabilization, marketization, privatization and restructuring were believed to support each other and result in growth and modernization. In the political system, competitive democracy and the rule of law seemed to be a winning combination promoted by local self-government, industrial democracy and—in the case of multi-ethnic states—by new (con)federal arrangements. As far as the social aspects of the transition were concerned, comprehensive Social Contracts were envisaged between the social partners, and a new entrepreneurial culture and the principle of solidarity seemed compatible with each other and with other principles such as environmentalism. These three spheres of society—economic, political and social—were expected to trigger mutual positive feedback. The well-known dilemmas of economic liberalism versus political democracy, freedom versus equality, etc., seemed to be solved through the process of conversion to capitalism.

Perhaps the most frustrating lesson to learn from the first stages of the post-communist transformation has been that the synergetic effects are frequently neutralized or offset by conflicts between the changes. To cite the one example that has probably most embarrassed the liberal economists in Eastern Europe recently: market reforms (e.g., price liberalization) have often counteracted privatization; at the same time, private property has sometimes contributed to the perpetuation of distorted markets. If such—inherently compatible—transformative tasks as privatization and marketization can disrupt each other, many transformers nowadays ask, how one could expect even limited harmony between, for example, these tasks and stabilization policies, not to mention the establishment of the rule of law or social justice.

* * *

As a contrast to the mainstream of current historiography of Eastern European transition, many of the chapters in this collection take a *history-of-ideas approach* to seek answers to questions like these. The aim of our research group[1] is to observe how the main theoretical paradigms, political ideologies and social values, applied by the scholars and politicians of Eastern Europe in understanding the communist heritage, have changed throughout the period of transformation, and continue to do so. Unlike most of the TD (Transition to Democracy) projects that have mushroomed in the last three years, our research group was *not* organised for the sake of a one-conference program; a program which tried to cover every possible aspect of the transformation under a comprehensive title such as "Why has communism fallen so rapidly, and why is capitalism emerging so slowly in Eastern Europe?" On the contrary, many of the members of the group have been working together on case studies of the transformation during the past three years, and they continue to observe the intellectual developments of the transition in the long run.

In principle, every transition process can derail in at least three ways: (a) if the transformer miscalculates his starting position; (b) if he chooses an unfeasible destination; and (c) if he insists on improper means and non-viable sequences of measures in managing change. In our research project we have decided to begin with the study of the *points of departure* of post-communist transformation. At this juncture, we try to reinterpret those alternative institutions, movements, ideologies, values, etc., which allegedly contributed to the erosion of the old regimes in Eastern Europe. As a result of this, one can arrive at a new typology of the heritage. The authors, a number of whom work as practicing transformers, portray the unofficial legacy of communism without nostalgia. They do not long for the good old days of anti-communist solidarity within the opposition and do not feel particularly sorry for the alternative movements which—like Winston Churchill—won the war but lost the peace.

Instead of gloomy prophecies about the "betrayal of the revolution", the reader will find quite a few cautiously optimistic predictions in this collection. Legacies are elastic social phenomena. Eastern Europe is currently witnessing, for example, how rapidly the members of the former *nomenklatura*, who were always considered a rigid component of the official heritage of communism, have turned into new entrepreneurs. Why should we exclude then the possibility of flexible adjustment in the case of the alternative heirlooms which already showed great variability under the old system?

* * *

Our book consists of *four parts*. The first three parts cover the economic, political and sociological dimensions of the transformation. The fourth one includes comparative observations on the basis of Latin American and South-East Asian experiences.

I

In the first part István Gábor examines why—contrary to the various theories of post-communist embourgeoisement—the private entrepreneurs of the "socialist" shadow economy in Hungary are reluctant to become pioneers of marketization and privatization despite the legal recognition of the freedom of private ownership. They are accustomed to weak competitors in the form of the state enterprises, to behind-the-scene transactions and to monopolistic behaviour. Therefore, any populist third-road strategy based on the further protection of this sector from foreign capital by the state may invalidate the overall liberalization of the economy.

János Mátyás Kovács portrays the intellectual heritage of the economic reformers of the old regimes in Eastern Europe, emphasizing the elements of continuity in their sociological status and theoretical attitude on their way to becoming transformers. Some years ago they did their best to modernize the Soviet-type system from above through regulating the market but—in most cases unintentionally—they contributed to the system's demise. In the author's opinion, instead of a kind of "Eastern neoliberalism" that has been predicted in the West, we rather see in the new democracies a large array of economists with a continued strong inclination for state intervention and social engineering.

Relying on the experiences of shock therapy in Poland, Jerzy Osiatynski provides a revision of the thesis, widely accepted in scholarly circles before 1989, that radical market reforms would be blocked by the "natural" resistance of the population. For a short period, the Poles were ready to accept a series of painful stabilization measures taken by the new government. To a great extent, this was due to the strength of the alternative political heritage of the Solidarity movement, and the temporary consensus created favourable conditions for economic liberalization. Another consequence of the same heritage, namely the replacement of the communist nomenklatura by the Solidarity elite in large segments of the state economy may, however, become an obstacle to further deregulation.

In their twin essay that connects the first two parts of the collection László Bruszt and David Stark take a genetic approach to explain the differences between the various types of privatization strategies and transformative policies in Eastern Europe by means of the diverse institutional legacies of the countries leaving socialism behind. After having compared the types of privatization in Czechoslovakia, the former GDR, Hungary and Poland, Stark concludes that the choice between statist versus market strategies for dismantling the public sector is also highly dependent on the mode of political extrication from real socialism in the given country. Thus, in Hungary the long reformist-liberal past of economic guidance may be counter-balanced by the interventionism of the new government; the opposite tendency may occur in Czechoslovakia; the Polish tradition of workers' self-management may restrain the privatization efforts of the liberal government, etc. In a word, the alternative heritage in economic matters does not inform the observer properly about the future paths of the overall transition.

II

This is the main message of Bruszt's paper, too, which provides a dynamic typology of the transformation programs in Eastern Europe.

In this typology the countries are arranged according to the speed of the transition and the ways of interaction between state and society in managing change. No matter how broad popular support was inherited by the new governments from the unofficial movements of the "civil society", says the author, the sympathy has in the meantime rapidly eroded. This calls for new Social Contracts, in which the terms of incorporating some old alternative heirlooms will be essentially redefined.

András Bozóki attributes the fragility of the new democracy in Hungary to a considerable extent to the political legacy of the Kádár regime. As a contrast to Poland, civil society in Hungary was characterized by "individualistic" economic strategies of survival rather than by political self-organization and mobilization. Nevertheless, even this late-socialist entrepreneurial culture is evidently not sufficient to avert economic crisis, the greatest danger in democratic transition. Because the new political elite can only partly derive legitimacy from its oppositionist heritage, it is difficult for it to neutralise the authoritarian-populist tendencies produced by economic hardships.

In his chapter Vladimir Gligorov examines the political spectrum in former Yugoslavia from the point of view of the breakdown of the political space of communism and the emergence of state nationalism. The alternative political movements became nationalist parties almost without exception. As a result, civil society has lost its strength that was not great anyway. The old collectivist structures were replaced by new nationalist, authoritarian ones, and the heritage of dissident liberalism could not grow into a right-wing democratic-liberal movement. In Gligorov's view the present civil war was preprogrammed by the conditions of the first Yugoslav state in the Balkans and there is no constitutional solution for the conflict based on a liberal approach to rights. What has been "left" from communism is not "right", concludes the author ironically.

Jan Gross is also concerned about the fate of the unofficial political legacy of the old system. In his opinion, the former opposition forces of Poland have proven unable to gain sufficient legitimation in their new democratic roles. Solidarity is swinging between its old anti-statist position and the daily requirements of establishing itself as a political authority. Moreover, the new order cannot get rid of the moral burden of the "illegal" roundtable deal made with the communists on important constitutional issues. This provides an opportunity for authoritarian-populist leaders to occupy large segments of the political space. The recent victory of the ex-communist parties in the parliamentary elections proves the legitimation deficit of the liberal forces.

National ideals, family, religion, etc.—these elements of conservative culture were supposed to accelerate liberal transformation after 1989. The alternative heritage of political conservatism, however, seems not to follow the dominant Western patterns, says George Schöpflin in his chapter. Rather the conservative thinkers of Eastern Europe in our days turn to the prewar illiberal traditions, to a kind of "underdeveloped" conservative culture in seeking answers to the questions of the future. Thus, despite the fact that the new conservatives situate themselves on the right, they are inclined to think in "leftist" (statist, collectivist) terms.

III

In the third part of the collection, Ivan Bernik re-interprets the role of the former marginal intellectuals, bearers of a large part of the unofficial heritage, in the light of the political revolution in Slovenia. Their influence became crucial (as compared with that of the technocracy) at the moment of change. Nevertheless, it decreased drastically during the establishment of post-revolutionary institutions. Messianism, non-conformism, innovativeness, etc., are not bestsellers in this phase; the former oppositionists are dispersed among the new parties; and their basic ideological differences are not obscured any more by a uniform anti-communist position. They have become just one small group of the new political actors.

In his chapter Marcin Król examines how the liberals might react to the reemergence of the church in Poland as a kind of "state authority". The author, who ironically calls himself an angel's advocate, considers the new hegemonic attempts of the church, a former adversary of communist hegemony, a natural consequence of Catholic teachings. Therefore, he rejects the possibility of both "liberalizing" the Catholic tradition and "catholicizing" the liberal heritage of the former opposition movements. Moreover, he suggests that a strict division of labour between the "law" and the "soul", a kind of *modus vivendi* between the liberal political forces and the church, may help avoid the former allies from becoming enemies in the period of the transition. The failure of the Christian parties in the 1993 elections provides lessons for both sides.

Martin Bútora, Zora Bútorová, and Olga Gyárfásová explain how nationalist legacies in Slovakia contributed to the "velvet divorce" of the two nations of Czechoslovakia. These legacies, rooted in pre-communist times, were reinforced by real socialism. The alternative movements, which were predominantly liberal, underestimated the vigor of nationalism in Slovakia. This paved the way for a political regime based on a combination of post-communist and nationalist forces; a combination of the official and unofficial legacies of communism.

The unofficial liberal heritage of communism in Hungary is surveyed in Antal Örkény's and György Csepeli's chapter by means of opinion research. Contrary to the expectations of social scientists, liberal values were represented by the tiny groups of urban intellectuals in the former opposition rather than by the millions of real participants of the late-Kádárist "socialist" market. Furthermore, the latter's views have become increasingly inconsistent during the first years of the transition: in the deep economic crisis the "Sleeping Beauty" of socialist-egalitarian values may wake up at any moment, and nationalist aspirations also have started to suppress the remaining liberal beliefs of the population. In short, the unofficial legacy of communism must be much more ambiguous than the analysts thought at the very outset of the transformation.

At the first glance, the case study written by Endre Sik about the Hungarian taxi drivers' strike of October 1990 seems to contradict the above thesis. The author portrays the strike, which was regarded by many as the first sign of large-scale civil disobedience against the new governments in Eastern Europe, as a normal corporatist action of interest representation. He derives the bargaining power of the taxi drivers from the late-socialist milieu of the Hungarian 1980s favourable for small entrepreneurship. Nevertheless, this entrepreneurial heritage also includes monopolistic techniques that were used to counter-balance state intervention under the old regime. The same techniques can be applied, however, to endanger the fragile institutions of the rule of law as well.

IV

The last part of the volume contains three comments made by scholars who look at the Eastern European transition from the perspective of European history, as well as of Latin American and Asian studies.

Peter L. Berger selects four cases (nationalism, the church, intellectuals and the shadow economy) to show how former virtues may become obstacles to post-communist transformation. This metamorphosis also stems from the fact that in Eastern Europe two distinct processes of transition are combined: the transition from socialism to capitalism and the transition from dictatorship to democracy. Comparative studies demonstrate, however, that the relationship between capitalism and democracy is asymmetrical. Furthermore, capitalism historically has tended to precede democracy (cf. most of the Asian cases of the transformation). If the establishment of democratic institutions precedes capitalist development, those who suffer the unavoidable economic pains of the transition may organise themselves to block marketization.

Barry Levine seeks Latin American analogies in his paper. However, it is very difficult to find examples of successful economic transformation on that subcontinent, and even the success stories (Mexico, Puerto Rico, Chile) are politically ambiguous. In these countries economic modernization was managed by authoritarian-interventionist regimes. At the same time, if Eastern Europe succeeded in linking political liberties with the market, this would be greeted with great acclaim in the developing world. In any event, the Latin America expert has already seen so many attempts at importing development schemes from the modern world that the only thing he can predict is that "what is transferred will be transformed": i.e., the transition from socialism will certainly surprise the social scientists with a new bunch of evolution patterns in the future.

Finally, Robert Weller's comments originate in that part of the world where the most spectacular examples of rapid capitalist transformation can be found in our time, East Asia. The fact that currently in Eastern Europe even part of the unofficial legacy of communism seems to inhibit the transformation process must not disappoint the observer. For in East Asia sometimes even official remnants of the pre-capitalist systems promoted the transformation. Family ties, patronage networks, religion, etc., could be used for new purposes instead of throwing them away. Marketization and privatization gained legitimacy from their final economic success in retrospect rather than from a democratic process running parallel to them.

Note

1. The Vienna Institute for Human Sciences launched a comparative project on contemporary economic and political thought in Eastern Europe in 1988 (cf. J.M. Kovács & M. Tardos (eds), *Reform and Transformation in Eastern Europe. Soviet-Type Economics on the Threshold of Change,* Routledge, London 1992). This research program was continued and enlarged first by the Institute's "Rediscovery of Liberalism in Eastern Europe" project in 1990 (cf. the special issue of *Eastern European Politics and Societies,* Winter 1991), then by the "Transitions to Democracy?" project from 1991 on. The Institute for the Study of Economic Culture at Boston University showed interest in our long-term research efforts and generously supported the preparations of this volume. Our book owes a great deal to Rosemarie Winkler and Elisabeth Zickbauer who so carefully prepared the manuscript for publication.

I

Entrepreneurs, Reformers, and Privatizers: On the Economics of Transformation

1

Modernity or a New Kind of Duality? Second Thoughts about the "Second Economy"

István R. Gábor

> Bourgeois development in Hungary suffered a setback of decades. In the form of household farming, a legal private activity of widening scope in the second economy resurged in traces from as far back as the 1960s. This course of embourgeoisement now has good chances to gather speed . . . But, even in case of acceleration, a full-fledged and mature private sector will take long years or even decades to establish. (Kornai [1989] p. 24)

> Both the old and the new elites are hesitating in how much they wish to have a new national bourgeoisie . . . it looks so obvious how economic decline or collapse could be avoided. Even if they do not bother about the state economy, simply by giving a free hand to that 25 percent of Hungarian citizens whose desire is a private undertaking they could release incredible sources of economic dynamism. (Szelényi [1989] p. 34)

Perhaps the most important result of the past one decade and a half of research on the second economy[1] in Hungary was the refutation of those early interpretations which had regarded this subeconomy as alien to socialism and thus transient, representing a remnant of the capitalist past, or a consequence of some technical imperfections of economic planning. Investigations from the late 1970s through the 1980s served to demonstrate the systemic character of the second economy, thereby revealing some systemic characteristics of the first economy as well.

However, at the end of the 1980s, when the transformation into a capitalist market economy became the order of the day, the very term "second economy" as a category closely linked to the declining state-socialist order was claimed to have lost its relevance. Nevertheless, this devaluation of the concept proved to be temporary. The initial difficulties of the transformation have provoked a renewed interest in the second economy.[2] These difficulties show the existence of a relatively large private economy as a "positive" legacy of socialism, and also the imprints that the past decades of state-socialist development have left on this economy and on the "memory" of its participants. Both aspects of the legacy of the second economy must be examined before we can reassess the potential evolutionary role of private entrepreneurship and small-scale production.

The Development of the Second Economy in Hungary

The history of this subeconomy dates back roughly to the mid-1960s. By then, as a result of repeated drives launched against private forms of production, all but a small minority of the active population was absorbed in the socialist sector. Paradoxically, it is precisely with this absorption that we can begin to speak of the process of organization of small businesses into an increasingly coherent market-oriented subsystem that coexists with the socialist sector in a symbiotic, i.e., partly complementary, partly competitive, relationship.

The first impulse to massive participation in the second economy was given by the rapid rise of living standards during the second part of the 1960s and by the relaxation of the policy of isolation from the West. Both lent momentum to the spread of consumption-oriented behaviour and of an instrumental relationship to work. With the concentration of the peasantry in large agricultural enterprises and the influx of huge masses of peasants into the manufacturing and building industries, the traditional rural values practically lost ground and gave way to acquisitive attitudes.

The most prominent factors supporting this development include the abolition of legal restrictions on change of workplace as a step preparatory to the 1968 reform, the appearance of a global labour shortage and, in the first years of reform, thanks to the recognition of the economic role of small business,[3] a more tolerant attitude towards private initiative. Those developments provided wider scope for calculative household strategies, including participation in the second economy.[4]

The Hungarian government cherished the hope that the reforms of the first economy would entail a decline of the second economy. Yet the second economy continued to expand in the 1970s, though, parallel with the cycle of the reform process, its administrative treatment changed from time to time. Restrictive and denouncing campaigns, with consequential short supplies, were followed by hastily adopted corrective measures to improve conditions for the second economy.[5]

Towards the end of the 1970s, the worsening prospects for economic growth prompted the political leadership to be more consistent in reckoning with the lasting raison d'être of the second economy. The fear from the worsening of supplies for the population and from the lack of small undertakings as potential subcontractors were also contributing to this policy change.

The change was reflected in a proliferation of legal forms of individual and collective small-scale enterprises, a widening range of business lines in the second economy, a lifting of some restrictions on their expansion, a simplification of the procedures for the authorization of new businesses, etc. The more balanced course of policy, coupled with economic pressures exerted on households by diminishing real wages, resulted in an unprecedentedly massive participation in the second economy by the late 1980s.

The advance of the second economy was accompanied by a falling ratio of full-time participation in it, a process which was in line with government intentions up to the second part of the 1970s. This trend, however, continued even in the 1980s. Only those of the new forms sanctioned in the early 1980s proved popular which could be combined with employment in the socialist sector or at least required no sizable financial investment.[6]

Dilemmas of Regulation

That the more pragmatic course of policy in the early 1980s could only bring about modest improvements may be traced ultimately to the "schizophrenic split" of the Hungarian economy. Two economies—a mostly large-scale socialist sector and a mostly small-scale entrepreneurial sector—were operating on different principles and regulated in different ways. By this we mean profound differences in the relative roles played by market coordination (money and prices) and bureaucratic coordination (hierarchical dependence and state paternalism).

Owing to the shortage-economy nature of the first economy in general, and to its chronic excess demand for labour in particular,[7] any increase in the volume of work performed in the second economy acted to relieve pressure on the first economy, to raise the standard of living and to mitigate shortages. At the same time, however, earnings acquired through the second economy weakened the incentive power of wages and eroded government control over income distribution. The more so since in a wide range of activities the second economy, thanks to its market-sensitiveness, had a definite advantage over the first economy in terms of the size of income that could be earned by a given amount of work, even if no rent-type or entrepreneurial income was acquired.

With this particular relationship of complementarity/competition that existed between the two economies, the government was left with the triple dilemma of (1) stimulating private activities while trying to keep incomes in parity with wage rates in the public sector; (2) stimulating private accumulation while seeking to restrict income differentials deriving from capital investments; (3) preserving the market-sensitive and self-financing character of small farms and plants while integrating them with the monopolistic organizations of the first economy. As a consequence of these dilemmas, periodical shifts were bound to occur in the official treatment of the second economy.[8]

This varying treatment gave rise to anomalies. In the first place, it contributed to the erosion of business morality: those acting in the second economy tended to strive for quick enrichment instead of pursuing a longer-term business policy. Secondly, it forced them to build up bribed connections in order to moderate the uncertainties of state regulation. Thirdly, it made full-time participation and business investments in the second economy marginal. Finally, while government restrictions were normally called forth by the "allegedly" excessive income differentiation, it was mostly those with exceptionally high incomes who had the financial reserves and personal connections necessary to weather these restrictions. This pattern of regulation blurred the boundary between legal and nonlegal transactions in second economy.

The shortage economy of the socialist sector perpetuated a state of affairs in which second economy units simply could not prosper without having recourse to illegal means in obtaining the necessary inputs. This led to the establishment of an extensive system of corruption sanctioned by custom (and not readily available to potential new entrants). Consequently, mute complicity as a rule of behaviour was continuously reinforced.

Dual Livelihood Strategies and the Labour Market

Since it was largely the same households that acquired income from the second economy as those whose members were wage earners in the socialist sector, second economy incomes tended to diminish the relative purchasing power of first economy earnings. This was both a cause and an effect of the fact that the Hungarian population felt compelled to do extra work in the second economy on a scale disruptive of family life and hazardous to health.

The weaker the relative purchasing power of wages, the smaller are the socially tolerable and the greater the economically desirable wage differentials, with unfavourable impacts on job performance and labour turnover in the first economy. Small wonder that government wage policies were simultaneously calling for a narrowing of the established wage scale for social considerations (namely that even the lowest wages should cover the modest living costs of at least one person) and pressing for a rise in the range of wage differentials for economic considerations (referring to the weak incentive power of the prevailing wage differentials).[9]

Managers in state firms, in determining earnings and performance requirements, had to take into account the workers' unequal opportunities for earning second economy income. This was made possible by the fact that wage negotiations typically took place in an informal manner, which resulted in extreme variances and excessive fluctuations in individual wages and wage/performance ratios.

Those workers who were least dispensable in view of their skills and local knowledge were given high wages and opportunities for extra earnings within the enterprise so as to counteract the temptation of earning additional income in the second economy. Often this could only be done at the price of making concessions on labour discipline and performance requirements for other groups of workers, thereby acknowledging, or even facilitating, their parallel participation in the second economy. Again, the situation was different for those workers—mostly in the service sector (e. g. waiters)—who were enabled precisely by their full-time jobs to earn income in the second economy, a condition which employers could use as a bargaining chip in negotiating wages. Finally, certain groups of workers, because of their underprivileged position in the labour market of the first economy, were hardly able to earn income in the second economy. Most of them were paid wages by result subject to tight work norms.[10]

From "Socialism and Market" to "Market or Socialism?"

The expansion of the second economy during the 1980s did not bear out the optimistic assumption that widening the legal frameworks for small business would alleviate social and economic conflicts arising from the duality of the Hungarian economy. In addition, the late 1980s witnessed an erosion of confidence in the decentralization of economic power without altering the predominance of state ownership. This scepticism questioned the assertion that publicly owned firms could successfully resist systemic pressures for short-term maximization of incomes and set targets to achieve long-term profitability.[11] With bureaucratic coordination renounced and market coordination unattainable, the policy of decentralization was increasingly seen as a course resulting in a coordination vacuum and therefore self-defeating.

Thus, a markedly different view of future prospects emerged: the concept of a "socialist mixed economy" in which the antagonism and interdependence of multiple modes of coordination would be explicitly acknowledged. Such a socialist mixed economy should differ from contemporary capitalist ones in that the second economy was presumed to remain the sphere of activities incurring losses for the governmental sector, whereas the state capitalist sector would include the actually or potentially profitable activities. Defined in contrast to state socialism, the decisive difference would be a shift of emphasis from the recognition of the second economy's practical role of meeting certain demands to the recognition of the functional role of the antagonism between the two economies, and of the fierce competition between the contradictory ownership forms.[12]

This view, however, proved to be neither readily acceptable even for the most enthusiastic advocates of market reforms nor particularly influential in public thinking. Nor could it become effective as a guide for policy-makers. Instead, government treatment of the second economy as well as mainstream reform proposals in the late 1980s were guided by illusions about the viability of economic regulation neutral to any particular sector. This principle of regulation came in handy for those lobbying for favourable regulation of their respective sectors and fuelled hot and inconclusive disputes about which of the two economies was in fact discriminated against, and in what aspects.

Thanks to a growing awareness of the incompatibility of state ownership and market coordination, the idea of sector neutrality was abandoned at the end of the 1980s. It is since that time that we can speak of the ascendancy of the (now majoritarian) view, according to which the government is assigned the dual task of resisting pressure for liberalization in the public sector while liberalizing the regulatory environment of the private sector.[13]

There appears to be no alternative to such a policy of liberalization of private enterprise. Nonetheless, the above mentioned features of the second economy suggest that this will be only a necessary but not sufficient condition for launching the desired process. Paradoxically, liberalization of private enterprise will possibly have to cope even with the opposition of private entrepreneurs themselves, who have long been accustomed to a non-competitive business environment.

Entrepreneurs against the Market?

The ambiguous process of re-embourgeoisement over the past decades has evolved a special type of private entrepreneur in Hungary who is simultaneously semi-proletarian and semi-bourgeois. Also, as compared to his Western counterpart, he is of "bourgeois" rather than "citoyen" orientation. In addition, horizontal links between private firms are sporadic, while a large part of private economic activities is "integrated" by the bureaucratic sector.[14]

The Hungarian entrepreneur learned to exploit the advantages of the relative security of the existence in the public sector as well as the extra income he could earn as a private producer in the second economy. He also learned to obviate chronic difficulties in getting the necessary inputs, and to circumvent bureaucratic uncertainties.

In any event, the spread of the second economy and its institutionalization in the 1980s are facts attesting to an increasing strength of civil society over the state. We can rightly suppose that in the new democracies the relative autonomy of the state vis-à-vis civil society is bound to decline further during the 1990s. Therefore, the key question for the outcome of the policy of liberalizing the private sector while maintaining (or even strengthening) the dominance of bureaucratic coordination in the public sector will be the measure of support such a policy can expect from the Hungarians who have geared themselves to a multi-pillar living.

Except for a narrow elite of private businessmen, even "full-time" entrepreneurs may adopt an attitude to full liberalization somewhat similar to the way—apologies for the profane parallel—"entrepreneurs" of the prostitution business in market economies would likely react to the full legalization and liberalization of their activities. In both cases we see institutions long branded as less than fully desirable, and not so much for the kind of service they provide as rather for its provision for gain. Again, in both cases the services face solvent demand, the jobs are relatively remunerative, and the markets cannot be abolished by administrative means. So the state cannot but make concessions in both cases: either ease the stringency of restrictive regulation or turn a blind eye to its infraction. All the more so since by forcing the institution in question into clandestinity or semi-clandestinity it would leave its entrepreneurs mortgaged to parasitic, corrupt and delinquent subcultures. Moreover, it would be compelled to exercise control of low efficiency involving large public costs.

Should the private entrepreneurs not fear, once entry into the business is easier, the emergence of a supply market and hence a sharpening competition, stricter quality requirements, loss of revenues, etc.? Not to mention the variety of one-time expenses they would incur when switching to legal operation, and the incomes which actors of the infrastructure supportive of illegal or semi-legal prostitution (i.e., hotel receptionists, panders and pimps, and the like) would definitely lose with the legalization.

But, once I have used a profane analogy, let us imagine the tormented state of mind of the private entrepreneur who was once convicted on trumped-charges and is now released from prison unexpectedly. He might have long dreamt of this day, but he is worried on the threshold of his discharge. With the passing of years in prison, he was getting on better, feeling his feet in the end, and since he stopped being a loudmouth he was not particularly maltreated, and found a way to get what he wanted. Can he benefit from what he has learned during the past decades, and will he be able to get along without all those skills that he has lost? He has grown unused even to the limited kind of rivalry he is now in for. But what is to become of him if his acquittal later turns out to have been a bona fide mistake or, God forbid, a mala fide empty promise?

Indeed, there are indications that the new liberal policies have not been met with an immediate change of behaviour on the part of the entrepreneurial stratum. According to a recent investigation, although the number of registered private entrepreneurs in Hungary increased remarkably from the end of 1989, there was a fall in their relative tax contribution. Moreover, private entrepreneurship remained overwhelmingly a secondary occupation, mostly in the least capital-intensive industries. The new entrepreneurs trustful of the stability of the new democratic institutions, operating in the full light of legality, and driven, instead of short-term rent seeking, by the purpose of establishing a soundly and solidly expanding enterprise, appear not yet to have been born.

Competition and Cooperation

At this juncture I have to express my full agreement with those who advocate the full liberalization of the private economy in Hungary. I am nevertheless afraid that this proposal will not necessarily be acceptable even for those who are in the process of embourgeoisement. Its implementation could at best amount to the restoration of a "natural" state previous to the enforced interruption in the late 1940s of the already delayed process of bourgeois development.

Can we entertain any hopes at all? It appears to me that this paradox cannot be resolved unless competitive conditions for the private economy are created parallel to industrial policies promoting cooperation within the private economy. With such policies absent or failing, the desirable shrinkage of the bureaucratic sector would probably leave the private economy in some sort of a "cooperation vacuum". Private business would be atomized to such an extent as to become incapable of offsetting the decline in the output of the bureaucratic sector.

To be sure, competition and cooperation appear irreconcilable only to doctrinaire minds. For evidence of their co-existence one can refer to the unexpected achievements in the 1980s of industrial regions like Emilia-Romagna, Province of Italy under communist-socialist local government or, say, Baden-Württemberg in Germany governed by

Christian-Democrats where, as is demonstrated in a special issue of *Economy and Society* (November 1989), the success of industry registered largely by small firms comes less from a life-and-death competition between atomized entrepreneurs than from comprehensive links of subcontracting based on cooperation and trust. While it would obviously be mistaken to argue that such local industrial strategies are a condition for prosperity everywhere, their relevance is based on the declining efficiency of macroeconomic management and the welfare state, and partly on certain developments unfavourable for mass production in the world economy.

The success stories of such regions may offer some lessons for Hungary also because they suggest "pro-embourgeoisement" industrial policies in the country's slump-ridden areas as opposed to a protectionist policy serving to conserve large enterprises; policies that may prove acceptable for the diverse political forces representing the civil society. In addition, they could serve as counterpoints to excessive macro-policy-centredness which is characteristic today of government advisory boards and ad hoc groups of experts (both Hungarian and international) thinking about economic transition in Eastern Europe. And, finally, they may also act to prevent Hungary from slipping into a new kind of economic duality: the simultaneous presence of a highly competitive private economic sector dominated by foreign capital and a poorly performing domestic sector representing an obstacle to modernization and a permanent source of political instability.

In Hungary small enterprises tend to increase differentiation in the level of development not only between the capital and the countryside or between towns and villages but also across regions. These enterprises are concentrated mostly in the capital, large towns and more-developed regions, and it is mainly young and skilled urban males who join them. Similarly, falling demand for labour in the first economy is often associated with low ratios of private sector employment, and vice versa. Moreover, the rapidly growing number of small firms and their share in employment in Hungary is in our days associated with a diminishing role of small firms as sellers or subcontractors to large firms.

As for foreign direct investments, they are concentrated in the same, relatively non-capital intensive, non-core industries (mostly in the service and commerce sector) which are the favourite targets of domestic, second economy entrepreneurs. This gives rise to a pro-protectionist attitude among them. The same attitude may result, however, from foreign takeovers of or shares in large, state sector firms. Indeed, domestic entrepreneurs having established strong business ties to state firms should feel threatened by the prospects of such takeovers.

Conclusions

Up to the mid-1980s, it was a typical view in Hungary that the dilemmas inherent in state control of the second economy would almost automatically be resolved by further reforms within the first economy. Correspondingly, the schizophrenic duality of the Hungarian economy was regarded as a transitory stage of evolution, and views only differed in the recommended pace and ways of relaxation of administrative constraints on the expansion of private enterprises.

By contrast, following the historic events of the past years, the overwhelming majority of economic experts, political forces and citizens in Hungary see the only way out of the country's critical situation in the preponderance of private property and in a democratic political order. This broad consensus implies a shift in perceptions of the second economy—once hostile, later ambivalent, and finally overappreciative. This latter view is only based on the positive features of the second economy (on private enterprise and the market) and attributes the adverse features to the continued predominance of state ownership and to discriminations against the second economy.

Ironically, just as the unquestionability a few years ago of state property, the current weakness of the Hungarian middle class of entrepreneurs again brings forth "third-roadism", i.e., a desperate search for a historically untested alternative path of modernization. Yet, while earlier third-road ideas envisioned some sort of a mixed economy which should be neither capitalist nor state socialist,[15] their current descendants adhere to Western-type capitalism and political democracy. At the same time, they refuse to believe that, with a weak national bourgeoisie, it is directly attainable here and now. Typically, they advocate protectionist policies providing preferential treatment to Hungarian investors and private entrepreneurs in order to block the road to a neocolonialist type of dependence on Western capital attended by a strong and powerful comprador bourgeoisie.[16]

I do not consider such fears to be unjustified. On the contrary, it is crucial to win the firm political support of the Hungarian middle strata.

Also, I agree that to the extent foreign direct investments discourage domestic entrepreneurs or compete them out of the market, they may delay the ongoing process of embourgeoisement. Moreover, those employed in the large-scale sector may be particularly hit by the shrinkage of opportunities for part-time participation in the second economy. This may generate a paternalistic nostalgia among them, which, in turn, could make them allies of certain entrepreneurs in delaying the state's withdrawal from the economy.

Yet the ambivalence of present-day Hungarian private entrepreneurs toward liberalization is much too deep-rooted to be eliminated simply by placing restrictions on the influx of foreign capital. Nevertheless, the policy of liberalization can be adopted consistently only if it is complemented, instead of protectionist policies discriminating against foreign entrepreneurs, with local industrial policies aiming to promote cooperation within the private sector.

This, however, brings me to the final question of whether, under conditions of transition, it is possible at all to elaborate any kind of local industrial policy acceptable by those concerned. After all, it was some kind of well-established corporative setting that in the Western countries allowed the interested parties to negotiate and reach consensus on local levels. Can we expect such consensus to emerge if there are no historically established corporative institutions representing local industrial groups?

Notes

1. Throughout this chapter the term "second economy" is meant to refer to the Hungarian private economy of the late 1960s up to the end of 1980s. It is conceived (in conformity with the definition put forward by the author in the late 1970s—see e.g. Gábor (1979a) as the aggregate of all income-motivated activities performed, whether legally or not, by individuals and households beside (i.e. instead of or, more typically, along with) employment in the state and large-scale cooperative firms ("first economy"). Correspondingly, the term "first economy" is used interchangeably with "socialist", "bureaucratic", "state" or "public sector".

   According to moderate estimations, in the mid-1980s at least one fifth of the total annual GNP, a net personal income equivalent to about one third of wage-type earnings in the first economy were generated by production and service activities performed in the second economy, mostly in the form of moonlighting, with a labour input equivalent to approximately one third to one half of the annual working time of the first economy. Similar in size was the amount of income acquired from non-productive second economy transactions directly related to employment in the first economy (job theft, bribery and the like), of which about one third concerned the redistribution of income among the population, whereas two thirds were at the expense of state-ownership. This means that for the three fourth of the population that received second-economy incomes, the second economy was on the whole a source of income of similar importance as the first economy, and a primary factor of income inequalities among the Hungarian population. (For more information on the overall size and sectoral composition of the Hungarian second economy of the mid-1980s see Gábor [1985] and [1989], Galasi-Sík [1988] and Balázs-Laki [1991].

2. These difficulties were nonetheless not entirely unanticipated; see Róna-Tas [1990].
3. This recognition was nevertheless reluctant rather than enthusiastic. As Rezsö Nyers, a leading reformer of the time put it in his [1968] programmatic article, "Today the petty bourgeoisie in Hungary represents 2 to 3 per cent of the population, and its weight in society is proportional to its economic activity. While they do not essentially work at cross-purposes with the development of a socialist society, they must be under constant control by the state, because they are a segment seeking profit, regarding their own gain rather than the welfare of society as their main goal".
4. Workers' calculative behaviour was brought into focus in the first years of reform by extremely high rates of inter-enterprise labour turnover, whereas entrepreneurial behaviour was most evident in the proliferation of auxiliary plants at cooperative farms; see Rupp [1983].
5. For evidence of such swings in the position of part-time farming and small-scale industry see Gábor [1985] and Gábor-Horváth [1989], respectively.
6. Among the new forms of small undertakings the VGMKs (Hungarian acronym for intra-enterprise business partnership), which neither needed capital investment nor required anyone to quit his full-time job in the socialist sector, spread most rapidly. David Stark pointed out that whereas enterprises in the market economies protect themselves against uncertainties by establishing bureaucratic internal labour markets, socialist large enterprises try to cope with their environmental uncertainties of bureaucratic origin and with the second economy by relying on internal market relations; see Stark [1986].
7. For my attempts at the explanation of labour shortage in Hungary, see Gábor [1979b]. See also Kornai [1980].
8. See Gábor-Galasi [1985] for the structural background of these dilemmas; and Gábor [1989a] for related fluctuations in government wage and employment policies within the public sector.
9. See Gábor [1989c]. Here I describe the paradoxical situation, what I call "wage-scale syndrome", in which the population as well as government authorities can justifiably find the prevailing wage differentials unreasonably small and unacceptably large at the same time.
10. For an analysis of the impacts of the second economy on the strategies and stratification of workers in the state labour market see Kertesi-Sziráczki [1985].

11. A few years later, Kornai [1990] takes it as a starting point that "those who stand for the dominance of state property have thereby accepted a 'package' which is bound to contain a huge portion of bureaucratic coordination. . . . If one really wants a larger measure of market coordination he must, by reason of that fact, accept a much higher and growing ratio of private property and private business." His position should be contrasted to early criticisms of economic reforms, in which the failure of those reforms was traced to the technical imperfections of indirect management. Later criticisms shifted the emphasis to the lack of political reforms. Even a few years ago, however, the property reform was still thought to separate administrative and economic control over state property by creating new types of public institutions for capital management (see Tardos [1988]).
12. For a general assessment of contemporary views of future prospects see Gábor [1986]. On the coexistence and competition of organizational forms see Stark [1989]. See also Szelényi [1989] for the concept of a socialist mixed economy he thought was being born.
13. This concept was elaborated and advanced by Kornai in his 1989 pamphlet. His insistence on the maintenance of bureaucratic coordination within the public sector and his rejection of the principle of "sector neutrality" coincide with the view set forth by György Kövári and myself from the mid-1980s in several writings influenced by Kornai (1980) in which we argued against the idea of wage liberalization (Gábor-Kövári [1989]) and sector-neutral regulation (Gábor [1989b]).
14. Szelényi [1988] points out that in the 1980s, typical agricultural households, accounting for 70 to 90 per cent of rural households, combine waged employment with commodity production on their small plots. Even those 5 to 10 per cent whom Szelényi identifies as entrepreneurs were formed by state socialism rather than by the earlier epoch of embourgeoisement. "Apart from some very limited groups . . . , the vast majority of those participating in the second economy are not in the trajectory most conceptualizations would prefer to assign them. Instead of moving to a bourgeois position, their life strategy can be characterized primarily as a survival strategy", concludes Manchin [1989]. A more recent survey on new entrepreneurs demonstrates that "their opinions on management have been shaped not by the market but by the conditions of the shortage economy" (Kuczi-Lengyel-Nagy-Vajda [1991], p. 143).
15. Cf. Szelényi's third way theory, in which he argued for the likely advent of a "socialist mixed economy", "a quite unique mixture of redistribution and market", as a "viable" and "durable new form of social organization" ([1988] pp. 212–13; see also pp. 16–18 and his [1989] pp. 231–32.). See also Kornai [1989] and [1990], for whom "market socialism is a sheer illusion", and who flatly rejects the possibility of any way neither capitalist nor state socialist.
16. As Szelényi, who changed his mind in the meantime, spelled out quite clearly in an interview [1990]), "there is no economic prosperity, no national independence, and no system of democratic institutions without a national bourgeoisie . . . A national bourgeoisie is to emerge from the ranks of present-day small entrepreneurs, of petty bourgeoisie slowly learning the laws of the

market in the second economy . . . The sellout of state property to foreign capital cannot but result in neocolonial, dependent type of development, in the reproduction of our social backwardness".

References

Brusco, Sebastiano-Ezio Righi [1989], Local Government, Industrial Policy and Social Consensus: the Case of Modena (Italy). *Economy and Society,* Vol. 18, No. 4 (November), pp. 405–24.

Gábor, István R. [1979a], The Second [Secondary] Economy: Earning Activity and Regrouping of Income Outside Socially Organized Production and Distribution. *Acta Oeconomica,* Nos. 3–4, pp. 291–311.

———. [1979b], "Munkaeröhiány a mai szocialista gazdaságban: kísérlet a jelenség elméleti magyarázatára" (Labour Shortage in Present-Day Socialism: An Attempt at the Theoretical Explanation of the Phenomenon). *Közgazdasági Szemle,* No. 2, pp. 171–187.

———. [1983], Second Economy and Socialism: The Hungarian Experience. In: Edgar L. Feige (ed.), *The Underground Economies: Tax Evasion and Information Distortion.* Cambridge: Cambridge University Press, 1989, pp. 339–60.

———. [1985], The Major Domains of the Second Economy. In: Péter Galasi and György Sziráczki (eds.), *Labour Market and Second Economy in Hungary.* Frankfurt-New York: Campus Verlag, pp. 133–78.

———. [1986], Market Reforms and Second Economy in 'State Socialism': Speculation on the Evolutionary and Comparative Economic Lessons of the Hungarian 80s. Invited paper prepared for the International Conference on Markets and Social Policy in Comparative Perspective. Santa Barbara (Calif.), May 8–11, pp. 36.

———. [1989a], Main Issues and Major Trends of Government Employment and Wage Policies. In: Tamás D. Horváth, Gerry Rodgers and György Sziráczki (eds.). *Flexibility and Rigidity in the Hungarian Labour Market.* Geneva: ILO, Research Series, No. 90, pp. 19–37.

———. [1989b], Second Economy in State Socialism: Past Experience and Future Prospects. The Case of Hungary. *European Economic Review,* Vol. 33, pp. 597–604.

———. [1989c], "Bérskálaszindróma és munkavállalói magatartás" (Wage-Scale Syndrome and Employee Behaviour). *Közgazdasági Szemle,* No. 12, pp. 1480–9.

Galasi, Peter [1985], Second Economy, State and Labour Market. In: Péter Galasi and György Sziráczki (eds.), *Labour Market and Second Economy in Hungary.* Frankfurt-New York: Campus Verlag, pp. 122–32.

Horváth, Tamás D. [1987], Failure and Retreat in the Small-Scale Industry. *Acta Oeconomica,* Nos. 1–2, pp. 133–53.

Kertesi, Gábor-György Sziráczki [1985], Worker Behaviour in the Labour Market. In: Péter Galasi and György Sziráczki (eds.), *Labour Market and Second Economy in Hungary.* Frankfurt-New York: Campus Verlag, pp. 216–45.

Kövári, György [1989], Can The Promises of the Hungarian "Wage Reform" Come True? Social Mechanisms of Wage Determination and the Competency of Wage Theories. *Acta Oeconomica,* Vol. 40, Nos. 3–4, pp. 307–18.

Kornai, János [1980], Economics of Shortage. Amsterdam: North-Holland.

———. [1989], "Indulatos röpirat a gazdasági átmenet ügyében" (A Passionate Pamphlet in the Cause of Economic Transition). Budapest: HVG RT, pp. 129

———. [1990], "A tulajdonformák és a koordinációs mechanizmusok affinitása: a reformszocializmus néhány tapasztalata" (Affinity Between Forms of Property and Modes of Coordination: Some Lessons from Reform Socialism). *Valóság,* No. 1, pp. 1–15.

Kuczi, Tibor-György Lengyel-Beáta Nagy-Ágnes Vajda [1991], Entrepreneurs and Potential Entrepreneurs: The Chances of Getting Independent. *Society and Economy,* No. 2, pp. 134–50.

Manchin, Róbert [1989], Individual economic strategies and social consciousness. In: Péter Somlai (ed.), *Changing Values in Hungarian Society.* Budapest: Coordinating Council of Program Ts-3, Research Review No. 2, pp. 81–91.

Nee, Victor-David Stark [1989], Toward an Institutional Analysis of State Socialism. In: Victor Nee and David Stark (eds.), *Remaking the Economic Institutions of Socialism: China and Eastern Europe,* Stanford: SUP, pp. 1–31.

Nyers, Rezsö [1968], "Az új gazdasági mechanizmus várható társa-dalmi és politikai kihatásai" (The Probable Social and Political Impacts of the New Economic Mechanism). *Társadalmi Szemle,* No. 3.

Róna-Tas, Ákos [1990], The Second Economy in Hungary: The Social Origins of the End of State Socialism. Ph.D. Dissertation (Sociology), The University of Michigan, 298 pp.

Rupp, Kálmán [1983], *Entrepreneurs in Red: Structure and Organizational Innovation in the Centrally Planned Economy.* Albany: State University of New York Press.

Sabel, Charles et al. [1989], Regional Prosperities Compared: Massachusetts and Baden-Württemberg in the 1980s. *Economy and Society* Vol. 18 No. 4 (November) pp. 374–404.

Sík, Endre [1991], The Vulture and the Calamity (cf. the chapter in this volume).

Stark, David [1986], Rethinking Internal Labor Markets: New In-sights from a Comparative Perspective. *American Sociological Review,* Vol. 51, pp. 492–504.

———. [1989], Coexisting Organizational Forms in Hungary's Emerging Mixed Economy. In: Victor Nee and David Stark (eds.), *Remaking the Economic Institutions of Socialism: China and Eastern Europe,* Stanford: SUP, pp. 137–68.

———. [1990], Bending the Bars of the Iron Cage. Sociological Forum, Vol. 4, No. 4.

Szelényi, Iván [1988] (in collaboration with Robert Manchin, Pál Juhász, Bálint Magyar and Bill Martin), *Socialist Entrepreneurs: Embourgeoisement in Rural Hungary.* Madison: University of Wisconsin Press, 255 pp.

———. [1989], Eastern Europe in an Epoch of Transition: Toward a Socialist Mixed Economy? In: Victor Nee and David Stark (eds.) [1989], *Remaking the*

Economic Institutions of Socialism: China and Eastern Europe, Stanford: S.U.P. pp. 208–32.

———. [1990], "Polgárosodás Magyarországon: nemzeti tulajdonos polgárság és polgárosodó értelmiség" (Embourgeoisement in Hungary: National Propertied Bourgeoisie and the Embourgeoisement of Intellectuals), *Valóság,* No. 1, pp. 29–41.

Tardos, Márton [1988], "A tulajdon" (Ownership). *Közgazdasági Szemle,* No. 12 pp. 1405–1423.

Zeitlin, Jonathan [1989], Introduction. *Economy and Society,* Vol. 18 No. 4 pp. 367–373.

2

Planning the Transformation? (Notes about the Legacy of the Reform Economists)

János Mátyás Kovács

> *Can the Ethiopian change his skin and the leopard his spots?*
>
> —Jeremiah

The Soviet-type system cannot be overthrown but it can be undermined. The *nomenklatura* cannot be dismissed but it can be confused and corrupted. State property cannot be privatized but it can be decentralized and informally appropriated. The mono-party cannot be rivalled but it can be pluralized internally. The planned economy cannot be dismantled but it can be marketized. . . . Nowadays, these truisms provoke at best a forgiving smile in Eastern Europe. Some years ago, however, thousands or—if China and the Soviet Union are included—tens of thousands of reform-minded social scientists, "socialist entrepreneurs" as well as government and party officials constructed their reform proposals in terms of such compromises in this corner of the world.[1] One part of these experts firmly believed in these second-best solutions of limited (simulated) liberalization, and built new "Third Road" models around them, while the other part—which rapidly grew in number as years passed—for want of better solutions, pragmatically accepted these compromises because they did not dare dream that one could think of first-best solutions in the near future.

In the meantime, the former socialist reformers have rapidly converted to the new faith of post-socialist transformation, in East-Central Europe. At present, the majority of them assume, almost axiomatically, that the above compromises and the well-known dilemmas they invoked in reformist thought have, together with the communist rule which is still considered to be the *only* reason for the former ambiguities of the theory of market socialism, disappeared once for all. Relieved for the moment, a great many ex-reformers feel uneasy about the past: when you hear them speak about the 1989 revolutions, it is not very likely that they will bore you with heroic stories about reformist "conspirators" who helped disperse the party-state from inside. Instead, they are scrupulous—they served too long, recognizing only too late that the emperor had no clothes. Nevertheless, scepticism concerning the past performance of the reformers is often complemented with cautious optimism with regard to their role in the future. The thesis of "what has not been permitted (feasible, reformable) thus far, is permitted (feasible, transformable) from now on" will occur in most of their self-portraits.[2] Of course, there may appear some new political obstacles to the transformation but these are dwarfed by the former communist limitations.

In their view, by touching upon the taboos of real socialism, the former *socialist* "liberals" can become genuine liberals who will complete the theoretical work started by the reformers back in the 1950s. Accordingly, there is no need for cathartic changes: the original premises of reform thinking should not be essentially revised but only supplemented with the missing elements of privatization and political democracy. The ex-reformer would say: despite the fact that we lent our expertise to the *ancien régime* for too long, intellectually we were not unprepared for the fall of the Soviet-type system. 1989 was preceded by a scholarly learning process and a kind of successive radicalization (secularization, liberalization) of reform thinking, in the course of which we covered a great distance from the early attempts at destalinization to the more recent proposals for a "crucial reform" of real socialism.

It would not be difficult to reinforce the self-accusations of the former reformers by demonstrating how ambitiously they helped the old system survive through rationalizing the dysfunctional mechanisms of real socialism for many decades, and how persistently they tried to maintain certain parts of the *status quo* in the form of an *Ausgleich,* a

Social Contract or a "Grand Coalition" with the *nomenklatura* even on the eve of the revolution.[3] Similarly, one could also easily share the pleasure these academics, managers and politicians feel now in experiencing the unexpected freedom of thought, the chance for *theoretically unlimited* reform-making in the period of transition from socialism to a liberal order. (Self-) censorship is over, from now on the creative imagination of the old-new experts will only be limited by technical (albeit huge) constraints. After so many years of distorted and reversed socialist reforms, it is the "transformer" who will be able to design coherent liberal reform projects—or so the ex-reformers say.

In what follows, I venture to take a contrary approach. The main thrust of this paper is a.) to illustrate the "*positive*" (unofficial) part of the legacy of reformers, i.e., their important contribution to the disintegration of the Soviet-type system, and b.) to point out the ambiguous effects of the reformist tradition as a whole on the way of conceiving of the new order by the transformers. A catalyst may become a retarder, the liberal imagination of the transformer may be blocked by his surviving reformer ego. It is often exactly those reformist attitudes which—in most cases involuntarily—helped loosen the fabric of real socialism in the past that may make it extremely hard for the ex-reformers to think in terms of a liberal order today.

* * *

The following notes are based on the results of a previous research project on "reform economics", a comparative study of the intellectual heritage of economic reformers (the most significant group in the reformist camp) in Eastern Europe. I owe special thanks to all the project participants.[4]

The Reform Economist as a Proto-Transformer

In some of my earlier writings[5] I have tried to counterbalance the excessive pride the reform economists felt in allegedly challenging the last prerogatives of the Soviet-type system with a new paradigm of economic science. Now, after socialist reformism has been politically deactivated, it would be unfair and futile to continue this line of critique, and present the reform economists as reform-mongers rather than brilliant theorists. What is more, the student of the history of economic thought cannot help putting in a couple of good words for the former reformers when he sees—to rephrase the German proverb—how many fathers the victory over communism has among the members of the new élite. Rehabilitation of socialist reformism? No, but why focus on the illegal struggle of the anti-communist rebels rather than on the legal activity of the reformist experts, on intended rather than on unintended change, on the spectacular demise of real socialism rather than on its former gradual exhaustion?

No doubt about it, the reform economists did form an integral part of the Soviet-type system after Stalin. Nevertheless, their work, although it did not result in a new Grand Theory of economics, became instrumental in the decomposition of the planned economy and one-party rule. In many cases they were even more instrumental than any of the overtly anti-communist opposition movements. I would suggest two "*subversive*" *features* of socialist reformism for consideration:

(1) "*Entzauberung*" of the planned economy. By disenchantment I mean a kind of delegitimation of the Soviet-type system through challenging its basic economic philosophy derived from the vision of the centralized and demonetized communist economy. While recently the reform economists were late in recognizing the agony of real socialism, in the first half of the 1950s they had been the first to diagnose the maladies of the Stalinist regimes. Willy-nilly, even the most naive proposals for perfecting the planning targets or decentralizing the command economy pierced—at that time still unnoticeable—holes in the balloon of the utopia of communism, holes that were not too hard to widen afterwards. The cure the reformists recommended to heal the wounds inflicted upon the economy by Stalinist policies made it increasingly improbable that the recovery would ever end up in "collectivist economic planning".

The partial rehabilitation of the concepts of market calculation, individual and group interests ("material incentives") and decision-making, competition, enterpreneurship and profit-making, freedom of consumers' choice and personal enrichment, as well as the renewed emphasis on economic versus political rationality ("optimization" vs "humanization"), informal versus formal relations, quality versus quantity, balanced growth versus acceleration, consumption versus investment, agriculture versus industry, civil versus military, light versus heavy industries, opening up to the West versus autarchy and cooperation with the East, etc.,—only a fraction of these concepts and shifts of emphasis would have proven sufficient to invalidate the communist discourse whose primary strength lay in its all-embracing and seemingly homogeneous character.

More importantly, this disenchantment—while robbing real socialism of its future (or at least making its prospects uncertain)—actually contributed to the end of the identification of the party-state with the idea of the common good. Furthermore, portraying the socialist state as an overregulated bureaucracy with vested interests that commits enormous "government failures" and which is far from becoming a welfare state took the sting out of the critique of modern capitalism, another pillar of the system's legitimation. Stressing the need for some decentralization and partial deregulation in economic life, combining the planning and market mechanisms, tacitly accepting the convergence theorem, etc.,—were only the first wavering steps of depriving the party-state of its integrative-messianic role. True, at any moment, reformist anti-statism could take the collectivist route of self-management, nonetheless in most cases it opened vistas for a series of technocratic (managerial) solutions, legal private small business and the shadow economy. In other words, the economic segments of the "civil society" had been supported by the reformers well before the term started to be used by the dissidents.[6]

Accordingly, reform economics managed to plant foreign bodies in the texture of Soviet ideology, bodies which this ideology was not capable of assimilating entirely. Instead, new hybrid concepts emerged, ranging from "socialist commodity production" all the way to the "economics of perestroika" (these were called "halfway houses" in the literature), which could not evolve into a new liberal paradigm of economic science but proved strong enough to prevent the rise of a coherent *ideology of restoration.* Though the Soviet-type system was cyclically able to reconstitute its main structures after consecutive shocks of reformation, thus integrating certain reformist techniques of control over the economy and polity, in the long run it lost its ideological self-esteem and decisiveness. Neutralizing alien concepts took much of its strength: tolerating the notion of "law of value under socialism" opened the way for the reformers to use the term "socialist" or "regulated market", and then "market" without euphemistic adjectives; proposals for marketization eventually led to advocating privatization; economic liberalization could not stop politely at the border of the political system for good, etc., etc. We know this story of the chain reaction of liberal concepts well from the "memoirist" literature published by the radical reformers in the second part of the 1980s.[7]

At that time, I made efforts to show that what they regarded as an essential scholarly refinement of the theory of market socialism was rather a process of political and ideological *radicalization.*[8] Reform economics became increasingly secular, almost profane, and by the 1980s it even developed a kind of "middle-of-the-road" transformation theory (political economy) on the basis of the new claim of marketization *cum* privatization. Back in the 1950s and 1960s, the reform economists had criticized the Stalinist planned economy primarily by means of technical arguments, confronting what they learned from Western mainstream *economics* with the obscure teachings of the textbook "*political economy* of socialism". As years passed, the general framework of economics proved, however, too tight for the radical reformers to construct a programmatic theory of the transition from socialism. So again and again, they began to flirt with political science. Though this oscillation between the two perceptions of economic science did not help market socialism become a Grand Theory, the combination of technical-scientific and political-ideological reasoning did inhibit the crystallization of any new *unified official concept* of socialist planned economy, should it be supported by Galbraithian, neo-corporativist or "Third Road"-type arguments. In the long run, the reform economists were able to make the official ideologues believe that they, the "revisionists", could produce the better (at least, better applicable) socialist theory.[9]

In other words, thanks to its ambiguous nature, reform economics provided munition against old-new ideological monopolies, while (relying on its own quasi-monopoly position in certain countries of Eastern Europe and periods of time) it could also put up a shelter to safeguard some traditional liberal ideas in economic and other social sciences, as well as to experiment with new reform and transformation projects. It is in this laboratory where the basic language of market socialism (I call it "plan-and-market discourse"[10]) was developed, which, as an alternative discourse to the official one, finally succeeded in rehabilitating even such concepts as private ownership, multi-party democracy, rule of law, etc., in an attempt to complete the disenchantment of the Soviet-type economy.

(2) Contamination through symbiosis. The above description of a kind of reformist subversion-via-language may arouse the suspicion of the reader. Why would the reform-minded experts have overthrown or

corrupted their bosses, he may justifiably ask. Were not the reform economists exposed to the mercy of politicians? Could they not be simply dismissed, silenced or forced to convert when in the slumps of reformation the need arose for restoration ideologies? Were they not interested in maintaining their limited expert power and status? Did they not therefore prefer to comply with the current requirements of the ruling élite, and "render unto Ceasar the things that are Ceasar's", at least temporarily?

I am afraid that one cannot answer these questions unless one breaks with the strictly hierarchical interpretation of the relationship between reform economics and political power in the Soviet-type systems. Why not consider the reformers' *intermediary position* between politics and academic life, government and opposition, East and West? Why not pay attention also to their relative sovereignty?

In real life the reform economist had many masters to serve. He was a historian, a "social engineer", and a fortune teller (he said, cynically, both a jester and an alchemist at the royal court), a critic of the orthodox and a supporter of the neologist wing of those in power. He represented the academic community, acted as a spokesman for social groups (managers, small entrepreneurs, etc.) interested in economic and political liberalization, and even played the role of an *ersatz* oppositionist who often channeled nonofficial views to the government and safeguarded the dissidents. Without becoming substantially more schizophrenic than the average socialist citizen, he could be simultaneously a mild oppositionist in the eyes of the ruling apparatus and a mild *apparatchik* in the eyes of the opposition. These diffuse roles presupposed a permanent cooperation with the political authorities but also involved day-to-day conflicts with them.

To exaggerate slightly, the reformer played competitive politics in a formally monolithic regime and represented various imaginary organizations: political parties, employers associations, sometimes even trade unions. As long as the diverging interests in the Soviet-type society were not protected by real political institutions, the reform economist was a kind of substitute not only for dissidents but also for politicians of a peasant party (say, in loosening up the agricultural cooperatives or increasing farming subsidies), for liberals (in fighting against monopolies and state tutelage), or for social democrats (in insisting on certain welfare schemes). Evidently, in many cases this political mix resulted in rather controversial positions, dilemmas, and even paradoxes in reformist thought and behavior.

Like every reformer in world history, the reform economist also had to decide whether he wanted to initiate social change with the help of the "monarch" against the "people" or the other way round. Reform—from below or from above? All at once or step by step? In economic life alone or in the political system as well? In the economic institutions or in economic policies as well? In a slump or during an upswing? Well-known practical dilemmas like these appeared on the theoretical level as paradoxes without proper logical solutions. Nevertheless, at the same time, they made it possible for the reform economists to cleverly manoeuver between the rocks of pseudo-reforms and revolution, to flexibly mix moderate and radical solutions, seeking ways that were acceptable to both below and above.

Presumably, however, the reformers' readiness and ability to find a *modus vivendi* would not have sufficed to convince the ruling oligarchy about the need of replacing the original communist techniques of self-legitimation by reformist ones. The reform economists also had to deliver reliable success stories, and, in order to exclude an alternative interpretation of these stories, it did not hurt if in the meantime they managed to get themselves built into the establishment as well.

What could the reformers promise to the ruling élite? Surprisingly many things. The reform economists did not conceal the fact that—to put it simply—the main commodity they offered was *survival.* In other words, they were selling guarantees for relative stability (i.e. for damping the hectic oscillation of the economic and political system), and also for an effective control both over the people through the apparatus of the party-state and over the apparatus through the leading oligarchs. Furthermore, they promised dynamic stability with the motto of "*plus ça change, plus c'est la même chose*" at an acceptable price. They pledged to attain most of the general objectives (growth, welfare, catching-up with the West, etc.) formulated by the early socialist regimes, and to represent many of the progressivist-professional values these regimes loved to proclaim with pride (technical superiority, efficient organization, flexible adjustment, etc). True, in exchange for a better performance the reformers required substantial change in the "mechanisms", to use their favorite term.

Mass mobilization, terror, central planning, etc., had to be replaced or supplemented by consolidation/corruption, power-sharing and the market, in such a way that the "commanding heights" remain as intact as possible. In any event, the reformist advisors added, incidental losses in their intactness would be compensated by gains in *real* power, i.e., by the substitution of inexecutable formal commands for instructions (accompanied by incentives) which would be actually obeyed by subordinates. If this were not always the case, "self-corruption" might offer some consolation for the decline of the political influence of the rulers.

Economic reformism was actually able to exhibit tangible results. Reform projects often kept their promises even in the most exotic economies of real socialism when the dysfunctions of the planned economy called for liberalization packages in order to prevent deep crises and accelerate modernization. Accordingly, reform economics as a normative doctrine appeared justified in the international arena for a long time. If the patient was getting better, it was the reform that cured him; but if he had a relapse, it was definitely the under- and not the overdose of the "reform medicine" that led to the recurrent crisis, or so the reformers said.

This "medical" theory was badly needed during the defensive phases of reformation. Power-sharing was tantamount to the victimization of influential groups of the *nomenklatura,* which from time to time launched vehement counter-attacks against the allegedly ultra-liberal reformers and their communist patrons. In many countries, however, the reform economists managed in the meantime to get "within the walls", mingling with the pragmatic defenders of the castle and making themselves indispensable as "social engineers" serving the Lord. This is the point (fairly neglected in the literature) that I would like to emphasize with the help of the term "contamination through symbiosis".

For during the last forty years, the reformers in Eastern Europe succeeded not only in irreversibly distorting the original dominant discourse of the Soviet-type system but also in *infiltrating,* in person, the ruling élite and thus, to a certain extent, in restructuring and reeducating it. Abandoning the strictly hierarchical interpretation, according to which the fate of reform economics was almost totally dependent on the political authorities (an interpretation that might have been correct in the late 1950s in Hungary or in Czechoslovakia after 1968), and at the same time doubting the rival thesis that the intellectuals have taken "class power",[11] we can arrive at a complex model of *bargaining.* This model includes the various forms of coexistence and interaction between the reformers and the *nomenklatura,* as well as the various degrees of the institutionalization of the reformist expertise (in the advisory activities, education, propaganda, etc.). It also examines the patterns of both the recruitment into the party-state apparatus and the circular migration of the reform-minded economists between party politics, government, business life, mass media and academia.

Understandably, the extent to which the ruling élite was willing (and able) to open channels of communication between itself and the intellectuals as well as autonomous social groups is a crucial variable in the model. Where the rulers, having once or twice already been disastrously misled by their own apparatus, wanted to rely on quasi-independent experts as well; where members of the Politbureau and the government could become directors of large enterprises and research institutes and vice versa overnight; where a certain amount of tolerance, common sense and pluralism was required to earn the benevolence of the West; and where the reforms recommended by the economic experts proved advantageous (and the counter-reforms disadvantageous) for those in power—in such countries reform economists could establish their political *métier* and obtain more than small bargaining chips.[12]

The partial integration (etatization) of reform economics was only one side of the coin. On the reverse one could discover in many countries of real socialism a.) a partly "domesticated" and "civilized" professional apparatus of the party-state in which quite a few leading posts (first of all in the so-called functional ministries) were occupied by reform-minded officials; b.) large industrial/agricultural lobbies which got the taste of limited autonomy and learned how to protect their interests against each other and the center by reformist means; c.) state universities which brought up ever new generations in the spirit of reformation. In some countries of Eastern Europe not only the traditionally conservative university departments of political economy but also the Central Party Schools, the *agit-prop* departments of the Central Committee and the national media became profoundly contaminated by reformist thought in the 1980s. The emancipation of reform economics contributed also to the liberation of other social sciences, first of all to that of economic history, law, and sociology.

Undoubtedly, the reformers lost many of the battles they fought together with their allies in the "*realo*" faction of the élite. Nevertheless, they could often weather out the hardships of anti-reforms on the periphery of the party-state and get back to the center in the next reform cycle. Also, not infrequently, the moderate members of the reformist group might appear on the other side, as advisors to the "*fundis*" in the leadership. A dismissed "liberal" communist party official might become for a while a deputy minister, a top manager or a head of a university department, with good chances for a comeback.

The principal values represented and policies pursued by the reformers also facilitated the *pluralization of the nomenklatura*: in many cases the emphasis on expertise led to conflicts between the more "ideological" party leaders and the more "professional" state officials; the requirement of market competition might pit the military apparatus against the civil lobbies, capital goods against consumer goods industries, those interested in the Comecon contacts against those cherishing Western relations, etc. New interest groups emerged: vertical dependence and rivalry were in this way replaced or complemented by strong horizontal ones; the system became increasingly polycentric. At the same time, those marketization and (clandestine) privatization measures recommended by the reform economists which were actually implemented also reinforced the centrifugal tendencies within the ruling élite. They opened up middle-class ("bourgeois") career lines outside the *nomenklatura* for deserters from the apparatus, which further weakened the internal cohesion of the party-state.

Finally, embourgeoisement was also forcefully urged by the reform economists from below. They made pioneering work in defending the case of private agriculture, legal small entrepreneurship and the shadow economy by providing some legitimation for formally illegal activities of the population. This kind of support greatly alleviated the tacit institutionalization of the second economy (and thereby of the civil society), which, as if in remuneration for protection, helped jeopardize the recurrent counter-reform moves of the conservatives. As a consequence, in many countries of Eastern Europe in the 1980s ruling élites with confused identities were facing nations with perhaps less confused identities. Their pragmatic rapprochement proved to be a necessary prerequisite for the "negotiated revolutions" of the region.

In a sense, contamination meant preparatory education. When, in the 1950s, the reform economists started to convince the communist *apparatchiks* of the advantages of the market, corruption, and westernization, and the disadvantages of planning, mobilization and autarchy, they did not hope that they thereby dissuaded them from using the latter techniques if the question of the life and death of communism arose. The reformers were in fact afraid of this moment and did their best to postpone its arrival. The majority of them did not want to overthrow the Soviet-type system, and were far from devising a plot against it: they *had* something to lose, and, strange as it may be, they did not trust the destructive power of their own truth and persuasion. Paradoxically, in 1989 they were at least as surprised by the peaceful revolutions of Eastern Europe as those observers who used to think, in place of the ambiguous categories of socialist reformism, in terms of a "heroic revolt of the civil society against totalitarian oppression".

The Transformer as a Socialist Reformer

In the light of the reformist "subversion" described above, one might expect that the socialist reform economists would enter the world of post-communism with a great élan, full of suppressed liberal fervor. No doubt about it, their radical faction became very active during the last couple of years in preparing the first stage of the transition. They have fully—and publicly—abandoned the strategy of improving real socialism by means of the project of "socialist market economy". In its stead the concept of *Soziale Marktwirtschaft* (social market economy) emerged with dazzling success as the main point of reference in the vocabulary of the new political parties in Eastern Europe. The "unofficial" heirlooms have fallen into good hands, one might assume. Or, to put it in another way, the reformers have executed a smooth landing on a ground which they had cautiously prepared in advance, a ground on which they cannot become anything else but liberal transformers.[13]

Let us now forget for a moment all the words of appreciation in the previous section about the involuntary anti-communism of the reform economist, and examine the bumps and pot-holes of this ground.

(1) Liberalism and social engineering: the "official" legacy. In a recent paper[14] I made an attempt to classify the theoretical components of what I called the "*deformed liberalism*" of the ex-reformers. This strand of tradition seems rather difficult to cut.

In the multiplicity of roles the reform economist played in the *ancien régime* there was one, that of the "social engineer", which could not be suspended for a long period of time. The reformer's cooperation with the political authorities was defined much less by his mediating activities, critique of the conservatives, or ability to make predictions, than by his tangible reform programs ("master plans", "Grand Designs") offered for sale to the pragmatic wing in the communist leadership. Hence, the whole intellectual ambiguity of reform economics may be expressed, with slight exaggeration, by this brief definition: the reformer was *planning—hand in hand with the planners—the taming of planning.* As we will see below, in this regard it does not necessarily make much difference if the planners disappear and the reformers become transformers who venture to make bolder plans than simply domesticating central planning. After all, the methodological structure of their discourse may remain similar.

The liberal aspirations of the ex-reformers may be blocked by the inherent *statism* (élitism, interventionism) and *constructivism* of reformist thought. The reformer wanted to "introduce", to "build up" the market economy, and—paradoxical as it may seem—had asked the regulators to help deregulate. The reform economist always had a positive reform program to experiment with, and found the idea of "*leben und leben lassen*" inadmissibly passive and non-professional. The reformer's nightwatch-state was often also awake during the day. Nevertheless, because he lacked a definite vision of the future (where does the "Third Road" end?), these positive expert programs tended to focus on the initial steps and the process of reformation rather than on its final stages. Consequently, if it makes sense at all to speak about liberalism in this context, reform economics embodied a sort of "*processual*" liberalism, rather than a liberal discipline derived from a definite—though abstract—ideal vision of the future or the past.

Even the radical reform concepts did not rely on a profound philosophical (ethical) basis, on strong arguments about the intrinsic "beauties" of the market and the virtues of private property, that is, on a radical liberal dream. Instead, the reformer saw the market in a *pragmatic-utilitarian* way as a device for "repairing" the Soviet-type economy. In his view, the market does not embody justice in itself. It is, however, capable of working as a machine (cf. the term "economic mechanism") which is geared, or even at times switched on and off, by the planners assisted by "social engineers". This sterile notion of a *simulated* market purged of property rights lent a *mechanical* character to reformist liberalism. Finally, as regards the principle of individualism, the reform economist did not consider it an indispensable element of market socialism. It was treated as something technically unfeasible as well as partly replaceable by *collectivist* experiments made in the field of self-management.

No doubt about it, these deformations were considerably reduced in the course of a learning-by-doing process, i.e., by realizing the consecutive failures of limited liberalization projects. Nonetheless, liberalism in socialist reform thinking remained *rootless* in double sense. On one hand, the pre-war liberal tradition in economics in Eastern Europe was weak or broken, on the other, it was only partly reconstructed by the theorists of market socialism through importing or reinventing the basics of Western liberalism. In the absence of a firm philosophical background, the trial-and-error procedures of reform-making could only lead to a pragmatic rediscovery of liberal thought. Liberal ideas resulted from practical choices, I would say, for want of a better solution, and were often against the moral conviction of the reform economists.

To be sure, the romantic anti-capitalist feelings inherited from Marxist teachings by the early reformers began to wane as the years passed. Churchill's *bon mot* that democracy is the worst except for all other political systems, however, is still very popular in Eastern Europe whenever economists discuss private property and the free market. Marketization *and* privatization tend to be considered musts, but they are regarded as necessary evils rather than "the best of all possible worlds". The latent animosity even some radical reform economists felt toward the allegedly inhuman market was supported by traditional arguments that defend the principle of equal opportunity. *Egalitarian* considerations (whether they came directly from the Marxian utopia of communism, Western social-democratic thought, or from recent critiques of new classical liberalism) always permeated reform thinking, even when liberal views did not need to hide behind the facade of post-Stalinist ideology. True, many ex-reformers have since suspended their egalitarian vigilance, arguing: first we must create the market in order to "humanize" it later.

You do not have to be an arch-libertarian to recognize that these heirlooms are less "unofficial" than the aforementioned ones, and may endanger the liberal transformation of the Soviet-type systems in Eastern Europe. It would be, of course, futile to deny that the reform economists also had a seemingly ultra-liberal group which based its proposals on the idea of small entrepreneurship and free competition.[15] Nevertheless, its adherents tended to trust the virtues of the spontaneous market process *only after* having already introduced their Grand Design by the center. I am afraid that the transformers have to face a very similar dilemma in our days.

(2) Controlling the transition. Can privatization be privatized, deregulation be deregulated? Or—to put it in Hayekian terms—can one reach, without "constructivist rationalism", a spontaneous order by starting out from an extremely non-spontaneous one? In the transforming countries of Eastern Europe a number of economists are desparately seeking answer to these questions. There are, however, a far greater number who consider these problems irrelevant or give a negative answer almost instinctively with a reformist reflex action. In excluding the possibility of *spontaneous evolutionary change* they select their arguments, according to their political taste, from among the following sources (they are not listed in order of importance).[16]

a. Beware of Survivors! Strict government supervision is indispensable both to the assembly of parts for the new economic system and the dismantling of the components of the old one, unless our objective is to make it easier for the old elite to capitalize—literally—on their political privileges. Spontaneous evolution favours the strong—however, it was mainly under the old regime that one could accumulate strength. If privatisation is spontaneous, the result will be capitalism for the *nomenklatura* only. To assure equal chances for all, it is necessary, at least in the beginning, to discriminate against the old ruling elite. Anyway, nobody expects a transsexual man to increase the country's birth rate.

b. Checking the Lobbies. The supervision of the transition will be ineffective unless it is coupled with the systematic dismantling of the economic institutions of the Soviet-type system and their accompanying lobbies, the breaking up of monopolies, and the disruption of the informal networks. If we deduct the state-party from the party-state, the result, unfortunately, will not be zero. Until the state economy has been fully demonopolized, a strong hand is necessary to keep the lobbies under control. The old monopolies must not be allowed to strangle, under the banner of *laissez faire,* the "young markets." A strong government must discipline the state sector before, during and after privatisation, keeping all possible budget constraints hard. Otherwise, inflation will spiral upwards, capital will leak away before it can be privatized, and stabilization will be obstructed by producers' strikes and financial chaos.

c. Old-New Socialism. Because the state economy might come not only under liberal but also collectivistic criticism, socialist hopes, egalitarian endeavours, self-managment programs and populist illusions may reemerge in the course of the old order's demise, especially in the case of a profound economic crisis causing rapid social polarization. To protect the liberal path of social progress, it is necessary to restrain socialist leanings that are reborn along with capitalism. Third Road type programs can, unfortunately, be built not only on the basis of the first (state) economy but also on the more market-friendly second (shadow) economy. The reviving trade unions should be counter-balanced by the government until the employers' organizations grow strong.

d. Horror Vacui. The death of the old is not tantamount to the birth of the new: unless we are careful in sequencing the economic measures of the transition, illiberal wizards with their self-styled recipes can easily find their way into the "no more communism—not yet capitalism" void. We must be armed with detailed plans for pulling down the old house as well as for building the new one, or both might collapse on top of us. It is in this "transitional" stage of the transition that fatal mistakes can be committed. Until the rule of law (legal state) is asserted, it is the state that represents the law. While the market is not fully in place, the state has no alternative but to assist in privatization. Until the private property becomes widespread, who else could launch marketization if not the state? As long as the market is incapable of stabilization, and so on . . .

e. Cleaning up the Mess. Transformation does not start with a *tabula rasa*: the first priority is to clear away the physical, spiritual and moral heritage of communism as quickly as possible. The real work ("unmaking the omelette", "remaking the aquarium from the fish soup") can only begin afterwards. Over the past decades, things have fallen apart, and one needs detailed instructions to put them all together again, if that is even possible. Reconstruction will probably be facilitated by innovative experimentation. It is a unique historical trick of communism that even the measures designed to eliminate it bear its distinctive characteristics.

f. The Missing Agent. In the absence of a strong middle class (entrepreneurs, civil society, etc.), the state must act as its temporary substitute. At the same time, it has to produce and train the natural agents of capitalist development. This is not the first time this will happen in this region—as demonstrated by Alexander Gerschenkron and Karl Polányi. Once again, a bourgeois revolution has to be launched with the subsequent approval of the emerging bourgeoisie. Indeed, the first thing we are building in our new house is the loft. To use the language of systems theory: the new economic order comes into being in an *autopoietic* way; that is, it creates the preconditions of its own genesis. We are not born to be entrepreneurs . . .

g. Transition Laboratory. Postcommunist transition is an unprecedented venture in the history of mankind. Similar transformations are either removed from us by centuries (early capitalism), are anything but liberal (Southeast-Asia), or tend to be unsuccessful (Latin America). Undoubtedly, there have been more recent, more successful and more liberal examples which may be instructive for Eastern European transformers (the reconversion of modern war economies, the German social market economy, privatisation in the United Kingdom, etc.). However, their success has rested on institutional conditions mostly lacking in Eastern Europe. One thing is for sure: the means we employ today should be at least as statist as those of the late 1940s and early 1950s, when the German economy was stabilized and freed from the legacy of Nazi rule. Until the appropriate techniques of transformation are found, there is a genuine need for macro-experimentation. At the same time, market simulation no longer works: there can be no more "Monopoly game" for adults played on a "plastic Wall Street." Instead, we have to choose between feasible capitalist arrangements, possibly even combining several of these, enriching them with new ideas. The only certain element in the transition is that every now and then the transformer will be confronted with uncertain developments.

h. Time Pressure. The liberal expedition sets out at a time of an acute economic crisis. The distance between the point of departure and even a moderately liberal stage of the transformation is so long, and the expectations of the population are so high (and their limit of tolerance so low) that the transition may easily lose its original momentum. Step-by-step modification may be neutralized, whereas across-the-board changes are technically unworkable and politically risky. Given the interdependence and inertia of—and frictions between—the tasks related to transformation, if we want to prevent the process from collapsing, we must strive for an effective breakthrough right at the beginning. Therefore, we have to guarantee the critical mass of measures at the outset, and we must be adroit in selecting and ranking the subsequent steps in order to accelerate or at least sustain the pace of change. We are witnessing a new era of *Sturm und Drang* and we should not be ashamed of that.

i. Technical, Logical and Political Dilemmas. There are numerous tasks that need to be performed simultaneously. (In the economy: marketization, privatization, stabilization, modernization, opening up to the West, etc; in politics: democratization, establishing the rule of law, reforming the public administration, institutionalizing social partnership, etc; in society: embourgeoisement, distributing the social costs of the transition, creating the "Capitalist Type of Man", etc.) By contrast, the working capacity of the transformers is limited. Moreover, the required tasks often support and, at the same time, counteract one another (some logically, some politically), and it is extremely difficult to compare the short- and long-term advantages and disadvantages of the qualitatively different processes. Thus, without a constant and occasionally daring rearrangement of priorities, the liberal transition will become too costly and painful. While accepting the truism that "once a leg has to be amputated, it should be done at once rather than bit by bit," shock therapy may be applied only to certain stages and spheres of the transition.

j. Transition is Intervention. A number of transformative measures require, almost automatically, government intervention in the economy. Resolute central guidance is part and parcel of processes such as macroeconomic stabilization, sectoral restructuring, comprehensive welfare reform, and liberalization of foreign trade. A " stabilization surgery" cannot be executed by an "invisible hand." After all, there must be someone present to regulate wages, consolidate the currency, distribute subsidies, and adjust exchange rates, taxes and rates of interest. Let us not forget, it was the party-state and not the state as such that became discredited this past half a century in Eastern Europe. There is a widespread desire for a strong but democratic government, administered by a highly qualified bureaucracy, which is capable of making limited and mostly temporary intervention in the economy. Such types of intervention create an appropriate environment for the market, without either replacing or distorting it. The history of capitalism cannot be started afresh: the free market tends to eliminate itself; it is better to have some minor intervention today than to have a major one tomorrow; the market should be protected from itself; in economic history mixed economies were not born by accident. Besides, what has become of the conservative revolution of the 1970s and 1980s in the West?

Relying on these sources, in which I have included some of the favorite metaphors used by the transformers, one can follow the "official" (statist, constructivist, élitist, experimentalist, etc.) traditions very closely and also from a certain distance, depending on which arguments one is ready to accept. Nevertheless, it would be too much to expect that the signals issued by the transition process will induce the ex-reformers to break the illiberal line of the legacy completely. Rather, the opposite case seems likely: the deformed liberalism of the reform economists may become less deformed by incorporating the crucial elements of large-scale private ownership and parliamentary democracy, the ex-reformers will, however, apply these concepts with basic limitations, according to the actual requirements of the transformation. And the foregoing list shows that the possibilities to make concessions to statism are innumerable . . .

Without evaluating the above arguments, it is clear that they portray the state as a "*chief architect*" of the transition. Furthermore, the state must be prepared to act as a construction manager, dispatcher, programmer, designer, laboratory assistant, tutor and arbitrator. *Horribile dictu,* it may even serve as a security guard (but not a night watchman!) and garbage collector. As far as the transformer is concerned, he supplies the government with pieces of (literally) constructive advice, and joins this crucial construction project primarily as a building engineer.

He speaks of tasks to be executed, programmes to be drawn up and deadlines to be met, and allows little time for observation and explanation. He is active, normative and programmatic. Yet, paradoxically, the uncertainties and theoretical dilemmas of the transition, as well as the general shortage of reliable information about the real processes of change, could just as reasonably argue not for but *against* state intervention.

By including the elements of privatization and democratization in the plan-and-market discourse, the economics of reform gets beyond the boundaries of Soviet-type socialism, and enters—to put it simply—the realm of social market economy. Here, this "Great Leap Forward" notwithstanding, the ex-reformers may theoretically choose the less liberal and more social-democratic (interventionist, welfarist) variants of the concept and vice versa. Similarly, they may be more or also less oriented to social-engineering within the limits of *Soziale Marktwirtschaft,* as far as their methodological attitudes are concerned. But one thing is certain, namely, that, as in the past, they will not be able to get along without major compromises between their statist and liberal selves in an attempt to create harmony not, as earlier, between Plan and Market, but between *Public and Private.* Also, they will hardly be able to avoid facing the old dilemma of *simultaneous liberalization and democratization.* Until recently, as reformers, they believed that their liberalization proposals had failed because there was too little democracy in the party-state. Now they may learn that too much democracy can also block marketization and privatization.

In any event, like reformation, transformation is also a trial-and-error process with the great difference, however, that in this experiment organic institutions such as market, private ownership and political democracy may come to the fore. Owing to their historical congruence (at least of the first two) these institutions may well ease the dilemmas and reduce the frequency of errors. Compromises will mean "halfway houses" again, though these houses will lie closer to the imaginary state of *laissez-faire* than the former reformist ones and, in principle, nothing would seem to prevent the transformer from moving them still closer to the ideal.

Let us return to the Hayekian dilemma of "how to arrive at a spontaneous order from an extremely non-spontaneous one, through evolution." After having absorbed the above ten arguments in favour of a "sound (defensive) interventionism", one should be astonished if the economists firmly opposed to social engineering represented more than a negligible minority in Eastern Europe.

It is very telling that even the most devoted advocates of spontaneity (who are also the least limited in their political influence) such as the team of transformers working with the Czech prime minister, Václav Klaus, act with a kind of "*delayed liberalism*" when cautiously defining the stages of "laying the foundations of capitalism". They assert that (a) spontaneous market selection is unsuitable for the rapid deregulation of an overregulated state economy; (b) resolute, so-called, "negative" reform measures should be taken by the government to accelerate deconstruction; (c) from among the components of monetarism, during the first stage of the transition, stress should be laid on restrictive rigour; (d) the initial steps of marketization and privatization have to be taken under strict government control; (e) to serve the right goal—"market economy without adjectives"—one should not even shrink from formally collectivist solutions (see *kupon* privatization); (f) the state should only withdraw, gradually, after the "*first push*" has been made and when the appropriate economic and legal infrastructure for market self-regulation has already been established.[17]

All in all, then, Friedman before Hayek. Confronted with the above arguments, innocent Western observers ask: what should we consider the appropriate infrastructure? That of the mixed economy of Sweden, Germany, the United States or Japan? Or that of South Korea or Mexico? Eastern observers, who are usually less innocent, may raise, full of anxiety, the following questions: who will decide when the appropriate stage of liberalization has been reached? Why should the state quit, and why should the government bureaucracy commit collective suicide after having been so successful during the heroic years of the transition? What if sooner or later the state abandons Friedman and falls in love with Keynes again? Finally, those with no innocence, who were reared on Lenin's teaching about the withering away of the state, would simply feel at home when they hear the familiar explanation about the need to substitute temporarily the state for the middle class. (This time it is not the proletariat that has to be replaced by its vanguard, the Communist party-state.)

As we have seen, it is not difficult to support the idea of a *strong "medium state"* with reasonable arguments even if one does not go so far as to long for a populist dictator or an enlightened monarch who would prevent the transformation process from derailing. Considering the mixed signals sent by the actual developments of transition, the only force we may put our faith in is that of *oblivion,* if we liked to see the transformers get released from the burden of the "official" reformist legacy. Could forgetting be sociologically stimulated? In principle, yes. However, as peculiar as it may be, the sociological status of the ex-reformers seems not to have greatly changed in Eastern Europe during the last couple of years.

Though 1989 put an end to the era of socialist reformism, the reformers did not leave the scene of Eastern European economics as losers. They probably did not have to leave the scene at all. They need not have withdrawn and sought refuge in the university libraries or buried themselves in business activities. As far as it can be estimated at this juncture, the majority of them were rapidly absorbed by the new élite, so they remained "within the walls". Moreover, owing to their contacts with the former opposition movements, to the insatiable demand for expertise in the new political parties and governments, and above all to the fact that these institutions were seeking experts exactly in "social engineering" to have them work out the new party programs and transition scenarios, the ex-reformers often could get closer to the "commanding heights" than ever.

Thanks to the vacuum of political control (the *nomenklatura* has already lost its power while the parliamentary system has not accumulated it yet), the early transformers could temporarily acquire a much greater elbow-room than their reformer predecessors. "Transformation-mongering" was a bit easier than reform-mongering had been before. In many countries of post-socialism, a series of long-term nation-wide comprehensive master plans of stabilization, privatization, etc., (or entire "programs for national salvation") could be initiated in the last three years without scrupulously filtering them through the new democratic polity.

Sociologically, the majority of former reformist experts could keep their intermediary roles between politics, business and academia. True, some of the moderate "collaborationists" who cherished close links with the communist party fell out of the élite. At the same time, however, the radical reform economists had good chances for being elevated to the supreme leadership of the new parties and government administrations. Symptomatically, most of them are grouping around social-democratic type parties (even if these organizations call themselves liberal), whereas many ex-reformers have simply changed their bosses and now lend their expert knowledge to parties with overtly authoritarian, populist, etc., ideologies. They sometimes even do not refrain from making concessions to collectivist, "Third Road"-type solutions.[18]

The Destructive Tradition

Are we actually witnessing the reformist legacy as a whole turning into a serious obstacle to the transition from socialism in Eastern Europe? Are the "official" components of the heritage more harmful now than before? For the time being, I would not risk to make such statements. Not because I would think that the "official" heirlooms of reform economics are about to disappear. Rather because I am afraid that, *practically,* without a little help from them, one cannot even achieve limited success in launching the transition process. *Planning the transformation?* Realistically, this is to be expected, even if, one hopes, with much less dirigisme than before.

To sum up, while under real socialism the reform economist would not have been able to survive and permitted to build up his “unofficial” legacy without the “official” one, and while nowadays this winning combination may help the transformer start the transition to a liberal order, it is very probable that this mix of traditions will considerably hinder him in completing the transformation in the foreseeable future. Paradoxically, reformism that, in the last analysis, proved *destructive* for the old regime may turn to have the same effect on the new one as well. Why? Because—in Hayekian sense—it tends to preserve its constructivist traits . . .

Notes

1. In this chapter I will focus on the so-called “reform countries” of Hungary, Poland and Yugoslavia. Nevertheless, because the theoretical and political aspects of socialist reformation will also be discussed, Czechoslovakia, China and the Soviet Union cannot be left out of consideration either.
2. See the answers of Leszek Balcerowicz, Aleksander Bajt, Wlodzimierz Brus, Karel Dyba, András Hegedüs, Branko Horvat, Gennadii Lisichkin, László Szamuely and Márton Tardos to the questions of *Acta Oeconomica* (1989/3–4) “On Socialist Market Economy”. See also Wlodzimierz Brus & Kazimierz Laski, “From Marx to the Market”, Oxford 1989; János Kornai,”The Road to a Free Economy”, New York 1990; Iván Szelényi, Eastern Europe in an Epoch of Transition—Towards a Socialist Mixed Economy? in: V. Nee-D. Stark (eds): *Remaking the Economic Institutions of Socialism,* Stanford, 1989, and Vaclav Klaus & Tomas Jezek, Social Criticism, False Liberalism and Recent Changes in Czechoslovakia, Eastern European Politics and Societies Winter 1991.
3. For the similarities between the “*nomenklatura*-buyout” programs in radical reformist/dissident thought, see János Kis & Ferenc Köszeg & Ottilia Solt, “Társadalmi Szerzödés” (Social Contract), *Beszélö* 1987; Elemér Hankiss, “Eastern European Alternatives—Are There Any?”, Oxford 1990; Jan Winiecki, “Gorbachev’s Way Out?” CRCE London 1988.
4. See János Mátyás Kovács & Márton Tardos (eds), “Reform and Transformation in Eastern Europe. Soviet-Type Economics on the Threshold of Change” London 1992; “Rediscovery of Liberalism in Eastern Europe” *Eastern European Politics and Societies* Winter 1991.
   For typologies of reform economists, see also Wlodzimierz Brus, “Institutional Change Within a Planned Economy”, in: M. Kaser (ed.): “The Economic History of Eastern Europe 1919–1975”, Oxford 1986; János Kornai, The Hungarian Reform Process: Visions, Hopes and Reality, *Journal of Economic Literature* December 1986; László Lengyel, “Végkifejlet” (End-game), Budapest 1989; and my Reform Economics: The Classification Gap, *Daedalus* Winter 1990.

The terms "reform economics", "economic reformism", and the "theory of market socialism" are used interchangeably in the chapter.

5. A reform-alku sürüjében (In the Thick of Reform Bargaining *Valóság* 1984/3; Reform Bargaining in Hungary, *Comparative Economic Studies* 1986/3; Compassionate Doubts About Reform Economics (Economic Science, Ideology Politics), in: Kovács & Tardos (eds), "Reform and Transformation . . . "
6. Cf. István R. Gábor, Reformok, második gazdaság, államszocializmus (Reforms, Second Economy, State Socialism), *Valóság* 1986/7; Kálmán Rupp: "Entrepreneurs in Red", Albany 1983; David Stark: Bending the Bars of the Iron Cage, *Sociological Forum* 1989/4; Iván Szelényi, "Socialist Entrepreneurs. Embourgeoisement in Rural Hungary", Madison 1988.
7. Cf.Tamás Bauer, Reforming or Perfectioning the Economic Mechanism?, *European Economic Review* 1987/31; Tadeusz Kowalik, On Crucial Reform of Real Socialism, *WIIW Forschungsberichte* October 1986; László Szamuely, "A magyar közgazdasági gondolat fejlödése. Bevezetés" (The Development of Hungarian Economic Thought. Introduction), Budapest, 1986. See also the works of Brus, Kornai and Lengyel cited above.
8. Cf. J.M. Kovács, Reform Economics . . . ; Compassionate Doubts . . .
9. Cf. J. Kornai, The Hungarian Reform Process . . . ; Alec Nove, "The Economics of Feasible Socialism", London 1983; Pekka Sutela, "Socialism, Planning and Optimality. A Study in Soviet Economic Thought", Helsinki 1984, and Reformability of the "Objective Economic Laws" of Socialism, in: Kovács & Tardos (eds) Reform and Transformation . . .
10. Cf. J.M. Kovács, Reform Economics . . . ; Compassionate Doubts.
11. Cf. György Konrád & Iván Szelényi, "The Intellectuals on the Road to Class Power", New York 1979.
12. For the role of experts and their bargaining power, see, for example, Aron Katsenelinboigen, "Soviet Economic Thought and Political Power in the USSR", Oxford 1980; Jacek Kurczewski, Power and Wisdom: the Expert as Mediating Figure in Contemporary Polish History, in: I.Maclean, A.Montefiore, P.Winch (eds.): "The Political Responsibility of Intellectuals", Cambridge 1990; and also my "A reformalku . . . " and "Reform Bargaining . . . "
13. For a discussion of how the Hungarian reformers became transformers, as well as of the sociological and intellectual similarities between the two groups, see my Szocialista vagy szociális piacgazdaság? (Socialist or Social Market Economy?) *Világosság* 1990/1, and From Reformation to Transformation (Limits to Liberalism in Hungarian Economic Thought) *Eastern European Politics and Societies* Winter 1991.
14. Cf. J.M. Kovács, From Reformation to Transformation . . .
15. Cf. István Siklaky (ed.): "Koncepció és kritika. Vita Liska Tibor 'szocialista vállalkozási szektor' javaslatáról" (Concept and Critique. A Debate on the Proposal by Tibor Liska of the "Socialist Sector of Entrepreneurship"), Budapest 1985; Tibor Liska, "Ökonosztát" (Oeconostate), Budapest 1988, and "Szent barmunk a politika alaprendje" (Our Sacred Cow—the Political System), Budapest 1989.
16. Cf. Janusz Beksiak & Tomasz Gruszecki & Alekszander Jedraszczyk & Jan

Winiecki: The Polish Transformation, CRCE London 1990; H. Bloomestein & M. Marrese (eds): Transformation of Planned Economies: Property Rights Reform and Macroeconomic Stability, Paris 1991; Csaba László: Közép-Európai rendszerváltás és stabilizáció (Systemic Change and Stabilization in Central Europe), Külgazdaság 1991/9; Marek Dabrowski: A lengyel stabilizációs program (The Polish Stabilization Program), Külgazdaság 1991/3; R. Dietz: Transformation: From Command to Exchange Communication, manuscript 1991; R. Dornbush & J. Edwards: The Economic Populism Paradigm, NBER Working Papers, May 1990; John Farrell: Monitoring the Great Transition, Comparative Economic Studies Summer 1991; Roman Frydman & Andrzej Rapaczynski: Evolution and Design in the East European Transition, 1991, manuscript; Gábor R. István: Második gazdaság, modernitás, dualitás (Second Economy, Modernity and Dualism), Közgazdasági Szemle 1991/11; Stanislav Gomulka: The Causes of Recession Following Stabilization, Comparative Economic Studies, Summer 1991; Irena Grosfeld: Privatization of State Enterprises in Eastern Europe. The Search for a Market Environment, Eastern European Politics and Societies Winter 1991; Tomasz Gruszecki: Privatization in Poland, Communist Economies 1991/2; Historical Precedents for Economic Change in Central Europe and the USSR, Oxford Analytica 1990; G.W.Kolodko: A lengyel hiperinfláció és stabilizáció (Hyperinflation and Stabilization in Poland), Külgazdaság 1991/2; Kornai János: The Road to a Free Economy . . . ; A privatizáció elvei Kelet-Európában (The Principles of Privatization in Eastern Europe), Közgazdasági Szemle 1991/11; Jiri Kosta: Ökonomische Aspekte des Systemwandels in der Tschechoslowakei, in: R. Deppe, H. Dubiel, U. Rödel (eds): Demokratischer Umbruch in Osteuropa, Frankfurt 1991; Robert Kuttner: The Dustbin of Economics, The New Republic 1991/2/25; K. Laski: Transition from Command to Market Economy in Central and Eastern Europe, manuscript 1991; Helmut Leipold: Die Politik der Privatisierung und Deregulierung. Lehren für die Wirtschaftsreformen im Sozialismus, in: Zur Transformation der Wirtschaftssysteme, Marburg 1990; Paul McCracken: Thoughts on Marketizing State-Managed Economies, Economic Impact 1990/2; John M. Montias: The Sequencing of Reforms, Challenge Sept-Oct 1990; W. Nordhaus: Soviet Economic Reform: The Longest Road, Brookings Papers 1990/1; Claus Offe: Das Dilemma der Gleichzeitigkeit. Demokratisierung und Marktwirtschaft in Osteuropa, Merkur 1991/4; Richard Portes (ed): The Path of Reform in Central and Eastern Europe, European Economy (special issue) 1991/2; Adam Przeworski, Economic Reforms in New Democracies. The Polish Experience, manuscript 1990; Inderjit Singh: Is There Schizophrenia about Socialist Reform Theory?, Transition 1991/7; Aleksander Smolar: Durch die Wüste. Die Dilemmas des Übergangs, Transit 1990/1; Jadwiga Staniszkis: 'Political Capitalism' in Poland, Eastern European Politics and Societies Winter 1991; David Stark: Privatizációs stratégiák Közép-Kelet-Európában (Privatisation Strategies in East-Central Europe), Közgazdasági Szemle 1991/12; Szelényi Iván: A magyar polgárosodás esélyei (The Possibilities of Embourgeoisment in Hungary), Hitel 1989/16; Alternative Futures for Eastern Europe, Eastern European Politics and Societies, Spring

1990; Jan Svejnar: A Framework for the Economic Transformation of Czechoslovakia, Eastern European Economics, Winter 1990–91; Tardos Márton: A tulajdon (Ownership), Közgazdasági Szemle 1988/12; The Soviet Economic Crisis: Steps to Avert Collapse, IIASA 1991; Jan Winiecki: The Inevitability of a Fall in Output in the Early Stages of Transition to the Market: Theoretical Underpinnings, Soviet Studies 1991/4.

17. Václav Klaus: A Road to Market Economy, Prague 1991; Das kann man nicht mehr kontrollieren, Weltwoche 1991/9/ ;V. Klaus & T. Jezek, Social Criticism, False Liberalism . . . ; The Evolutionary Approach, Financial Times 1989/12/13.
18. For the faulty, exaggerated expectations of a neoliberal breakthrough in Eastern Europe, see Ellen Comisso, Property Rights, Liberalism, and the Transition from "Actually Existing" Socialism, *Eastern European Politics and Societies* Winter 1991, Vladimir Gligorov, The Discovery of Liberalism in Yugoslavia, *Eastern European Politics and Societies* Winter 1991. See also my "From Reformation to Transformation . . . ".

It would take many pages to list the names of those former reform economists who work for the new parties and governments in Eastern Europe. Nevertheless such names as Dyba, Dlouhy, Klaus, Komarek, Kouba in Czechoslovakia; Bauer, Bod, Kádár, Matolcsy, Soós, Surányi, Tardos in Hungary; Balcerowicz, Jozefiak, Lewandowski, Osiatynski, Mujzel in Poland; Aven, Gaidar, Jasin, Petrakov, Popov, Shatalin in the former Soviet Union; or Bajt, Kovac and Mencinger in the former Yugoslavia may help indicate the contours of the group.

3

Opposition against "Market Breakthrough Reforms" Revisited

Jerzy Osiatynski

Introduction

In an earlier paper I discussed various types of market reforms in traditional centrally planned economies (TCPE) and examined sources of actual or potential opposition to such reforms, concentrating on what I called a 'market breakthrough reform' (Osiatynski, 1992). The exercise was largely of a speculative nature as at the time the Great Transformation From Plan to Market has been on drawing-boards only. Now I have a chance to re-examine the issues I raised in 1988, in the light of the actual experience of some 16 months of implementing the 'market breakthrough reform' in Poland (with some passing references to the respective experience of Hungary and the Czech and Slovak Republics).

Following Brus (1986), I distinguished three fundamental features of a TCPE: (i) the state monopoly in ownership of the means of production, (ii) the centralized system of organization and management of its socialized sector, and (iii) at the heart of the system, the communist control over all organized forms of public life, including the subordination of economic decision-making and management to communist party administration, the politization of the state-owned enterprise, and the dominance of polity over the economy.

Clearly, replacing these features with their respective counterparts in a market economy and political democracy may be accomplished only in a long process. This, however, must be preceded by a stabilization policy package which may also give rise to various oppositions. Therefore in what follows I shall distinguish between the opposition which relates mainly to the stabilization package of the Great Transformation, and that which relates to the process of systemic transformation itself. Then I shall return to re-examining some opposition to replacing the fundamental features of the TCPE, encountered in practice.

However, it may be useful already here to deal briefly with one aspect of fundamental feature (iii), i.e. with the dominating role of the communist party. While any discussion of conditions under which it ends goes beyond the scope of this paper, the experience of the Central and East European countries clearly indicates a strong positive correlation between the public conviction that the Great Transformation is tantamount to an end of the communist system in the country in question on the one hand, and the public support for the 'breakthrough reform', including its readiness to accept even large short-run losses in standards of living, on the other hand. This banal truth explains why the first post-communist government in Poland could get away with about 30% reduction in real wages after the reform was started, in January 1990, whereas its communist predecessor was not allowed a reduction of about 8% only a year earlier. The importance of mass support for the 'breakthrough reform' was noted in my 1988 paper but the practical consequences of public enthusiasm for the first post-communist rule were, I feel now, underrated.

Opposition against the Stabilization Policy Package

The stabilization package consisted in Poland of (i) tightening fiscal policy through a radical reduction of the budget deficit, mainly through better execution of budget revenues and cutting budget subsidies, tax exemptions, etc.; (ii) a tight monetary policy, among others through restricting subsidized credit and a very large rise in interest rates (in pursuit of positive interest rate policy) on new credits as well as on the old ones; (iii) a restrictive income policy involving high taxes upon the rise in wages exceeding a predetermined (very low) norm.

The systemic transformation measures which were introduced with the stabilization package with the aim mutually to reinforce each other, comprised of: (iv) a price liberalization which reduced the share of government controlled prices from about 50% to about 15%; (v) the introduction of convertibility of the zloty, the rate of which was sharply devalued (from 1800 zl to 1 US dollar in September 1989, to 2400 in October, 3800 in November, 6500 in December, and to 9500 zl to 1 US dollar ever since 1 January 1990); (vi) a removal of all forms of administrative allocation of goods and services, foreign exchange including; (vii) liberalization of the foreign trade regime; (viii) elimination of an automatic, non-interest bearing crediting of budget deficits by the banking system.

The first result of the stabilization measures and price liberalization was a corrective inflation which was determined by three factors of a 'negative legacy' nature: (a) the repressed inflation (or 'inflationary overhang') and domestic market disequilibrium prior to reform, (b) the depth of direct and indirect budget subsidies, and (c) maladjustments of demand and supply. Clearly, the stronger is the influence of factors (a) and (b) the higher the corrective inflation has to be. This was appreciated in my 1988 paper, but the importance of factor (c) was not. Yet, as witnessed, for instance, by the Czech and Slovak Republics, even under relative market equilibrium, the changing of factors (b) and (c) generates price rises, because it takes time before supply adjusts to new demand patterns.

There is also a 'positive legacy' which I did not well appreciate in this context. In the late phase of a centrally planned economy there develops a phenomenon which was labelled 'shortageflation' (and examined in some detail by Kolodko and McMahon, 1987). Its essence is that when government increases prices the economy diverts even further from market equilibrium instead of approaching it, mainly because of expectations that price rises will not generate re-allocation of resources that would help counter shortages. Hence shortages become even more acute. Consequently, although prices rise, goods are even harder to come by. For this reason, when prices are not merely government-increased, in order to meet requirements (i) and (ii) of the stabilization package, but genuinely liberalized, the shortage expectations disappear, as do the shortages themselves, and this generates some measure of public approval for the initial corrective price rises. Since with time the public's acceptance of price rises declines, the bulk of necessary price adjustments of (a) and (b) type should be concentrated at the very beginning of the 'market breakthrough reform'.

Another pillar of the stabilization package in Poland was incomes policy which came close to a wage freeze in the first four months of 1990, to be somewhat relaxed later on. The very low coefficients of wage indexation with respect to retail price index were maintained even though the actual price rise in the 1st quarter of 1990 was nearly twice as high as expected in the stabilization program. Nonetheless, opposition to such a drastic fall in real incomes was much less than I had anticipated, for reasons explained above. However, already after a few months the public approval for incomes policy largely subsided and on the turn of 1991 it was passionately opposed by trade unions, workers' self-management councils, and firms' managements. Yet, incomes policy is, I believe, an important instrument of preventing a return of high inflation rates, although the particular form of this policy applied in Poland should be replaced by a system of personal income tax.

One may therefore wonder if this opposition against incomes policy could not have been at least partly avoided. True, some of it was generated by plain populist demagogy spelled out in the course of presidential election in Poland, in the autumn of 1990, and continued later on. However, there remains the question of whether such a drastic fall in real incomes as that which actually occurred in the first quarter of 1990 was indeed necessary, and whether incomes policy would not be less opposed to if an alternative variant of it was followed in the light of so much higher time path of price rises. Moreover, it may be asked if an alternative profile of incomes policy would not find a more sustained public approval, e.g. one which instead of very low indexing of all incomes would index only those below some minimum level, thus protecting the real value of some minimum income? (For elaboration of this point, see Nuti.)

A negative legacy of the pre-reform economic position of both the household and the enterprise sectors was their excessive liquidity, an overhang of forced savings, and the dollarization of money circulation. In order to combat these phenomena the stabilization package introduced tight monetary policy which implied a large rise in interest rates on new as well as on old debts. These measures were facilitated by a positive legacy of the last communist government, which in August 1989 liberalized agricultural prices without attempting to control money incomes and firms' profits; the hyperinflation which followed destroyed a large part of excess liquidity before the 'market breakthrough reform' was started. This positive legacy was well appreciated by economic policy makers of the Mazowiecki government.

The taxation of old debts (by increasing interest on them) could be called into question, as well as the pursuit for positive real interest rates in the midst of corrective, largely government-induced inflation; yet a discussion of these problems goes beyond the scope of this chapter. What is more relevant for its main subject is a rather specific pattern of behaviour of households' savings. Although on the whole in the first 16 months rates of interest on deposits have been negative in real terms, nominal interest rates were significantly increased and offered better remuneration than interest on deposits of foreign exchange (at a fixed rate of exchange of the zloty). This induced not only a large transfer from foreign exchange denominated deposits to zloty denominated deposits but also a very large rise in households' savings in terms of zlotys; indeed this could have well been at the time the single most important nominal anchor in Poland. The importance of this factor (which in part can be explained by accumulation of small savings which could not be invested in real property, nor—in the absence of capital market—invested otherwise, but which offered at least some protection against inflation) was not sufficiently appreciated when the stabilization package was under discussion.

Opposition against Systemic Transformations

Let us start with changing the ownership structure and privatizing state owned enterprises. The arguments on government sector being much too large and domestic private capital assets much too limited to permit so fast a privatization as would otherwise be sensible proved correct, as did the forecast that it would be easier to expand private sector on 'no man's land' than to sell out public companies to private hands (Osiatynski, 1992). Much less appreciated were difficulties in creating capital and financial markets that could do the job (Czekaj and Sopocko, 1991).

Firstly, in the absence of available funds, acceleration of selling out state owned companies is possible only if non market instruments of privatization (e.g., capital vouchers) are used on a large scale. Yet, the importance of markets as regulators of allocation of resources is thereby undermined, the functioning of various segments of capital market is made internally inconsistent, and claims escalate that everyone should get free of charge a 'fair share' of state owned assets. Nevertheless, vouchers might be considered a fair price to pay if only a genuine restructuring of large public companies could thereby be achieved. It is not clear, however, that the thus 'privatized' firms would indeed significantly change their present pattern of behaviour.

Secondly, there are great practical difficulties in evaluating the capital assets of state owned companies, and the recent Polish experience shows that even if foreign experts are contracted to do the job there is a strong tendency to overvalue these assets.

Thirdly, the underdeveloped banking system is unable to cope with a large increase in supply of stocks and other commercial papers, and when priority is given to these operations this often negatively affects standard credit operations of the banks in question. Related to this is the lack of skills and knowledge about the use of various instruments of financial markets (which in turn affects the allocative functions of these markets).

Fourthly, continued economic recession not only adds to difficulties in evaluating firms' assets but it also prefers purchase of bonds to stocks. The tendency for bond rather than stock trading could be considered useful from the viewpoint of a harmonic development of financial markets, were it not for the pressing need to advance a massive transformation of the property structure as quickly as possible.

Fifthly, the creation and expansion of financial markets as well as the process of privatization itself require additional outlay and supply of money (to finance increased transactions on money markets). There is no guarantee, however, that this increase in money supply will not enter markets for goods and services thus undermining tight monetary policies aimed at combating inflation.

Summarizing the Polish experience with respect to changing the fundamental feature (i) it may be argued that the importance of potential difficulties of institutional and 'technical' nature was underestimated. Concentration on developing capital markets, with some neglect of parallel development of financial markets, should have been avoided. Also privatization of commercial banks should have preceded that of the state owned firms or at least go step by step with it.

Finally there is the legacy of illegal and/or wrongful nationalization of the late 1940s and later. The claims for reprivatization present all sorts of problems: political, economic and social, were reprivatization to imply actual restitution of property rights. The problem is much discussed in the press and there is no need to restate the main arguments of the debate here.

With respect to changing fundamental feature (ii), with the end of all forms of administrative allocation of goods and services the position of state-owned firms became, formally speaking, similar to that of the private ones. Equal treatment of public and private sectors was officially declared. In practice, however, apart from an ideological and indiscriminate campaign against all state owned companies, on the one hand their soft financing has been maintained and banks continue to tolerate their bad debts and finance enterprises which are in tax arrears and do not show prospects of economic feasibility. On the other hand, a policy of fiscal discrimination against state owned enterprises was vigorously followed. It was pursued in Poland already earlier, but compared to 1989 the differentiation in the tax burden of the private and the public sectors increased in 1990 about fourfold (from a shift to private sectors' advantage of 20.4 percentage points in 1989 to a shift of 82.3 points in 1990; see Bolkowiak, Relewicz, 1991). With time also incomes policy was limited to state owned firms, and tax allowances were granted if they were transformed into government owned joint stock companies, which was considered a first step to their privatization.

However, with the prospects of privatization of individual state owned firms unclear, and privatization procedures complex and lengthy, this policy made the position of management and workforce of these firms extremely unstable. This, next to colliding the managerial powers of enterprise management, workers' councils and trade unions' representation, was responsible for predominant interest, at the enterprise level, in short-run survival and wage rises, and it left hardly any room for longer-run development strategies and/or other ways of microeconomic restructuring and adaptation. Yet the lack of microeconomic response of state owned companies to instruments of macroeconomic policy is the Achilles Heel of Polish economic transformation.

No wonder there is an urgent need for these companies to know where they stand, and to subordinate their management and workforce to external rigors of the market mechanism, even when their present property structure is retained. This involves devising motivation systems that would encourage public firms' managers and workforce to consider long run profitability of their firms; a task long overdue in ex-socialist countries and not properly taken into account before the 'market breakthrough reforms' started there.

Related to this is the problem of overlapping powers of the enterprise workers' council and trade unions' representation on the one hand, and those of the government, representing the rights of the owner, on the other hand. The most important area of conflict is the ill-defined authority of all the parties to hire, promote and fire enterprise managers.

That workers' representation should have such an authority has been vigorously demanded in Poland, at least since 1956. The powers that were once granted (as in 1956 or 1980) were either soon taken away (1957), or largely neutralized (1980s). Yet, in a centrally planned economy the power of workers' representation to influence the selection of managing directors of their firms was practically the single protection against the nomenklatura 'merry-go-round' from one failed managerial position to another. The device was also hoped to gear enterprise management to look after the interests of their firms and their workforce, and under an appropriate system of incentives to follow market signals rather than instructions of their government and Party authorities.

The device was not very effective in majority of the state owned firms because workers' councils were not very experienced in controlling everyday enterprise business, but where it was effective (i.e. in about 10 % of firms where workers' councils could be founded) it clearly improved economic performance. Moreover, in the mid 1980s, when communist hard-liners attempted to discontinue an economic reform that had been devised under some influence of 'Solidarity' trade unions but was introduced already under the Marshal Law regime of General Jaruzelski, workers' councils effectively defended the reform and political liberalization.

Unfortunately, a 'market breakthrough reform', if it is to bring the desired microeconomic adjustments and macroeconomic development, requires enterprise managers often to reduce employment, curb wage rises, re-allocate resources (man-power including), etc. These decisions, no matter how critical they are from the viewpoint of enterprise's survival, will not be readily made if workers' representatives and trade unions retain their respective powers to hire and fire enterprise managers, because then in effect the latter become hostages of the former.

Hence the urgent need to re-define the role of workers' representation and trade unions in this area.

Clearly, the question discussed above has a strong political dimension and the process of finding its satisfactory solution appears slow and painful. Moreover, with respect to the powers of trade unions at the enterprise level the problem is even more thorny and borders on an important aspect of changing fundamental feature (iii).

In my 1992 paper, I emphasized the politization of the state owned firms and the special position of the local Communist party organizations, which in fact directed the firm but assumed no responsibility for its workings. Their interference and supervision were outside any explicit legal framework and therefore implied no public accountability. In the new political balance of power this role can no longer be performed by the Communist party, but it does not follow that the problem of politization of the enterprises altogether disappeared. The temptation to assume the position of the enterprise Communist party leaderships is not infrequent among 'Solidarity' trade unions leaders, and also among the leaders of the competing, communist-run trade unions. The former were often leading the opposition against communist rule in the factories or regions during the past decade, or are granted the credibility of their predecessors if they themselves were not personally involved in the underground activities before 1989. One way or another their political authority and influence are usually higher than those of managers of their enterprises. The latter fight for political and organizational survival and therefore feel compelled to take even more militant position than their opposite numbers from the 'Solidarity'.

The dilemma—to limit and regulate the powers of trade unions at the enterprise level at a risk of undermining the political position of the most important supporter of the Polish 1989 revolution, or to leave things as they are and pay the price of non-adjustment on the part of state owned firms—is very acute. Thus, changing fundamental feature (iii) also presents not wholly foreseen difficulties.

Post-scriptum

At present, possibly the most important factor limiting the pace of transition is the lack of a political and social base for continuing tough monetary and fiscal policies including rigid controls of wage rates, and for some forms of privatization, involving an inflow of foreign private capital. The actual reductions in living standards in the early phase of transition, increased income differentiation, and growing job insecurity on the one hand, and lack of market infrastructure and patterns of behaviour on the other hand, plus some mistakes of the first post-communist governments, are all responsible for the fact that the popular support of 1989 for the 'anti-communist peaceful revolution' turned out short-lived.

In Poland, 'Solidarity' trade unions too soon became victims of political profiteering by various groupings which through populist demagogy sought to improve their political positions. Local, presidential and parliamentary elections, all in the period of less than 18 months, gave way to propaganda which destabilized the political positions of even those reformers who clearly demanded corrections that would put greater stress on combating recession and improving the supply response of the economy. With 'Solidarity's' support for the economic transformation largely weakened, its political base fragmented, and counter-reform pressures from various quarters intensified, we face now in Poland an urgent need to build up not only market infrastructure, but also a political infrastructure that would help consolidate the support for both parliamentary democracy and a market economy.

This is easier said than done. In the absence of middle classes it is difficult to define the social base of the would be reformers. Mass privatization is vehemently opposed by senior 'Solidarity' trade union politicians and advisers. Maybe a civil-rights approach to defining and consolidating political support for the transition started in 1990 would be more promising in this context than other, more traditional ways of forming such a support. Moreover, in the absence of a well established network of democratic institutions and modes of behaviour, corporatist approaches and structures—even if we are aware of their dangers—as well as a widespread participatory democracy could be of great value.

Finally let me mention yet another bottle-neck of transition: the crisis of public finance. This is a combined effect of the collapse of budget incomes, mainly due to a dramatic reduction of tax revenues from state-owned enterprises, of a large rise of the necessary budget spending, following the growth of unemployment, the earlier retirement of those threatened by loss of employment, and of a lack of systemic changes in the field of welfare benefits, social services, etc., long overdue but difficult to introduce for political considerations.

References

Bolkowiak I., Relewicz E. (1991), 'Reforms of the Tax System in the Process of Market Transformation', contribution to the conference on 'Financial Policy—Stabilization—Transformation', Ministry of Finance and Institute of Finance, Wilga, April 24–6, 1991 (in Polish).

Brus, W. (1986), 'Institutional Change within a Planned Economy', in M. Kaser (ed.), *The Economic History of Eastern Europe, 1919–1975,* Vol. III, Clarendon Press, Oxford, Chs. 23–6.

Czekaj J., Sopocko A. (1991), 'Financial Markets in the Transition Period', contribution to the conference on 'Financial Policy-Stabilization-Transformation', Ministry of Finance and Institute of Finance, Wilga, April 24–6, 1991 (in Polish).

Kolodko, G.W., McMahon W.W. (1987), 'Stagflation and Shortageflation: A Comparative Approach', *Kyklos,* 40/2.

Nuti, D.M., 'Lessons from Polish Stabilization', *Cambridge Journal of Economics.*

Osiatynski, J. (1992), 'Opposition against Market-type Reforms in Centrally Planned Economies', in: J.M. Kovács & M. Tardos (eds), *Reform and Transformation in Eastern Europe,* London, Routledge 1992.

4

Paths of Extrication and Possibilities of Transformation

László Bruszt and David Stark

With the installation of legitimate governments chosen via free elections and the establishment of new political institutions, the East Central European polities of Czechoslovakia, Hungary, Poland, and the former East Germany have completed the stage of *extrication* from monocratic state socialism. These societies are now entering the second stage of transition in which the critical questions concern whether and how democracy will be consolidated and whether and how their economies will be transformed.

The two papers that follow are the result of our collaborative efforts exploring the relationship between the stage of extrication and that of consolidation/transformation. Their starting points are based on a characterization of the transitions in East Central Europe as differing not in degree but in type. That is, the collapse of communism throughout the region did not vary from case to case simply in speed or in the relative strength of democratic impulses. Instead, the mode of extrication was through capitulation in some cases, through compromise in others, and elsewhere through electoral competition itself.[1] Recognizing these different patterns in the first stage suggests the likelihood of patterned variation in the subsequent stage and the formative constraints of the former on the latter. In short, in analyzing the creation of a new social order from the ruins of the old we argue that differences in how the pieces fell apart have consequences for how political and economic institutions can be reconstructed in the current period. In the papers that follow we argue that the distinctive patterns of transformative politics that we can observe in contemporary East Central Europe in this second stage of transition are shaped by institutional configurations produced in the process of extrication from state socialism.

Our goal in these papers is to develop a comparative framework for understanding the already visible differences in the general strategies of transformative politics and the more specific strategies of privatization in the region. By *transformative politics* we refer to the twin (and intertwined) processes of transforming economies and securing social peace. To this end, Bruszt charts the courses of action pursued by the newly elected governments in the first year (or year and a half) of their rule. His task will be to explain the zig-zag courses taken in each of the cases not simply in terms of the fundamental dilemmas generic to the post-communist transition but in relation to the country-specific structural and institutional legacies inherited by each new regime. Stark develops a similar model to explain characteristic differences in the more specific *strategies of privatization* among our four cases.

Central to our common argument is the concept of path dependence: pre-existing institutional configurations *constrain choices* and *shape actions*. The concept of path dependency should not be confused with the many variants of purely historicist argumentation often organized around essentialist cultural features such as "Poles have always had ambivalent attitudes to authority" or "Hungarian culture has long been characterized by its entrepreneurial spirit." Nor can it be reduced to a simple organizational inertia, as if organizations can only follow the least resistant course of the most familiar. On the contrary, the true strength of the concept of path dependency is its analytic power in explaining outcomes where strategic actors are deliberately searching for departures from long-established routines and attempting to restructure the rules of the game. It is precisely when attempting to modify institutional arrangements that underlying institutional configurations are manifested. Only from the theoreticist plane of clairvoyant rational choice models can actors choose from a universe of abstract possibilities. In the world of historically constituted action, by contrast, actors who seek to move in new directions find that their choices are constrained and shaped by the existing set of institutional resources.

The dramatic industrial restructuring currently being attempted in East Central Europe is so shaped and constrained. Some strategies will be excluded by the absence of certain institutions of interest intermediation and conflict resolution. For example, corporatist solutions based on centralized bargaining among peak associations of capital, labor, and the state will not even be contemplated in those cases lacking employer associations and strong trade unions. Other strategies will be more readily perceived and selected that correspond with (or, at least, are not entirely alien to) the inherited set of institutions. And because the full array of institutions cannot be redesigned with a single stroke across the board, any given strategy will eventually confront obstacles imposed by those institutions not yet dismantled or transformed. For these reasons, we anticipate that continuities and not ruptures will mark even the most radical transformations.

This view of transformation stands in sharp contrast to the prevalent approach that argues that economic development requires a rapid, radical, extensive (even exhaustive) *replacement* of the current institutions, habits, and routines of the former centrally planned economies by an entirely new set of institutions and mentalities. Such grand experiments and utopian blueprints ignore the fact that economies are embedded in a complex configuration of social institutions in which societies (and hence economies) are reproduced. It is in these institutions that dispersed agents will act to transform the transformers. The alternative to utopian experiments anticipates a process in which transformation is taking place throughout society. It thus argues that the *structural innovations* that will bring about a dynamic transformation will entail a process of complex *rearrangements* of institutional elements rather than their immediate replacement.

Note

1. This argument is elaborated and illustrated in László Bruszt and David Stark, "Remaking the Political Field in Hungary: From the Politics of Confrontation to the Politics of Competition," in *The Journal of International Affairs* (June 1991) (also published in Ivo Banac, ed., *Eastern Europe in Revolution,* Ithaca, NY: Cornell University Press, 1991).

5

Path Dependence and Privatization Strategies in East Central Europe

David Stark

Introduction: Capitalism by Design?

Across the ruins of Communism, a clear breeze blows from the West. Like the "fresh winds" hailed from the East across the ruins of war more than four decades earlier, it promises prosperity through sacrifice. Like the old vision with its road maps to the promised land, this new vision comes with packaged formulas for applying economic science to the grand project of institutional reconstruction. In 1991, no less than in 1948, devastation is seen as mandating boldness of action but also as presenting an opportunity: the collapse of the old order demands ambitious experiments and offers the occasion to build anew, this time, with a fresh start to create capitalism by design.

As the juxtaposition of postwar Bolshevism and post-Cold War designer capitalism suggests, this paper is highly skeptical about

---

A version of this chapter appeared in *East European Politics and Societies* 6:1 (Winter 1992):17–54. Research for this paper was supported by grants from the National Science Foundation. My thanks to László Bruszt, Valerie Bunce, Janusz Dabrowski, István Gábor, Péter Gedeon, Peter Katzenstein, János Lukács, Gerald McDermott, Peter Murrell, Victor Nee, László Neumann, Andrzej Rychard, Jan Szomburg, Márton Tardos, Eva Voszka, and especially Monique Djokic Stark for helpful criticisms and suggestions at various stages of researching and writing this paper.

analyses that approach the economic transition in East Central Europe as a problem to be solved by the rationalist design of economic institutions. Three sets of reasons inform this skepticism.

First, proposals for all-encompassing institutional change according to comprehensive blueprints suffer from an inadequate comparison of socialist and capitalist economic systems.[1] Misled by the superior performance of capitalist institutions, such proposals mistakenly conclude that these institutions can be replicated according to instructions. But the deeper comparative lesson is that the failure of socialism rested precisely in the attempt to organize all economic processes according to a grand design. The notion that more rational institutions can be implemented by conscious design thus duplicates the rationalist fallacy from the introduction of socialism, for example, the Leninist notion that property relations could be changed overnight by decree. Moreover, the premise that efficient institutions can be drafted at the systemic level ignores, as Peter Murrell observes, the actual operations of existing capitalisms.[2] The origins of capitalism in the West were not by blueprint, its development has not been directed by conscious design, and, as recent research in evolutionary economics and organizational ecology has demonstrated, its processes for selecting technologies and organizational forms are governed more by routine than by rational choice.[3]

The second reason to be skeptical about cookbook capitalism is that the systems designers and international advisory commissions who fly into the region with little knowledge of its history approach the problem of "the transition" exclusively through the lenses of their own general models. Through such a gaze, differences among the countries in the region are merely differences in degree (the timing and rapidity of collapse, the strength of elite commitment to reform, the speed of introducing new policies, and the like). As a consequence, their analyses of developments in the region are the simple measurements of the degree to which a particular strategy conforms to or departs from a given therapist's prescriptions. Instead, we should regard East Central Europe as undergoing a plurality of transitions in a dual sense: across the region, we are seeing a multiplicity of distinctive strategies; within any given country, we find not one transition but many occurring in different domains—political, economic, and social—and the temporality of these processes are often asynchronous and their articulation seldom harmonious.[4] Most important, because their models of economies are abstracted from the social institutions in which societies (and hence economies) are reproduced, analyses that begin with blueprints ignore how actual policy makers are shaped and constrained by the citizens of the newly emergent democracies of East Central Europe. Capitalism cannot be introduced by design in a region where forty years of experimentation by a rational hand have made citizens cautious about big experiments. A new social order cannot be created by dictation—at least not where citizens themselves want a voice in determining the new institutions. And these voices will be loudest where economic transformations are, as they must be in East Central Europe, painful and difficult. Attempts to reduce production costs and lower transaction costs can only be successful where society is willing to bear the transition costs.[5]

Because the actions of policymakers will be shaped by their perceptions of society's tolerance of these burdens, we would do better to analyze their resources for securing support instead of focusing exclusively on their recipes for change. Such resources are not likely to be evenly distributed across the countries in the region. Even more important, these resources are not simply material, financial, or economic, but are above all political. They entail the historically-shaped patterns of mediation between state and society that differ qualitatively from country to country. In such a view, social change is not a process either directed from above or initiated from below but is a result of interactions in which the designs of transformation are themselves transformed, shaped, and modified in response to, and even in anticipation of, the actions of subordinate social groups.[6] By attending to these interactions, our examination shifts from preoccupation with the "one best way" to manage the transition scientifically to a more comparative analytic strategy deliberately attuned to diverse institutional configurations differing among the countries not in degree but in kind.

The third reason for skepticism about analyses that begin with blueprints is that they often take the "collapse of Communism" to indicate the existence of an institutional void. Indeed, this myth of "starting from scratch" explains some of the academic fascination with the region and the hasty proliferation of marching orders to create capitalism in six steps or sixty. But the devastation wrought by Communism and the quick demise of its party-states have not left an institutional vacuum. My concern here is not with lingering traces of socialist ideology or with the reconstructive surgery that gives new anatomies to the old nomenklatura but with the institutional legacies of the transitions themselves. To extend the metaphor of collapse: It is in the ruins that these societies will find the materials with which to build a new order. Therefore, differences in how the pieces fell apart will affect how political and economic institutions can be reconstructed in the current period.[7] In short, it is the differing paths of extrication from state socialism that shape the possibilities of transformation in the subsequent stage.

The analysis below thus takes as its point of departure a proposition that is implausible only on first acquaintance—the economic transformations currently attempted in East Central Europe will be marked by "path dependence". The hypothesis is unlikely from the vantage of the drafting board where the designer sketches new institutions on a *tabula rasa*: Why should we expect continuities where departures are imperative? The strength of the concept of path dependence, however, is precisely its analytic power in explaining outcomes where strategic actors are deliberately searching for departures from long-established routines and attempting to restructure the rules of the game.[8] Actors who seek to move in new directions find that their choices are constrained by existing institutional resources. Institutions limit the field of action, they preclude some directions, they constrain certain courses. But institutions also favor the perception and selection of some strategies over others.[9] Actors who try to introduce change need resources to overcome obstacles to change. This use of existing institutionalized resources is a principal component of the apparent paradox that even (and especially) instances of transformation are marked by path dependence.

Such a view does not preclude the possibilities of dramatic change. But it departs emphatically from those all too prevalent approaches that argue for a rapid, radical, extensive (and even exhaustive) replacement of the current institutions, habits, and routines of the former economies by an entirely new set of institutions and mentalities. Such wholescale replacement is rejected not because of some illusions or nostalgia for socialism but from an appreciation of the evolutionary character of capitalism. If the massive social engineering that would be required to create it is undesirable, it is also unlikely.[10] It is for these reasons that I argue that the structural innovations that will bring about dynamic transformations are more likely to entail complex reconfigurations of institutional elements rather than their immediate replacement.

From this perspective, we become more circumspect about such notions as "the transition to capitalism" or "the transition to a market economy"—alert to the possibility that behind such seemingly descriptive terms are teleological constructs in which concepts are driven by hypothesized end-states. Presentist history finds its counterpart here in futurist transitology. Thus, in place of transition (with the emphasis on destination) I analyze transformations (with the emphasis on processes) in which the introduction of new elements takes place most typically in combination with adaptations, rearrangements, permutations, and reconfigurations of existing institutional forms.

This paper examines these transformative processes by comparing strategies of privatization in the four East Central European economies: Czechoslovakia, Hungary, Poland, and the former East German territories. The purpose of such a four-way comparison is not to construct some essentialist model of privatization against which the respective cases differ only in degree but to produce a comparative framework in which the specificity of each case will be revealed through its simultaneous mutual contrast with the other cases.[11] The comparative study of East European capitalisms is best launched not by taking its point of comparison in a general model of capitalism nor even of the plural models of existing capitalisms (in which the East European cases are various approximations of West European counterparts) but by an analysis in which the specific content of the analytic categories is developed through a relational comparison of the East European cases themselves.[12] The privatization programs of the region offer an opportunity to adopt such a methodological strategy. Despite broad and pervasive similarities in the systemic problems encountered, there are significant differences in the privatization programs that typify transformative processes across the four national cases. In the concluding section, these differences in the first phases of transformation are traced to differences in the earlier stage of extrication. We shall see that these privatization programs are not derived from master blueprints but are shaped by the specific institutional resources that are the legacies of the path of exit from state socialism. Seen from this vantage point, transformative processes taking place in contemporary East Central Europe resemble less architectural design than bricolage, construction by using whatever comes to hand.

Specifying the Dimensions of the East European Variant(s)

"Privatization" in this paper refers to the process of transferring ownership rights of productive assets held by the state. Although in the contemporary East European context such transfer is conventionally seen as the principal means of creating a private sector in an economy dominated by a public sector, the two processes should not be confused or conflated. First, transferring ownership from state to private hands is unlikely to be sufficient to create a dynamic private market economy.[13] Second, such a marketized private sector might be produced more effectively by measures to stimulate the start-up of new ventures and expansion of existing units in the nascent private sector (formerly, the second economy) than by transforming state assets into private assets.[14] Nonetheless, each new government in the region looks to privatization, i.e., ownership transfer, as the fundamental step toward the creation of a market economy. This paper brackets the question of that causal relationship and focuses on the variation in privatization strategies across the cases. How do the ways these new governments differ in their policies for transferring ownership of the assets of state enterprises? While acknowledging similarities among the cases, it identifies the distinctive privatization programs that typify each new government's strategy during its initial period in office.

For a typology to portray these differences, I propose three dimensions reflecting three central questions that must be addressed by any program of privatization: (1) How are the state's assets evaluated? (2) Who can acquire these assets? and (3) With what resources are ownership rights acquired? In the following section I specify the categories of these dimensions for the East Central European variant(s) of privatization strategies.[15] I then analyze the country cases and identify those programs exemplifying the various combinations of methods of asset evaluation, identities of participants, and resources for participation in privatization.

Valuation of Assets. The polarities of this dimension are straightforward. At one pole, assets of the large public enterprises are evaluated by administrative means. At the extreme we would find a single agency responsible for every aspect of the privatization process. That bureaucratic agency would assess the economic viability of firms, selecting some for foreclosure and others for privatization, and would seek out buyers for those to be privatized. Although bureaucrats might solicit economic assessments of market performance for these evaluations, decisions would be made on the basis of administrative measures rather than spontaneous market mechanisms. Here policymakers see markets not only as an outcome of privatization but also as a means of privatization. At the extreme we would find spot market transactions in the form of public auctions where auctioneers could, as with the sale of farm implements, announce a figure at which bidding could begin; but the final selling price would be determined by the competitive bidding.

The two poles, however, do not entirely capture the complexity of this dimension. Between them are some mechanisms of price formation and valuation that are either combinations of bureaucratic measures and market mechanisms or alternatives to them. Examples of such hybrid mechanisms would be *relational contracting* (in which state agencies contract the task of privatization to consulting firms based on their international reputation or in anticipation of long-term associations in which agency and firm would share information through channels not easily expressed in market terms), or *bargaining* (a loose term denoting patterns in which price setting is strongly influenced by network connections that differ from purely market transactions or political considerations that differ from purely administrative criteria).[16]

Actors Targeted to Acquire Assets. In constructing a strategy of privatization, the governments of these emergent democracies can present privatization as a process that will increase the wealth of the nation. Firms will be more accountable, more likely to economize on costs, and more oriented toward effective and efficient performance, they can argue, when property rights are exercised by private owners instead of state bureaucrats. But if privatization will increase the national income, it will also increase private wealth. Regardless of how they choose to portray private gain as contributing to the public good, governments that undertake privatization on a scale so potentially vast as that in East Central Europe (where over 85 percent of productive assets are state property) must address questions of distributive justice.[17]

We are thus interested in the question of whether these new governments will attempt to forge an explicit link between the economic objectives of privatization and the new civic principles of the emergent democratic polities. Specifically, is citizenship (that most fundamental civic principle with its attendant concept of the abstract equality of the citizen) invoked as a principle for distributing property rights? At issue is not whether individuals are favored over collectivities but whether individuals are explicitly targeted in their capacity as citizens to receive property rights in the privatization of large public enterprises.

Some governments will use civic principles to target citizens as recipients of the state's former assets, and others will use purely economic principles to target corporations. In this latter case, although private persons might participate in some programs of privatization (in agriculture, retail shops and restaurants, for example), the fundamental strategy of the privatization of the large state enterprises will be to distribute property rights to incorporated units. In short, privatization strategies will differ according to whether the state specifically seeks to involve civic persons (citizens) as participants or, alternatively, eschews civic principles in favor of designing large-scale privatization around legal-economic persons (corporations).

Resources Used to Acquire Ownership Rights. Privatization strategies can also vary according to the kinds of resources that are used, or converted, to acquire ownership rights. Monetary or financial resources are the obvious first category along this dimension. But, in addition to being differentiated according to their financial holdings or monetary savings, actors in the transitional societies of East Central Europe also differ according to the powers and capacities invested in their positions. In fact, the prohibition of private property in productive assets meant that the stratification systems of state socialist societies were organized more around differences in positions than in wealth. Thus, at the very moment when these economies embark on privatization, they must deal with a continuing legacy of the stratification system of state socialism in a society where advantages accrued to positions.

Thus, the third dimension contrasts privatization schemes and strategies that are organized primarily around the use of monetary (including credit or other financial) resources with those in which the participating agents capitalize on their positional resources. The concept of position and of "positional property," carry connotations of office holding.[18] I also start from that Weberian conception, but find it useful to extend the concept from office holding to a broader set of organizational posts and positions. This attention to positions should not be interpreted as a narrow preoccupation with the fate of those who held political positions in the old order, and whether and how they are converting their political capital into economic capital.[19] The concern here is more with economic job holding than with political office holding. Some privatization strategies will be structured in such a way that the occupants of certain positions will be able to use their position to an advantage in acquiring property rights. Managers, for example, might be able to use positional resources to gain ownership rights. Similarly, privatization strategies that place importance on employee ownership plans are instances of inclusion/exclusion in which ownership rights are acquired through position.

The three dimensions are cross-classified in Figure 1 to yield a preliminary typology of privatization strategies in East Central Europe. The dimensions referring to actors targeted to acquire assets and resources to acquire ownership rights form a two-by-two table. The remaining dimension referring to the method of evaluating assets is represented through shading ("administrative" lightest and "markets" darkest with "bargaining" in between). Also located on Figure 1 are

FIGURE 5.1
A Typology of Privatization Strategies in East Central Europe

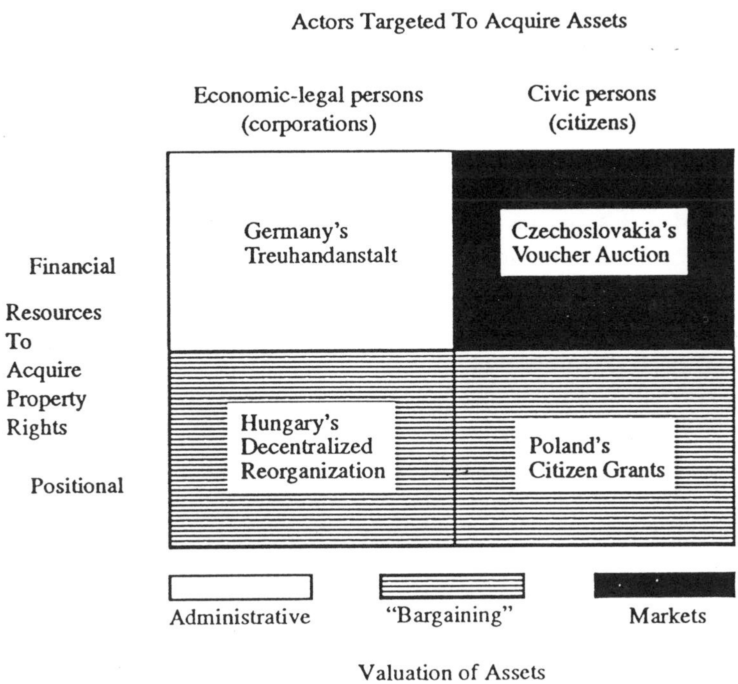

those strategies for privatizing large public enterprises that most closely exemplify four of the possible combinations of the categories along the three dimensions.

To avoid possible misunderstandings in interpreting this typology, we should state at the outset how we have delimited its object of study. First, the typology addresses the privatization of large public enterprises, but does not include schemes for privatizing retail trade, catering establishments, and agricultural cooperatives.[20] Second, our decision rule for placing country cases within the typology was to find cases that exemplify particular intersections of its dimensions. Our task here is to identify distinctive traits rather than to produce an exhaustive description of the full range of privatization programs in each country. Location of a particular country case in a given cell is not meant to capture all aspects about its privatization.[21] Third, the typology focuses on the strategies of policymakers in approximately the first year of the newly elected governments. How these strategies will be reshaped during later interactions with the relevant social actors must be the subject of a later investigation.

Distinctive Features of the Country Cases

Germany's Treuhandanstalt

Our discussion of privatization strategies in Figure 5.1 begins with administrative evaluation of assets favoring corporate actors that use predominantly monetized resources. No privatization strategy better exemplifies this particular combination of elements than Germany's Treuhandanstalt. Charged with the task of performing triage on the wounded enterprises of the formerly East German economy, the Treuhandanstalt, or Trust, has single-handedly carried out functions that are performed elsewhere in the region by government units scattered across the ministries of Industry, Planning, Finance, Labor, and Privatization. Following the monetary union of the two Germanies in July 1990 and their unification on October 3, 1990, the Treuhandanstalt became the world's largest industrial holding, with a staff of 2,500 to privatize and monitor the operations of the former East German state enterprises employing more than 3 million wage earners.[22] By May of 1991, the Trust had privatized 1,670 firms out of the approximately 7,000 that had been operating in the former East German lands, making its largest strides in the branches of energy, food stuffs, construction, trade, and tourism. Ninety percent of these properties were sold to West Germans (primarily corporations), five percent were purchased by foreign (that is, non-German) capital, and five percent are now held by their former managers. In preparation for further privatizations, the Treuhand has also split up 316 *Kombinat* (mega-conglomerates in the old socialist economy) into 8,500 smaller firms involving some 45,000 plants.[23]

This aggressive posture of attacking a problem through a strong bureaucratic agency with an almost unquestioned mandate to impose radical rapid restructuring is the defining feature of the German privatization strategy. But if the German state has moved with greater speed and determination than other Central European governments in the first stage of privatizaton, there are indications that its greatest difficulties lie ahead. Recent developments indicate that these obstacles will not be met with an even quicker pace and stronger administrative measures, but that the difficulties facing the Treuhand will retard its speed and lead to modifications of its methods.

The irony of the East German case is that the very strength of the West German economy, which was presumed to yield a more smooth transition (relative to its neighbors) has proven initially also to be a source of problems. In particular, the dramatic surge of demand for consumer goods in the newly incorporated lands was met at first by expansion of output by West German firms. If it might be the case that the "wealthy brother" will save the situation by buying firms in the long run, in the short run he began by selling goods to his desiring and poorer sibling. Uncompetitive on the world market, unable to sell goods on the West German market, and now uncompetitive on their own territory, the former East German enterprises saw their markets evaporate within weeks. With no orders and no work, millions of employees in these failing enterprises have been receiving a scarcely disguised unemployment compensation in the form of "short-time work" in which they remain on the payroll with little or nothing to do at their place of employment.[24]

For some intellectuals who attempt to shape German public opinion, the most attractive solution to this problem is massive migration. "Everyone who is willing to work hard can find a job here in our prosperity," they say. But even if such westward migration could absorb a significant proportion of those seeking work, the consequences might prove catastrophic to the social fabric and devastating to the local economies they leave behind. Massive migration, even on a scale far lower than some policymakers have in mind, could lead to a massive devaluation of the human capital of the economy of the former East German lands. Such devaluation would be triggered not simply by the aggregrate loss of highly skilled individuals, but also by the destruction of the work teams in which those skills had previously been used. Not as a direct outcome of foresight and planning but as an unintended consequence of the macroeconomic mismanagement of state socialism, the organization of work in the micro sphere of the redistributive enterprise had evolved into a forced autonomy and a distorted flexibility.[25] At the level of the shop floor, work teams were forced to develop ways to adjust quickly and flexibly to supply shortages and other irrationalities of central mismanagement. Such adaptations should not be idealized—they were constrained and distorted—but they had evolved into work units in which the human capital of the teams was more than the sum of its parts. In such a case, the departure of two or three from a team of a dozen can shatter a small but potentially significant resource that might otherwise be a basis for reconstructing a failed economy. In short, migration stimulated by the close proximity to prosperity on the same national territory might alleviate unemployment, but it might also erode organizational capacities and retard the development of a dynamic economy in the former East German lands.

Unemployment and severe economic crisis will have important consequences for the further work of the Treuhandanstalt. As the situation inside the Eastern enterprises deteriorates, it will prove more difficult to find buyers for them. Meanwhile, as unemployment explodes pressures will mount to slow the pace of liquidation. Firms that can be neither sold nor shut down (which will number in the thousands) will remain under the bureaucratic authority of the Treuhand, and that state agency will be forced to intervene directly in reorganizing these properties using subsidies to keep them afloat in the meantime.[26] But we can expect relentless pressures on the Trust to demonstrate that it remains committed to a determined course of privatization. After all, its mandate was for sweeping and rapid privatization—federal politicians and governmental officials will not look favorably on an agency that resorts to subsidizing instead of privatizing, and bureaucratic superiors will frown at subordinates in the agency whose quarterly record of completed privatizations falls below the norm. Therefore, we can expect that the

Treuhandanstalt will increasingly look to current managers as a pool of potential new owners for the failed but salvageable smaller units that have been or will be broken off from the large state enterprises. In this scenario, the evaluation of assets is likely to take place increasingly through bargaining between the agency and enterprises, with managers using their position to exercise expanded property rights. A recent study indicates that this process has already begun, and restructuring has become the critical task of the Treuhand. To organize the market for potential buyers, firms first must be reorganized.[27] The Kombinate are too big to sell all of a piece; and the parts that can be broken off and sold by themselves are too small to make a difference. Restructuring thus often entails the dismantling of several large enterprises and the strategic recombination of these newly available parts (from across different enterprises) to create new ventures.

Czechoslovakia's Voucher-Auction Program

In strong contrast to the decidedly statist orientation of the German privatization strategy, the Czechoslovak strategy of evaluating assets directly by the market involves participation on the basis of citizenship, and uses monetary resources. In fact, this combination of categories along our three dimensions is represented in a single institutional innovation in the Czechoslovak strategy—the use of citizen vouchers in public auctions of shares of the large state enterprises.

The program that the Czechoslovak economic authorities have devised involves the distribution of over fifty percent of the equity of more than a thousand large public enterprises through a citizenship voucher scheme. Each Czechoslovak citizen over eighteen years of age receives vouchers equal to a thousand "investment points." These investment points can be exchanged for shares in the enterprises designated for privatizaton through the voucher program. But if every citizen receives these vouchers as a matter of right, only those who pay a registration fee of a thousand korunas will be able to use the vouchers in the public auctions.[28] To indicate that the equity shares obtained through the voucher program are not a free gift from the state, to signal that there will be risk involved, and to filter out citizens with no serious interest in share ownership, the Czechoslovak officials have designed a voucher scheme that combines citizenship participation and monetary resources.

The actual process of exchanging vouchers for shares is fairly complex and the Czechoslovak authorities have undertaken a major program to educate the public about its basic principles and its logistical intricacies. The first round of the voucher-auction began May 18, 1992. For each wave of privatizations, the Ministry of Privatization designates the enterprises whose equity will be distributed through auction.[29] For each enterprise, the Ministry posts an initial asking price for the shares of that particular firm. To understand the principles of the auction, it is important to note that this "price" is not expressed in monetary units but in terms of investment points. Basically, the state announces the number of investment points at which it is willing to exchange a share of a given enterprise. A single share of a blue-chip company, for example, might begin at an initial level of 200 investment points; a share of a firm with a less prominent record or less promising future prospects, on the other hand, might be posted at only ten investment points. In the first round of the auction, then, one citizen might decide to place all of his 1,000 investment points on five shares of the blue-chip company; another could indicate his willingness to exchange all of his 1,000 points for 100 shares in the less promising venture; and a third could diversify his "portfolio" of investment points across firms with differing initial asking prices.

Equally important in understanding the principle of asset evaluation represented in the voucher-auction, it should be stressed that the auction is conceived as an iterative process occurring in multiple rounds. That is, although the economists in the Czech and Slovak Ministries of Privatization must conduct a rough and ready evaluation of the performance of firms to set the initial price of shares in the first round of bidding, the final price in investment points in the simulated market of the voucher-auction (and, more important, the later price of shares bought and sold on an actual market) will be determined by the supply and demand for these shares. What Václav Klaus and his team in the Ministry of Finance seem to have in mind is a kind of Walrasian auctioneer.[30] The auctioneer (actually a computerized network) accepts offers to buy shares of a given enterprise at a certain asking price in investment points. Unlike a commodities exchange (or the typical auction we might know from an estate sale or of objects of art) the bidder-citizens are not, strictly speaking, bidding up the price in a given round. At the end of the first round, the auctioneer identifies those shares for which demand exceeded supply, as well as those in which the reverse was the case. As the seller, the state can then accept offers from that round, or adjust prices upwards or downwards for the next round to be held two weeks later. The auction proceeds for three of four rounds, with the state accepting offers or revising prices. One concept currently in circulation among the designers of the voucher-auction program is that the state should accept offers where the demand for shares of a particular enterprise is lower than their supply (the number of shares for each firm in the auction is fixed) and revise prices upwards for those shares where demand exceeds supply.

This is not the place to elaborate all the technical and political complexities of the voucher-auction. For example, what percentage of assets will the state retain even for the auctioned firms and how will this influence the bidding process? What are the likely consequences of different decision rules about when the state should accept offers or when to revise "prices" upwards or downwards? What if the overall participation rate is so low that virtually all shares are under-subscribed?[31] Our attention here is instead addressed to the major principles that underscore the voucher-auction as an important feature of the Czechoslovak strategy of privatization.

Most important, the Czech leadership appears committed to using a simulated market to rapidly achieve an actually functioning equity market in the shares of a significant proportion of the former state enterprises.[32] The question of whether "investment points" reflect the real value, even a true relative value, of shares is beside the point, since the purpose of the voucher-auction is to get shares in private hands where they can be actually bought and sold.[33] According to the designers of the auction, it is in such a market (where speculators are not to be disparaged but encouraged) that the real evaluation of assets will take place.[34] It is for this reason, rather than primarily because of the registration fee, that we locate the Czechoslovak privatization strategy in that cell representing the intersection of market evaluation and monetary assets.[35]

Second, with a capital market organized around the stock exchange stimulated by the voucher-auction program, the Czech economy appears to be heading in the direction of raising investment funds through markets (typical of the Anglo-American system) rather than through the Japanese or German system, in which banks play a more central role in monitoring and directing the performance of their creditor firms (for a contrast, see the Polish case below).

Third, the Czech leadership appears prepared to accept relatively dispersed ownership in the initial stage of its privatization program in hopes that later transactions in the actual capital market will yield relatively rapid concentration of ownership in mid-level enterprises. Several design features currently being discussed (the combination of offering the shares of some firms at initial low asking "prices" and accepting offers where the supply of shares exceeds demand) suggest that the Czechs hope that some enterprising individuals will quickly buy up these relatively cheap shares and gain controlling interest in these firms. Such a scenario would likely be accompanied by continuing dispersed ownership in the most highly prized enterprises, where the economic leadership has more confidence in the enterprises' managerial talent and is therefore more willing to tolerate the managerial control that comes with highly diffused shareholding.[36] These same features also suggest that the Czech leadership is aware of the likelihood of resistance to the voucher-auction on the part of managers of the enterprises designated for auction, and is designing some features to help neutralize or mitigate this resistance. At the bottom end, firms whose shares find no buyers might be more easily liquidated after a strong vote of "no confidence" by the citizen "investors." At the top, economic officials can point to the likelihood of diffused shareholding in the blue-chip companies to persuade their managers (precisely the ones with the most bargaining power) that the auction is not against their interests and should not be resisted.[37] For that broad range of enterprises in between, the Czech ministers can probably count on resistance from managers, but they seem to hope that relatively quick concentration of ownership will bring these firms under control of the new owners.

Poland's Universal Citizen Grants and Employee Shareholdings

The story of Poland's privatization strategy begins in Gdansk, the birthplace of the first and, for a time, the largest independent trade union in Eastern Europe. But Solidarity and the most famous offspring of the Lenin shipyards who is now the president of the Polish Republic are only half the story. Not without historical irony yet not entirely by coincidence, Gdansk was also the birthplace of Polish neo-liberalism. During the mid-1980s, while the intellectuals of Warsaw and Budapest debated in urban coffeehouses, a group of young private businessmen and young provincial intellectuals in Gdansk formed a Liberal Club and at its meetings began reading and discussing major theoretical statements on property rights. From the practical experiences of these entrepreneurs and the circle of intellectuals close to them arose the Liberal Congress, a small but extraordinarily influential party that has produced Jan Krzysztof Bielecki, a former Prime Minister, and a disproportionate share of cabinet ministers in the government formed after the election of President Walesa.

Privatization in Poland, of course, did not begin under the leadership of Walesa's Polish liberals but instead under Jaruzelski's Polish Communists. During the power vacuum of 1989, an untold number of apparatchiks landed comfortably ("not perestroikists but parachutists," went the expression) as the new owners of promising units carved out of the former state enterprises. The liberals thus came to office (first with Finance Minister Balcerowicz and later with Prime Minister Bielecki's larger retinue) in a period in which the scandals of such "nomenklatura capitalism" could be heard in public circles, narrow and wide. Property reform was clearly on the agenda and the Mazowiecki government announced a program of clean privatization, with the promise of foreign investors and large public offerings along the British model at its centerpiece. But foreign investors were slow and few (looking more to Hungary and to Eastern Germany) and the public offerings made little dent in the state-owned assets of the large socialist enterprises. In fact, the major achievement of the first year of the Ministry of Property Transformation, a few unrepresentative foreign buy-outs aside, was privatization through liquidation—a dubious achievement, given the stated aims of the Ministry, since the assets of 159 of these 160 so-called privatizations were leased to the managers and employees of the liquidated firms.[38]

After the election campaign in which he had promised "acceleration," President Walesa turned to Janusz Lewandowski, the new Minister of Property Transformation from Gdansk, and asked him to elaborate and specify the sweeping program for "mass privatization" that Lewandowski had proposed years earlier together with his Gdansk compatriot, Jan Szomburg (currently, Director of the Research Center for Marketization and Property Reform).[39] The young transformers confronted two obstacles. First, from the other side of the Gdansk story, they faced the Workers' Councils, reactivated after 1989, which viewed property transformation as their opportunity to solidify employee ownership.[40] Second, they faced the enormous problem that domestic savings could cover only a fraction of the assets of the large state enterprises. On this subject Lewandowski had been heard to say that "privatization is when someone who doesn't know who the real owner is and doesn't know what it's really worth sells something to someone who doesn't have any money."[41]

The program of mass privatization formally announced in June 1991 calls for the property transformation of some four hundred Polish enterprises in the first stage of its operation. Contained within the program is a major peace offering to the Workers' Councils: employees in the privatized firms will receive 10 percent of the shares of their companies for free. That is, lacking savings and credit, employees will be able to use their positional resources as jobholders to gain an ownership stake in their enterprises.[42]

At the center of the mass privatization program, however, stands a universal citizenship grant in the form of share vouchers issued to every Polish citizen. In marked contrast to the Czech program, no registration fee is required to participate. By this signal, and through all its rhetoric, the Polish government seems eager to send the message that this is emphatically a free gift from the state.

Unlike the Czech schemes, moreover, the Polish citizen will not exchange his vouchers directly for shares in a privatized enterprise. Instead, the vouchers will be exchanged for shares in one or another "asset manager" who will, in turn, exchange the vouchers for shares in the transformed enterprises that it chooses (or is assigned) to manage. Current proposals call for this role to be played by experienced foreign companies, perhaps as few as ten. These asset managers should not be confused with the managers of pension funds or mutual funds with which they bear only superficial resemblance. According to the intentions of the program's designers, these asset managers will not influence firms indirectly by buying and selling shares on the market but, instead, exercise authority through active and aggressive property management directly involved in formulating the policies and business strategies of the firms under their control.[43] Thus, in place of the Czechs' imitation of Anglo-American practices, the Poles seem to be looking to models in Germany and Japan.[44]

Several other features of the Polish program of mass privatization complete the contrast to the Czech voucher schemes. According to Polish officials and experts, the situation in the immediate future is not likely to be developed enough to establish an "open-ended" program in which citizens are free to withdraw shares and change asset managers. Presumably to avoid inflation, citizens will be limited at first to collecting dividends from the results of the voucher-asset manager program. That is, for an indeterminate period (but certainly lasting for several years) citizens cannot capitalize their shares by turning them in for their nominal value. The system is further "closed-ended" by prohibiting citizens from changing to a different asset manager. Because they will not be exposed to the discipline of disappointed shareholders who seek higher dividends elsewhere, the mass privatization program will include a complex incentive program for the executives of the limited number of asset managing companies. The hopes, meanwhile, are that the managers of the former state enterprises will now be under the firm discipline of the foreign asset managers. Obviously more concerned than the Czechs about the consequences of dispersed shareholding, the Poles are hoping to target citizens as "owners" while using the universal citizenship grant as a vehicle to achieve extraordinarily concentrated corporate control.

Thus, with its unrestricted access, the Polish voucher program is more inclusive than the Czech schemes. Yet its citizens' participation is almost entirely passive. What can the Polish citizen do with his share? He cannot capitalize it, nor can he withdraw that share from his current asset manager and deposit it with another. In exchange for his passivity he gets a dividend, and that alone.

But why then have a voucher program at all? The answer lies in the goals of the Polish program to yield aggressive property management to foreign companies within the constraints of a politicized citizenry. No Polish politician or official could propose an outright giveaway of Polish firms to foreign asset managers, and, strictly speaking, this is not what they will do. In a legal and political sense, they will have given the ownership to the Polish citizenry and the stewardship of the citizen-owned assets will rest in the hands of presumably competent managers. The Polish voucher program will not be "popular capitalism" in the sense of millions of small active investors with an interest in the ups and downs of the market. Instead, its designers hope to increase the chances that a capitalism with quite concentrated effective ownership can be made popular with the Polish citizenry.[45]

Hungary's Institutional Cross-Ownership

The fourth cell in our typology is exemplified by Hungary—characterized by the combination of bargained evaluation of assets, corporate owners, and positional resources. Although Hungary's centralized State Property Agency (SPA) has a strong legislative mandate (and a firmly-established bureaucratic office) to supervise and control all aspects of the privatization process directly, asset evaluation in Hungary is not conducted through administrative means, as in Germany. And although the shares of Hungarian firms can be sold on an embryonic stock exchange, the evaluation of assets, unlike the auctions in Czechoslovakia, is not primarily performed by market mechanisms. Since it is between the polarities of administrative and market evaluation, it is represented in Figure 1. as "bargaining," yet this residual or negative definition fails to convey the more precise institutional character of asset evaluation performed by the Hungarian authorities. In the spontaneous and controlled transformation of property rights that is occurring through decentralized processes initiated by the large public enterprises, bargaining is indeed the prevalent form. But within the State Property Agency itself, and especially for the very largest firms designated by that agency to be sold to foreign investors for hard currency to reduce the state deficit, the mechanism of asset evaluation would be more accurately characterized as relational contracting.

Within months after taking office in the spring of 1990, Hungary's coalition government under Prime Minister József Antall of the leading party, the Hungarian Democratic Forum, responded to the criticisms of the opposition parties by adopting the opposition's call for the "privatization of privatization." The central feature of this measure was a dramatic increase in the role of international investment banks and leading consulting firms in the privatization of the large state enterprises. When it nominated a list of twenty enterprises to be sold in the first round of privatization, the State Property Agency also announced an open invitation to investment banks and consulting firms to place proposals with the agency indicating, in general terms, how they would evaluate assets, arrange credit, and find a buyer for a given enterprise. That is, the agency put up for tender the rights to manage the restructuring of a particular company. The investment and consulting firms that won this competition would be compensated with a percentage of the final selling price. In an important sense, the SPA was not directly selling enterprises, but instead was selling the rights to lead and manage their privatization.

Dozens of consulting firms and investment banks responded to these tenders, and whole rooms in the Property Agency were stacked high with proposals from floor to shoulder height. Several of the most internationally prominent firms (Solomon Brothers, Goldman Sachs, Barclays, Price Waterhouse, Coopers and Lybrand, and others) submitted prospectuses for eight or even more of the tenders. Each firm thought that, if selected on its merits, it would be leading several of the reorganizations. But when the SPA announced its decisions only three weeks later, it became obvious that its assignment of the tenders was based less on careful reading of the proposals than toward the aim of increasing the number of cooperating partners in the first round: the twenty enterprises slated for privatization were distributed among twenty different leading banks and consulting firms.

In more recent months it is becoming clear that these organizations are forming the core of a relatively stable set of participants involved in an ongoing relationship with the Agency. In assigning tenders (and even in selecting enterprises to be restructured) in later privatizations, the SPA is working closely with the international partners with whom it had positive experiences in the first round. Invitations are not entirely open; in some cases the Agency approaches only a few international firms to sound them out about plans for this or that enterprise. And, although we have no documentary evidence, we should not rule out the possibility that decisions are being made before the announcement of a competitive bidding for the rights to manage a particular restructuring. When making contracts in these cases, both sides are calculating not simply in terms of the immediate contract at issue but in terms of past performance and in anticipation of future exchanges. Our purpose here is not to denounce a too cozy relationship between the Property Agency and the communities of international banking and consulting. On the contrary, these practices have an economic rationale: relational contracting provides a mechanism in which both parties can gain more information than through more restricted market transactions. On the side of the SPA, such relational contracting lowers transaction costs (for example, the administrative costs of handling an overabundance of bids, or the costs in time and resources in working with too many partners) and can yield more extensive and better information (about capital markets, about international investors, about the marketing and production strategies of foreign companies, and the like) than might be obtained when contracts are made through open competition on a strictly case-by-case basis.[46]

We would seriously fail to understand the process of privatization in Hungary, however, if we focused our attention too narrowly on the State Property Agency—for although the SPA has the legal authority to supervise privatization, the predominant processes restructuring the ownership rights of the large public enterprises is not taking place at its initiative. Instead, the prevalent form of transformation in Hungary should be characterized as the decentralized reorganization of property. Simplifying from a more complicated web of transactions and a wider network of connections, the basic course of such reorganization can be outlined as follows: Under the pressure of enormous debt, declining sales, and threats of bankruptcy or (in the cases of more prosperous enterprises) to forestall takeovers or to attempt to increase autonomy from state ministries, directors of many large public enterprises are taking advantage of several important pieces of legislation that allow state enterprises to establish joint stock companies (RTs) and limited liability companies (KFTs). To be clear, in the typical cases of such reorganizations the state enterprise is not itself transformed into a joint stock enterprise; rather, the managers of the enterprise are breaking up the organization (along divisional, factory, departmental, or even workshop lines) into numerous corporations.[47] As newly incorporated entities with legal identities, these new units are nominally independent and are registered separately, with their own boards of directors and separate balance sheets. The more interesting question is, of course, who owns the shares of these new units? An examination of the computerized records of the Budapest Court of Registry indicates that the controlling shares (in overwhelming proportions) of the corporate satellites launched around the large public enterprises are held by the state enterprises themselves.[48] For this reason, we prefer to use the term VKFT (in Hungarian, *vállalati-KFT*, or enterprise limited liability company) to denote their semi-autonomous organizational status and to indicate their continuity with an organizational innovation of internal subcontracting (the VGMK) that had appeared in the earlier stage of transition.[49]

Property shares in these satellite organizations are not limited, however, to the founding enterprise. The typical cases involve patterns of more mixed ownership. Top and mid-level managers, professional and other staff, and (more rarely) highly skilled workers can be found on the lists of founding partners. But their shares are not large and should not be taken as evidence of "managerial buyouts." More important than private persons is the participation in share ownership in a given corporate unit by other joint stock companies and limited liability companies—sometimes by other VKFTs in a similar orbit around the same enterprise, more frequently by joint stock companies or VKFTs spinning around some other enterprise with lines of purchase or supply to the corporate unit.[50] Most important among the outside owners are banks. In many cases, the establishment of VKFTs and other corporate forms is triggered by enterprise debt, and in the reorganization the creditors, whether commercial banks (whose shares as joint stock companies are still predominantly state-owned) or other credit institutions (also state-owned), exchange debt for equity.

What then is the fastest growing new ownership form in the Hungarian economy?[51] The terminology is cumbersome but it reflects the complex, institutionally intertwined character of property transformation in Hungary: a limited liability owned by other limited liability companies owned by joint stock companies, banks, and large public enterprises owned by the state.

Has the decentralized reorganization of property rights taken place beyond the control and outside the purview of the governmental agents responsible for privatization? Consistent with its campaign rhetoric in the elections for Parliament, the new Hungarian government, upon taking office in May 1990, adopted a deliberate strategy that promised to slow down privatization and to provide for its centralized management.[52] But within months, the State Property Agency seems to have realized that it has neither the capacity nor the ability to oversee the privatization of thousands of state enterprises directly. Toleration of decentralized reorganization appears to be its current posture. This statement should not imply that the Property Agency is unaware of the particular character of these reorganizations. Each corporate spinoff of the kind described above involving assets valued above thirty million forints (approximately $400,000) or a series of such spinoffs that represents in the aggregate more than fifty percent of the assets of the state enterprise must be approved by the Agency. Although not virtually automatic, the approval rate of such proposals is extraordinarily high.[53] This high rate of approval suggests that negotiations with the Property Agency precede the submission of a proposal for reorganization. Moreover, case studies and summary reports of corporate reorganizations indicate that the dominant form of asset evaluation in these cases is unquestionably "bargaining."[54] Whether at the level between the state enterprise and its affiliated corporations or between the enterprise and the state agency, actors exploit every available means of bargaining power.

In which direction will corporate reorganization evolve? Any answer would be premature but the alternatives can be clearly stated. In the first scenario, the current ambiguities in the distribution of property rights will be clarified in favor of the managers of these enterprises. That is, decentralized reorganization will lead to a further concentration of managerial control.[55] In the second scenario, decentralized reorganization sets the stage for a later round of genuine privatization. That is, although senior management might have broken up enterprises with the aim of buffering the firm from inevitable bankruptcies or increasing its autonomy from state authorities, the establishment of even semi-independent corporate forms might create inviting opportunites for take-over by foreign firms or indigenous private entrepreneurs with limited means to acquire properties when they were more closely bound within the large state enterprises.[56] In the third scenario, decentralized reorganization is but the first phase of a reconsolidation of state ownership.[57] This outcome might be only seemingly paradoxical. State elites may be willing to tolerate corporate reorganization (even on a wide scale and together with some genuine privatization of the smaller units[58]) provided that the controlling shares remain in institutional hands over which the state can continue to exercise control.[59]

Whatever the outcome, we can observe in the meantime that the predominant form of the transformation of property relations in Hungary is the outcome of bargaining about asset evaluation and takes the form of institutional cross-ownership in which enterprise managers use their resources as officeholders to extend their effective exercise of property rights. For these reasons, Hungary exemplifies that cell in our typology representing the intersection of bargaining, corporate owners, and positional resources.

Paths of Extrication and Patterns of Transformation

The typology of privatization strategies and the discussion of the country cases presented above was to provide a preliminary analytic framework that might stimulate more systematic comparisons of these cases. The eventual outcome of these strategies will be shaped by the continued tug and pull of politics and the interaction of the state and various social groups in these societies. But whatever these outcomes, it is not too early to observe that the privatization strategies in East Central Europe are beginning from four quite distinctive starting points.

How can we explain these differences? In my view, an explanation of these distinctive strategies of privatization must begin by taking into account their distinctive paths of extrication from state socialism—reunification in Germany, capitulation in Czechoslovakia, compromise in Poland, and electoral competition in Hungary.[60] These diverse paths of extrication, and the preceding differences in social structure and political organization that brought them about, have had the consequence that the current political institutions and forms of interest intermediation between state and society differ significantly across our four cases. The collapse of communism in East Germany resulted in the colonization of its new political institutions during incorporation into the powerful state of the German Federal Republic. The capitulation of communist authorities in Czechoslovakia after decades of suppressing almost all institutions of civil society resulted in the rapid restructuring of its political institutions with few remnants from the earlier period.[61] Communism did not collapse in Hungary and Poland; its demise was negotiated in both countries. Faced with a powerful, indeed mono-organizational, opposition with deep roots in society, Poland's communists attempted a compromise. The legacies of this path of extrication, with its institutional guarantees for Jaruzelski and company, remain today in the compromised parliament, strong presidency and nationwide, though weakening, workers' movement. Hungary's reform communists, by contrast, attempted to salvage some of their power by entering into direct electoral competition with a seemingly weak political opposition. That political opposition, of course, is now in the government and the Parliament, but the legacy of Hungary's peculiar path remains. In the nearly two years since its roundtable negotiations, Hungary has seen its political parties flourishing without roots in society, its weak labor movement becoming further fragmented, and its enterprise managers (as the best-organized social group during the previous decade) becoming the most powerful actor in the society.

Thus, it is the relationship between different types of democracy and different types of capitalism, rather than the abstractions of democracy and capitalism, that holds the clue to explaining differences in contemporary Eastern Europe.[62] The diverse paths of extrication from state socialism yield distinctive patterns across a triangle formed by the state, the market, and the society. It is in terms of these patterns, that I conclude the discussion of privatization strategies in East Central Europe.

With their political incorporation into the German Federal Republic, the citizens of the former East German territories found their futures charted by a political leadership with a strong commitment to thorough marketization. But together with an abiding confidence in the market, this political leadership has profound confidence in the state. This trust, moreover, is accompanied by a deep, and almost indiscriminate, distrust of East German society. Forty years of communism, according to the German leadership, have produced a terrible human tragedy—the personality structures, habits, dispositions, expectations, and mentalities of the citizens of the new lands make them unfit and incapable of managing their affairs. It is not their fault, but they are no longer trustworthy. They must be remolded and re-educated not simply with industrial skills but with new mentalities. Those too old or too thoroughly spoiled by old habits and inclinations must be prevented from obstructing the new course; in the yet undamaged youth of the Eastern lands lies good fortune.[63] It follows that the German leadership will use the state to transform the economy and reconstruct the society.

The Czech leaders also have profound confidence in the market. Unlike the Germans, they lack a strong state; yet unlike the Poles, they are not faced with deeply rooted institutions in civil society that might negate their leadership. From this it follows that the Czech political leadership is trying to use the market to transform the economy. So deep is their confidence in the market that they will use it to privatize the economy. Citizen vouchers there are not an ideological means to win support through some extra-economic means but are instead the institutional vehicle to achieve the direct economic goals that will provide the basis for short-term and longer-term social support. It would be entirely misleading, therefore, to interpret the Czech leadership's use of a civic principle as an indication of its deep and abiding commitment to equality. In fact, if leaders do, indeed, proceed with the auctioning of the assets of the large public enterprises at the pace and scope proposed, that scheme is likely to give rise to a relatively rapid differentiation of wealth—because some individuals (not without certain risk, of course) will be able to acquire properties at truly bargain basement prices.

Hungary, by contrast, is in many ways the opposite of the Czech case. There we find a state elite that is profoundly ambivalent about the market, so much so, that we can say that it distrusts the market. But at the same time, this is a state elite that is highly uncertain about society's trust in its leadership. The current government was popularly and legitimately elected. It enjoys legitimacy but that legitimacy does not convey confidence that the burdens that will necessarily accompany marketization will be accepted by the population. Nor could the likely replacement government formed from parties of the same political elite anticipate greater confidence. Lacking intermediary institutions (such as strong and cohesive trade unions) with whom it could publicly negotiate, that elite has very few means to know where the limits of society's tolerance might be. Thus, it avoids taking decisive steps in fear of society's reaction. And all the while, it engages in a cyclical process of here tightening, there loosening the reins on the galloping enterprise managers.

If the German state leadership trusts the state to remake the society, the Czechs trust the market to remake the economy, and the current Hungarian leadership distrusts the market while being distrusted by the society, Poland is that case where to keep the trust of society the state must win society's faith in the market. Like the Czech voucher program, the Polish citizenship vouchers are intended to perform an economic function of promoting privatization where domestic savings are too little to cover the value of the assets. But unlike the Czech program, the Polish strategy of appealing to the civic principle is not simply auxiliary to, or instrumental for, an economic logic. Whereas in the Czech Republic the voucher system is a means of achieving a market that is seen as self-legitimating, in Poland, the citizen voucher system is a means of legitimating the market.

Conclusion: A Market Economy or Modern Capitalism?

These programs will inevitably be modified as the work of the transformers is transformed by the societies of East Central Europe. The resulting process will resemble innovative adaptations that combine seemingly discrepant elements, bricolage, more than architectural design. We should not be surprised, however, if the blueprints of foreign experts continue to figure in the transformative process. Although the grand designs of cookbook capitalism will not be used faithfully as guidelines for action, they will, nonetheless, be useful resources. This hypothesis stems from a view of contemporary East Central European policymakers as located between populations that must bear the transition costs and international agencies and foreign governments that may provide capital, aid, and access to Western markets.

Master blueprints are not substitutes for stabilization measures, but which East European finance minister would dare enter into negotiations with international lending institutions (the World Bank, the IMF, the European Bank for Reconstruction and Development, and the like) without one? With the diffusion of grand models from one economy to the next we should expect, however, that formulas for external legitimation will be "decoupled" from actual practices.[64] At the same time, we should note the possibility that politicians might present their own policy preferences as mandated by international agencies. ("The IMF made me do it.") The question of who is legitimating what and by which means is much more complicated than a matter of powerful international agencies dictating to East European politicians who have no choice but compliance.

Will this bricolage result in market economies? Definite prognosis is, of course, premature. But functioning markets are more likely to come from trials and errors that can be corrected, and new opportunities are more likely to be perceived and exploited when transformative processes are decentralized than when grand experiments are centrally imposed on society.

The more important question is whether the most far-reaching marketization of all aspects of economic life should be the policy goal in contemporary East Central Europe. Advocates of such a goal suffer from two analytic shortcomings: (1) they mistake one possible means as the end itself, and (2) they operate in a theoretical universe in which the dichotomies of state or market exhaust the range of viable coordinating mechanisms in modern economies. But surely the goal of marketization has been, among other ends, to modernize the production processes and improve the international competitiveness of these damaged economies. Yet, as various currents of thinking in political economy indicate, there are sectors in which the most competitive forms of economic coordination are neither market nor statist, but new forms whose operations we are only beginning to understand and identify (with such preliminary labels such as "networks," "alliances," "inter-firm agreements," and the like).[65] An exclusive policy of all-encompassing marketization across all sectors would therefore pose a new obstacle and not a means to international competitiveness.

Such a tragedy is likely so long as the policy debate in the transitions from state socialism is dominated by those who mistake the triumph of capitalism as the triumph of the market and look only to the "market revolutions" of Reagan and Thatcher when the real victories went to the industrial reorganizations in Germany and Japan that were neither market nor hierarchical. But modern capitalist economies should not be reduced to only one of their constitutive parts: markets are but one of many coexisting coordinating mechanisms in modern capitalism.[66] Transformative schemes that rely on an exclusive coordinating mechanism do not emulate existing capitalism as much as they echo the implementation of state socialism and, like it, carry the danger of sacrificing dynamic efficiency and flexibility that depend on diversity of organizational forms.[67]

Notes

1. See, for example, Merton J. Peck and Thomas J. Richardson, eds. *What Is To Be Done? Proposals for the Soviet Transition to the Market.* New Haven, Yale University Press, 1992.
2. Peter Murrell, "Conservative Political Philosophy and the Strategy of Economic Transition," *East European Politics and Societies* 6:1 (Winter 1992).
3. See especially Michael T. Hannan and John H. Freeman, *Organizational Ecology* (Cambridge, Mass., 1989); Richard Nelson and Sidney Winter, *An Evolutionary Theory of Economic Change* (Cambridge, Mass., 1982); Paul David "Understanding the Economics of QWERTY: The Necessity of History," in *Economic History and the Modern Historian*, edited by W. Parker (London, 1986), pp. 30–49; and Brian W. Arthur, "Competing Technologies and Lock-in by Historical Events: The Dynamics of Allocation under Increasing Returns," *Economic Journal* 99 (1989), pp. 116–131.
4. Sensitivity to these differences is obscured by the very events that brought so much attention to the region. "1989" was a double conjuncture—both in the near simultaneity of events across the countries of the region, and in the rapid acceleration and reciprocal effects of changes across political, economic, and social domains. But "1989" will stand in the way of understanding developments in the region if we take it as a universal beginning or culmination. That

is, we must begin to disaggregate "the transition," perhaps even dispense with it as a concept, and try to understand how changes in the different countries and in the different domains have very different temporalities. Changes in social institutions, for example, are not simply slower but might have been taking place much before more easily observable political developments. If pace and timing differ across domains, we should also not assume that changes within them necessarily move in the same directions.

5. See László Bruszt, "Transformative Politics: Social Costs and Social Peace in East Central Europe," in this volume.
6. Unlike the designer's schemes, in which the actions and preferences of subordinate social groups are a hindrance to the speedy enactment of the prescribed formulas (or at most take only a reactive role at the voting booth to approve or remove programs and parties), in the perspective adopted here, the institutionalized interactions between state and society play a formative role in shaping actual strategies.
7. I take this to be the key analytic insight of Theda Skocpol's *States and Social Revolutions* (Cambridge, Eng., 1979). See László Bruszt and David Stark, "Remaking the Political Field in Hungary: From the Politics of Confrontation to the Politics of Competition," in Ivo Banac, *Eastern Europe in Revolution* (Ithaca, N.Y., 1992), pp. 13–55.
8. By "path dependence" I am not referring to some processes whereby the societies of Eastern Europe are seen to return to the natural "historical trajectories" of the interwar period from which they had temporarily deviated (see, for example, the argument of Ivan Szelenyi in *Socialist Entrepreneurs* (Madison, 1988). Unlike these notions of already existing roads or the concept of trajectory in which one can calculate destination from knowledge of initial direction and thrust, the concept of path dependence is not that of a vector.
9. My conception of institutions as embodied routines, and my emphasis on practices instead of preferences and on predispositions instead of rational calculations draws on the work of Pierre Bourdieu, especially, *The Logic of Practice* (Stanford, 1990). For a similar conception of institutions as not simply constraining but as enabling, see Paul DiMaggio and Walter Powell's introductory essay in *The New Institutionalism in Organizational Analysis* (Chicago, 1991), pp. 1–38.
10. The pertinent lesson of state socialism is that large scale social engineering might so badly tear the social fabric that its damage will take decades to repair and preclude the longer term calculations so central to the efficient functioning of economic institutions. That is, the greater the scope of an experiment, the greater the risk of catastrophe. (See Murrell, *East European Politics and Societies*.) My intention here is not to denigrate institutional design. Institutional designs do matter and can be for the better, especially if they are delimited in scope to solve particular problems of governance and coordination for specific sectors or localities (rather than as global solutions to the problems of an entire economy). In place of grand experiments, we should hope for more, not fewer "designs"—partial solutions to limited problems in which transformation becomes a process undertaken by a multiplicity

of dispersed agents at many institutional sites.

11. For the use of a similar comparative methodology see David Stark, "Rethinking Internal Labor Markets: New Insights from a Comparative Perspective," *American Sociological Review* 51:4 (August, 1986), pp. 492–504; and David Stark, "Bending the Bars of the Iron Cage: Bureaucratization and Informalization under Capitalism and Socialism," *Sociological Forum* 4:4 (1990), pp. 637–664.
12. This is the major limitation of Ellen Comisso's interesting argument in "Political Coalitions, Economic Choices," *Journal of International Affairs* 45:1 (Summer 1991), pp. 1–29. For Comisso, the "options" available to the economies of Eastern Europe are given by the array of existing West European national economies, e.g., the "French model," "the Swedish model," "modified Thatcherism," etc.
13. David Stark, "Privatization in Hungary: From Plan to Market or from Plan to Clan?" *East European Politics and Societies* 4:3 (Fall 1990), pp. 351–392.
14. János Kornai, *The Road to a Free Economy* (New York, 1990); and Stark, "Privatization."
15. Instead of explicating these dimensions as a strictly logical deductive exercise, the analytic categories are given content in terms of the specific historical and social setting that is contemporary East Central Europe. The Weberian notion of historically grounded concepts should be familiar to most sociologists. My method here is antithetical to the hollow antinomies of "deduction versus induction" or "theory versus historicism" resuscitated in the recent rational choice literature, e.g., Edgar Kiser and Michael Hechter, "The Role of General Theory in Comparative-historical Sociology," *American Journal of Sociology* 97:1 (July 1991), pp. 1–30.
16. On relational contracting and other forms of coordination between firms that lie between (or outside) the dichotomy of markers and hierarchies, see Oliver Williamson, *The Economic Institutions of Capitalism: Firms, Markets, and Relational Contracting* (New York, 1985); and Rogers Hollingsworth and Wolfgang Streeck, "Countries and Sectors: Concluding Remarks on Performance, Convergence, and Competitiveness," in Rogers Hollingsworth, Philippe Schmitter, and Wolfgang Streeck, eds., *Comparing Capitalist Economies: Variations in the Governance of Industrial Sectors* (New York, 1992).
17. Strategies of justification thus lie at the core of strategies of privatization. Although I raise these issues explicitly in this subsection, processes of justification are an important aspect of each of our three dimensions. My intention here is not to unmask them as after-the-fact ideologies or false rationalizations mystifying some underlying injustice but to see how the specific work of justification can vary from case to case as shaped by the broader transformative politics. On strategies of justification in the transitional period on the shop floor, see David Stark, "La valeur du travail et sa rétribution en Hongrie," *Actes de la recherche en sciences sociales* 85 (November 1990), pp. 3–19 (available in English as "Work, Worth, and Justice in the Hungarian Mixed Economy," Working Papers on Central and Eastern Europe, Center for European Studies, Harvard University, 1990, no. 5). For an ambitious theory of

justification see Luc Boltanski and Laurent Thevenot, *La justification: Les economies de la grandeur* (Paris, 1991).

18. We think obviously here of the work of Pierre Bourdieu on different forms of "capital" in modern societies. See, for example, his "Forms of Capital" in John G. Richardson, ed., *Handbook of Theory and Research for the Sociology of Education* (New York, 1986), pp. 241–258.
19. The old political capital suffered a massive devaluation and, in the current period, the publication of memoirs is one of the few remaining avenues of such direct conversion. In fact, there are good reasons to expect that in the current period monetary rather than positional resources will be more important as an avenue to ownership for those former apparatchiks whose earlier assets were exclusively political (that is, whose political capital had not already been combined with certain forms of cultural capital to yield economic positions in the managerial ranks).
20. A more comprehensive examination would also have to address the disposition of real estate and the question of the reprivatization of property. Restitution or compensation of former owners is an important question with significant implications for the timing, pace, and methods for privatizing the large public enterprises. In particular, uncertainties about reprivatization can pose serious obstacles that inhibit potential buyers and delay privatization in the state sector.
21. For example, our location of "Hungary's decentralized reorganization" in the lower left hand cell indicates that policymakers there have, to date, designed ownership restructuring around corporate owners, through bargaining processes, favoring positional resources. It does not imply, for example, that financial/monetary resources are not mobilizable in Hungary nor that positional resources are not mobilizable in Germany. Similarly, the use of citizen vouchers in Poland and Czechoslovakia does not exclude incorporated actors from participating in privatization in those economies—although it is interesting to note that the governments of Germany and Hungary have, thus far, excluded the principle of citizenship from their strategies for privatization.
22. *The World Bank/CECSE* 2:5 (May 1991), p. 3.
23. For a description of the work of the Treuhand in its first months of operation and a balanced analysis of the difficult problems facing it in the near future see Roland Schönfeld, "Privatization in East Germany: Strategies and Experience," *Transformation der Wirtschaftssysteme in Ostmitteleuropa*. Munich, Südosteuropa Gesellschaft, 1993, pp. 159–170. On later developments see especially Gernot Grabher, "Eastern Conquista: The Truncated Industrialization of East European Regions by Large West European Corporations," in H. Ernste and V. Meier, eds., *Regional Development and Contemporary Industrial Response*. London, Belhaven Press, 1992.
24. Such short-time work was originally scheduled to expire on June 30, 1991, prompting some estimates that there would be 3.5 to 4 million unemployed (as high as 45 percent of the previously active earners in 1989) by the end of the summer of 1991. See, Schönfeld, "Privatization." These worst nightmares were not realized, in part, because short-time work was extended beyond that

deadline. By late 1991, high-level Treuhand officials acknowledged an effective unemployment rate of about 30 percent. See Horst Kern and Charles F. Sabel, "Between Pillar and Post: Reflections on the Treuhand's Uncertainty About What To Say Next," (Paper presented at the Conference on the *Treuhandanstalt*, Harvard University, November 1991; and comments by Treuhand officials at that conference.)

25. Stark, "Rethinking," and János Lukács, "Organizational Flexibility, Internal Labor Market, and Internal Subcontracting, Hungarian Style," in Rudolf Andorka and László Bertalan, eds., *Economy and Society in Hungary* (Budapest, 1986), pp. 15–34.
26. Schönfeld, "Privatization," and Kern and Sabel, "Pillar and Post."
27. Kern and Sabel, "Pillar and Post."
28. Presumably to increase participation rates, the registration fee has been reduced from initial proposals that called for 2,000 korunas (equivalent to about half the average monthly earnings of industrial employees). The designation "Czechoslovakia" is used in this section because the voucher-auction program was designed and initiated prior to the separation of Slovakia and the Czech Republic at the end of 1992. Slovak policy can be expected to diverge from the Czech strategy.
29. By late 1991, the Ministry had received 3,588 privatization projects from some 900 enterprises. Some 2,800 of these projects were in conformity with the requirements of the voucher scheme. I am grateful to Gerald McDermott for providing these figures.
30. We might also observe that the Czech voucher-auction has some resemblance to the schemes of Oscar Lange for setting prices through a simulated market within a socialist economy.
31. According to public opinion polls at the beginning of 1991, interest in participating in the voucher-auction program was very low. See, Franz-Lothar Altmann, "The Transformation of Property Rights in Czechoslovakia." *Transformation der Wirtschaftssysteme in Ostmitteleuropa*. Munich, Südosteuropa Gesellschaft, 1993, pp. 155–158. For an excellent account of the economic landscape in which the Czechoslovak privatization programs are occurring, see Gerald A. McDermott and Michal Mejtrik, "The Role of Small Firms in the Industrial Development and Transformation of Czechoslovakia," *Small Business Economics* 4 (1992), pp. 51–72.
32. The Czech leadership appears prepared to accept relatively high transaction costs (the voucher-auction will be costly) in the distribution of shares in its privatization strategy in anticipation that these one-time transition costs will quickly reduce overall transaction costs in the newly privatized economy.
33. To the problem that the citizenry might not have information about the market, the Czech strategists also seem to have a market solution in mind: investors who take risks will want better information and the demand for information will stimulate the business of gathering and selling information. The simulated market, they believe, will help to set in motion the secondary institutions (brokerage houses, market analysis, etc.) required for smoothly functioning capital markets.

34. Prominent among the Czechoslovak citizens who will have money to speculate on the stock exchange that is to be the product of the voucher-auction will be former Communist officials and black-marketeers. The cynicism of the architects of the Czech privatization strategy is undisguised: “It’s sure there is dirty money here,” said Tomas Jezek, Czech Minister of Privatization. “But the best method for cleaning the money is to let them invest it.” *New York Times*, January 27, 1991, p. 10.
35. The architects of the Czechoslovak voucher-auction programs hope that a simulated market will stimulate a market. There is an element of learning by doing built into the program. By playing the voucher market (and this is really playing a game) at least some groups of citizens get accustomed to “buying and selling” and might be drawn into really playing the market. (For a very different conception, see the Polish case below which highlights the distinctiveness of the Czech case.) The question of whether the institutions of a stock exchange can be created in such a manner, of course, remains to be tested.
36. For those enterprises at the very bottom of the list (where citizens were not willing to exchange points for shares) the state will, of course, face the difficult decision of whether to close them or to continue operating them under state management.
37. Anticipation of managerial resistance would lead us to expect that there should be active bargaining between ministries and enterprises in the initial asset evaluation determining the initial asking “price” in the first round of the auction. Such an observation does not threaten our typology since that initial asset evaluation is only a preliminary one to set in motion the auction (and the later market for shares) in which the effective and determinate asset evaluation will take place.
38. See Jan Szomburg, “Poland’s Privatization Strategy: Evolution and Features.” *Transformation der Wirtschaftssysteme in Ostmitteleuropa*. Munich, Südosteuropa Gesellschaft, 1993, pp. 135–154. For an overview of the ambitious goals but limited achievements of the early privatization efforts in Poland, see Tomasz Gruszecki, “Privatisation in Poland in 1990,” *Communist Economies and Economic Transformation* 3:2 (1991), pp. 141–154.
39. Lewandowski and Szomburg had proposed a stock distribution plan as early as 1988. See their “Uwlaszczenie jako fundament reformy spoleczno-gospodarczej” (Property change as a fundamental aspect of socio-economic reform) in *Propozyce Przeksztalcen Polskiej Gospodarki* (Warsaw, 1989), pp. 63–81. A similar program of mass privatization was later elaborated by David Lipton and Jeffrey Sachs, “Privatization in Eastern Europe: The Case of Poland,” *Brookings Papers* (1990), pp. 293–341.
40. Ownership claims coming from the Workers’ Councils arise in some places from strong bargaining positions while in others arise from weakness. For an excellent analysis of reorganization at the level of enterprises that cautions against any global statements about the activities of “workers,” “trade unions,” or “management,” see Janusz Dabrowski, Michal Federowics, and Anthony Levitas, “Stabilization and State Enterprise Adjustment: The Political Economy

of State Firms After Five Months of Fiscal Discipline." Working Papers on Central and Eastern Europe, Harvard University, 1990.

41. Szomburg, "Privatization Strategy."
42. Debated but not yet resolved is the question of whether Workers' Councils will be disbanded in all transformed enterprises. If so, workers would be asked, in effect, to exchange a set of implicit organizational rights inherited from the transition period for a set of explicit ownership rights in the new period of transformation. The question will not be answered without much bargaining.
43. See, for example, Janusz Lewandowski and Jan Szomburg, "The Strategy of Privatization," (Paper presented at the Research Centre for Marketization and Property Reform, Gdansk, October, 1990.)
44. The distinction between "credit based" and "capital market based" (roughly, banks versus a stock exchange) is presented in John Zysman, *Government, Markets, and Growth* (Ithaca, 1983).
45. By late 1991, Poland's program of mass privatization showed signs of unravelling. The 400 firms scheduled for the voucher program had been reduced to 230, and the program was under attack from all quarters. See Ben Slay, "Privatization and De-Monopolization in Poland," unpublished manuscript, Research Institute, Radio Free Europe/Radio Liberty, November 1991. If citizen vouchers recede in importance, we should expect that the locus of privatization/reorganization will shift even more to the level of firms and localities and especially to the Workers' Councils—one of the most important institutional legacies in the economic realm of Poland's extrication from state socialism. For an excellent analysis of decentralized reorganization in Poland, see Janusz M. Dabrowski, Michal Federowicz, and Anthony Levitas, "Polish State Enterprises and the Properties of Performance: Stabilization, Marketization, Privatization," *Politics and Society* 19:4 (1991), pp. 403–437.
46. To the legitimate objection that such an arrangement should be designated as a "market" because it bears strong resemblance to the organization of some capital markets in developed economies, we have three replies. First, see below on the continuing nature of these contracts. Second, the observation might lead some researchers to further explore features of "relational contracting" in such capital markets in Western economies. (Such research is already ongoing. See, for example, the extraordinary analysis of networks in investment banking by Joel Podolny, Ph.D. dissertation, Department of Sociology, Harvard University, 1991.) Third, for the purposes of our typology, the institutional arrangement (so prevalent in the Hungarian case) deserves some distinctive terminology to set it apart from the use of spot markets (auctions) in the Czech case.
47. Such a restructuring would require preparation of a comprehensive transformation program, under the guidelines of the 1989 Law on Transformation, with the direct involvement of the State Property Agency.
48. I am grateful to László Neumann and Eva Voszka for providing me with these data.
49. The term VKFT is not my invention but comes from workers I interviewed

(in collaboration with János Lukács) in January 1990 during field work in several Hungarian factories. With that acronym these workers were alluding to an earlier hybrid organizational form, the VGMK (enterprise work partnership), involved in a primarily internal system of subcontracting. Although they were free to make contracts and had significant autonomy in organizing production and allocating their "entrepreneurial fees," in the VGMK form the ownership of fixed assets remained in the hands of the parent enterprise. With the term VKFT these workers were denoting the semi-autonomous character of the new limited liability companies spinning around the enterprise. On the VGMK as a hybrid organizational form and precursor of new mixed property forms see David Stark, "Coexisting Organizational Forms in Hungary's Emerging Mixed Economy," in Victor Nee and David Stark, eds., *Remaking the Economic Institutions of Socialism: China and Eastern Europe* (Stanford, 1989).

50. See especially the important study by Eva Voszka, *Tulajdon—reform* (*Property—reform*) (Budapest, 1991), and also her "From Twilight to Twilight. Transformation of the Ownership Structure in the Big Industries." *Acta Oeconomica* 43:3–4 (1991), pp. 213–230. For an excellent case study of such reorganization, see Eva Voszka, "Rope Walking: Ganz Danubius Ship and Crane Factory Transformed into a Company," *Acta Oeconomica* 43:1–2 (1990), pp. 285–302; see also Mária Móro, "Az állami vállalatok (ál)privatizációja" (Pseudo privatization of state enterprises) *Közgazdasági Szemle* 38:6 (1990), pp. 565–584.
51. In the past eighteen months the creation of new economic units has increased by two-and-one-half times, but the number of corporations has grown by seventeen times (Voszka, "Rope Walking"). If we preferred to measure by capitalization instead of counting units, the new semi-autonomous corporate forms would be even more preponderant.
52. In this phase, as Eva Voszka succinctly describes, on issues of privatization the government was much more preoccupied with the question of who should be the seller rather than who should be the new owner. Voszka, "Rope Walking."
53. After consulting with the leading Hungarian experts in this field, our best estimates are that only about ten percent of such proposals are rejected at the level of the SPA. According to the best available data, the official rate of approval of corporate reorganization is seventy percent. But most practitioners in the field acknowledge that many rejected proposals are approved after minor technical changes (or, on occasion, with no revision).
54. Voszka, "Rope Walking," Móro, "Pseudo privatization" and Lászlo Neumann, "Labour Conflicts of Privatization." *Acta Oeconomica* 43:3–4 (1991), pp. 315–330.
55. This first scenario envisages a further extension of patterns of institutional cross-ownership and suggests a research agenda to investigate patterns of interlocking directorates in the Hungarian economy.
56. In this scenario, the debt for equity exchange so prevalent in the first round of reorganization could play an important part in the second. The overwhelming

problem of enterprise debt (some owed to banks, some in the disguised form of inter-enterprise debt as firms increasingly delay paying their suppliers in the state sector) is resulting in problems of solvency in the banking sector. There are recent indications that at least some banks are beginning to act like owners—demanding dividends from the KFTs and RTs affiliated with the state enterprises. Where profits are low to non-existent, some state enterprises may be forced to sell some of their affiliated units to pay such dividends. But the prospects for privatizing these units to domestic entrepreneurs are far from encouraging. Where will they receive the capital to make such investments? The same financial crisis that triggers the sales also places restrictions on credit.

57. In such a scenario, the relationship between enterprises and the state would take the form of bargaining and would reflect the continuity of ambiguous property relations in Hungarian state enterprises from the 1968 reforms to the present. But there would be discontinuities as well: in place of the earlier "plan bargaining" and the later "regulatory bargaining," under decentralized reorganization and reconsolidation of state ownership, the new relationship would be characterized as dividend bargaining. For a discussion of the continuities and discontinuities in these bargaining relations, see Erzsébet Szalai, "A hatalom metamorfózia?" (Metamorphosis of power?) *Valóság* 6 (1991), pp. 1–26.

58. Encouraging, but limiting, such privatization would be consistent with a policy choice that sought to rationalize the state's ownership role (trimming down the size of its assets) while consolidating its ability to intervene in the economy as an (indirect) owner.

59. In this case, as in all the scenarios, the question of who controls the banks is of fundamental importance. The dismissal in June 1991 of three bank presidents following a sharp dispute over the banks dividend policies indicates that the state is attempting to use its authority in appointing senior banking officials to control the shares in state enterprises held by the banks. It remains to be seen how the state's influence over banks will be changed by the new banking law that took effect on December 1, 1991. Under that legislation, only banks or other financial institutions may hold more than 25 percent of the shares of a bank. The state has until 1995 to reduce its direct ownership of shares in commercial banks.

60. For an elaboration of these concepts, see László Bruszt and David Stark, "Remaking the Political Field in Hungary: From the Politics of Confrontation to the Politics of Competition," in Ivo Banac, ed. *Eastern Europe in Revolution* (Ithaca, 1992), pp. 13–55.

61. Czechoslovakia's current trade unions, for example, bear relatively little resemblance to the pre-1989 unions—in contrast to Hungary, where the old official union remains the largest (if tired) trade union federation, and to Poland, where both Solidarity and the OPZZ are the continued legacy of the 1980s. See Bruszt, "Transformative Politics."

62. Bruszt, "Transformative Politics." On the concepts of different types of capitalism and different types of democracy see the insightful work of Philippe

Schmitter, "Modes of Sectoral Governance: A Typology," unpublished manuscript, Stanford University; and Terry Karl and Philippe Schmitter, "Modes of Transition in Latin America, Southern and Eastern Europe," *International Social Science Journal* 128 (March 1991), pp. 269–284.

63. The reader who suspects exaggeration here would benefit from reading, for example, Werner Gumpel's "The Mentality Problem in the Transition Process from Centrally Planned Economy to Market Economy." (Paper presented at the Conference on Transforming Economic Systems in East-Central Europe, Munich, June 1991.) I have paraphrased Professor Gumpel in the passage above. To quote him directly: "It will take a long time to reeducate them. These people must be made to unlearn most of what they were brought up with." *Transformation der Wirtschaftssysteme in Ostmitteleuropa*. Munich, Südosteuropa Gesellschaft, 1993.
64. The rapidity with which some packages of innovation have become institutionalized (that is, come to be taken for granted) has been extraordinary. No one was shocked, for example, when Yeltsin announced shock therapy for the Russian economy. On diffusion across national boundaries, see David Strang and John W. Meyer, "Institutional Conditions for Diffusion," (Paper presented at the Workshop on New Institutional Theory, Department of Sociology, Cornell University, November 1991.) On the decoupling of formal structures celebrating institutionalized myths from actual organizational practices, see especially John W. Meyer and Brian Rowan, "Institutionalized Organizations: Formal Structure as Myth and Ceremony," in Walter W. Powell and Paul J. DiMaggio, eds., *The New Institutionalism in Organizational Analysis* (Chicago, 1991), pp. 41–62.
65. See especially the research presented in Rogers Hollingsworth, Philippe Schmitter, and Wolfgang Streeck, eds., *Comparing Capitalist Economies: Variations in the Governance of Industrial Sectors* (New York, 1992); Schmitter, "Modes;" Robert Boyer, "The Transformations of Modern Capitalism in Light of the Regulation Approach and other Theories of Political Economy." (Paper presented at the Conference on Comparative Governance of Economic Sectors, Bellagio, June 1989); and Walter Powell, "Neither Market nor Hierarchy: Network Forms of Organization," in B. Staw and L.L. Cummings, eds., *Research in Organizational Behavior* (Greenwich, Conn., 1990), pp. 295–336. The key analytic move in this new literature is to shift from the preoccupation with micro- or macro-phenomena to a meso-level focus on sectors. These studies suggest an exciting agenda for similar meso-analysis of sectors and localities in contemporary Eastern Europe.
66. On the multiple meanings of the term "market," see the excellent paper by Robert Boyer, "Markets within Alternative Coordinating Mechanisms: History, Theory, and Policy in the Light of the Nineties." (Paper presented at the Conference on the Comparative Governance of Sectors, Bigorio, Switzerland, April 1991.)
67. Michael T. Hannan and John Freeman, *Organizational Ecology* (Cambridge, Mass., 1989), esp. p. 3; and David Stark, "Coexisting Organizational Forms" esp. p. 168.

II

Democracy and/or Liberalism: On the Politics of Transformation

6

Transformative Politics: Social Costs and Social Peace in East Central Europe

László Bruszt

Marketization and Democracy

The various approaches to the political dilemmas of economic transformation in East Central Europe are based on three uncontested assumptions and one highly debated question. The three uncontested assumptions are: (1) marketization will lower transaction costs, (2) privatization will lower production costs and increase the performance of these economies, (3) marketization and privatization will have high transitional social costs. The contested question is whether these societies will accept these costs—simultaneously a question of the capacities of the new democratic regimes to solve social conflicts.

Those who answer this question negatively do so by raising doubts about the compatibility of the social costs of economic transformation and the newly created rules of democratic politics. For them, the transitional social costs are too high and the worst-off will resist the changes, using the newly installed democratic rules to block the economic transformation and/or to undermine democratic governance. The argu-

Research for this chapter was supported by grants from the National Science Foundation. My thanks to David Stark and Monique Djokic Stark for their helpful criticisms and suggestions on earlier drafts of the paper.

ments in this approach are based either on the legacies of the past regimes in economic and social structures, or simply on the contradictions of the logic of economic change and democratic governance. The "structuralist" argument runs basically as follows: due to the peculiarities of the interests of the social actors, determined by the inherited social structures and cultures, they (usually the workers in the more concrete arguments) will resist economic transformation. Those social groups that would support both economic transformation and democratic consolidation are absent.[1] The existing social groups have interests that contradict the logic of marketization.[2] The formalist version of this argument offers a set of paradoxes: (*a*) the consolidation of democracy requires marketization, (*b*) marketization of these economies is impossible without democracy, (*c*) democracy does not allow for marketization, (*d*) if there will be marketization, it will undermine democracy, (*e*) the lack of marketization will also undermine democracy.[3]

The affirmative answer to the same question is based also on the same two factors, arguing that there are ways to minimize the social costs of transformation and to gain society's tolerance of these costs.[4] According to the most elaborate study using this approach, people would support radical programs with high transitional social costs if they were confident in the future.[5] In the view of Adam Przeworski, the most likely successful road to a market economy is not the one that minimizes social costs but the radical one that is able to move ahead with economic transformation and simultaneously generate popular support. The political conditions favorable for economic transformation can either be created through centralizing political decisions and neutralizing or marginalizing those forces that could resist the transformation. Or they can be created by generating social support for, or at least passive tolerance of, the economic changes through different types of inclusive politics that increase the range of democratic institutions and political actors included in the decision-making process on reforms.

According to Przeworski, this road is certainly not a linear one. Economic reform can erode its social basis and reforms can go in cycles. The basic question is whether the periods of moving ahead will result in a critical mass of changes, upon which the next reforms can go even further. On the other hand, both the centralizing and the decentralizing strategies of generating favorable political conditions for economic change have their own limitations; and similarly to the stop-and-go process of economic transformation, politicians will vacillate between de-mobilizing resistance to the changes and mobilizing social support for transformative politics.

To amplify the "compatibility thesis" of Przeworski, I analyze the strategies of transformative politics in four East Central European countries during the first year after the completion of the initial stage of transition to democracy. First I will present a simple analytic framework for describing the differences in the strategies chosen and the courses of action taken and, moving then from description to explanation, I will argue that we need to move a step beyond the proposals of Przeworski. While accepting his arguments in general, I will argue that a deeper analysis of transformative politics must examine the differences in the structural and institutional legacies of these regimes; linking the modalities in transformative politics to the differences in the paths taken before and during the transition to democracy. Based on the differences in the pre-transition solutions to the dilemmas of harmonizing economic growth and social peace, the institutional outcomes of state-socialist modernization, and the extrication, we should expect differences in the various strategies chosen.[6]

This approach draws from the recent studies of the relationships between the types of political regimes and the success of economic transformations in other regions of the world. One of the main conclusions one should draw from these studies is that there is no general rule of the relationship between democratic or authoritarian rule and economic transformation. Economic hardships are mediated by various preexisting institutional arrangements for managing political conflict and by divergent abilities of the political elites to maintain the support of the key groups in the society.[7] It follows that the chances for survival of the same types of regimes, authoritarian or democratic, will differ. In some countries the resistance to the social costs of economic changes lead to the collapse of both democratic and authoritarian regimes, under other regimes, whether democratic or authoritarian, political conditions would allow them to survive even deeper crises.[8]

Strategies and Legacies

In analyzing the changes in the courses of action taken in the first year of the post-communist governments in the four Central European countries—Hungary, Czechoslovakia, Poland, and the eastern part of Germany—the framework I propose is organized around the two major aspects of transformative politics: (1) choices concerning the speed of transformation and hence the timing of social costs and (2) the means of securing social support or toleration of these costs. The two major aspects are combined to create a two-dimensional space where we can then locate the initial choices of strategies among our four cases and chart subsequent changes in these strategies, and then analyze the linkages between the strategies and legacies.

Speed (The Timing of Social Costs). The two dimensions of transformative politics are interrelated, but their relationship is far from being direct.[9] Decisions about the speed of economic changes always take into account assumptions about the level of tolerance of different social groups, the capacities of the different actors to organize resistance, and the capacities of the reformers to mobilize support, and/or neutralize resistance. On the other hand, these decisions are always also influenced by such pressures from within as the internal structural problems of the economy, and/or from without, in the form of the pressure from private creditors, international financial organizations, and the like. To put it differently, decisions about the speed of economic transformation are always interconnected with calculations of the different time-frames of transformative politics. The latter is partly determined by the parliamentary business cycle, that is, on calculations by reformers to get visible economic improvement by the last year of their term, while holding the coalition of their supporting forces together during the hard times. Decisions concerning speed are also strongly influenced by the time given by the structural conditions of the economy, and also by the grace period provided by external creditors. Finally, the time frame given by the different extra-parliamentary political actors, first of all trade unions, is of increasing importance.[10]

While the slow-gradual approach dilutes the social costs of the economic transformation in time, the fast-radical strategy attempts to concentrate them. The gradual path seeks to partition the costs associated with systemic change evenly among the various segments of society, while proponents of the radical strategy do not take the social inequalities into account when calculating the net social cost of reform. The gradualist approach seeks incremental changes, accompanied by piecemeal monetary compensation to alleviate the gradually growing burden on the population, thereby seeking to placate them. In contrast, the radical strategy, or shock therapy approach, aims at minimizing the duration of this period of anesthetization within which the radical surgery altering the economic system is carried out, thereby minimizing the net cost.

Social Peace. The strategy of maintaining the social peace is again related to the choice of economic strategy, for example, in the form of calculations about the capacity of the reformed economy to create for various social groups the potential to accommodate themselves, the capacity of the new institutions to mobilize resources, and the interrelated capacity of the state to centralize them in order to "buy the social peace." The choice of this strategy is shaped by calculations of the capacities of existing institutions to generate a minimal level of political support as well as by calculations about the resources of potential opponents and the like.

Strategies of maintaining social peace can oscillate between two extreme solutions: they can either rely on the coercive capacities of the state to suppress, marginalize and/or neutralize resistance, sometimes combined with, centralized welfare-redistribution but usually not enough. Or, at the other extreme, the maintenance of social peace may be brought about through support, organized by the independent forces of civil society.[11] While these are the extremes of the potential strategies, the actual strategies may be located between the two poles of maintaining social peace based on the centralized means of "stick and carrot," or on "socializing the problems of the economy," by including the institutions of parliamentarism and the multitude of organizations of civil society into the decision-making process.[12]

On the one pole we will find different types of extreme centralization of power, from strong presidentialism with a populist-type leader to a one-party government with strong exclusionary and suppressive policies. Moving in the direction of the other pole we will find the different types of extension of the social and/or political basis of transformative politics: the extension of party coalitions, social pacts with parties and peak associations of labor and business, different types of corporatist arrangements, including trade unions, into the framing of transformative policies, and finally social movements supporting the politics of "there-is-no-alternative" on a moral basis.

Based on these two variables we can create a preliminary two-dimensional space for locating the different types of transformative politics (Figure 1). The horizontal axis indicates gradual versus radical economic strategies; the vertical axis runs from the extreme pole of the statist strategy of maintaining social peace, to the purely theoretical strategy of the support organized solely by civil society and includes between them the various forms of inclusionary policies.

Figure 6.1 is a first attempt to illustrate the modalities and strategies and actual courses of action. Because of the hesitations of policy-makers (that is, to the changes in the course of action between the publication of the economic programs and their implementation), to decide about the placement of the different cases was not easy. Moreover, in some cases, the change in the course of action is still more at the level of strategic considerations than at the level of actual policy, and the question-marks refer to such cases. Bearing in mind the tentativeness of the placements, Figure 1 does suggest that the political leadership in three out of the four countries initially chose various forms of statist strategies, and, with the exception of Hungary, the strategies aimed at a radical departure from the old economic status quo.

The Choice of Strategy. With these locations in mind, our task is now to connect the modalities of transformative politics to the different ideologies and legacies of the "transformers," focusing first on the institutional legacies of the extrication. Our analysis begins with the choices of the initial strategies and the role played in those choices by differences in the ideologies of the newly elected political leaders. We then turn to the different institutional and structural legacies that constrain these strategies.

In the choice of the initial strategies an important role was played by the different ideologies of the newly elected leaders. These ideologies were organized around two poles: the conservative "social-market" ideology of the Hungarian governing coalition, and in a moderate form, of the German government; on the other extreme the Thatcherite liberal views of the Czechoslovak "transformers." Somewhere between the two lies the more pragmatic liberal approach of the Polish economic policy-makers. Behind these different ideologies we can discover different views about the role of the market, the state, and civil society in the process of economic transformation.

The cautious "social market" ideology of the Hungarians, while accepting a market economy as the final destination of transformative politics, does not trust the market as the dominant means of the economic transition and places its trust more in the transformative capaci-

FIGURE 6.1
The Modalities of Transformative Strategies and Their Changes

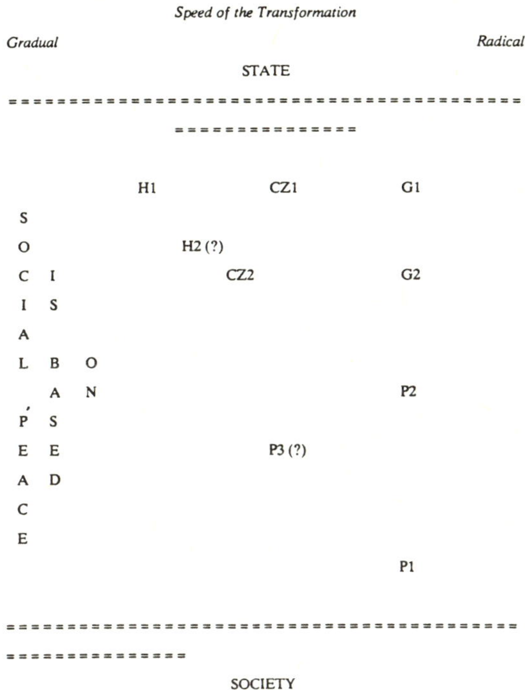

ties of the centralized state bureaucracy insulated from society.[13] The process of marketization, on the other hand, is seen by them as a dangerous experiment which can undermine social peace, and which has to be counterbalanced either by the welfare services of the centralized state or by a strategy of placing burdens on the society only gradually.

At the opposite pole we find the fast-statist ideology of the Václav Klaus type liberals in Czechoslovakia. According to this view, the market is not only the outcome of the economic transformation but itself can serve as a means of bringing about the economic changes. Moreover, instead of undermining social peace, the process of marketization can be designed in such a way that will help to generate support for the changes.[14] "Social-market" ideology holds that it is the state's role to coordinate economic transformation, while the fast-statist strategy sees the neutralization of potential social resistance as the major role of the state.

Finally, the pragmatic liberals in Poland hold that while the market can be used as a means of economic stabilization and transformation, the process of economic transformation needs the support of society despite the burdens placed on it. In this view the central role of the state is to maintain society's support of the unavoidable changes.

The initial views of the new governments about the social peace were strongly influenced by the institutional legacies of the extrication. With the exception of Poland, the institutionalization of intermediaries and civil society organizations started only after the transition, and the links were weak between the new power-holders and different social groups.

In Hungary the early promise of free elections during the first stage of transition resulted in a fast transformation of the majority of the existing political groupings into parties. There remained some weak new independent trade unions and small groups of environmentalists, but the post-election political scene was clearly dominated by the six parliamentary parties. The negotiated transition in Hungary allowed for a much stronger continuity at the level of intermediary political organizations. The old unitary trade unions are still the strongest. They have generally splintered from within and formed new confederations.[15]

In Czechoslovakia the level of political organization was lower at the time of extrication than in Hungary, and the political scene was dominated by organizations which were mixtures of proto-parties and social movements. In Hungary the negotiated nature of the transition allowed for strong continuities at the level of the intermediary organizations, but in Czechoslovakia the capitulation of the old regime resulted in a discontinuity at this level. Here the six thousand strike committees, set up at the time of the preparation for the general strike during November 1989, occupied the old Communist trade unions from within and created the strongest new trade union confederation in the region.[16] At the time of the formation of the initial strategy of economic change the trade unions were only in the first stages of formation.

In the former GDR the organizations of the extremely weak political society were marginalized by the political organizations of the "western brother" and during and after the electoral campaign the "Eastern" political scene was "colonized" by the West German parties and political organizations.

The lack of well-developed political societies in Hungary, Czechoslovakia, and the former GDR invited statist initial strategies, but in Poland the existence of the strongest social movement in the region (combined with the rapid deterioration of the economic situation) forced or allowed for a radical program of stabilization, based on large-scale social support.

These differences are reflected in the divergent views of the new rulers about the role to be played by the organizations of the civil society in maintaining the social peace. The Hungarian governing coalition cannot rely on the organizations of the society, the Czechoslovak reformers did not want to rely on the society, and the German government thought that social peace could be bought by the infusion of billions of Deutschmarks. Only the Polish reformers could rely, at least in the first critical phase of the economic stabilization, on the organized support of the society.

Finally, in the formation of the initial strategies an important role was played by the different institutional and structural legacies inherited from the previous economic regimes. With the exception of Hungary, the experiments with economic reforms were at a low profile in the pre-transition period in these countries and the institutions of the market economy were absent for the most part. Although in Poland there was an immediate pressure to stabilize the economic situation, in Czechoslovakia and the former GDR it was the lack of previous reforms that invited *tabula rasa* strategies, a fast departure from the old regimes. In Hungary, by contrast the new governing coalition succumbed to the temptation to continue the politics of gradual reform adopted by the previous governments with only slightly different methods. In the choice of the statist-gradualist strategy in Hungary an important role was played also by calculations related to the growth-capacities of the largest second economy in Eastern Europe.[17] The expectation that a tight monetarist policy (combined with a gradual extension of market institutions and change in the property relations) would quickly result in the improvement of economic performance and thus increase the capacity of the government to reduce indebtedness and finance the material compensations for the worst off was evident.

To sum up, alongside the differences in ideologies, the choice of the initial strategies was influenced in all cases except Poland by the initial weakness of the political societies in these countries. The choice of a radical strategy was prompted by pressure for rapid stabilization in Poland, but it was the lack of basic institutions of the market that invited the choice of fast strategies in Czechoslovakia and the former GDR. Finally, in the choice of the gradual-statist strategy in Hungary an important role was played by the existence of the institutional legacies of previous economic reforms.

The Constraints. In each country, these initial strategies were met by different constraints shaped by specific institutional legacies of the past. Common to all has been that the erosion of the initial support was fast, with the pressure from below to "renegotiate" the terms of transformative politics increasing rapidly. This erosion of support, however, was not signalled in the same ways and did not always have the same effects since its expression and influence were mediated by specific institutional differences shaped by the differing paths of extrication.

In Hungary and the former GDR during the first period of the new governments street demonstration was the only way for the society to communicate with the authorities.[18] Czechoslovakia showed a different pattern where a strike alert called by unions throughout November 1990 and later threats of a general strike were enough to convince the government that negotiations were needed.[19] In Poland, first the sporadic strikes of early summer 1990 and later the electoral support given to Tyminski were clear signs of the diminishing support of the people for the government.

It is important to note that the speed of the erosion of the support was not directly related to the speed (and thus the level of social costs) of the economic changes. In Poland, the fast economic stabilization program in its initial phase was tolerated by society much better and longer than the cautious gradual-statist strategy of the Hungarian government with lower social costs. And in Czechoslovakia it was not the price increases that prompted trade unions to change their initially strong pro-market slogans, but instead the attempt of the government's technocrats to disarm the trade unions through the introduction of a highly restrictive strike law that brought about the change in the unions' posture. Throughout the region the differences in the speed of the erosion of support were mainly related to the level of trust in the new political leaders and thus to the relationships that had emerged before and during the first stage of transition between political elites and society at large. Because there was no serious public debate about the major elements of the economic programs in any of the countries, people were unprepared for the hardships to come. But while the population in Poland had ten years to establish a strong identification with the Solidarity movement, in the other countries the initial identification with the new leaders was based mainly on their performance during the extrication and the electoral campaign.

Changes in the Course of Action. As Figure 6.1 illustrates, there were attempts to turn to more inclusive strategies (that is, in the direction of the lower end of our space), with the exception of Poland, and there were attempts to broaden the political basis of transformation. But the specific institutional vehicles for attempting to secure such support differ. In Czechoslovakia, the institutional basis for the renegotiation of the terms of the economic strategy existed in the form of the strongest and most unified trade union in the region, while in the former GDR the old trade unions have disappeared and this has not yet allowed for the emergence of trusted intermediaries. In Hungary the seven competing trade union confederations were too weak to negotiate in the name of labour.[20] As a result, the changes in the course of action in Hungary (and partly also in the former GDR) are more in the planning phase and the turn to more inclusive policies is constrained mainly by the lack of intermediaries. There are, however, some initiatives on the side of the political leaders in both countries that indicate the direction of the potential change in the strategies. In Hungary, the creation of the "Hungarian Moncloa Pact" was proposed in the middle of 1991 and, according to the original plans, would have brought together the six parliamentary parties to work out the conditions of the political support for the government's politics of economic transformation similar to the social pact made in Spain after the conclusion of the first free elections.[21] The idea of increasing the political basis of the government with a pact between the parties of the governing coalition and the parties in opposition failed because of disagreement on the political preconditions of such support. During the preparatory talks, the parties could agree only on one question, namely, that they have to solve the problem of the lack of intermediaries. They have agreed that trade union elections should be held to solve the problem of competing representative claims of the seven confederations and that the assets of the old confederation should be redistributed according to the outcomes of these elections.[22]

It is ironic that it was the Czechoslovak leadership who signed the first corporatist agreement on macroeconomic questions in Eastern Europe. The most important role in the change of the course of action of the government was played not by the resistance of the society to the social burdens, but by the reaction of the trade unions to the attempt of the Thatcherite technocrats to neutralize potential social resistance by a restrictive legal regulation of strikes. Warning with the threat of a general strike was enough to change the strategy of the government. The compromise resulted in the extension of trade-union rights, in a liberal regulation of strikes, and the joining of the trade unions of the tripartite Council of Social Accord in which the unions accepted a maximum 12 percent drop in real wages for 1991.[23]

Poland's institutional legacy (that is, the unitary social movement functioning simultaneously as a trade union, as a government, and as a legislature) allowed for the fast program of stabilization in the initial period. Later, as the support for the politics of transformation eroded, the same legacy became a liability for the major political actors who have differed among themselves as to what could be saved from the old Solidarity movement but have agreed that the regeneration of social support (to continue economic transformation) and the prevention of a regime crisis (in the absence of an organised alternative to the Solidarity government) presupposed the separation of the different "Solidarities."

The process of adaptation to the new situation was not the outcome of any conscious political design but instead the result of infighting within the unitary social movement that resulted in the formation of the first "post-Solidarity" parties, the division of the unitary movement into "Solidarities" along institutional lines.[24] There was also the institutionalization of the remnants of the charisma of the leader in the form of a strong president.[25] While the course of the transformative politics in Poland turned in the fast-statist direction after the presidential elections, the massive strike waves in 1991 showed the possibility of a new change in the direction of a more inclusive politics.

The Art of the Impossible? The first year of transformative politics in East Central Europe was therefore also the last year when economic change was solely the business of economic experts and politicians—as it had been for forty years during the old regimes and as it was everywhere in the initial period of the changes immediately after the extrication. The short period is over in which popular support for the politics of economic transformation was based either on moral support or only on the popular mandate given by the first free elections. What has just started in the region is the renegotiation, or more precisely the negotiation, of the terms of economic transformation. While the direction of the arrows in Figure 1 indicate the possibility of that change, it does not say anything about the feasibility or the durability of the new, inclusionary policies. As the initial strategies differed because of differences in ideologies and different configurations of the legacies of these countries, the chances of the more inclusive strategies will be different. There is a general tendency, however, to depart from the initial situation in which the programs for economic change were based mainly on a non-existing class, that is, the class of new middle-class entrepreneurs.

The strategies of the extension of the social basis of transformative policies are different, depending mainly on the differences in the balance of forces in the given country. In Hungary, for example, due to the weaknesses of organized labor, the first sign for an attempt for coalition formation was the stabilization and the strengthening of the positions of the state bureaucrats, and of the managers of the large public enterprises, vis-à-vis the workers. Due to a different balance of forces, in Poland the government until now did not touch upon the exemptionary participatory rights of the workers at the workplace level. Instead it attempts to include workers into marketization by a deal in which participatory rights would be exchanged partly for higher wages, partly for property rights.

The first year of transformative politics was also perhaps the last year when economic change was blocked by the mutual weaknesses of states and societies. Communist states were weak; unable to change not only because of their limited sovereignties, overpoliticized bureaucracies, or decrepit ideologies, but also because of the fears of their own societies. That fear was all the bigger when they have faced disorganized societies, lacking political organizations, leaders, and opposition strategies. They did not know how people would react to programs of economic liberalization or stabilization. How could they know the limits of tolerance of their societies or predict when people would start to march in the streets? In the last few years of Communist rule several economic programs have collapsed in Hungary and Poland in their initial stages due to the fear of the leaders of the sudden and uncontrollable reactions of the people. In both countries that fear was the biggest impetus for change: a partner was needed who was able "to sell" society the costs of economic transformation, a solid political basis to start with the programs of inevitable economic change.[26]

The first year of transformative politics thus validates, at least partly, those reformers within the old regimes who sought "partners for dialog". The durability of statist strategies, both gradual and fast, was short everywhere, and those states were stronger, that is, able to continue to execute their economic policies most consistently where, due to the level of the political organization of the society, it was possible to organize at least the passive toleration of the social costs of the economic changes. While that fact supports the old argument about the need of a "partner" and the need of democracy to start economic transformation, the first year of transformative politics does not give us enough evidence yet to strongly support or refute the thesis about the (in)compatibility of democracy and the continuation of the economic reform. Even at this stage, though, we have enough evidence to slightly reformulate the basic dilemma presented in the introduction of this paper about the compatibility of marketization (economic transformation) and democracy. According to this reformulation, the dilemma is not that of the compatibility of democracy and marketization in general but that of different types of democracies and different types of marketization, that is, different paths, not to a general market economy, but to new types of economies with different mixes of market and non-market elements.[27] While the reformulation does not negate the existence of the generic problem of transformative politics, it suggests that instead of studying that relationship at a general level we should study the different capacities of the different mixtures of democratic institutions and policies, the different types of coalitions, the different types of market and non-market solutions in the economy, and the theoretically seemingly impossible mixtures of different organizational principles.

Whether transformative politics is "the art of the possible" or "the art of the impossible" will be decided in the future. What we can observe now is the plurality of paths taken, problems faced and solved. To remain with the topic of this paper: the first one year of transformative politics brought with it six different mixtures of strategies in East Central Europe. It saw the failure of several policies which were thought to be "the only" feasible solutions to this dilemma. It saw in Czechoslovakia the failure of the neo-liberal statist strategy which wanted to solve the generic dilemma of economic transformation by anesthetizing society, reduce not only its time of reaction, by disarming it. We could witness the erosion of the support for the sole civil society based fast marketization strategy in Poland. 1991 also proved in Hungary that the gradual statist strategy of trying to minimize the political risks of economic change can be very risky, and lead to a fast erosion of the political support. Finally we have seen the failure of the "social peace can be bought" strategy in the former GDR. But we have also seen the creation of new mixtures: the fast-populist strategy in Poland based on the remnants of the charisma of the "leader," and the strange mix of neo-liberal-corporatist strategy in Czechoslovakia. Perhaps such unorthodox approaches to politics, the capacity to mix up the most different principles, might yet be the proof that transformative politics is, in the end, the art of the possible.

In 1992 and 1993 one could observe the continuation of struggles over the alternative paths of transformative politics shaped and constrained both by longer term legacies of past regimes and the shorter term institutional outcomes of policies taken by the new democracies.

After the separation of the Czech and Slovak Republics, the Czech government continued its more inclusionary transformative strategy while the new political elites in Slovakia, constrained by a much deeper economic crisis and facing a weaker civil society, turned in the direction of an exclusionary corporatist strategy. In Poland exclusionary policies prevailed in these two years. They were shaped by the fragmentation of political forces both within and outside the parliamentary arena. Despite the tripartite pact on privatization, struck in 1993, the larger part of society felt excluded from the changes. At the 1993 parliamentary elections they voted for forces which, rightly or wrongly, were perceived as representing more inclusionary *and* paternalistic alternatives. In the former GDR continuity rather than change characterized the ups and downs of economic transformation. Finally, in Hungary the coalition government concluded two socio-economic pacts with the representatives of labor and business in 1992 and 1993. While these pacts signified a departure from the previous exclusionary strategy, due to the weakness of labor and the internal fragmentation of the governing coalition, the formation of transformative policies is still dominated by state bureaucrats and party politicians insulated both from the parliamentary and the corporatist arenas.

Notes

1. The more concrete arguments here refer to the lack of a new "moneyed" middle class of owners.
2. The most sophisticated arguments of this sort can be seen in George Schöpflin, "Central and Eastern Europe over the Last Year: New Trends, Old Structures," in *RFE Report on Eastern Europe*, February 15, 1991, pp. 26–28., and David Ost, "Shaping a New Politics in Poland." (Paper presented at the conference on Transition from State Socialism in East Central Europe, Center for European Studies, Harvard University, Cambridge, March 15–17, 1991.)
3. See especially Claus Offe, "Privatisierung der Ökonomie als demokratisches Projekt? Paradoxen des 'politischen Kapitalismus' in Osteuropa." (Paper presented at the Zentrum für Sozialpolitik Universität Bremen, March 1991) and Jon Elster "The Necessity and Impossibility of Simultaneous Economic and Political Reform," University of Chicago, 1991, unpublished manuscript.
4. See especially Adam Przeworski, *Democracy and the Market* (Cambridge, 1991), pp. 136–188, and Andrew Arato, "Revolution, Civil Society and Democracy," New School for Social Research, New York, 1990, unpublished manuscript.
5. Przeworski, *Democracy and the Market*.
6. For example, one can accept, in principle, that the costs of the strategy of market-shock can be lower than the cost of the strategy of gradual change. But, based on the analysis of the above mentioned differences, we can also explain why certain countries will hardly even attempt to experiment with that strategy, why in others only the reformers will be shocked by the degree of popular resistance, and why, in a third country, the bitter pill strategy will be the one with a high level of temporary social support.
7. See especially Stephan Haggard and Robert Kaufman, "Economic Adjustment and the Prospects for Democracy," 1991, unpublished manuscript.
8. Haggard and Kaufman, "Economic Adjustment".
9. Concerning the relationship of the two variables also see Przeworski, *Democracy and the Market*.
10. In 1991/92 there were several general agreements between governments and trade unions in various Eastern European countries, in which usually wage-restraint and/or strike-stop was exchanged for the extension of trade union rights and some form of less than 100 percent wage indexation. In these agreements trade unions gave the green light for but 3 to 12 months in which the government may proceed unchecked with the transformation of the economy. Examples for the shorter one are the agreements made between the Bulgarian or Romanian trade unions and governments; for the longer, the example is the one struck between labor and government in Czechoslovakia.
11. The two strategies can be related to two different theoretical arguments about approaches to the political preconditions of transformative politics. According to the first school of thought only a strong, centralized state can transform the state-socialist economy, because of the peculiarities of social structure, i.e., there are no social groups that would be interested in capitalism, and the

state has to create those structural groups that would then support transformation.

According to the second approach, the success of the transformative politics will depend on the strength of the civil society, because of the contradictory logics of transforming structures and maintaining social peace. An example for the first approach is Jadwiga Staniszkis, "Dilemmata der Demokratie in Osteuropa," in R. Deppe et al., eds., *Demokratischer Umbruch in Osteuropa* (Frankfurt); an example for the second, Andrew Arato, "Revolution, Civil Society, and Democracy," New School for Social Research, New York, 1990, unpublished manuscript.

12. This expression comes from our conversation with Alfred Stepan.
13. See an example of the politics of privatization in the paper by David Stark, "Path Dependence and Privatization Strategies in East-Central Europe," in this volume.
14. Ibid.
15. The two independent confederations, created during the first stage of transition in 1989, are still weak, and together represent less than 10 percent of the active labor force. In the slow formation of the new trade unions, an important role is played also by the existence of the second economy and the economic strategies of the laborers, related to the second economy. While in Poland the working-class elite is busy in trade unions, e.g., the elite workers in Hungary are part-time entrepreneurs within or outside of the public enterprises.
16. The united Czech and Slovak Confederation of Unions (CSKOS) contained about 80 percent of the active labor force.
17. About the limitations of this strategy, and the ambiguous evolutionary potential of the Hungarian second economy, see the paper of István R. Gábor in this volume.
18. On the Hungarian taxi drivers' strike, see Sik's paper in this volume.
19. It was hard for the new leaders in Czechoslovakia to forget that it is possible to carry out a general strike. It was the general strike warning in November 1989 that resulted in the final capitulation of the old Communist rulers.
20. There exists in Hungary a corporatist institution for the mediation of conflicts between government and the representatives of business and labor, but this "National Council of Reconciliation" is mainly for the renegotiation of minimal wages. The government still hesitates to decide whether it has to divide, marginalize, or strengthen the trade unions.
21. Note one important difference from the Spanish Moncloa pact. While in Spain the trade unions were part of the negotiations, in Hungary the absence of the trade unions was the expressed preference of the designers of the negotiations.
22. The same solution, with the same ideology, is used in Romania to solve the problem of competing trade unions. David Stark and I interviewed the Romanian Minister of Labor, who made the following argument for holding trade union elections in Romania: "We cannot negotiate with several confederations, competing with each other, unable to agree on a single question with each other. We need a partner".

23. It was signed in January 1991 by the representatives of the three governments—Czech, Slovak and Federal—and the representatives of the employers' and trade unions. In the slowdown of the fast-statist strategy in Czechoslovakia, an important role was played also by the peculiar institutional outcome of the extrication, i.e., the consociational character of the federal state and parliament, which limited the use of exclusionary strategies based on simple parliamentary majority.
24. That is, the separation of the Solidarity Trade Union from the Solidarity government and the legislature.
25. Actually, the strength of the president is due more to the weakness of the parliament, due to its questionable legitimacy, than to the strong latitudes of the president.
26. See László Bruszt and David Stark "Remaking the Political Field in Hungary: From the Politics of Confrontation to the Politics of Competition," *Journal of International Affairs* 45:1 (June 1991), pp. 201–245.
27. On the concepts of different types of capitalism and different types of democracy, see the insightful work of Philippe Schmitter, "Modes of Sectoral Governance: A Typology," Stanford University, unpublished manuscript; and Terry Karl and Philippe Schmitter, "Modes of Transition and Types of Democracy in Latin America, Southern and Eastern Europe," Stanford University, *International Social Science Journal* 128 (May 1991), pp. 269–284.

7

From Soft Communism to Post-Communism (Authoritarian Legacy and Democratic Transition in Hungary)

András Bozóki

In order to understand East Central European democratic transitions, first the nature of the discredited communist system should be studied.[1] The proposition that a close relationship can be identified between the nature of the old system and the type of political change seems to be well founded. Transition began in the less autocratic systems, where it took more peaceful, slow and evolutionary shape. The more the earlier regime had limited human rights, the more drastic separation was.

The post-communist transition is a new case in history, where not only a dictatorial political system is replaced by a more liberal, or democratic one, but also a collectivized economy is replaced by a market economy based on private ownership. Trends of *renewal* and *restoration* are simultaneously present in transition because of this dual nature of change. Successful transition means the establishment of a democratic system based on human rights, and 'remedying'[2] the blind alley of development, a return to capitalism in the region. In this respect the paradoxical term *'conservative revolution'*[3] seems to be appropriate. The political agents can be characterized by their desire to return to a pre-communist system, or by emphasizing the transformation of the communist system in a new democracy. In the Hungarian Parliament there are 'historical' parties looking back to the past and emphasizing the continuity with the pre-communist system (Independent Small Holders' Party, Christian Democratic People's Party), as well as modern parties stressing the importance of a new beginning (Alliance of Free Democrats, Federation of Young Democrats). Both approaches are present in the largest governing party, the Hungarian Democratic Forum. The Hungarian Socialist Party has been transformed into a modern parliamentary party out of the old state-party: it is rather difficult for it to get rid of its own depressing heritage.

In Hungary a systemic change in the narrower sense of the term was completed with the local elections in the autumn of 1990, as far as the institutional transformation of the central and local authorities was concerned. The transformation of the economic system is a slower and longer process. The present paper mainly deals with the issue of the *political transition.* Despite the different nature of the old regimes there are similarities between the East Central European and the earlier South European and Latin American transitions. In most of the East Central European countries (with the exception of Romania) the old systems could not be described fully by the concept of totalitarianism. From the sixties onwards these countries were rather authoritarian dictatorships which tried to retain some elements of the former totalitarian regimes.

The Nature of Authoritarian Rule in Hungary

East Central Europe's mixed social structure contains both Western and Eastern elements. It has the traits of embourgoisement as well as byzantinism. Soviet-type societies[4] started out with a program of surpassing both feudal and bourgeois societies. The requirement of transcending the existing system called for a program-ideology[5] which, for a period, guaranteed the revolutionary legitimation of the new regime. A small group (the vanguard party) was the carrier of the "revolution" which projected its program onto a chosen minority of society, the working class. With the belief of this-wordly salvation the vanguard created a closed ideological system which attempted to realize its promises about economic modernization through forced development of certain industries.

It was an inorganic modernization directed from above; the promises concerning the economy and welfare gradually gave way to the vision of a militant, homogeneous mass of the disciplined society. "It destroyed the one essential prerequisite of all freedom which is simply the capacity of motion which cannot exist without space."[6] This system was characterized by the parallel dominance and disappearance of politics. The centralization and monopolization of power overshadowed politics as an activity of social groups. Administrative planning and the system of periodic purging took its place. The civil society disappeared, and the informal sector fell into the background.

In Hungary, after the suppression of the 1956 revolution, the communist leadership gave up the total politicization of the society after the reprisals. It abandoned the idea of permanently mobilizing the citizens in order to legitimize the system. It was satisfied by the fact that the people had resigned themselves to their inability to change their destiny by collective political acts, therefore their aspirations were pushed back into the depoliticized world of individual progress. The post-Stalinist paternalistic system, hallmarked with János Kádár's name, was based on the political neutralization of the citizens.[7]

This authoritarian rule had two stages: stabilization and consolidation. *Stabilization*, in my view, was the stage, in which the stability of power could be maintained only by force. Open political conflict was over but the peace did not come yet. This was the case in Hungary between 1957 and 1962–63.

The second stage, *consolidation*, started after 1962. The leadership made the system better by economic reforms and the practice of the so-called "material compensation". Citizens accepted the system because it offered certain advantages within the given possibilities. The social peace, i.e. loyalty, acceptance and obedience was guaranteed. The system was based on a "negative consent" which did not bring about legitimacy, because people had no right to choose among political alternatives. Negative consent means only an assent, which comes from the fact that social groups mutually and yet tacitly gave up some of their initiatives, rights, opportunities. Political leadership in Hungary abandoned the totalitarian type of control over the society in order to keep its monopolized position in politics; while the members of the suppressed society refrained from anti-systemic political actions in exchange for more space in the private sphere.[8]

Although in such a situation, as compared to the totalitarian model, society became more colorful, more varied, its duality was sustained in one respect. Since politics remained the privilege of the bureaucratic elite, there was a clear split between the "political society" (the party-state) on one hand, and the "antipolitical society" on the other. In this duality there was no room for civil society in the sense of political consciousness and economic autonomy. There was a society made infantile, which escaped into private life and hoped for the "good king" during the decades after 1956.

Survival became the most important life strategy of people. For this purpose they joined the informal networks of lobbying, which made life easier to endure, as contrasted to the hopelessness of passive resistance.[9] Hence a significant part of the society had something to lose when the system began to disintegrate: the protective net of informality had to be abandoned. This kind of consent was possible as long as the system was relatively effective. A recession could challenge the whole political regime. Since citizens perceived even stagnation as recession, the need for legitimation was insatiable. In the East Central European post-Stalinist systems negative consent was the abandonment of the imperative of system-*integration* in exchange for system-*stability*. Since political leaders in most of the countries in the region resigned from an ideocratic control of society, these regimes could be characterized as authoritarian.

The communist leadership in Hungary of the eighties reacted upon the erosion of the system with liberalization measures so that a collective political protest of social dimensions could be prevented by the division of social groups. Thus the tiny groups of political opposition evolving from the late seventies onwards, could be isolated from the society. As the reformability of the command economy proved to be illusionary, the leadership needed economic autonomies (small semi-private firms) to maintain social peace, but even these autonomies, free of politics, got into conflict with the system in the long run. The economy of "neither plan, nor market", the intricate mechanisms of bargaining only aggravated the crisis of the system. In Hungary, systemic change could be peaceful because the circle of people under political discrimination was relatively narrow; while the circle of those who could safeguard their own future exclusively by the maintenance of the regime was also getting narrower within the political leadership. The second generation of the communist party elite consisted primarily of technocratic intellectuals with a convertible expertise, who were not existentially exposed to the party.[10] The growing petty bourgeoisie, emerging from the seventies onwards as a positive legacy of Kádárism, gradually disrupted and disintegrated the monolithic structure of the system, independent of the original intentions of the political leadership.[11] Thus Gorbachev's ascent to power in the Soviet Union did not launch, but encouraged and justified the process of transformation slowly unfolding in the daily routine of the Hungarian society.

On the Concept of Transition

Transition in its *broad sense*—according to O'Donnell's and Schmitter's definition—is an *interval between two different political systems.*[12] It includes the dissolution of the old authoritarian system as well as laying the institutional foundations of the new one. The definition concentrates only upon the fact of change between systems, irrespective of the fact *how* this change takes place. In this approach transition is a *collective concept* of systemic change which can include a revolution or a coup just as much as slow evolution. It is the advantage of this approach that the often inextricable linkages of the forms of change can be interpreted historically with greater flexibility, and there is no need to make strict distinctions among the forms whether change had started from above or from below, whether it had been violent or peaceful, whether it had been accompanied by the mobilization of the masses, or not, etc. But it is a disadvantage that the concept of transition may become relativistic. To some extent it is left to the decision of the social scientist which interval he considers a transition, and when would he regard a transition completed. Hence excessively normative interpretations may also fit into the definition.

In a *narrower sense* transition is essentially an *alternative of revolution.* In this approach such a change accomplishes the objectives of a revolution while avoiding its sacrifices. Thus transition shows the features of reform as well as revolution, yet it is fundamentally different from both. According to this approach, democratic transition is *a controlled transformation from a more illiberal state to a more liberal one.*[13] Transition begins when the authoritarian system is unable to observe its own rules and makes allowances for the extension of the rights of individuals and groups. Hence its legitimacy is challenged, and the regime may get into the condition of *anomy* in Durkheimian sense, resulting in a power vacuum. Transition can be regarded successful if the life chances of the people improve in the evolving institutional system. From this angle the 'Glorious Revolution' of 1688–89 in England was the first successful *transition* according to Ralph Dahrendorf, whereas the French Revolution of 1789–93 can be really regarded as *revolutionary* change.[14]

Post-communist change in 1989 went beyond the framework of reform everywhere, but—with the exception of Romania—it did not take the shape of classical revolutions. In describing the changes the analysts are using terms such as 'negotiated revolution', 'peaceful revolution', etc. Timothy Garton Ash reached the conclusion that the conventional categories cannot be employed, therefore he created a third term out of the words reform and revolution: *refolution*.[15]

It is the advantage of the narrower interpretation of transition that it lays emphasis on the manner of change, thus offering a more sophisticated typology. Also, this interpretation is suitable to grasp shorter historical periods on the basis of certain formal criteria (such as free elections). Its disadvantage, however, is that every transition can be compared too comfortably by the means of formal elements, and the typology may become unrealistic.

In this paper a relatively short historical period is under survey and as I do not consider these changes as 'revolutions', I attempt to summarize their general features by employing the narrower interpretation of political transition.

Political transition can be isolated from other forms of political change as follows:

	Reform	**Coup**	**Revolution**	**Transition**
Start:	from above	from above	from below	from above and below
Process:	peaceful	peaceful or violent	mostly violent	peaceful
Opposing Agents:	conservatives vs. reformers	rival power groups	old elite vs. social opposition	*leadership*: conservatives vs. reformers *opposition:* moderates vs. radicals
Relationship to Society:	demobilization	demobilization	mobilization	mobilization and demobilization
Result:	usually the system does not change	usually the system does not change	systemic change	systemic change

Of the East Central European changes in the past decades the policy of the Hungarian 'new phase' (1953–54) and the 'New Economic Mechanism' (1966–72), the 'Prague Spring' (1968) starting as a reform but launching independent social movements in Czechoslovakia, and the Soviet perestroika (from 1987 onwards) can be characterized as *reform efforts*. There were two *revolutions* in the classical sense of the term: in Hungary in 1956 and in Romania in 1989 (accompanied by a coup-like replacement of the leadership). The Polish "self-limiting" revolution of 1980–81 occupies a special place in the history of the region. It could not become a successful political transition, though it could destroy the legitimacy of the communist system.

As history shows, no democratic transition is possible starting from a totalitarian regime. In such regimes the ruling group is not responsible to any elected body, and it is impossible to remove it from power by any institutionalized, peaceful method.[16] The creation of a more tolerable authoritarian system by reforms following, or substituting revolution, or by a coup is a more typical process (see Hungary in 1956 or Czechoslovakia in 1968). In 1989 the outbreak of the revolution was accompanied by a well organized coup in Romania. The new leadership applied the strategy of demobilization as well as the channelling of emotions into nationalism. After the consolidation of power, the new elite has created a setup anti-communist in its rhetoric but semi-democratic in its practice. Revolution, as an alternative to the democratic transition is usually a risky solution accompanied by extraordinary sacrifices, which, in most cases does not bring the expected results: it may develop into a dictatorship of revolutionary extremists, as it was the case with the Jacobin terror, or the communist dictatorship after the democratic change of 1918 in Hungary. All this may lead to attempts by the conservative regimes at restoration in the long run. Learning from the lesson of 1956 and 1968, the Polish, Czech and Hungarian opposition groups of the late seventies elaborated a new strategy: *new evolutionism* based on a critical publicity, constitutional legality and human rights instead of open confrontation.[17]

In 1989 and 1990 a democratic political transition took place in most of the countries of East Central Europe, which was characterized by negotiations between the authorities and the opposition in Poland and Hungary, and by mass protests in the GDR, Czechoslovakia and Bulgaria.

The Process and the Chief Actors of the Democratic Transition

Three phases of the transition can be distinguished: (1) *the erosion of the old system*, which was accompanied by the appearance of the new, autonomous movements; (2) *the moment of extrication*, when the basic features of the regime changed; and (3) *the consolidation of the new regime*, the phase of institution building. *Liberalization* characterizing the first phase of the transition can also be distinguished from the following *democratization*, as suggested by O'Donnell and Schmitter. The former expands the framework of the system based on autocracy and creates a liberalized autocracy (*'dictablanda'*), while the latter surpasses it and at first creates a limited democracy (*'democradúra'*), and next a full fletched political democracy.[18]

The chief actors of the transition are the '*makers of politics*' (representatives of the old and the emerging new political elites), and the pressure groups, or the *civil society*, which manifest their political will in a less articulated form, not only, or not primarily through parties.

Conservatives and *reformers* can be distinguished among the representatives of the old system, whereas *moderates* and *radicals* occur within the new opposition groups. All the four groups have a significant role in the process of systemic changes. During the first phase of the transition usually it was the struggle of conservatives and reformers within the state-party which affected the process the most. It was followed by a confrontation between the power elite and the opposition. Finally, the struggle of the moderate and radical opposition forces become dominant after the retreat of the old power elite. As political transition is nearing its completion, the significance of concepts such as 'moderate and radical'—which indicated the relationship of the opposition forces to the communist system—is gradually pushed into the background, and competing ideologies and party programs come into the fore. The extent of moderateness and radicalism cannot always be identified with the proximity to, or the distance from the ideology of the *ancien régime*. For instance, the Hungarian Christian Democratic People's Party has always been very moderate and sometimes even loyal to the representatives of the old system during the negotiations of the Opposition Roundtable, whereas it had been the farthest away not only from the socialist-communist, but even from the leftist liberal values in its ideology.

In the first phase of the transition the opposition forces are still weak and unorganized, their voice does not reach the broad layers of society. They project a possible critical behavior toward the existing system, and spread the culture of a critical language, different from party jargon, in the "second publicity" created by themselves. Initially, mostly writers and artists appear besides the marginal intelligentsia, who know the metaphoric language of the critique of the regime. The influence of thinking differently gradually reaches the students and young intellectuals, who organize clubs, circles and networks, who participate in the development of new subcultures, or in the not directly political peace and environmental movements. At this stage they locate themselves *between* the authorities and the opposition, thus blurring the borderline between bipolar publicity (directed press versus *samizdat*).

What are the causes of transition? Why does the political leadership feel that the government cannot continue along the old lines? Why does a society feel that 'time has come', and it can turn against the regime with good chances?

A great number of causes are enumerated by comparative analysts of political transitions.[19] One possible case is *defeat in a war*. The most important cause of the democratic transformation of West Germany after 1945 was the overthrow of the Nazi regime from outside. Armed conflict had a role in the 1973 changes in Greece as well. The fall of the Salazar-regime in 1974 was greatly motivated by the fact that the army had been unable to retain the colonies. The Falkland war was a significant component of the change in Argentina. Though no real war had a role in the 1989 changes, the Soviet bloc *lost the Cold War* in the eighties.

The process of transformation can also be launched by *conflicts within the power elite*. They can become particularly sharp, when the person symbolizing the system dies, or has to give up his leading position by some other reason. Succession and the replacement of whole generations inevitably emphasize the internal divisions and may become a catalyst of the transformation. This is what happened in Spain after the death of Franco, and in Hungary when Kádár and his inner circle were removed from the leadership almost by a coup at the 1989 May party conference.[20] The intra-party struggle between conservatives and reformers characterized the years after the death of Brezhniev in the Soviet Union as well.

A further cause of liberalization can be the success or decay of the *social and economic efficiency* of the system. It was the economic success of the autocratic system which encouraged the reformers to launch changes and to establish contacts with certain social groups in Chile and in South Korea, and at the end of the 1980s a similar process started in China too, but there it was terminated by the merciless reprisal at the Tienamnen square. Economic decay had a role in the East Central European changes. In Hungary the leadership attempted to extend its rule by loans from the West. However, economic dependence upon the West, further constrained the mobility of the conservative leadership. In fact any further loan would have come forth only if stability had been guaranteed, which could not be maintained by forcing people to do overwork and to exploit themselves beyond a certain point. Thus political 'opening up' ensued, at first by introducing free travel, then by broadening the freedom of the press and also by acknowledgeing the demand right to free association. *Changing international environment* may also play an important role in the commencement of the transition. Gorbachev was an encouragement for the reformers of the communist parties and the opposition movements. When in 1989 he openly gave up the Brezhniev doctrine, the protective umbrella helping the ruling parties disappeared, and the crisis of legitimation of the system suddenly became obvious.

If the conservative communist leadership retains its unity, the transition may start from *below,* bursting forth. Demonstrations and strikes break out, emigration from the country becomes a movement, autonomous initiatives develop, etc. Adam Przeworski differentiates between two different models of the East Central European transitions: the '*top-down*' model starting from above (Poland, Hungary), and the '*bottom-up*' model starting from below (GDR, Czechoslovakia, Romania).[21] However, it is important to stress the role of the society even in the so-called 'top-down' model, partly because its desire for freedom had already been manifest in the earlier, suppressed revolutions; and because the leadership by itself would not go beyond the reforms.

Liberalization starts with the policy of 'opening up', when certain liberties are redefined and extended. However, this is only allowed within the sphere defined by the leadership. (For instance, police and criminal procedures are relaxed, censorship is limited or abolished, the sphere of private enterprise is extended, etc.) Liberalization is a result of the mutual influence of the power groups within the leadership on one hand and the leadership and the autonomous groups of the society on the other. The policy of opening up is expressed by such concepts as the 'new phase' (1953), the 'new mechanism' (1968), or 'unfolding' (1987) in Hungary, *'apertura'* (opening) in Spain, *'odnowa'* (renewal) in Poland; *'distensao'* (reduction of tension) in Brazil; or *'ottepel'* (melting, 1953), *'glasnost'* and *'perestroika'* (1987) in the Soviet Union.[22]

If the conservatives become dominant within the leadership, *repression*, a more or less violent halt of liberalization ensues. If it is successful—as it was in the post-Khruschevian Soviet Union—the dictatorship may survive, but on a narrower basis of power; if it fails then a revolutionary situation may develop and an uprising may take place, the outcome of which is always uncertain (see China, 1989; Romania, 1990). Therefore the conservatives do not always turn against liberalization right from the outset, as they may be confident to be able to control the process and compromise the reformers.

If the reformers succeed in squeezing out the conservatives from the leadership—which took place in Hungary at the party conference of 1988, and between February and June, 1989—the question will be whether there should be *reform or democracy*. At this stage the hitherto offensive reformers are suddenly forced into the defensive. What is at stake here is no more the extension of certain rights but a general *acknowledgement* of these rights. While liberalization means the redefinition of certain legal statuses, democratization means the acknowledgement of formal rights on the level of the individual as well as public institutions and governmental procedures.

During this period the role of experts (lawyers, economists) becomes increasingly important within the opposition; experts who are able to criticise the operation of the system violating human rights and the malfunctioning of its economy on a professional basis with a political edge. The strategy of the opposition may be based on the ideology such as 'civil society against the state'.[23] As this is not a revolution, but its peaceful alternative, the role of the moderates grows within the opposition during this period. They may facilitate the beginning of negotiations by being nearer the reformers. In Hungary, for instance, the reform communists agreed to negotiate because they could hope in reaching a compromise with the moderate forces of the opposition.

However, the democratic transition is rarely a linear process. The reformer leadership may not wish to proceed toward political democracy but to maintain a reform policy managed from above for a longer period of time. Democratization may be avoided by *cooptation*. The leadership may try to lift the moderate opposition groups into power, thus channelling social dissatisfaction. By creating a new power centre, the leadership may effectively turn against the radical groups labelled as extremists, and push them to the margin of politics. A typical example of cooptation is the setting up of pseudo-movements of a Popular Front character in order to strengthen the support of the reformist leadership. These solutions are usually encouraging 'unity', the 'joining of forces', and 'appeasement'. In Hungary the meeting at Lakitelek in September 1987 was a demonstrative act of the reformers within the communist party and the moderate national minded opposition. It is not quite clear whether the reformers met the moderates, excluding the radical opposition, with the intention of coopting them into power, or it was only an opening toward the society, the beginning of liberalization. The intentions of the participants may have included the broadening of the social basis of the forces of reform, the elaboration of a new, popular socialist alternative, the rearrangement and possible extension of the power centre, and the creation of germs of political pluralism in Hungary. The so-called Movement for a Democratic Hungary, set up for the support of Imre Pozsgay's presidential candidacy in the summer of 1989, without effective social backing, can be regarded as an attempt at cooptation.

The longest period of liberalization was achieved by General Jaruzelski in Poland, who introduced a number of democratic institutions (constitutional court, administrative court, ombudsman, a 'consultative council' of intellectuals, etc.) in the eighties, but while the system absorbed neo-corporative elements (state party—the Church—trade unions), its basic structure remained unchanged. Jaruzelski's 1986 decree on amnesty was also issued in the spirit of liberalization, but it became the starting point of the democratization of the political system.[24]

Once the process of democratization starts, the reformers, who have hitherto attempted to control the process, have to decide whether they return to autocracy, or allow the emancipation of the society and the opposition. It is a trap because there is *no correct decision whatsoever* as the reformers may be squeezed out of power in either case: by the conservatives in the case of restoration, and by the opposition in the case of democracy. It is a self-extinguishing enterprise because even the collapse of the system buries under itself the reformers for some time.

As the legal and political outlines of systemic change become clear, the difficulties of the opposition also grow. They know that the anti-dictatorial forces have to act jointly for the success of transition, but they also know that they have to compete with one another in the evolving democratic system. Hence nothing else is left to them but a 'two-front struggle'. This was the case in Hungary at the end of the negotiations between the party-state and the Opposition Roundtable, after the agreement of September 18, 1989, which was signed by some and rejected by others.

A too early separation of the opposition forces, or their keeping together too long is equally dangerous for the success of the democratic transition.[25] If moderates and radicals break up too early, they make the job of their common political adversary too easy. This was the case in South Korea recently, where the representative of the earlier regime won the elections against the two opposition candidates. But if the different wings of the opposition do not separate from each other, the new regime may become rather similar to the old one: (see Romania after the landslide victory of the National Salvation Front, led by Iliescu).

An understanding between the reformers and the moderates is important for the peaceful nature of change. At the same time, the radicals have a significant role in avoiding halts in transition, and hindering the development of a new power centre consisting of reformers and moderates.

From the angle of 'policy makers' transition is nothing else but a successive process of agreements and the annulment of agreements.[26] Temporary pacts, as the corollaries of elite politics constitute a part of peaceful transition almost everywhere.

Another, often anonymous chief actor of democratic transformation is *civil society*. The chances of the success of systemic change are better in those countries where there had existed a civil society before the authoritarian regime came to power and a democratic political culture had evolved. Di Palma argues that the chances of democracy in East Central Europe are better than in the developing countries, because a "new structure of normative thinking"[27] could evolve in the region out of the heritage of dissidence and the success of 'cognitive mobilisation' launched by it. Apparently, civil society is a precondition as well as a result of democratic transition. Where embourgeoisement was rudimentary, and the space of the informal society was narrow, democratic transition may turn toward a new authoritarianism.

Civil society may grow strong economically or politically, but the success of the transition becomes doubtful in the long run, if the two are not linked.[28] In Hungary a depoliticized, 'withdrawing' behavior, an 'entrepreneurial type social strategy, seeking individual ways of success, and a defence against state expropriation by extra work were characteristic during Kádárism, whereas in Poland there was a politicized, mobilizing workers' resistance of 'trade unionist type', asserting interests collectively, which was encouraged by the Church.

The political transition is usually accompanied by *demonstrations*, by the celebration of certain political anniversaries by the opposition, and the related *symbolic acts*. They build up identity: it is in these events that the atomized society meets itself in *great masses* for the first time. Fear is relaxed, inhibitions, hitherto hindering social pressure from below are dissolved. The mass—no matter how disorganized it is—offers a sense of security to the participants. In this respect the demonstrations of hundreds of thousands in Leipzig, Berlin, Prague and Sofia, the reburial of the martyrs of the 1956 revolution in Budapest, and the self-sacrificing Timisoara protest, launching the Romanian changes, played a significant role in the collapse of the Soviet bloc. Mass movements may contribute to the political institutionalization of the opposition and exercise pressure on the representatives of power, so that liberalization should not be followed by reprisals, but by democratization. In June 1989 Li Peng ordered firing at the students in Beijing, but neither Honecker, nor Jakesh dared to do the same in October and November.

Transitions are often void of the moment of *euphoria* and *catharsis*. When transition is achieved by negotiations, the liberating experience that systemic change was forced by the masses is missing. There was such a cathartic moment in Portugal (1974), in Chile (1989), in the GDR (1989) and in Czechoslovakia (1989), but in Hungary, for instance, many people spoke about a 'morose revolution', and the same thing happened in Poland. But with the passage of time political 'hangover' occurred even in countries where the changes had been accompanied by the enthusiasm of the masses. Social mobilization *cannot be identified* with civil society; as extensive mobilization does not necessarily mean the strengthening of civil society, so no (or decreasing) mobilization does not mean that the civil society is on the retreat. Rather it means a return to daily life after a period of politicization. The success of democratic transition can be measured, among others, by the ability of civil society to political self-organization in new conflict situations in the wake of the first free elections.

The process of political change in the East Central European countries is summarized by the following Table:

Country	Former System	Way of Change	New Regime
Poland	authoritarian regime with limited neo-corporatist type pluralism	roundtable negotiations, limited free elections, presidential elections	opposition gained power although it still had to share it with the communists ('dyarchy') parliamentary democracy with strong presidency
Hungary	liberalized authoritarian paternalistic regime	roundtable talks, referendum free & fair elections	parliamentary democracy with competitive parties after the elections
GDR	authoritarian regime (no changes from above)	emigration waves, mass demonstrations, limited power-sharing, free & fair elections	parliamentary democracy with competitive parties after the elections
Czechoslovakia	authoritarian regime (no changes from above)	mass demonstrations, limited power-sharing, free & fair elections	parliamentary democracy after the elections
Bulgaria	authoritarian regime (no changes from above)	mass demonstrations, provisional government, free elections	fragile parliamentary democracy
Romania	totalitarian or 'sultanistic'[29] regime	popular uprising, coup d'état, provisional government, free elections	unstable democratic institutions, anti-democratic pro-government movements

The Polish and Hungarian transitions were dominated by negotiations, the East-German, Czechoslovak and Bulgarian transitions were based on non-violent mass mobilization, whereas the Romanian transition was launched by an uprising.

Systemic change in politics took place in two phases in Poland. The roundtable negotiations and the subsequent free elections constituted the first phase, when the communists acquired parliamentary representation in advance, irrespective of the election results, and Jaruzelski became the first President of the republic. During the second phase, half a year after the elections, Jaruzelski was pressed to resign and Lech Walesa was elected President.

The Hungarian transition was continuous. The opposition did not conclude a self-restricting pact with the authoritarian leadership, and the presidential claims of the communists, wishing to follow the Polish example were hindered by a referendum.

The East-German, Czechoslovak and Bulgarian transitions are similar in so far as the communist leadership did not show any inclination towards political reforms by itself before the emergence of the social movements. Transition had begun from below and the reformers in the ruling party (Krenz, Modrow, Urbanek, Adamec, Mladenov) appeared in public only afterwards but were sooner or later squeezed out of politics. New governments were formed before the free elections in all the three countries: in the GDR and Czechoslovakia the representatives of the opposition, and in Bulgaria the reform communists were included.

In the GDR and in Czechoslovakia the opposition (the CDU, and the Civic Forum respectively) won the elections, whereas in Bulgaria the reform communists (Bulgarian Socialist Party) retained power, a fact soon becoming a source of new conflicts. In Romania, too a reform communist group took over after the December coup. This group projected itself as the heir of the national revolution and thus it could safely win the elections.

The opposition movements of the earlier regime could only ascend to power in Czechoslovakia and Poland. In the GDR the New Forum could not even enter Parliament, and the heir of the Hungarian 'democratic opposition', the Alliance of Free Democrats, though it has become the second largest party of the country, has become a Parliamentary opposition only. However, since then pluralization has gone far within the victorious political forces in Poland as well as in Czechoslovakia.

The political actors of the East Central European countries have learned a great deal from one another during the period of transition. The Hungarian opposition gained a lot from the experiences of the

Polish roundtable talks, whereas the East German opposition learned a lot from both country stories. In Hungary one part of the erstwhile communist state-party (HSWP) entered the political arena of the new system under a new name (HSP), with new faces and a social democratic program. Its example was followed by the Polish, East German and Bulgarian communist parties.

During the course of transition some leaders of the communist parties realized that they had to give up their rigid policy in their own interest and had to anticipate change. Gorbachev's visit to Berlin in October 1989 was accompanied by demonstrations against the regime, resembling those of Peking, but Krenz and his comrades hindered Honecker in applying violence, and a month later they opened the Berlin Wall. Miklós Németh's government in Hungary offered consultations with the opposition and, under pressure, dissolved the Workers' Guard, a paramilitary force of the communist party before the plebiscite of November 1989, and banned the organization of parties at the work places. In the meantime some communist leaders realized that they could defeat the opposition forces of weaker organization and with little access to the mass media if the free elections were to be held as soon as possible. This strategy was applied by the National Salvation Front in Romania, by the Socialist Party in Bulgaria, and by the Labour Party in Albania.

In Hungary political transition was completed by the local elections in the autumn of 1990. In the towns the liberal opposition parties, and in the villages the independent candidates had a landslide victory.

However, the most conspicuous lesson of the elections was the loss of society's confidence primarily in the governing coalition, but also in the parliamentary parties in general. During the first round of the local elections 60, and during the second round 70 per cent of the electorate absented themselves from the polls. In 1989–90 there were six national elections held in Hungary, of which participation was above 50 per cent only on two occasions: at the referendum of November 26, 1989 (58 per cent), and at the first round of the parliamentary elections on March 26, 1990 (65 per cent). In both cases the issue was the rejection of the *ancien régime*. Thus the society knew what it had *not* wanted, but it was far more uncertain how to approach the desirable future.

The Parliament 'freely floating' above the society was working with full capacity on legislation, but in the meantime the parliamentary parties often engaged themselves in unnecessary ideological disputes. Privatization was delayed, inflation and unemployment was growing and the society had become uncertain in whether the Hungarian Democratic Forum, posing with the slogan of being the 'calm force' was really safeguarding its security. The conservative-gentry-national rhetoric of the governing coalition evoking the twenties and thirties was irritating for a good part of the intelligentsia shaping public opinion. Parallel to it, the opposition parties, earlier called 'Thatcherist', became more open to social issues. The Hungarian society voted for a *power balance* at the local elections.

Local elections have established a three-tiered power system approaching bipolarity in Hungary. It is *bipolar* in so far as in the beginning socialist-social democrat forces played a marginal role in political life, thus the opposed political forces can be separated on the basis of conservative-national and liberal-social liberal values. The Hungarian political setup had the potential of evolving into a two party system (or a two bloc system) by the end of 1990, but with the growth of social tensions the left, underrepresented in Parliament, reemerged. The power structure became *three-tiered* in so far as the Parliament and national politics are dominated by the conservative right-of-the-centre forces; the capital and the settlements of more than ten thousand inhabitants by the liberal parties; whereas in the villages the independents, the majority of whom had been members of the HSWP, have acquired a decisive influence.

In current political sociology two marked views can be distinguished regarding the issue *when a transition can be considered accomplished*. According to the *minimalist* concept the main criteria of democratic consolidation are the following: (1) each major political force acknowledges that democracy has no alternative; (2) nobody challenges the legitimacy and right to action of the democratically elected decision makers. The *maximalist* concept regards democracy consolidated only if (1) all the elements of a democratic institutional system have evolved; (2) the party system is consolidated; (3) power is first shifted from the governing parties to the opposition parties.[30]

The political transition in Hungary is very near to meeting the minimum conditions of a self-supporting democracy, though claims of political discrimination still occur in the ruling coalition parties. Nevertheless, it sounds exaggerated to link democratic consolidation to the stabilization of the party system and to the first shift of power. The changes of the party system—provided some other conditions exist—do not necessarily mean the fragility of democracy. Also, there were democratic parties where the shift from government to opposition did not take place for decades after the political transformation.

Apparently, it is indispensable for the success of a democratic political transition that:

- the majority of social conflicts should be channelled into democratic institutions (parliamentary system, local self-governments, democratically elected organs of interest representation);
- the outcomes of democratic decision making should not be predetermined, or subsequently modified by non-democratic means;
- a democratic change of power should be possible;
- efficient civilian control should be exercised over the armed forces.[31]

The new East Central European democracies have not yet reached this level of a self-supporting democracy. However, the inefficiency of democratic arrangements in itself cannot be identified with the lack of democratic consolidation.

The Fragility of the New Democracy: A Danger of Populism?

The post-communist transitions have again sharply exposed the question: is democracy possible in poverty? Can a democratic system be maintained during an economic crisis threatening with collapse? Can a freely elected Parliament, and a government responsible to it, retain its legitimacy if the country becomes ungovernable? Can strikes, collective disobedience movements and civil wars be prevented? Can it be avoided that the losers of transformation should drift towards nationalist-populist extremes?

It is not accidental that we find stable democracies in those parts of the world where there are advanced market economies. Elsewhere—like in Latin America—the unfolding new democracies had to face the possibility of loss of social confidence and a military takeover. Until the forties, Argentina was among the richest countries of the world, but her development slowed down during President Perón's populist system. Whereas in South Korea it was the economic boom that produced the possibility of a systemic change: the interests of the prospering middle class were hurt by political autocracy. The only lasting exception is India, where poverty has not shaken the institutions of democracy, though it has repeatedly given birth to bloody violence. In the eighties a series of countries have set out on the path of democratization outside East Central Europe. There are such backward countries among them as Bangladesh, Pakistan, Namibia, Bolivia or Peru. Thus the issue of the relationship between democracy and relative wealth is still open.

The destiny of the former communist countries has been different from those in which political dictatorship did not limit economic growth. The task of the East Central European opposition movements was to attack the system at its strongest, and not the weakest points. As the pillars of the system had been *political* ones, it was quite obvious that only the dismantling of an outdated political setup could create chances for economic prosperity. However, many in the opposition have inferred from this that systemic change can be realized only simultaneously in politics and in economics as the two were inseparable.

Actually, political and economic transition have been torn apart, and the political changes have not brought along automatically the restructuring of the economy. Transition has reached a delicate imbalance, where the emotions of the increasingly impoverished strata are leashed out against the newly established democratic institutions.

Just as revolutionary situations produce their own revolutionaries, so the spokesmen of the dissatisfied society, left to itself may come forth from anonymity, who in the best case take the lead of autonomous interest representations, or in the worst case organize political movements against the democratic system. Theoretically, the new political forces can be incorporated into the democratic mechanism with the help of new elections. A not yet consolidated democracy, however, may be destabilized by too frequently held elections, because the political campaigns inevitably push the long term ideas of consolidating democracy into the background.

Up to now, Hungary and Poland have been able to avoid the dangers of turning the new democracies into nationalist-populist systems despite their grave economic situation. In Poland, after the epoch of varying ex-Solidarity governments people voted for ex-Communists and the democratic pendulum turned again to the Left. In Hungary the conservative government, after a long period of internal fights, could "discipline" or expel the rightist extremists of its own camp. In Czechoslovakia, after the "Velvet Revolution" we could witness a sort of "Velvet Separation" between Slovakia and the Czech Republic, which was a result of the fact that Czech and Slovak political elites were unable to make compromise over the future of a federal state. This separation, however, did not shake the basically democratic institutional order of these countries.

The development of the organizations of interest representation and local self-government may create links between the 'political class' and the civil society. In that case there is a chance for democracy to survive the economic crisis.[32] The experience of the successful democratic transitions after World War II show that there is no direct casual relationship between the economic situation and the nature of the political system. In some cases the *commitment* of the society to democracy may be a crucial factor. This becomes manifest when democracy is endangered.

There was a moment in Hungary in 1992, when István Csurka and his nationalist circle, the movement of *Hungarian Road*, launched an attack in an extreme rightist spirit against his own party, the Hungarian Democratic Forum (MDF), and indirectly against the new democracy as well. Utilizing social dissatisfaction, Csurka demanded in his manifesto that the MDF nationalists remove the "liberal" Antall-government or press it to settle the political conflicts by force and not by compromise.[33]

Nevertheless, Csurka failed to address the middle class, for which welfare values proved more attractive than the nationalist (and sometimes neo-Nazi) exclusivity of the *Hungarian Road*. In his later writings he did not strive to create a new national middle class but tried to mobilize the "bitter hinterland" of the underclass.[34] Though he sensed precisely the growing inequalities in the Hungarian society, he was wrong assuming that he would be able to mobilize those who are falling back by anti-elitism and nationalism. Thus Csurka has found himself in the political pigeon-hole of extreme rightist radicalism: he became the Hungarian Le Pen. He was unable to build a semi-democratic populist coalition against the governing elite, and expelled from MDF, he had no other choice than form a new party on the rightist margin of the political spectre. True populism wishes to solve the existing social tensions, on the basis of anti-elitism and social justice, in a realistic way. It does not want to adjust the existing people to an imaginary political ideal. Csurka could not become a credible populist politician, his political message was not open and admissive, but isolating and exclusive.

Ironically the Kádárist legacy, and not only the commitment to democracy, played an important role in Csurka's failure in Hungary. Despite the occasional legitimation deficit of the new Hungarian democracy,[35] the chances for nationalist (right-wing) and/or socialist (left-wing) populist policies are *limited* because of the following reasons:

- in the Kádár-regime the majority of society followed individualist strategies of survival, and became less and less susceptible to political demagogy;
- despite the deteriorating conditions, the circle of those who have nothing to lose is limited, and this keeps away people from supporting actions of political adventurism;
- politics appealing to the people and to social justice assumed extreme forms (fascism, communism) in the past;
- the soft dictatorship of the Kádár-era created opportunities of informal interest assertion along patron-client lines, and the costs of economic transformation can be compensated within this framework;
- the Hungarian society does not see any attractive alternative to Western-type democracies;
- the small size of the country and its dependence upon world economy limits the space of autarchy, which is a corollary of populism;
- the Hungarian society had experienced the disadvantages of "personality cult" under communist rule, therefore people have a skeptic attitude towards politicians;
- no massive aversion against the penetration of Western capital can be experienced in the Hungarian society, and people strive to share its benefits;
- there is an influential intelligentsia committed to the values of autonomy and civility;
- the concepts of liberalism and democracy, capitalism and democracy still seem to be linked together (or at least found difficult to be separated from each other) for those social groups which would be able to produce Latin American-type populism, and simultaneously demand democracy and authoritarian paternalism;
- populism evolves in places where considerable social groups believe that there is much to be distributed, so they hope they may get in a favourable position exclusively by the alteration of the internal proportions of redistribution, but no such signs are apparent in Hungary;
- a characteristic feature of populism is confidence in the state, but in Hungary such a confidence is missing;
- paradoxically, the traditional anti-state attitude of the Hungarian society does not only weaken the credibility of the new democracy (which cannot be strong without an accepted authority of the state), but it also hinders the development of populism.

Thus in Hungarian society it is not so much the spread of populism that can be expected. The dissatisfied groups, sinking into poverty and falling behind, might orient themselves towards some fragments of the extreme right, the ex-communist socialists (HSP), or towards the organizations of interest representations (especially the ex-communist trade unions). It is also possible that large segments of the underclass will refrain from voting in the next elections, broadening the gap between politically active and passive citizens. The danger is not so much a populist inter-class coalition attacking democracy, but a deprived, nostalgic, fragmented society, living behind the facade of democratic institutions.

The new political system in Hungary is basically democratic but the everyday routine of people did not change much. The legacy of the former "soft" authoritarianism had a twofold impact on democratic transformation. On the one hand, Kádár's reform-minded policy in economic matters gave a certain advantage to Hungary to manage a relatively smooth transition as compared to other post-communist countries. But the logic of Kádárist rule was like the logic of governance in a colony of a foreign empire. It created hidden, informal networks under the level of official political society. "Second economy", "second publicity", "second culture" was born, like in Poland, but the Kádárist leadership was successful in isolating or integrating them in the society, excluding the emergence of any Solidarity type opposition. After the change in the political system, the development of capitalism in Hungary highly depends on the ability and willingness of society to get rid of its Kádárist legacy of informality and clientelism. Critics of the post-communist Antall-government say that the new system is similar to Kádárism but without communists. If Hungary gets over this legacy, it will have better chances to avoid slipping down to the "developing world". To be sure, even in that case Hungarian new capitalism will rather go on the way of a "Mediterranean" type of development, than the German or Scandinavian one.[36]

Notes

1. There are a great many concepts of communism as a system. Totalitarianism had the greatest impact among them, of which classic explanations were the works of Hannah Arendt and Friedrich-Brzezinski in the fifties. Other important approaches were the idea of *new elite* or *new class* (Trotsky, Djilas, Konrád-Szelényi), which examined the rule of party-bureaucracy (nomenklatura) and of technocratic intellectuals; the theory of *group conflicts* (Skilling); the con-

ception of *clientelism* (Oi-Walder), which emphasized the role of patron-client relationships, and of informal networks; the theory of *syncretic society* (Campeanu), which pointed out the co-existence of different historical structures in communist systems; the conceptions of redistribution, bureaucratic coordination, *state socialism* (Kornai, Szelényi); the approaches which understand communism as *cultural phenomenon,* political religion (Bell); and that paradigm which finds strong correlation between the forced and centralized industrialization attempts of the economic *periphery,* and its power concentration (Wallerstein, Gerschenkron, Nove) etc.
On these concepts see: András Bozóki-Miklós Sükösd "Honnan, hová, miért?—a magyar átmenet megértése felé" (From Where to Where and Why? Toward the Understanding of the Hungarian Transition) *Mozgó Világ,* No.8. 1990, pp. 3–9.
2. Jürgen Habermas: *Nachholende Revolution.* Frankfurt am Main, Suhrkamp, 1990, pp. 179–204.
3. Jürgen Kuczynski is quoted by Habermas, op. cit. p. 180.
4. György Bence—János Kis: *A szovjet típusú társadalom marxista szemmel.* (Soviet-type Society from a Marxist Point of View) Paris, MFK, 1977.
5. Miklós Szabó: "Programideológiák és állapotideológiák" (Program-Ideologies and Conservative Ideologies) *Világosság,* No. 2. 1978.
6. Hannah Arendt: *Totalitarianism.* New York, Harcourt Brace Jovanovich, 1985, p. 164.
7. See in details: Miklós Szabó: "A legitimáció történeti alakváltozásai" (Historical Changes of Legitimation) In: Miklós Szabó: *Politikai kultúra Magyarországon, 1896–1986.* (Political Culture in Hungary 1896–1986) Budapest, Medvetánc, 1989, pp. 275–306.
8. On the concept of "negative consent" see more: András Bozóki: "Confrontation and Consent," A paper presented at the 20th convention of the American Association for the Advancement of Slavic Studies (AAASS) Honolulu, Hawaii, November 18–21, 1988.
9. József Böröcz finds *informality* as a systemic feature of Kádárism in Hungary. See: József Böröcz: "A kádárizmustól a parlagi kapitalizmusig" (From Kádárism to Rough Capitalism) *Mozgó Világ,* No. 8. 1990, pp. 61–66.
10. See in details: Erzsébet Szalai: *Gazdaság és hatalom* (Economy and Power). Budapest, Aula, 1990, especially pp. 169–176.
11. See in details: Iván Szelényi: *Socialist Entrepreneurs. Embourgoisement in Rural Hungary.* Madison, The University of Wisconsin Press, 1988.
12. Guillermo O'Donnell-Philippe C. Schmitter: *Transitions from Authoritarian Rule* Vol. 4. *Tentative Conclusions about Uncertain Democracies.* Baltimore, Johns Hopkins University Press, 1986, p. 6.
13. Ralf Dahrendorf: "Politik, Wirtschaft und Freiheit" *Transit,* Heft 1. Herbst 1990, p. 38.
14. Dahrendorf, op. cit. p. 37.
15. Timothy Garton Ash: *The Magic Lantern. The Revolution of '89 Witnessed in Warsaw, Budapest, Berlin and Prague.* New York, Random House, 1990, p. 14.

16. Juan J. Linz: "Transitions to Democracy" *Washington Quarterly,* Vol. 13. No. 3. Summer 1990, p. 144.
17. Adam Michnik: "A New Evolutionism". In: Adam Michnik: *Letters from Prison and Other Essays.* Berkeley-Los Angeles-London, University of California Press, 1987, pp. 135–148.
18. O'Donnell-Schmitter, op. cit. Vol. 4.
19. Alfred Stepan mentions ten different versions: (1) internal restoration after external reconquest; (2) internal reformulation after external liberation; (3) externally monitored installation; (4) redemocratization led from within the authoritarian regime; (5) transition initiated by the military as government; (6) extrication led by military as institution; (7) society-led regime termination; (8) transition through a pact of political parties; (9) violent revolt; (10) Marxist-led revolutionary war. Alfred Stepan: "Paths toward Redemocratization: Theoretical and Comparative Considerations." In: O'Donnell-Schmitter-Whitehead (eds.) *Transitions from Authoritarian Rule.* Vol. 3. *Comparative Prospectives.* Baltimore, The Johns Hopkins University Press, 1986, pp. 64–84.
20. See in details: George Schöpflin-Rudolf Tôkés-Iván Völgyes: "Leadership Change and Crisis in Hungary" *Problems of Communism,* September, 1988, pp. 23–46.
21. Adam Przeworski, op. cit. p. 193.
22. Ibid., p. 195.
23. On this idea see: Andrew Arato: "Civil Society vs the State." *Telos,* No. 47. Spring 1981; Andrew Arato: "Empire vs Civil Society. Poland 1980." *Telos,* No. 50. Winter 1981/82; Andrew Arato: "Civil társadalom, társadalomelmélet és államszocializmus" (Civil Society, Social Theory and State Socialism) *Századvég,* No. 3. 1987, pp. 46–52.
24. David Ost: "Towards a Corporatist Solution in Eastern Europe: The Case of Poland" *East European Politics and Societies,* Vol. 3. No. 1. Winter 1989, pp. 152–174.
25. Adam Przeworski, op. cit., p. 198.
26. Ibid., p. 207.
27. Giuseppe Di Palma: "Why Democracy Can Work in Eastern Europe" *Journal of Democracy,* Vol. 2. No. 1. Winter 1991, pp. 21–31.
28. According to Iván Szelényi, the two social "heroes" of the Hungarian transition were the enterprising petty bourgeoisie and the critical intelligentsia. Iván Szelényi: "Polgárosodás Magyarországon" (Embourgeoisement in Hungary) *Valóság* Vol. 33. No. 1. 1990, pp. 29–41.
29. The term "sultanistic" was derived from Max Weber and reformulated by Juan J. Linz. See Juan J. Linz: "Transitions to Democracy" *Washington Quarterly,* Vol. 13. No. 3. Summer 1990, pp. 145–146.
30. See in details: Juan J. Linz op. cit. pp. 157–160. The author argued for the minimalist concept of democratic consolidation.
31. Ibid. Linz, pp. 159–160.
32. As Dahrendorf skeptically put it: "This is not exactly an encouraging story. Political transition leads to economic frustration which results in instability

and unrest; economic transition leads to political frustration which also results in instability and unrest. Either way liberty is victim". Ralf Dahrendorf, op. cit. p. 42.

33. István Csurka: "Néhány gondolat . . ." (Some Thoughts) *Magyar Fórum,* August 20, 1992, pp. 9–16.
34. István Csurka: "Keserü Hátország" (Bitter Hinterland) *Magyar Fórum,* December 24 and 31, 1992.
35. János Kis: "Gondolatok a közeljövöröl" (Thoughts on the Near Future) *Magyar Hirlap,* December 24, 1992.
36. See András Bozóki, "The Hungarian Transition in a Comparative Perspective" in: András Bozóki, András Körösényi and George Schöpflin (eds.): *Post-Communist Transition: Emerging Pluralism in Hungary.* London, Pinter; New York, St. Martin's Press, 1992, pp. 163–191.

8

Is What Is Left Right? (The Yugoslav Heritage)

Vladimir Gligorov

> Two men travelling on the highway—the one east, the other west—can easily pass each other if the way be broad enough; but two men reasoning upon opposite principles of religion cannot so easily pass without shocking, though one should think that the way was also in that case sufficiently broad and that each might proceed without interruption in his own course. But such is the nature of the human mind that it always lays hold on every mind that approaches it, and as it is wonderfully fortified by a unanimity of sentiments, so it is shocked and disturbed by any contrariety. Hence the eagerness which most of the people discover in a dispute, and hence their impatience of opposition even in the most speculative and indifferent opinions. (D. Hume, "Of Parties in General")

The outcome of the Yugoslav crisis is still far away. The country has disintegrated, and everything else has fallen to pieces. At this moment there is a civil war going on, there are new independent and semi-independent states and regions, thousands of dead and wounded people, destroyed cities and villages, a huge and growing tide of refugees, private and officially private armies and mafia, growing unemployment, unrest and a running inflation. However, the main problem is that there is no political solution in sight.

In this paper I try to explain the political dead-end that Yugoslavia

---

This chapter complements an earlier study of mine: Vladimir Gligorov, "The Discovery of Liberalism in Yugoslavia", East European Politics and Societies, 1, 1991. It is followed by a paper on "Balkanization, A Theory of Constitution Failure," East European Politics and Societies.

has come to. In order to do that, I describe the essentials of the breakdown of the communist political space; I discuss the political fundamentals of the country; interpret the developments in the different regions; and speculate on the eventual outcome of the crisis.

I discuss only the political aspects of the Yugoslav crisis, leaving the historical and economic considerations and explanations aside. I will argue that the political legacy of communism not only contributed to the eruption of the crisis, but it also deepened it. Besides the crisis, the civil war was also chosen by the political actors. They have chosen it rationally in view of the political interests they had committed themselves to. Though everybody in Yugoslavia blames the past or the enemy for what is going on, the plain truth is that the crisis is a predictable outcome of political aims with wide legitimacy. And the crisis will not end until the political strategies of the dominant nations are changed.

In civil wars both (in this case, all) sides fight for a just cause. In the Yugoslav case, the just causes are the national identities, interests and rights. That is why the war is so violent, brutal and destructive. In principle, in a war between states, natural rights are respected (and many legal and other conventions). In a civil war, no rights are recognized. Both (all) sides want to completely destroy the legitimacy of the rivals.[1] So, the Yugoslav crisis is about rights and power, and that is what is left.

The Center Does Not Hold

The dominant theory describes totalitarianism as a totally controlled social system, as a system without ideological, political or economic competition. This picture has been criticized by many, but the alternative interpretation rested mainly on the sociological idea of growing functional differentiation. Judging by the evidence, the anti-totalitarians were right. However, the totalitarian model proved to have more predictive power, because it asserted that the system tended toward a collapse. The alternative model predicted a smoother transition. Still, both models lacked a theory of the political dynamics of the transition period. They failed to look at the specifics of the political space as it developed through political competition under communism. In what follows, I will draw a very simple picture of the communist political space.[2]

The totalitarian theory saw the communist system as one vertical line of authority. The revisionist theory argued that there were different dimensions of authority, and they drew a number of vertical lines. The elements of competition were seen to emerge on the horizontal levels between these lines. A typical example is a bunch of ministries competing for authority and resources. The competing factions were described in terms of “reformists” and “hard-liners”, or “liberals” and “conservatives”. Sometimes the metaphors of “left” and “right” were used, mostly in the way introduced by Stalin.[3] It was believed that because the communist system was not legitimate under one party rule, there was no need to introduce the citizens into the political model. An exception was made in the discussion of nationalism, but it was not clear how this factor was supposed to influence the overall picture of totalitarian communism.

That proved to be a huge flaw in communist studies. It left the profession without any serious answer as to what would happen when the totalitarian system collapses and the people become influential, and the power has to be redistributed. The only way in which the individuals and the nations entered these models was that of the consumers. It was believed that the system would get into trouble at a point when it fails to provide for the needs of the population. However, explicit political needs were left out of analysis.[4]

In fact, the communist political space was more simple and at the same time more complex than what the above models described. If we only take the revisionist idea that there were a number of lines of authority, it should have been expected that they not only competed for influence over the power center, but also for popular support. If that is correct, there were a number of factions in the ruling communist party struggling for the support of the various parts of the population. Thus, though there were no meaningful elections, the population “voted” in many other ways, and a quasi-pluralized political space developed. However, it had an equilibrium point somewhere between the center and one of the extremes. Following Stalin, I will call the side where the rulers are the “left” and that where the population is the “right”. The question is: How does the behavior of the political actors influence the dynamics of this political space?

If the population is not indifferent as to what policies are pursued, and if that can be exploited in the competition for power, there will be at least two factions in the communist party, one of which would be more to the right than the other. If the masses of the population are to the right of the ruling party, the policies of the right faction of the communist party will be more popular. As a matter of fact, the further to the right the population goes, the closer to the center the power center can be moved. However, the left-wing faction can block this development by going even further to the left. So, an equilibrium emerges with most of the population moving to the right, the ruling communist party together with the real power center moving to the left, and with the "right-wingers" holding the space in equilibrium by creating a center that is to the left of the one where the power would have settled after a few rounds of regular free elections (see Appendix I).

This communist equilibrium is not stable. In terms of power, the political space is never left-wing enough. On the other hand, in terms of the beliefs of the majority, it is never right-wing enough. Therefore, it can rest only on force, fear, and corruption. Force, because otherwise a rival party would emerge trying to represent the will of the majority. Fear, because otherwise the routinized compliance and cooperation with the authorities could hardly be explained. Corruption, because no level of force and fear can rationalize the prolonged stability of an otherwise unpopular regime. However, the fact that the center of communist political space diverges from what would have emerged had free elections been held, creates all kinds of moral and political problems. In some communist countries, the moral disgust is the basis for political unrest, in others political irrationality induces moral considerations.[5] Whatever the case, the center cannot hold for long.

At least two outcomes are possible. One is for the majority of the population to join the party or party controlled organizations. The totalitarian system might get transformed into an authoritarian one. In this case the right-wing faction of the ruling party and especially the state officials are captured by the population, while the power center would end up being an isolated, autocratic ruling body. This I would call, somewhat ironically, a "liberal solution".

The second possibility is for the political space to break down. If the ruling party remains under the control of the left-wing faction, the population will be driven to the far right extreme, and when this becomes, for whatever reason, politically unsustainable, the whole political space will start falling to the right almost indefinitely. I will call this a "populist solution". An interesting variant of the "populist solution" is when a "liberal" faction gets hold of power just before or immediately after the collapse of the political equilibrium. However, the "liberalization" attempt, if it comes too late or in an already "populist" political space, will prove to be unsuccessful. The defeat of the "liberal communists" may even move the whole political space further in the populist direction.

As I will show in a moment, the way the political space will change does not depend only or even decisively on the characteristics of the space, but also on what I will call the political fundamentals.[6]

The Fundamentals

In describing the political fundamentals (see Appendix II) of Yugoslavia, I will pay attention to the crucial conflicts first.

Yugoslavia is a construct, it is not a "natural state". Philosophically, of course, this is a debatable point, because in a sense every state is a construct.[7] However, in Europe states tend to be nation-states, and in that sense they have a "natural foundation". Yugoslavia was constructed without such a justification, though the very name ("the state of the South Slavs") implies that the nations which lived in Yugoslavia are ethnically close to each other.[8] Anyhow, due to the political space under communism, no continuous horizontal line was constructed. The different regions might choose different solutions on their way out of communism. And this is what happened.

If there is one fundamental fact of Yugoslav history and politics this is it. National interests were the reasons both for the construction and the destruction of Yugoslavia. The state was created as an expression of the "right to self-determination" of nations which were previously grouped together within the Austro-Hungarian Monarchy. Thus, national interests were taken to be the "natural foundation" of the newly created state. Nevertheless, it soon became obvious that some old national conflicts would only aggravate in the new state and also, new ones would emerge. In fact, it is the understanding that national interests are "natural" that makes the construct like Yugoslavia "unnatural".[9]

Yugoslavia was reconstructed several times, but never in a satisfactory way. The first Yugoslav constitution of 1921 was democratic (even social-democratic in some respect), but not federalist. It was passed by the dominant Serbian parties while Croatian and Slovenian parties were in the opposition.[10] As a consequence, the main political problem in Yugoslavia up until the Second World War was the so-called Croatian question.[11] In 1939, the Cvetkovic-Macek agreement federalized Yugoslavia in an asymmetric way, that is, it created a Croatian province (state) without federalizing Yugoslavia as a whole. Nothing symbolizes the basic political conflict in Yugoslavia better than this chimerical solution.[12]

The numerous constitutions of the second—Communist—Yugoslavia were federalist, but not democratic. They recognized both the necessity of giving autonomy to all the nations in the country (the principle of self-determination was reasserted in every post-war constitution), and of a full-blown federalism (even con-federalism). However, federalization was imperfect because it copied the model of the Soviet Union, and the system was socialist. Federalism and socialism work against each other. Decentralization aggravates every regional conflict in a comprehensive socialist system.[13] Federalism justified various sorts of decentralizations, and the Yugoslav system was much freer and more market oriented than those of the other Eastern European countries. However, everybody felt that the rival region got a better deal in the socialist game of distributing and redistributing resources.[14]

Yugoslavia's record of national tolerance is better than that of the majority of other states in the region. Though Yugoslavia was not a proper federation and was only for a short while a democracy, it was not harshly anti-nationalist if all seventy odd years of its existence are taken into account. If Yugoslavia is compared to other countries in the region or to the nation-states created during World War II on Yugoslav territories, it is clear that the Yugoslav state did not systematically go against the national emancipation of the citizens. It is true that every emancipation had to be won through sometimes bitter political struggle but, in the end, the rights of Croats, Slovenes, Macedonians, Muslims, Albanians and Hungarians were recognized and steadily enlarged. And it would be hard to prove that the rights of Serbs and Montenegrians were frustrated.[15] However, that depends on how the rights are perceived, that is, on the national interests one is committed to.[16]

Yugoslavia was constructed and reconstructed according to the will of the dominant political forces. Neither the first nor the second Yugoslavia were a mistake or a ploy. There have always been theories of Yugoslav history that claimed to have shown "once and for all" that "the other side" tricked the "right side" into the bargain. However, the state was constructed in accordance with the interests of those living in it. As is easy to see now, the dominant idea of all Yugoslav nations is a centralized, unitary state.[17] Some nations could never hope to dominate Yugoslavia, so they advocated a federal or a confederal constitution. Some, on the other hand, did dominate it, and they tried to shape it as centralized as possible. Even socialism was accepted by some as one way to centralize.

However, no construction proved to be stable. This is because the only way in which a state like Yugoslavia could have achieved stability would have led through a liberal constitution. However, liberal forces were always very weak in Yugoslavia as in the Balkans in general. Thus, though democracy and federalism are necessary ingredients of an acceptable Yugoslav state, they would not be sufficient for the stability of that state. Only with a liberal constitution could Yugoslavia survive. But, as in many other countries, the liberal elements were and are nationalist, and the populist elements are not liberal. So, the chances for a liberal constitution were never explored.[18]

To solve the "Croatian question" is to open the "Serbian question". The above said refer to the fundamental political fact of Yugoslavia, that is, to the conflicting political strategies or national interests of the two dominant nations, the Serbs and the Croats. Croats want to live in a separate state. They claim that they have never renounced that right, though during almost all of their history they have not been able to create their nation-state.

Serbs all over Yugoslavia want to live together in one state. This is how they have perceived their national interest for more than a century now. Serbian state expanded through wars and in other ways to end up as a dominant element of the first Yugoslavia. After World War II, Serbian national aims were somewhat frustrated. But according to the prevailing view at that time even a federal Yugoslavia was acceptable as long as Serbs could feel that they were all living together in the same state.

The nature of the conflict was well recognized after the Cvetkovic-Macek agreement had been signed in 1939. Once Croats' rights to state autonomy were acknowledged, there was a marked change in the way political problems were perceived in Yugoslavia. The leading Serbian politicians and intellectuals became aware that with the "solution" of the "Croatian problem" the "Serbian problem" emerged, for at least three reasons. First, the Croats had their autonomy in Croatia, while Serbs had no such state entity. Second, Yugoslavia ruled directly over all the other parts of the state, except for Croatia. In other words, Croats could influence the decisions at the federal level concerning all other parts of Yugoslavia, while Yugoslavia, that is, all the other Yugoslav nations, had to respect Croatian autonomy. Third, as every asymmetry tends to elicit demands for symmetrical treatment, all the other nations demanded to be treated like the Croats, so that further federalization was inevitable. That, of course, meant a further erosion of the power of the Serbs as well as a further aggravation of their national and territorial problems. The basic issue is simple: If Croatia is created, and if every nation is given a right to self-determination, where are the borders of the Serbian state to be drawn? There is still no answer to that question.

The national interests of Serbs and Croats are irreconcilable. One glance on the map of Yugoslavia will make it clear that, given the ethnic distribution of the population, Serbs and Croats cannot both gain. For Croats to have a separate state, Serbs would have to give up what they perceive to be their fundamental national interest. Also, for Serbs to all live in one state, Croats would have to give up what they believe is their one thousand year old national interest. The only way that either of these outcomes could be achieved is for one side to prevail over the other. And that means war.

Therefore, once Serbs and Croats become committed to a political strategy which is in accordance with their long-term national interests, civil war in Yugoslavia is inevitable. For these strategies to be adopted, populist movements have to come to power. This is precisely what happened in Serbia and Croatia. And, as I tried to show, the development of communist political space made this outcome possible.

All the other national conflicts can be, in principle, reconciled inside Yugoslavia or through secession, but not in any other state construct. Apart from the conflicting interests of the Serbs and Croats, those of other nations can be satisfied inside a Yugoslav federation or confederation, or in independent states. For instance, Slovenian, Macedonian, Montenegrian, Muslim and even Albanian interests can be satisfied inside a Yugoslav state which respects equal rights of all individuals and nations. Also, the interests of all these nations (except for the Muslims) could be satisfied without further political deterioration of Serbian or Croatian interests if they were to create independent states or, in case of the Albanians, if they were to unite with Albania.

The problem of Albanian separation is difficult, but the territories they live on are ethnically homogeneous now. Also, no national interests of other nations are really severed because of Slovene and Macedonian independence. This is true for Montenegrians too, though they feel that they are not only Montenegrians but Serbs also. Still, with the exception of the inter-war period, they have always had their autonomous state and it is unlikely that they would be ready to give it up completely now.

However, the problem of the Muslims is different. They cannot live without autonomy, but they can hardly create an independent state. The regions that they populate, Bosnia and Hercegovina and Sandzak, seem doomed to be provinces in search of a state. The best solution they can hope for is to be a federal or confederal unit in a Yugoslav state. But if such a state is impossible, they are left in a void. They, as well as other nations in the region, cannot become a part of a different state construct, for instance of Serbian dominated "smaller Yugoslavia" or of a "greater Croatia".

There is no solution of the Yugoslav crisis without a Bosnian crisis being created. Bosnia and Hercegovina is populated by Serbs (just over 31%), Croats (about 17%), and Muslims (more than 45%).[19] All possible mixtures exist. In some regions one nation predominates; in others Serbs live mixed mainly with the Muslims, and Muslims are mainly mixed with the Croats; but in large regions the three nations are mixed in such a way that only the relative majority changes from one town or village to another.

Therefore, Croats can hardly live in a Bosnian state with no strong ties with Croatia, and the same goes for the Serbs. Muslims cannot accept a solution that deprives Bosnia of political autonomy, because that would drastically infringe upon their national interests. As long as there is a Yugoslav state, the national problems can be solved in terms of individual and collective rights. If Yugoslavia disappears, there are national rights to be observed. And how they could ever be reconciled is hard to see. This is not to say that there are no political solutions; it is to say that it is hard to expect that they will be in accord with nationalist perceptions.

Even if a solution to the Serbo-Croat-Muslim problem is found, there is still the Albanian question to be solved. Today in Eastern Europe there is no way that the Albanians will give up their goal of creating a nation-state. Albanians live on nationally homogeneous territories in Kosovo (that is Serbia), Macedonia and Montenegro. All these territories border on Albania. Even if Yugoslavia were to survive, the Albanian question would be all but impossible to solve. Almost as many Albanians live in Yugoslavia as in Albania[20] and they are divided only by the border. Therefore, it is only a matter of time when these Albanian regions will be united. This is so irrespective of the changes in the political regimes of Serbia, Macedonia or Yugoslavia, and for that matter in Albania, too.

Apart from the above difficulties, there are Middle European and Balkan problems left. On the fringes of all these conflicts there are the Slovenian, Hungarian and Macedonian questions to be solved. Slovenia is the easiest case, though it stood for some time as a proxy for Croatia, fighting over every possible political issue with Serbia. However, there are no conflicting national interests between Serbia and Slovenia.

The Hungarian question is more difficult, because there is a sizeable Hungarian minority in Serbia and Croatia. They have expressed serious misgivings with the new nationalist regimes, especially with the Serbian one (most of the Hungarian minority lives there). However, once the conflict between Serbs and Croats is over (that, unfortunately, may mean never), the Hungarian minority problem is about national and cultural rights which should not be politically difficult to solve. Contrary to that, the Macedonian problem displays the very essence of all Balkan conflicts. As it does not belong only to the Yugoslav crisis, I do not go into details here. Nevertheless, it is not going to disappear quite soon.

Nationalism and not multi-nationalism is the real problem. To sum up, Yugoslavia was not openly nationalist or anti-nationalist, though it was neither, for most of the time, a democracy nor did it ever work as a liberal federation. It did not develop into a modern liberal state, because it chose communism in a very dark moment of its history. Communism resulted in a political space that was not favorable to a liberal solution, at least on the federal level. Theoretically, however, there was a chance for a liberal solution, which was frustrated by a resurgence of populist movements playing on the long-term national interests of the dominant Yugoslav nations.

Therefore, in general, it is not the existence of different nations that makes it impossible for a multi-national state like Yugoslavia to preserve its stability and its very existence in the long run. Nationalist political interests are the real problem.[21] They express a demand for security and equal rights for the equals. In that sense, national interests are a demand for coherence between the personal and public identity of the people. However, they imply a potential discrimination of those with different national identities in terms of security, rights and policy.

Asymmetrical Symmetries[22]

Why did the populist parties take over in Serbia and Croatia? The simple answer is that this is what the majority of Serbs and Croats wanted. Their decisions were based on rational judgements on their national interests. That is to say, they anticipated that the ensuing conflict will be brutal, and mobilized the resources which they believed would prove to be the most effective.

Let us compare the developments in Slovenia with those in Serbia and Croatia. Slovenia was the first to realize the possibilities which were opened by collapsing communism.[23] It moved towards democracy and greater independence from the rest of Yugoslavia, and eventually succeeded in relying on a coalition between the liberal faction in the Slovenian Communist Party and the moderate nationalists. So, the otherwise typical communist space of Slovenia broke down and approached what I have called "the liberal solution".

To achieve the same goals, Croats chose "populism". The "liberal coalition" was badly defeated in the elections, and a curious coalition of hard-line communists and a far right-wing party took over. This was explained as a reaction to the revival of Serbian nationalism. However, this is hardly true. The Croatian political space was more severely twisted in the orthodox communist direction and that made the populist outcome more likely.[24] The political elite and the electorate was convinced that their national interests were not achievable without a populist party taking over.[25]

On the Serbian side, there was almost a resurgence of Stalinism. The right-wing faction of the Communist Party was defeated long before the collapse of communism was in sight. The main reason for this was that it did not respond severely enough to the demands of the Albanian nationalists. The left-wing faction of the Serbian Communist Party expected that with a show of force and with the help from the federal party and the army it would be able to take over. However, it misjudged the constellation of the political space in the other Yugoslav regions and also in the federal state. At the same time, it almost grotesquely misjudged the overall development of Eastern Europe, and fatally the Russian changes. Eventually, it had to move and even jump to the extreme right, nationalist position. The Communists led the populist movement with a promise that they can use the Yugoslav army to represent the Serbian national interests. The electorate understood the message and voted the Socialist Party of Serbia in.[26]

Therefore, once the elections in Croatia and Serbia were over, the war could be safely predicted. As a matter of fact, the populist parties in Serbia and Croatia did not hide their militant ambitions. For them nothing short of war seemed to be efficient. The war rhetoric actually started during the prolonged Kosovo crisis. Albanians argued that they were in overwhelming majority in Kosovo, and that in their sovereign republic Serbs would be guaranteed all the minority rights. Serbs answered by saying that Albanians were a small minority in the whole Serbian state, and that they would enjoy all the minority rights in the Serbian state. And the same argument was repeated all over Yugoslavia. When the Croatian nationalists came to power, they were ready to respect all the minority rights of the Serbs living in Croatia. The logical answer went as follows: "Why should we be a minority in your state, when you can be a minority in our state?" The ultimate consequence of this slogan is not to have a state at all. This is exemplified by the situation in Bosnia and Hercegovina. There Muslims are only in relative majority. Therefore, Bosnia cannot be either a theocracy or a nation-state. It lived in some kind of con-societal political space, that was never democratic and liberal, but showed a reasonable degree of tolerance. Consequently, the only direction this region can move in, if left alone, is towards some kind of pluralized democracy with regional autonomies. The multi-national character of Bosnia and Hercegovina is not an unsurmountable obstacle. Both Serbs and Croats offer the Muslims the prospect of being a respected minority in their, Serbian or Croatian, state, while some Muslim nationalists assure both Serbs and Croats living in Bosnia and Hercegovina that their minority rights would be fully respected in the Muslim state.

The problem is not only that nobody wants to be a minority in somebody else's nationalist state, but that every nation can offer the same prospect to the rival nation. At this point, given the rational expectations concerning the fact that national interests are, for the first time in history, within reach—this prospect produces violence even in those regions which lack particular reasons for that.

The situation is somewhat different and also more complex in Montenegro and Macedonia. These two republics contributed almost nothing to the disintegration of Yugoslavia. In a sense, they have been dragged into the conflict and pushed into directions that do not necessarily represent their best considered interests. However, once the conflict between Serbs and Croats erupted, all nations had to search for a place in the world.

Macedonia is a contested territory, where the people[27] are as nationalistic as everywhere else, but where there are no gains to be anticipated by relying on the use of force. The populist option did not win in Macedonia. True, neither did the liberal one. If a clash between the Serbs and the Albanians emerges it is impossible to tell what will happen to the whole region. Barring that, Macedonia has problems with all its neighbors. Greece on the South objects to the name of the nation and the state. Macedonians are Slavs that have adopted the name of the region which does not coincide geographically with the ancient Macedonian territories. Therefore, Greece demands that the "Yugoslav" Macedonians choose a different name. However, a new name would not solve the problem, because the territories themselves are contested. As a matter of fact, certain changes in the nation's and state's name may even aggravate the territorial problems. If Macedonians were to declare themselves Bulgarians, the territorial claims of a larger Bulgaria might even be more forcefully put. (Bulgaria does not recognize the existence of a Macedonian nation.) Finally, the medieval Serbian state incorporated Macedonia, and that was actually a reason why Serbs fought wars against Turkey and Bulgaria.

A major internal problem of Macedonia is the existence of a large Albanian minority. It is unlikely that the Albanians, who live on compact national territories, will not struggle for their nation-state incorporating Albania, Kosovo and Western Macedonia (perhaps even parts of Montenegro). How the Macedonians will react is impossible to see. Thus, even though Macedonia presents no threat to anybody, it is a medium through which threats are generated and transmitted. As a contrast, in Montenegro the main problem is how close that state wants to be to the Serbs. There no serious contests over the state territory exist, though almost 30 percent of the population is either Muslim or Albanian.[28]

To sum up again, the basic problem of Yugoslavia is that national rights can hardly be universalized without a multitude of violent changes. For instance, the right to self-determination, if universally applied, would require not only drastic changes in the existing borders but huge migrations in all directions. At the same time, asymmetrical solutions are not acceptable to the majority of the population no matter how the rights are distributed.

For a symmetrical solution to be found, national rights would have to be seen as derived (not fundamental). Unfortunately, there is no state that could credibly guarantee the respect of equal rights of all its citizens regardless of their nationality. As a result, there is a widespread feeling that individual rights can be credibly protected only inside a nation-state. So, in order to feel safe, citizens demand asymmetrical rights, which elicit similar counter-demands. One arrives at a complicated problem of multi-criteria classification which is impossible to solve even in principle.

The Rights Left

Yugoslavia has disintegrated though it is still not clear into precisely what. Nevertheless, the new states and the states that are coming into existence have either written their constitutions or have announced their political intentions. In the following, I will discuss national, human, economic, political and basic citizen's rights briefly relying on these documents. I am not going to pay attention to the letter of the constitutions only, but to their spirit, too.

1. All the new states are nationalist in the sense of expecting their citizens to value their nation more than their own life, wealth and rights. The basic constitution of all the new states is founded on national obligation. Therefore, though they may be formally democratic, they are constitutionally authoritarian states, because the duties and obligations of the state and of the citizens are derived from the interpretation of the national interest and not from the constitutional, legal or democratic procedure. In practice this means that the political space in these states will move to one of the extremes. In a sense, there will be a relapse into the same political space that was characteristic under the communist rule in some of these states; in others, there will be an authoritarian restriction on the freedom of political organization.[29]

2. The new states all have constitutions that implicitly or explicitly discriminate on the basis of nationality. The constitutions of the newly created states define these states as nation-states or give preferential

treatment to the dominant nation and its culture. Thus, nations that have constituted new states relying on the right to self-determination deny the same right to other nations.

If nationalism is not explicit in the constitution it can be detected from the way cultural diversities are treated. The most telling is the treatment of the language and the alphabet. Serbs and Croats speak the same language which can be written both in Latin and Cyrillic alphabets. However, they not only use their national name for the language, and they not only deny that the language is the same, but they discriminate against the other's alphabet. Thus, Serbian constitution prefers the Cyrillic alphabet, while Croatian prefers Latin. Of course, both alphabets are neither Serbian nor Croatian, but are regarded as such because the other alphabet is preferred by the other side.

On the basis of such distinctions further discriminations follow in terms of citizenship rights, employment, promotion, education, etc. In Serbia, thousands of Albanian teachers were fired because they did not accept the new school programs based on the new constitution (and thousands of Albanian workers and professionals have lost their jobs for political reasons). In Croatia, the new government has instituted quota requirements to give preferential treatment to Croats over Serbs.

3. The new states have shown an inclination to rely on nationalist interpretation of economic rights and economic policies. All the privatization schemes have strong nationalist overtones, and these states have already experienced all kinds of protectionist policies. They have all nationalized or declared the intention to nationalize their currencies. They have created huge public corporations and introduced tax differences on the basis of state or national affiliation.

4. All new states (except Slovenia and perhaps Bosnia and Hercegovina) treat freedom of speech in an instrumental way and even restrict it in many explicit and implicit ways. The political propaganda is unbearable and in many places there is a much more effective censorship than in the final years of the communist regime. In all the new states the dominant newspapers and TV networks have been nationalized, so that the government can tightly control public opinion.

5. Finally, the general level of protection is very low, not to mention that of the rule of law. While communism was a system of comprehensive dependence on the people in power, the new states have developed a system of dependence characteristic of typical authoritarian regimes. Again there are regional differences. While one can discover many

elements of a typical police state in both Serbia and Croatia, with a high level of lawlessness and mafia type protection agencies, in other states all this is present but to a much smaller degree. In some states this situation will probably change through normal legal and democratic evolution. However, in the key states of Serbia, Croatia and Bosnia and Hercegovina democratic transformation will be possible only after the nationalist character of the new systems is changed.

Permanent Instability

The process I have described is covered by the term of "Balkanization".[30] It is characterized by internal disintegration and permanent international involvement. One thing is sure: no, not even a quasi-stable outcome is possible without international help. At this point, there are as many as seven Serbian states or autonomous regions.[31] Apart from that, there are republics of Croatia, Slovenia, Macedonia, Bosnia and Hercegovina, and Kosovo. All seceded in time. The secession of Slovenia created huge problems, but it was in the end recognized that no national interests of the others are at stake. Macedonia managed to secede even without inciting any violent clashes, but it failed to gain international recognition because of Greece. In principle the secessions of Slovenia and Macedonia leave the rest in Yugoslavia no worse off in terms of their national interests.

Nevertheless, the Serbian states and regions intended to create a new, smaller Yugoslavia that would on the one hand effectively terminate the existence of Bosnia and Hercegovina and would abort Albanian intentions to have their republic of Kosovo. It would also make the state of Croatia all but chimerical. On the other hand, Serbian territories, regions and states can hardly be run over by Croatia, Bosnia and Hercegovina, and Kosovo.

Croatian strategy is to grant the Serbs in Croatia significant rights of autonomy. This is difficult to achieve, especially after the civil war, but is not inconceivable. In that sense, a Croatian state is possible in principle, especially if it is affiliated with the European Community (that, however, does not mean that it will ever be accepted as legitimate by the Serbs living there). However, a creation of a viable state of Bosnia and Hercegovina is difficult to imagine. The best hope for this region is to be put under some kind of a prolonged international protection. But, in that case, the Serbian problem will hardly be solved. It is difficult to see that the Serbs would be willing to give up all their territorial aspirations, especially because they would be left with the Kosovo problem. As soon as the Yugoslav and Bosnian crises are solved, whatever that means, the Kosovo crisis will erupt.

Therefore, Serbia is the central problem. The positive Serbian contribution would be a turn to Western Europe. Isolated, Serbia is experiencing extremely hard times. With a liberal and democratic government, Serbia could have looked for more promising solutions of its national interest.

The end of the old Yugoslavia is widely accepted, and Slovenia, Croatia and Bosnia and Hercegovina are recognized as independent states. The Serbian government aimed at recreating a smaller Yugoslavia, including Serbia, Montenegro, Bosnia and Hercegovina (or at least Serbian territories there), Macedonia and Serbian territories in Croatia. Now, it has, for the time being, settled for a much smaller Yugoslavia, consisting only of Serbia and Montenegro. However, the name of Yugoslavia is used to signal that the long-term goal has not been changed. Only when all the "Serbian territories" are incorporated, the name of the state will be changed from Yugoslavia to Serbia.

The strategy of the international community was to first secure the independence of Slovenia and Croatia and only then to start to worry about the rest. The rest was a Serbian dominated territory with millions of Albanians, Muslims and Macedonians and hundreds of thousands of other national minorities. This country could hardly become anything but a dictatorship of one kind or another. Thus, the process of further Balkanization was opened. With Macedonia proclaiming independence, and with the Yugoslav Army pulling out of the region, the problem did not change much because the Serbian state was left with huge Albanian and Muslim minorities. So, the process of Balkanization went on and will go on.

Even if Serbia turns to democracy and even if all the other states temper down their nationalisms, the stability of this region is difficult to envisage. The best one can hope for is that fightings will stop and a process of political emancipation will start. But it is more likely that a kind of permanent instability will be the outcome of the creation of nation-states and lawless provinces.

Nonetheless, international influence could help. The fundamental problems of Yugoslavia (and the Balkans in general) are connected with rights and security. It is hard to expect that the newly created states would be able to guarantee equal rights and security to their citizens, even if they recognized each other's national interests.

In terms of rights, it would be a significant step forward if the new states were to accept the jurisdiction of the European Community court in Strassbourg (or some other international court). In terms of security, some states and regions should be demilitarized and some like Bosnia and Hercegovina should be put under the protection of the United Nations. In the long run, these regions will have to be integrated in the newly emerging European order. Until then, they must not be left to their nationalist leaders.

The "international community" has not been acting altogether responsibly during the whole crisis. At the same time, partly because of mixed international signals and mostly in disregard of anything else but their narrow nationalist interests, the Balkan countries (not only those of former Yugoslavia) have been going on with their destructive policies.

With the failure, first, of decisively influencing the democratic process in Yugoslavia; second, of recognizing the dangerous policies of Belgrade; third, belatedly of acknowledging the seceding republics; fourth, of unevenly treating their requests; and fifth, with a rejection of the independence of Macedonia, both the USA and the EC have revealed a worrisome inability to even formulate some principles of the "new world order" let alone to act on them. It seems that the international community aims to get involved in ways that I do not think they themselves are aware of at this point. Macedonia and Kosovo, for example, are both encouraged and discouraged to seek independence. It is ironic that the stability of the whole region in the South of former Yugoslavia depends on the political prudence of Albanians and Macedonians, who are expected to search for peaceful solutions under pressure and complete lack of understanding from every side.

The costs of permanent instability cannot be computed even in principle. In 1993, there were only few strategic changes. The break-up of Yugoslavia proved to be an inconclusive process. With the exception of Slovenia, which is generally recognized as an independent and viable state, all other republics are still referred to as "former Yugoslavia." There is an international effort to keep Macedonia out of the Balkan conflict, but it is still not clear what is to be done with it. Everything else is unstable and deteriorating.

In terms of security, the idea of extending recognition to the former

Yugoslav republics proved insufficient. It is hard to see at this point how permanent instability in Croatia, Bosnia and Hercegovina, and Yugoslavia (consisting now of Serbia and Montenegro) is to be avoided. In terms of rights, the acceptance of the principle of ethnic division of Yugoslavia and of the creation of ethnic states has predictably led to huge violations of individual, civil, and other human rights and thus to long-term political problems. For some reason it needed the horrors of the destruction of Bosnia and Hercegovina for that to be recognized. Unless the ethnic principle is given up, or rather unless liberal and democratic principles are adhered to, there will be more of the same sufferings in the future.

Appendix I

Politics is but geometrical purity
embracing the law of the jungle.
— Joseph Brodsky, "Less Than One"

Political space can be represented even by a straight line.

```
          *         *         *         *         *
________ ________ ________ ________ ________ ________
 left     A         B         C         D         E   right
```

At C there is the "true" center. Power would settle here if free elections were held regularly. At A there is the "ideal" communist power center. At B there is the "liberal" communist power center. At D the majority of the citizens are grouped, when the "liberal" communist faction is in power. E is where the center is pushed if the political space breaks down.

If the state is a federation, the political space may be fragmented so that no general horizontal line exists at all. In that case, all combinations are possible. In some cases, the political space will settle around the "true" center, in others it might go to the left or to the most extreme right. This in fact means that there is no state any more.

In a federation of nationalist states there are no single-peaked preference spaces. Then, the permanent instability theorem applies with two consequences: first, there are no stable majorities, and, second, every political stability is perceived as imposed.[32] Provided that the political space breaks down along national lines, the non-existence of single-peaked preferences will not only end up in the lack of a common horizontal line but also in a breakdown of the state itself.

Appendix II

By political fundamentals I mean the way in which fundamental political goods are supplied and demanded.

The fundamental political goods are security and rights. Supplier is the state, the demand comes from the citizens. If the supply and the demand do not cross, there is no credible state. That means that, fundamentally, the citizens are not identifying themselves with the state they live in. One way to elicit this identification is to invoke national rights. A citizen feels more secure if he shares his identity with the state. Also, he can demand that his rights be respected in his own nation state. Therefore, the national identity of a state becomes a surrogate political good which generalizes all other political goods.

Supply and demand of basic political goods can be constituted in different institutional arrangements. It can be constructed as a contract, it can be based on power, or follow the rules of an ancient constitution. Though every state is a construct, not every state is a constitutional construct. There are no obvious or natural rules of inclusion and exclusion in a state. On the other hand, the state cannot be constructed on power alone. Because, though there are no clear criteria of the state's optimal size, there do exist criteria of individual inclusion in cultural and other groups and societies. A generalized type of such criteria is belonging to a nation.

The fundamental problem of nationalism is seen when it is universalized. If every state should be a nation state, no state can have national minorities. Therefore, not only voluntary migration is not to be allowed, but also there has to be some compulsory migration, if nations live mixed on the same territory. Civil war is one way to achieve forced migration, and discriminations are the political way to check undesired migration.

Appendix III

By a liberal constitution I mean an institutional arrangement that is based on the Bill of Rights. The essential characteristic of such a constitution is that the rights it relies on are universalizable. In other words, the state is founded on the notion of protection of individual freedoms.

Liberal constitution does not have to be based on a contract. But it differs from a nation-state constitution because the latter is founded on a special non-contractarian quality of individual origin. A nation-state is a state that:

a) includes those who are of specific origin, whether by birth or by choice;

b) treats those who are of a different origin in a different way;

c) follows a national interest.

The last element is well described by Lord Acton:

" . . . The national theory marks the end of the revolutionary doctrine and its logical exhaustion. In proclaiming the supremacy of the rights of nationality, the system of democratic equality goes beyond its own extreme boundary, and it falls into contradiction with itself . . . Nationality is a more advanced system than socialism, because it is a more arbitrary system . . . Nationality does not aim either at liberty or prosperity, both of which it sacrifices to the imperative necessity of making the nation the mould and measure of the state. This course will be marked with material as well as moral ruin, in order that a new invention may prevail over the works of God and the interests of mankind. There is no principle of change, no political speculation conceivable, more comprehensive, more subversive, or more arbitrary than this. It is a confutation of democracy, because it sets limits to the exercise of the popular will, and substitutes for it a higher principle . . . Thus, after surrendering the individual to the collective will, the revolutionary system makes the collective will subject to conditions which are independent of it, and rejects all law, only to be controlled by an accident."

On national rights Lord Acton says the following:

"The greatest adversary of the right of nationality is the modern theory of nationality. By making the State and the nation commensurate with each other in theory, it reduces practically to a subject condition all other nationalities that may be within the boundary. It cannot admit them to an equality with the ruling nation which constitutes the State, because the State would then cease to be national, which would be a contradiction of the principle of its existence. According, therefore, to the degree of humanity and civilization of that dominant body which claims all the rights of the community, the inferior races are exterminated, or reduced to servitude, or outlawed, or put in a condition of dependence."

Appendix IV

> *If we take the establishment of liberty for the realisation of moral duties to be the end of civil society, we must conclude that those states are substantially the most perfect which, like the British and Austrian Empires include various different nationalities without oppressing them. Those in which no mixture of races has occurred are imperfect; and those in which its effects have disappeared are decrepit. A State which is incompetent to satisfy different races condemns itself; a State which labours to neutralize, to absorb, or to expel them, destroys its own vitality; a State which does not include them is destitute of the chief basis of self-government. The theory of nationality, therefore, is a retrograde step in history.*
>
> —Lord Acton, "Nationality"

The process of "Balkanization" can be described in the following way. Suppose that there is a Tiedbout process of spontaneous state creation. That is, people use institutional or violent means to organize a state only for those citizens that happen to share certain similar characteristics. Suppose that a stable solution is given by a distribution of power (as a function of a tax level chosen by different proto-states that want to be independent).[33] Then, the process of "Balkanization" is described by two properties:

a) every distribution of power is worse than some other for at least one proto-state;

b) every decentralization of state authority reveals a new preferred decentralization or centralization of state authority.

That is to say, "Balkanization" is a process that constantly changes the distribution of power due, among other impacts, to international groupings and regroupings. It is a process that never reveals the "true" preferences of all those concerned. In the latter sense, it is a process of constitution destruction.

However, even the Tiedbout process is not an adequate framework for analyzing the process of Balkanization because it is presumed on state, federal or confederal jurisdictions being clearly drawn so that people can "vote with their feet". If, on the other hand, the boundaries are not clearly drawn, then there is a degree of freedom that strengthens the two outcomes mentioned above. There is no distribution of power which is independent of the way the boundaries are drawn, and there is no state that equilibrates the level of public goods, because that depends on the nationalist preferences, that is, on the process of revelation of the preferences for the domain of state authority.

Both processes bring in the international factor that makes the problem of power politics even more complicated.[34]

Notes

1. There are no "innocent victims" in a civil war. While in a war armies fight, in a civil war there are no armies and there is no civilian population. In that sense, Carl Schmitt was right: the fundamental and, in fact, the only distinction is the one between the friend and the enemy.
2. A detailed discussion can be found in V. Gligorov, "Buharin i strategije desnice", *Argumenti*, 1, 1979, and V. Gligorov, *Gledista i sporovi o industrijalizaciji u socijalizmu*. IDN, 1984.
3. The criterion is simple: everything bad is on the right side.
4. See, for instance, J. Kornai, *The Economics of Shortage*. North-Holland, 1980.
5. See V. Gligorov, "Justice and Privatization", *Communist Economies and Economic Transformation,* 4:1, 1991.
6. The above examples are based on a minimal political space that I need for clarifying my approach. In reality, everything is much more complicated.
7. For a critique of the contractarian approach in political philosophy see my forthcoming book: V. Gligorov, The Political Genre.
8. Of course, history can be interpreted differently. On the one hand, Yugoslavia was created in 1918 (at first as a Kingdom of Serbs, Croats and Slovenes; it took the name of Yugoslavia only in 1929) following the rule of the "self-determination" of nations. On the other hand, a mythology of common linguistic and cultural roots developed in some intellectual and political circles in the future republics. However, no nationality was ready to give up its national identity in exchange for the common one.
9. I discuss the relationship between natural and national foundations of a state in the context of a "liberal constitution" in Appendix III.
10. On the first Yugoslav constitution see S. Jovanovic, *Ustavno pravo*, Beograd, 1928.
11. This is not to say that no other national conflicts existed. However, the Croatian question was recognized as the central one.
12. The ethnic principle was used to determine the borders of the Croatian federal unit. The borders did differ from those drawn after the Second World War, but not as drastically as one might suppose when listening to the heated debates about the "unjust borders" of federal Yugoslavia.

13. More on that in V. Gligorov, "Liberalna federacija", *Kulturni radnik*, 2, 1990.
14. However, the economic profession did not support the popular opinion. Only a minority of economists believed that it was exactly their nation that was exploited by the rival one. The influence of this minority grew precisely when communism broke down and they were able to use the authority of the nationalist parties they joined or of some national institutions (like the Serbian Academy of Arts and Sciences that in an infamous "Memorandum" declared that "Serbs were exploited by the Slovenes and the Croats from the time Yugoslavia was created in 1918"). Most of the explanations for the long-term exploitation of certain regions in Yugoslavia are coached in Marxist jargon. Some Marxists say that the more developed regions exploit the less developed, while their Marxist opponents from more developed regions contend with the same terror that only the less developed regions can exploit the advanced ones.
15. There are many versions of the process of national emancipation in Yugoslavia. Some deny that any nation except the one they belong to really exists. There also used to exist strong sentiments of self-denial. In fact, Yugoslavia was conceived of as a state based on ethnic similarities of the different nations living there. There was a widely shared belief among influential intellectuals of all the leading nations in the nineteenth and twentieth century that Slovenes, Croats and Serbs are one nation consisting of three tribes. Having had all kinds of wrong ideas as to who Serbs, Croats, Slovenes, Macedonians, Muslims and others had really been, they were all very surprised to find out that the differences are far greater than the similarities.

    So, the current Yugoslav national conflict has to be seen, admittedly rather benignly, as a growing understanding of who they really are. If this is defined as "cultural difference", then given how huge it was and how primitive historical knowledge and how strong cultural prejudices were, the level of national tolerance in Yugoslavia was not too low. For instance, Serbs fought to liberate their compatriots in Macedonia only to learn to their amazement that the majority of the population there had not been Serbian for quite a long time. Even well educated and liberal intellectuals could never reconcile themselves to the idea that the center of Serbian Kingdom in the Middle Ages is not populated by Serbs any more.
16. In defining what it means to be committed to national interests, I accept Lord Acton's characterization in his essay on "Nationality" in *The History of Freedom and Other Essays*. The Liberty Press, 1990 (see the Appendices).
17. All the constitutions of the newly independent Yugoslav republics define highly centralized states (the only exception is Bosnia and Hercegovina which allows the formation of regions, and in a sense, Serbia that nominally has two autonomous provinces).
18. For what I mean by a "liberal constitution", see Appendix III.
19. The figures are based on the latest census (spring, 1991) which was not very reliable.
20. The Albanians boycotted the last census, so the numbers used by the analysts are highly speculative.

21. See Appendix III for more on this. Lord Acton believed that any state that was not multi-national was "imperfect" (see his article quoted above). See also Hayek's last chapter on federalism in his *Individualism and Economic Order*.
22. For the failure of Yugoslavia to accept universal principles, see my "The Discovery of Liberalism in Yugoslavia".
23. This happened in 1988. Otherwise, Slovenia was as thoroughly a socialist state as any other in Yugoslavia. As a matter of fact, one could very well argue that Slovenia was a model socialist state, because, unlike the other regions in Yugoslavia, it had almost full employment, relatively high social services, and very little opposition. The Slovenian communist leadership had certainly been more conservative than, for instance, the Serbian one during the eighties before Milosevic took over.
24. This was due to the way the 1971 political crisis in Croatia had been resolved. Communist rule broke down in Croatia and nationalists were close to taking over. However, Tito, relying on the hard-liners in the party and in the Yugoslav army, staged a political counter-attack and a hard-line communist system was reintroduced.
25. For more on this, see V. Gligorov, "The Survival Coalition", *Danas*, March, 1989.
26. For more on the developments in Serbia, see V. Gligorov, "Ustav iz 1990. za 1914", *Demokratija*, June, 1990; V. Gligorov, "Vojno resenje", *Vreme*, December, 1990.
27. The population consists of Macedonians, Albanians, Serbs, Romas, Turks and a number of other nationalities. Albanians are about 25 percent of the population.
28. Nevertheless, in the course of the civil war, a conflict between Montenegro and Croatia has emerged over Prevlaka (a strip of land on the coast). There are national tensions in Ulcinj and some other Montenegrian regions, too where Albanians and Muslims are in majority.
29. As everything has an original and a caricature in Yugoslavia, the constitutions of the new Serbian states in Croatia and Bosnia and Hercegovina represent such extreme nationalist cases. All the worst nationalist ideas can be found there together with constitutional declarations of respect for universal human rights.
30. For more on that, see Appendix IV and my "Balkanization, A Theory of Constitution Failure."
31. They are the following: Serbia, Montenegro, Krajina, Zapadna Slavonija, Istocna Slavonija, Baranja i Zapadni Srem, Bosanska Krajina—there are even more, but these seven are going to play important roles. By now, the Republic of Serbian Bosnia and Hercegovina had been proclaimed (consisting of all the "Serbian regions"); also the Republic of Serbian Krajina was proclaimed (consisting of all the "Serbian regions" in Croatia); finally, the new Federal Republic of Yugoslavia was proclaimed in May 1992, consisting of Republics of Serbia and Montenegro.
32. For this theorem, see T. Schwartz, "The Universal-Instability Theorem", *Pub-*

lic Choice, 37 (1981), 487–501.

33. On the size of a state as a function of its tax base, see D. Friedman, "A Theory of the Size and Shape of Nations", *Journal of Political Economy, 85* (February 1977), 59–77.
34. On that see M. Wight, *Power Politics*. London: Macmillan, 1977.

9

Poland After the Revolution—the Obfuscated Autonomy of Politics

Jan T. Gross

The 1989 revolution in East Central Europe calls for simultaneous reconstruction of economy, administration, and political authority. Countries of the region must learn anew how to produce material goods, how to run their bureaucracies, and how to govern themselves. The three tasks, interrelated as they are, are also to a substantial degree autonomous. I take interest primarily in the latter. I will argue that at the current stage of the Polish revolution the relative autonomy of the political factor has been unduly obfuscated. To some extent this has resulted from the force of circumstances. Yet, while simply registering that this has occurred, I do so with a sense of regret. In part, because laying out careful foundation for legitimate authority might have been easier, perhaps less time consuming, and certainly cheaper than setting up new bureaucracies or introducing market economies. But it is also possible that this should have been a priority task. For when all is said and done and the time will come to consider to what degree the East European revolution was a success or a failure, when people will ask themselves whether transition has been accomplished, the answer will not be given in terms of GNP per head, or unemployment figures, or the rate of inflation. Instead, we will want to know how strongly entrenched institutions of representative government had become.

A new phase in the political articulation of liberty currently took hold of East Central Europe. It involves enfranchisement of the state. Nations of East Central Europe, which at the civil society[1] stage of their emancipation have but demonstrated that they are real living entities, are now constituting themselves as polities. They are in the process of authenticating their institutions.

In this transition from civil society to a political nation an altogether different environment for articulation of liberty has been created. For the change that has occurred cannot be simply exhausted by pointing out that people who used to be in the opposition are now in the establishment (i.e. exchanged the role of a critic for that of a proponent of a positive program and assumed responsibility for carrying it out). What is crucial, rather, is that as opposition the—let us call them Solidarity/human rights activists—implemented liberty in an uninstitutionalized context (creating civil society in the process), while as establishment they are bound to operate within the confines of institutions (creating, in the process, a political nation).

To state that liberty became institutionalized may seem trivial today. Yet but some years ago the main protagonists who brought about the 1989 revolution were not quite aware that this was about to happen.[2] Some years ago decent people, i.e. the architects of the 1989 revolution, shunned state institutions and if they partook in them it was only as a concession, as a necessary evil. Lech Walesa, the only politician with complete freedom of action, i.e. the only one without a Walesa to bully him to do things he didn't quite want to do, deliberately chose to stand outside of the institutional order.

And then the unexpected happened. Unlike in 1980/1981 when Solidarity came into existence, the 1989/1990 developments in the surrounding countries were uniquely favorable to the Polish revolution, but the consequences for the domestic Polish politics were paradoxical. That USSR dropped its imperial claims to East Central Europe with such alacrity, that Hungary, Czechoslovakia, and East Germany so rapidly shed their Communist establishments (these stunning developments in the Soviet Union and in Eastern Europe which allowed for the depth of the Polish transformations and their irreversibility) rendered the mid-1989 strategy of the opposition obsolete. For while Solidarity activists operated as if their task was to consolidate the gains of civil society, events thrust them already into the role of architects of a political nation. The clearer it became that the then President Jaruzelski and Minister of Interior Kiszczak were willing to play along with the transition, that the Soviet Union effectively abandoned its claims to Eastern Europe, and that sweeping changes are taking place in all neighboring countries, the more obsolete became the role of an outside arbiter, mediator, and source of authority that Walesa prudently cast himself into at the beginning of the process.

Its very success and its becoming a government party much more for real than it anticipated fractured the Solidarity movement. Suddenly, rhetoric of several most outspoken and articulate revolutionaries—by then occupying parliamentary, governmental, or editorial offices—filled with a new idea: that of strengthening and preservation of the state. A polity was in the making. Institutions were being authenticated. And some people were in positions of authority while some were out. And among those out was Walesa. Issues of personality (or, rather, personalities) aside, sources of the protracted political crisis in Poland after the June 89 elections are institutional, and the novelty of suddenly institutionalized liberty is responsible.

For when Walesa realized what has happened he decided to insert himself promptly (forcefully bending the rules if necessary) into the institutional order. As a result, legitimacy of state institutions already appropriated by society was weakened. The institutionally well positioned group of Solidarity leaders, on the other hand, also displayed a certain lack of foresight. They suddenly (and not entirely in good faith, I am afraid) adopted a strictly law and order etatist attitude, promoting in effect a version of Polish politics without an identifiable place for Lech Walesa. This did not work very well either.

Notice that when positions of power and authority in a state get filled with incumbents who have an authentic mandate[3] the realm of liberty extends enormously compared to what it had been when free association could manifest itself only within the boundaries of civil society. Strangely enough, however—even though, I stress, the sum total of liberty multiplies manifold in such a polity—for political actors the transition is experienced as a move from abundance to scarcity. It is so because liberty in the framework of a political nation is institutionally well defined and its bulk is available in a finite number of well circumscribed positions. Consequently, active exercise of it becomes a zero-sum game and as such a new experience altogether. For while there was little liberty in the confines of civil society, its supply—because it could be created by spontaneous action—was infinite. Anybody could partake in it by launching a new initiative—whether a newspaper or a political action group—and, if successful, this would redound to the benefit of all by creating yet another precedent and enlarging the domain of free association; by empowering in some fashion yet another segment of society. Today society is empowered all right but power is confined, predominantly, to a small number of well defined positions.[4] Over which therefore there is bound to be competition. The necessity of competition is what makes the exercise of liberty in the confines of a political nation so radically different from what it had been in the confines of civil society. It is all right to want somebody else's job even if it is that of a president, or a prime minister, or a senator. One needn't be a scoundrel, or a traitor to harbor such desires. The greatest and most difficult mental leap necessary at this stage is for recognition not so much that pluralism but that competition is legitimate in politics.

An unavoidable ambiguity of revolutionary processes has to do with the following: strategies or events winding down and closing up ancien regimes are also (without being construed with an eye to play that role, however) foundation events of the new order. They don't merely stand at an end of an epoch, but also at the beginning of a new era. And in this latter capacity they may become a liability, since there is no compelling reason for the cleverest, most ingenious and effective end-game that overpowers or neutralizes the old regime to be just as clever, or even simply fitting, beginning of a renewal in collective life. Take the phenomenally successful and ingenious device of the Round Table discussions and the June 1989 elections in Poland.

The round table negotiations were set up outside of the institutional framework of the Polish People's Republic. Its participants were an ad-hoc gremium which, on the one hand, embodied the authorities (the state/party decision making circles) and on the other, society. I use "embodied" rather than "represented" because just as there was no delegation of authority from the state/party governing institutions to the group of the government side negotiators (there simply could not be—the parliament could not delegate its authority to make laws or amend the Constitution, for example) so their interlocutors were not, strictly speaking, representatives of society.[5]

In one sense we should appreciate that the illegality of this ad-hoc arrangement was unavoidable. The round-table was, after all, an instrument of a radical transformation of the extant regime (in fact much more far reaching than any of the participants understood at the time), and as such it probably could not be accommodated within the officially recognized procedures. Political regimes of a non-democratic sort do not, typically, carry legal arrangements to provide for their own extinction. And in the known arsenal of revolutionary means the round table's "illegality," its "lawlessness," were of a milder sort. Thus, as an end to an era the round table was a most ingenious device, a "velvet revolution" indeed. But as it was also the foundation of a new era—the era of a *Rechtsstaat,* of a state based on law—it would expose the legitimacy of Mazowiecki's government to a plausible accusation by unfriendly critics that it rested on "a deal" made by impostors, a self-serving agreement between two like-minded segments of Communist and Solidarity elites.[6] Then came the hands off policy by Solidarity when 33 out of 35 prominents of the regime, who ran unopposed on the National List in the June 1989 elections, failed to obtain the necessary absolute majority. Because of a proviso of government-drafted electoral law that there are no second round elections for national list candidates (it must have seemed redundant to government lawyers, since the seats were uncontested), they could not recuperate from the loss. Solidarity consented to the law being changed retroactively in the midst of electoral process—to allow for the additional 33 coalition seats to be filled in the second round of elections. On July 19, the spectacle of General Jaruzelski's doctored presidential election was played in front of the entire nation (literally so, for parliamentary debates broadcast over the radio and television were diligently followed by the Poles). As a number of deputies from the so-called coalition parties would no longer be disciplined to vote for Jaruzelski a number of prominent Solidarity deputies ensured his election. They waited until all the votes were tallied in the National Assembly and then deliberately invalidated their own ballots so that Jaruzelski could be elected by one vote.

Once again, these were mild forms of lawlessness by revolutionary standards. But as this was also a mild kind of a revolution, with a stated purpose to establish a *Rechtsstaat,* it mattered that in the process the successor political camp was overtly instrumental vis-à-vis the most important legitimizing procedure of the new polity, namely elections. It was also not without consequences that the leading personalities identified with this instrumentalism were key figures of what later was to become the pro-Mazowiecki government wing of Solidarity. They were the ones who in the subsequent conflict with Walesa advocated strict observance of due process, slow pace of transformation, and support for institutions of the state as a good in itself. Against them, in turn, the pro-Walesa wing used the argument of "acceleration" and the idea of an interventionist president ("running around with an ax," in Walesa's own words), calling in effect for results at the expense of due process.

Thus, at the very beginning and in full public view a conflict emerged between formal and substantive, or procedure- and outcome-oriented understanding of the public good. Public good in this case consisted on the one hand in the need to respect the law and accept election results and, on the other hand, in making sure that the outcomes of elections do not lead to aborting of the whole transition process by the old regime which still controlled the apparatus of coercion. In time, in a very short time, electoral outcomes which the new political stratum deemed so important to ensure, would prove irrelevant. And the stunning success of the Polish revolution would reveal ambiguity of the very strategies that brought it about. For once associated with promoting outcome-oriented politics the first Solidarity-spawned government opened the way for anybody espousing an issue of sufficient priority to argue for its immediate enactment irrespective of binding legal provisions. In the ensuing debates we witnessed a rapid depletion of authority of all state institutions.

Poland, together with the rest of East Central Europe, developed a rather peculiar self-understanding of the political process it is going through. Having parted with Communism and the vocabulary of Marxist analysis in an ironic twist it got captured by the fundamentals of Marxism. Economics revealed itself with a vengeance to be the key determinant of regime transformation. To be sure Marxist principles were reversed and private ownership appears as indispensable foundation for a well ordered politics; for a stable, normalized, condition of society. But the framework remains unchanged: circumstances of material life, indeed property relations, are posited as foundation of politics. The kernel of economic and political reform in East Central Europe is privatization.

Thus, not surprisingly, the essential point of reference, the shorthand designation, the symbol associated today with the Polish revolution is not a Solidarity logo, or one or another of Walesa's irreverent *bon mots.* Rather, it is a certain blueprint for economic reform—the Balcerowicz Plan. The 1989 East European revolution is encapsulated in a set of technical prescriptions. It stands or falls, apparently, on the accuracy of experts' advice. I think this a major theme that requires reflection, for such development represents a radical shift in the spiritual elan of the revolution, in its ideological (though it shies from the term "ideology") impact, and in its ability to produce new ideas and therefore sustain involvement, not to say enthusiasm, of the population.

Revolutions used to be export commodities presumably because they had a blueprint for a better society to offer or, in any case, because they represented something new. This one, judging by the number of outside experts criss crossing Eastern Europe (from business school graduates to constitutional lawyers), apparently can be imported in. Evidently there is a know-how somewhere—experience, ability, resources, knowledge, certainly money—which simply needs to be transplanted in, to carry the task to successful completion. It is so because unlike what the circumstances had been for its predecessors (i.e. other great revolutions), the future, the destination, the end point of this revolution is well known. It actually exists. It can be reached by an overnight train. And a lot of people from East Central Europe have seen that future. And it works.

Over the last fifteen years, at the civil society stage of articulation of liberty in East Central Europe—as society was emancipating itself from the constriction of imposed state institutions—this was an immensely intriguing and creative process, self-conscious of its novelty in gradually winnowing away from the grip of Soviet imperialism and Leninist organization of power. It created a new vocabulary, a literature, a strategy of social action, and a good many well deserved reputations. Now the conceptual/spiritual/ideological referent of collective action changed decisively. Poland (East Central Europe) knows where it wants to go. It said so, with so many voices, on different occasions. It wants to return to Europe. A truly challenging, multifaceted and provocative demand when articulated in the context of Soviet imperial rule (it unambiguously stood for liberty at the time) it loses today, I think, much of its energy. For, in effect, it says—we want what Western European societies have (now with material goods palpably mixed in) though, of course, in the foreseeable future we wouldn't expect to get exactly as much of everything.

The hidden message—we will settle for less—is thus, certainly, different from the one which sustained East Central Europe over decades, some would say over centuries, but which certainly was coded into this latest process of emancipation through its beginning years. It proclaimed with confidence that Poland is accumulating a unique experience, that it is travelling a road nobody had travelled before, that it is somehow special. Can the Polish society settle now—and mobilize for sustained and demanding collective effort of reconstruction—with the aspiration, instead, to eventually become second rate?

I want to return briefly to this phenomenon of expertise replacing and subordinating politics in East Central Europe. The East European revolution carried the day, refreshingly, against and despite the advice and diagnosis of assorted experts. One may consult vast libraries of sovietological writings and the wrongheaded or plainly shameful record of foreign policy experts' advice[7] to realize that this was so. Now again, with massive dispensation of advice, a lot of academic reputations will be in jeopardy. But there is more to worry about than the fate of academic profession, because when rhetoric of expertise permeates domestic political discourse in a republic it puts in jeopardy the foundation of democratic process. It stifles public debate and leads to disenfranchisement. As experts are allowed to claim discovery of the only right solution in matters of public importance, the faculty of citizenship becomes meaningless.[8]

Naturally, there is room for expert advice in all matters. But in public affairs we must be vigilant against subtle encroachments of citizens' prerogative to decide on their own. Democratic government is predicated on the assumption of equal competence of all citizens with respect to public business. It is a naive, indeed demonstrably wrong, assumption but a political regime built to implement it has so far yielded less pernicious consequences for mankind than any other known form of government. And while politicians might be of the opinion that people have not yet grown mature enough to govern themselves (and some might even express such views publicly) they could never state them in defence of democracy.

Politics, in short, has been treated in the 1989 revolution as a derivative rather than autonomous sphere of collective experience. It has not been reflected upon with intensity commensurate with importance it takes in the life of a community under representative government. For when political authority and power does not flow from the barrel of a gun, or from God's will, but from mutually agreed upon rules (concerning proper procedures for aggregation, articulation, representation, and implementation of collective interests) they must be laid bare, scrutinized and made transparent especially at the time of foundation. Legitimacy of authority rests on clarity in these matters. But there is little such clarity nowadays, and virtual absence of constitutional issues from the public debate in Poland. The political meaning of the 1989 elections has never been properly understood for example. And this ambiguity remains a nemesis of Polish politics ever since.

It is often said that the first post-communist Polish parliament was not representative because 65% of the seats in the lower house were not openly contested. Yet its status was far more dubious and, to be sure, for other reasons. Take, for example, the generally accepted view that there were free elections to the upper house, the Senate, in June of 1989.

People in Poland were fond of a *bon mot* coined at the time by a rising star Communist politician Aleksander Kwasniewski. Even a cow, he said, provided it carried the Solidarity logo (and certainly if it were photographed for its campaign poster together with Lech Walesa, as all but one Solidarity candidates had been) would have won in the contest with the government-sponsored candidate. People recognized the truthfulness of Kwasniewski's observation and gleefully laughed at it. But when they stopped laughing they should have asked themselves a question. In what sense would a cow elected to a Senate seat from a certain voivodeship become its representative? And if it wouldn't (because, of course, it wouldn't) did any of the incumbent senators become representatives of the voivodeships where they were elected? (After all each of them could have been substituted by a cow on the ballot?)

To dismiss such silly questions it is necessary to realize that not an election was held in June of 1989 in Poland, but a repudiation. The Communists were shown the door by the people at the time—a momentous, historical, event no doubt, but not an election. It was a plebiscite, a referendum, and the difference between the two is very important. Plebiscites, unlike elections, are issue-specific. They provide resolution with respect to a narrowly defined, concrete question. In June 1989 a plebiscite was held whether continued rule by the Communist Party is acceptable to the Polish society. And the overwhelming majority of the society answered "no." It was, to repeat, a momentous, historical event, but nothing more. And while Poles were throwing Communists out in June of 1989, they were not empowering legislators. They were not giving a mandate to make laws to anybody. It should have been understood that June elections were but a costume for a "velvet" revolution and nobody elected at the time should have considered himself or herself an empowered representative of the people.

Since the issue of representation has come up let me pursue it one step further with reference to the Senate. A point to remember: a representative body is by definition derivative, it is but a reflection of something else. With the lower house, the Sejm, the matter is straightforward—the mechanism of representation is grounded in the principle of equality of citizens. They are represented in the Sejm. The citizens are sovereign. On the other hand Senate elections do not guarantee political equality of individuals. Citizens' votes have a different weight depending on whether they live in more or less populous voivodeships. It is voivodeships not citizens who are represented in the Senate. They are treated as sovereign by the electoral system which guarantees them equal input into the construction of that representative body.

And so again we have to ask ourselves a series of questions: in what sense is *pilskie, bydgoskie, leszczynskie,* or any other voivodeship, a sovereign? What would such sovereignty entail? What does collective identity of a voivodeship consist of? Nobody, I am afraid, could provide informative answers to these questions. It is impossible to tell collective identities of particular voivodeships, and it makes no sense to speak of them as sovereign. In fact, they don't really exist (I mean by that that they don't have socially rooted identifiable boundaries). They are a 17-year old artificial creation of a party boss who tried to protect what seemed like a good job against his colleagues' intrigues. Accordingly, he fragmented the country into small and awkward administrative units to deprive his potential future competitors of a power base. Voivodeships didn't perform well even this highly specialized assignment as Edward Gierek (the first secretary of PUWP who implemented administrative reform of the country) was overthrown not by his *Parteigenossen* but by the 1980 wave of workers' strikes. Since we are not concerned here with the history of People's Poland but with contemporary politics however, it is befitting simply to point out that something which does not exist cannot be sovereign and also cannot be represented.[9]

In general, I think, the issue of collective identity—indeed, collective identities—in Poland of the 1990s must be seriously considered. After half a century of application first of Hitler- and then Stalin-inspired meat grinders Polish society is indeed beaten up into an unfamiliar, featureless shape. Social bonds, group identities, have been shattered and they have to be identified, newly discovered, or nurtured back to reconstruct orderly political intercourse. Because political institutions are merely an instrument, they are but a transformation device, they have an input and an output and they must be shaped depending on what that input (i.e. collective identities) is like.

Senate mimicking the American arrangement in its present form makes no sense in the Polish Diet (though it makes sense in the US Congress), because of the difference in the political history and make-up of American and Polish societies.[10] Instead, perhaps a corporatist second chamber would be called for (i.e. would provide opportunity for representation of really existing collective identities) in Poland? At least one perplexing issue of Polish politics would go away if Solidarity did not have to invent a new identity for itself (as it has been repeatedly urged to do since June 89 elections) but could instead run a slot of candidates for a chamber of legislature. If collective identities with a nation-wide scope are so difficult to discover—just think of the impossibility of the political parties to take off in Poland—perhaps local or regional politics (where these identities ought to be more transparent, easier to discover or to nurture back) ought to be given more institutional backbone? (Say, truly empowered local assemblies in historical regions.)

I do not think there are easy answers to such questions and I am not surprised that good, "fitting," institutions are not yet in place. What worries me deeply however, is a lack of sustained, public debate of these issues. As if there were other more pressing things to decide first.

When Lech Walesa began to stake his presidential claims early in 1990, and the procedural issue concerning mechanics of presidential elections came up, his allies initially favored election by the parliament. This seemed most expedient at the time. Objection was voiced that the parliament is not representative because 65% of its lower house has been put there by the old regime. To this the then leading pro-Walesa politician (since then they have quarreled and are no longer on speaking terms) senator Jaroslaw Kaczynski replied that "even non-representative bodies can produce representative decisions." Less catching perhaps than Marie Antoinette's "let them eat cake," Kaczynski's *bon mot* is nonetheless far more ominous. For it has been uttered not by a royalty leaving historical stage but by an influential politician just entering upon it. Irrespective of the difficulties with privatization and restructuring of post-socialist economy the state of mind of the Founding Fathers of each republic will matter greatly for the future of liberty in East Central Europe.

One must conclude, unfortunately, that the 1989 revolution has temporarily lost its bearings. Its original inspiration to which we all bore witness was to constitute liberty not to repair a malfunctioning economy and overcome poverty—a fundamental distinction as we know from Hannah Arendt's discussion of legacies of the French and the American revolutions. But the 1989 revolution has disembowled itself with respect to "the political." It got rid of the vocabulary and in consequence abdicated political discourse. In Poland even the word "party" is shunned by all political actors. For many years, all over Central Europe one could not at all articulate a left of center position as the entire "collectivist" vocabulary was suspect. And, not surprisingly, it turned out that when half of the spectrum of the political discourse is eliminated the other half can no longer carry politics at all because it loses the power to discriminate.

So what remains is personalities and general appeals to common interest—a lukewarm, or not so lukewarm, nationalism. As the issue of privatization, demands for settling old scores (de-Communization through lustration laws), and personal recriminations tend to dominate in public debate for the outside observer it appears, increasingly, that the revolution has lost the sense of what it was all about—namely, institutionalization of liberty. In any case, it does not talk about it anymore.

But autonomy of politics remains for ever strong, and plays practical jokes on participants in the political process. The September 19, 1993 elections gave two thirds of parliamentary seats to successor parties of the Communist establishment—precisely what the then government coalition wanted to get in June of 1989. Primarily, this was an artifact of political circumstances: a combined result of a new electoral law which introduced thresholds, and fragmentation of the center-right spectrum of political parties. As a result, in a country which is 99% Catholic, there is no Christian Democratic party of any kind in the parliament, while post-Solidarity political parties—drawing altogether about two third of the popular vote—can do little but watch as the post-Communist parties put through a new constitution.

We should keep, of course, these critical observations in proper perspective. For the strides which have been made in East Central Europe on the way to pluralistic democracy are nothing short of miraculous. And if the public opinion over there is about equally divided (as national surveys across the region show with surprising consistency) as to what is the most important, defining feature of democracy—economic prosperity or ability to freely participate in the political process—it may be so, because free elections, freedom of assembly, and freedom of speech are already being taken there for granted. Such shared, matter-of-factly accepted convictions would be as important a stepping stone, metaphorically speaking, on the way back to Europe as written constitutions.

Notes

1. The notion of civil society has been elucidated over the last decade in numerous writings stemming from (and generated by) interest in East Central Europe. Narrowly constructed, civil society refers to the process of gradual empowering of society outside the framework of official institutions provided by the Communist state. It emphasizes, with perhaps a certain myopia—after all Communist establishments ought to be given some credit for having contributed to their own demise—that emancipation of East Central Europe did not require taking over the extant institutions. From the Worker's Defense Committee, through Charter 77 and Solidarity, up to the *Neues Forum* and the *Obcanske Forum,* enclaves of freedom where collective action took place were deliberately constructed apart and outside of them.
2. The subsequent chairman of the Citizens' Parliamentary Club, the most influential deputy in the Diet of the renewed Polish republic, Bronislaw Geremek, did not want to stand in the 1989 elections and agreed to run only when threateningly admonished to do so by Lech Walesa. Tadeusz Mazowiecki ironically dismissed in an editorial note Adam Michnik's precocious idea, "Your President, our Prime Minister," but later he was tapped by Walesa to assume the very office on behalf of Solidarity. And most importantly, Lech Walesa did not let himself be elected into the parliament or appointed as head of government. In addition, he deliberately handed the office of presidency to General Jaruzelski the first time it was for the taking. Two symbolically most important Solidarity activists after Walesa, Wladyslaw Frasyniuk and Zbigniew Bujak, also did not enter any institutions and for over a year (until ROAD was established in July 1990) could not find a place for themselves in the new reality of Polish politics.
3. This authentication was not carried through to the end in Poland but was far enough advanced to create the sense of state institutions having been reappropriated by society.

4. It can still be created by spontaneous association, of course, but this introduces only marginal differences since there is so much of it in institutionally well defined locations.
5. The opposition could hardly be blamed for this state of affairs as there were no provisions then under the law to construct such a representation at all and, in any case, the organization which was de facto sitting on the opposition side of the table—Solidarity—was at the time illegal.
6. Once improvisation replaces behavior according to rules, it tends to proliferate. Accordingly, there was a round table within the round table negotiations proper—a series of meetings between Walesa and Interior Minister Kiszczak with a small entourage of their closest advisors—to quietly negotiate over the most difficult issues. They were held in a secluded government villa at Magdalenka. And the specter of this Magdalenka returned to haunt the first Solidarity sponsored government of Tadeusz Mazowiecki. Simultaneously with Walesa's challenge, since early spring of 1991, insinuations were passed around that secret deals advantageous to the Communists were made at Magdalenka. Presumably this cast a shadow on Mazowiecki's team and the group of Solidarity activists which spearheaded the challenge to the old regime and masterminded the transition—the Geremek, Kuron, Michnik, Bujak milieu. It was conveniently forgotten that Walesa was present at Magdalenka as indeed were key figures from the Catholic hierarchy as well. The atmosphere soured enough for the Secretary of the Episcopate, bishop Alojzy Orszulik, to issue a denial on June 7, 1990 stating that no secret agreements were concluded at Magdalenka. It didn't help when his office simultaneously declared that no transcripts of negotiations were kept by anyone. The legitimacy of the Mazowiecki government was seriously undermined by recurring rumors on the subject.
7. Just think of the guru of foreign policy expertise, Henry Kissinger, making sure that President Gerald Ford does not receive Aleksandr Solzhenitsyn in the White House. For this far sighted *Realpolitiker* undoubtedly Leonid Brezhnev and his successors embodied the future of the Soviet Union.
8. What a coincidence indeed—to a problem of acknowledged unprecedented complexity (transforming wholesale a socialist into a market economy)—there is suddenly only one solution and the man who got it right happens to be the economics czar. How lucky you can get. For Poland this is certainly the first time around in its long history of repeated bad luck and misfortunes.
9. I understand that the arrangements for setting up the upper house of the Polish Diet were hastily put together during Round Table negotiations, that they were purely opportunistic, and that they were a wonderful scoop of the opposition for they allowed to show unambiguously how thoroughly the Polish society rejected Communist rule. But this was some years ago. Since then the business of politics was not to throw out the Communists but to construct legitimate authority.
10. Individual states have had real, distinct collective identities in America. The bloodiest war in US history was fought over the issue of states' sovereignty.

10

Conservatism in Central and Eastern Europe

George Schöpflin

The first problem in any consideration of conservatism in Central and Eastern Europe is to define one's terms. At the simplest level, the word "conservative" has two different meanings. It can either refer to the desire to maintain the old and a corresponding reluctance to accept the new or it can refer to a political current which nominally expresses these attitudes to continuity and change. These definitions immediately give rise to new difficulties. While the concepts of old and new may be straightforward enough, their politicisation is far from clearly delineated. Besides, "old" and "new" cannot be absolute categories, rather they involve choice of which elements of the old to retain and which to discard, thereby raising the problem of criteria and content of conservatism. Hence these cannot in any sense be "pure" terms, but are conventional and contingent, dependent on the historical, political and geographical context.

Conservatism as a political philosophy starts from the proposition that tension cannot be eliminated from human relations, only eased by various arrangements and that the quest for an ideal or perfect society is liable to create greater imperfection than minimal intervention. Consequently, it rejects the liberal argument that an ideal set of institutions will allow for humanity's inherent goodness to flourish; that satisfactory institutions can be legitimated by reason, for rationalism is no more than the distillation of existing political traditions; that the human will has unbounded capacity to shape human destiny; and that popular sovereignty will invariably produce good government.

The proponents of ordered and planned change under modern conditions, be they liberal or socialist, take the view that social and political relations must be determined by the impersonal character of society that is framed by a juridical order that gives no special status to any one member of the community. In an ideal-typical way, reference to the past, to blood-ties, religion or ethnicity are not regarded as relevant to this, on the contrary. Conservatism as it has been expressed in democratic politics can broadly be regarded as the political current that seeks to combine elements of the modern with appropriate elements of the past and coming to terms with transformation gradually.[1] The motto of the true conservative, therefore, is "We must change a little, in order that we may remain the same".[2]

The German tradition of conservatism has its intellectual roots in the reaction to the French Revolution, which it completely rejected, together with any idea of popular participation and popular sovereignty, preferring to call upon the concept of an unchanging social order in which hierarchy and state predominated. To an extent, this fused with nationalism and one development of it led to National Socialism. However, with the defeat of the latter, German conservatism was discredited and potential conservative currents were incorporated into Christian Democracy. In the post-war period, it found expression in its emphasis on order, discipline and hostility to the democratisation of social and economic life.

At the same time, there are numerous expressions of conservative behaviour that are not linked with conservative politics, but can and do influence the political order. This paper will attempt to look both at conservatism as a political current in Central and Eastern Europe and, equally, at aspects of conservatism and conservative attitudes in post-communist politics and societies, but the two will be kept conceptually separate.

Conservative Political Parties

In Western Europe since the Second World War, conservatism as a political movement has had two contrary propositions to integrate into its frame of reference. It has had to accept and manage the political arrangements derived from the welfare state paradigm, while at the same time, it has sought to make some provision for individual choice. It has, therefore, looked for legitimation in two separate areas, one traditional and one modern. Its compromise with the welfare state is argued in terms of social protectionism, the traditional community, religion in the case of Christian Democracy and the values of the past, whilst the protection of individual choice is structured by reference to freedom not bound by tradition. What is largely missing from the current armoury of the right is reference to nationhood or empire and, for that matter, religion is much more an ultimate value than a day-to-day one. The inherent tension between traditional conservatism and what is termed the neo-liberal wing of conservatism has not impeded Western European conservative parties in their quest for power; indeed, it is likely that this tension has been creative.

The situation in the post-communist world is very different. The modernisation of conservative agendas has not taken place for the very simple reason that under communism, there was no reason or utility in conceptualising conservatism at all. In as much as there was a political debate during the communist period, it took place within the broad framework of Marxism. With the disappearance of communism, however, a large number of political groupings reemerged into the daylight with little or no idea of what it actually meant to be conservative in the conditions of the 1990s.[3]

The particular irony of the situation in the post-communist systems of Central and Eastern Europe, which goes beyond a mere semantic reference, is that in as much as a conservative looks to preserve the past, he will be faced with the choice of which past, the immediate past or the pre-communist past. Strictly, it can be argued a conservative's remit is to keep whatever elements from the past that he regards as the most valuable and most stabilising for the purposes of society. Yet in the present circumstances, this would lead to the paradoxical conclusion that a conservative's task is to preserve communism. This is obviously nonsense, so that a more complex model must be adopted.

To look at a historical precedent of constructing a post-revolutionary order, the French conservatives after the post-Napoleonic restoration had a simpler task. They took some of the elements of the ancien régime when they came to construct a new order in 1815, central to which was the reestablishment of a monarchy as the dominant legitimating principle. In this sense, there was a clear reaching back into the pre-revolutionary political order for creating the key institutions of the new framework. By contrast, the conservatives of the post-communist world are in a state of confusion. They would like to reject the whole of the communist experience, which is obviously impossible; they would like ideally to go back to the pre-communist system; while at the same time they are committed to building a liberal democracy. These are difficult to reconcile, essentially because the establishment of a liberal democracy involves conservatives in innovation, not least because the pre-communist régimes were hardly democratic and, equally, liberal democracy has been thoroughly reshaped in the intervening period.

Innovation is not, of course, entirely alien to conservatives; but the question, as already suggested, is what to change and by what criteria. The broad objective of liberal democracy and market economy is set and cannot be altered, not least because it is safeguarded by the legitimating principle of the transformation and by the international order. The question is how post-communist conservatives should deal with the processes engendered by democracy and markets.

The situation is further complicated by the fact that the left, as conventionally understood, suffered an enormous, epoch-making defeat with the collapse of communism. This has placed an extra burden on the movements that define themselves as the "right", in as much as they are called upon to begin the process of formulating alternatives to the programmes of the left, to clear up the economic, political and social mess left behind by communism and to create a wholly new political system with a degree urgency. The movements describing themselves as conservative have been looking at the experience of the West and their own history, but neither can be adequate guide for present, because the countries of Central and Eastern Europe have been through a non-Western experience and pre-communist past cannot be an adequate guide for these societies, precisely because they have been thoroughly transformed by communism. Thus the traditional peasant question has disappeared—the Polish and Hungarian peasantry have different values from those of the 1930s or 1940s; industrialisation has created new social structures, aspirations and disciplines; and these countries now have some of the elements of a modern legal-rational type of bureaucracy.

Consequently, those who call themselves conservative in the new post-communist order are engaged in defining their agendas and are doing so in a state of some confusion. These agendas on the evidence to date are significantly different from those of their nominal counterparts in Western Europe. In effect, what these movements have been engaged in is to look for ideologies rather than policies and to find these in nationhood, religion, morality and status. Thus tradition and religion have a saliency far greater than in the West. The right under post-communism has been tending to emphasise nationhood, patriotism and also includes populist elements in its make-up. Furthermore, the evidence from Poland and to a lesser extent Hungary suggests a desire for charismatic leadership; this is also present in Czecho-Slovakia (see the career of Václav Klaus), but it would be, for example, difficult to associate Havel with conservatism as such.

Havel is unusual in one respect, in that he is one of the few post-communist leaders whose views on what kind of a society he would like to see are a matter of public record. What emerges, in summary form, from what Havel has written is that he has a rather organic, anti-political view of the political process, with a distrust of organisation and an insistence that the political system should be the expression of the actions of the sum total of responsible individuals. Constitutions, the law, structures, ideologies and institutions tend to be distrusted in Havel's philosophy and there is more than a hint of his belief in a kind of social harmony, based on the authenticity of experience and not on alienating modernity. Indeed, there is a flavour of an anti-technological Romanticism in his writings and an implicit suggestion that a Third Road between capitalism and communism is possible. To be fair, there has been no indication on Havel's part that he actually intends to put any of this into practice. There is an interesting parallel here with the intellectual career of Thomas Masaryk, who similarly entertained organic concepts of the state before he moved into active politics, but made no attempt to translate these into political practice when in office.[4]

What is very clear, however, is that post-communist conservatives have a strong commitment to the state and to étatism. This, of course, has several explanations. There are étatist legacies from the inter-war period, to which reference is made as a source of conservatism; a clear inclination to rely on paternalism, given a tacit belief that élites are better fitted to govern than the people; from the hyper-étatism created by the communists; and from the structures and practices inherited from the communist system. The fact that this goes parallel with pro-market rhetoric should not be allowed to obscure the reality of a strong state role, in which previous habits, like a patronage system that bears of certain resemblance to the *nomenklatura* and appointments are made on the basis of party political loyalty rather than technical expertise, either remain or have revived. There is much to be said for the proposition that the natural response of post-communist conservatives is to turn to state regulation rather than accept the apparent "disorder" of the multiplicity of individual action.

There is another factor that enhances rather than hinders this approach. The communist tradition has instilled a rather curious concept of change in the countries of Central and Eastern Europe, albeit this has its pre-communist roots. Rather than regard change as a constant, steady process, communism conceptualised it as a single, one-off event, which then needed no further attention. Once something was, let us say, built, it could then be left alone, because it had been achieved. This attitude probably had its roots in the utopian triumphalism of the Soviet-type culture and is at variance with liberal democratic ideas of constant readjustment to new impulses. The pre-communist roots derive from the peasant view of change as being something to be equated with messianic change, i.e., a single overwhelming event, to which may be added the romantic nationalist concept of "revolution" as a more or less desirable way of effecting change, rather than viewing it as a failure of the political system. All this adds up to a paradoxical, contrary perception of change as something sudden and radical, then followed by periods of inactivity. The upshot is a surprisingly static and suspicious approach to political reform.

Factors of Conservatism

At this point, the conceptual distinction between conservatism as a political movement and conservatism in society becomes operative. However, it is now necessary to define the criteria against which this second type of conservatism should be understood, i.e., what is to be regarded as non-conservative. Essentially, this is the cluster of factors and processes to do with change, complexity and choice—the central components of modernity—and the factors that impede or retard these can be described as conservative in the second sense as used in this paper. At the operational level, factors that can be analysed as in some way being antagonistic to the introduction and functioning of liberal democracy will be classified as conservative. It should be understood that the following list is far from exhaustive and that these currents assessed in the following may frequently interact and should not be seen in isolation.

Thought-Worlds

Of considerable significance in this list, not least because it potentially affects a very wide range of phenomena, is the nature of the thought-worlds of post-communist societies.[5] The political élites of these states, as well as economic, bureaucratic, intellectual and similar élites, have been enfolded in particular thought-worlds—those of Marxism-Leninism and the opposition to Marxism-Leninism—and are, presumably, looking to escape from these confines. The essential characteristics of this thought-world may be defined as a certain propensity to see processes in black-and-white terms, to treat compromise with suspicion, to be reluctant to practise the tolerance needed to sustain competing points of view, to be slow in adapting to new situations and to the flexibility in the face of new developments that democratic practice requires for effectiveness. The communist legacy is antagonistic to these attitudes, given its utopian, perfectionist and reductionist characteristics. Inevitably, the opponents of Marxism-Leninism have come to resemble what they opposed—a common enough phenomenon—and, precisely because they felt that they had to develop a fundamentally negative approach to the ruling communist value system, which they regarded as illegitimate, they tended to adopt many of its features. Ultimately they can all be described as the infantile disorders of societies that have lived with closed systems.[6]

In this process, one can single out a number of factors. Thus there is a certain tendency in these post-communist polities to use words as a substitute for deeds, to regard high-flown language, a declaration of principle as tantamount to action. Second, there is strong current of conspiracy-mindedness, a firm and unshakeable belief that there is a link, usually a causal nexus, between seemingly unconnected events and a rejection of attempts to offer alternative explanations as "naive". Frequently accompanying this view of the world is the automatic assumption that hostile intentions hide behind apparently innocent words and the rejection of explanations that suggest coincidence or chance as factors. In this thought-world, an explanation is found for all phenomena that justify the initial assumptions and data that do not conform are simply ignored or given an explanation consonant with the original assumption. When confronted with empirical reality at variance with the assumptions, the proponents of this thought process reject it.

Next, there is a strong, sometimes unshakeable belief in the "single truth", that it is possible to know with absolute certainty and reject epistemological doubt. This near naive insistence in there being a single "scientific" truth was strongly argued by Marxism-Leninism, but the exaggerated respect for "learning" in pre-modern societies must also have played a role here. Correspondingly, there is a rejection of ambiguity, the dogmatism of which is at times close to morbid, as if the very idea that there could be more than one answer to a particular question was inherently threatening. Coupled with this is the unstated belief that the world is black and white, that there is only one answer to questions, in a word that things are knowable in a one-dimensional fashion. This kind of epistemological certainty has largely disappeared in the West. This legacy makes compromise difficult, not least because for the bearers of this world-view, compromise is dishonourable and ignoble.

There is, too, a flight into abstraction, a reluctance to establish a clear link between word and concrete reality. Indeed, there is a broad pattern in these cultures which distrusts factuality and prefers abstraction and pathos, making the real situation hard to assess in certain circumstances.[7] This particular phenomenon has several sources feeding it, notably a tradition of communication by inference and allegory deriving from the constraints of censorship. A long term tradition of powerlessness on the part of society and the experience of attempting to communicate indirectly has inevitably given rise to patterns where abstraction is no longer seen as a faute de mieux reaction to oppression, but has acquired a life of its own and even a legitimacy that is inimical to more concrete modes of expression. An illustration of this may be found in the complex, abstruse quality of the language used by Hungarian samizdat in the 1970s and 1980s; intended to side-step the problem of censorship and self-censorship favoured in the Kádár period, the language of the Hungarian opposition was as convoluted as that of officialdom. Czech and Polish patterns were not that different.

It has also been suggested that the lateness and suddenness of absorbing a more or less fully fledged intellectual tradition from the

West, the repeated experience of top-down transformation from abroad, may likewise be relevant in this connection. Rather than the organic process of developing a culture over time in response to direct challenges, in Central and Eastern Europe intellectuals were regularly faced with the problem of catching and sought to do so by importing ideas wholesale from the West, without ever having had time to adapt these to local conditions. This has inevitably left these ideas floating in the air somewhat, as the concepts they were supposed to denote were still in the process being defined, rather than the other way round.

Another relevant factor in this section is the problem of overpoliticisation. In systems where everything has been given a political significance, it is impossible to create neutral space. Spheres other than the political sphere—economic, legal, aesthetic etc.—cannot be easily defined by their own criteria, but are politicised. Thus when the political actors in a particular situation see everything in political terms, it is automatic that all questions will be judged by political criteria. It is an easy step from here to impute political motives to all manifestations, whether regarded as positive or as negative, and from there to assume political conspiracies as the best explanation.

This is then legitimated by reference to one's own sophistication and the other's naiveté. In this mind-set, it becomes naive to see things in terms of accident, happenstance or coincidence. This is effectively a kind of political paranoia or hysteria, a closed intellectual system. If everyone acts as if all the actors were politically motivated, then self-defence breeds a political reaction and thereby perpetuates the intellectual paranoia through a self-fulfilling prophecy. The real danger of this phenomenon, for which there is any amount of evidence from the post-communist world, is that for all practical purposes it reproduces something akin to the Soviet-type system, in as much as it denies the possibility of the middle ground and works on the presumption that all games are zero-sum. This makes compromise and bargaining virtually impossible.

Finally in this section, there is the problem of exercising choice. Choosing is not a natural, automatic response to situations, but has to be learned. Societies which have been starved of the range of choice or actually prevented from choosing at all, as these societies were under Stalinism, develop immune reactions, devices for avoiding the externally imposed powerlessness.[8] By the same token, the Soviet-type approach to decision-making was calculated to diffuse individual responsibility by insisting that it be collective. A collective decision imposes no responsibility on anyone, but ensures that the factors involved become vague, hard to pin down and generally "soft".[9] This diffuseness is hard to reconcile with the demands of democracy, which does not mean that it is unknown in the West, but the scale of it and the way in which it is regarded as the norm indicate that it poses problems of a particular difficulty in the post-communist world.

Religion

Religion has played a contradictory role in Central and Eastern Europe. It has simultaneously been a democratising and an anti-democratising force, especially in the countries of Latin Christianity. Christianity is, of course, entirely irreconcilable with the bases of Marxism-Leninism and notionally it must be in total opposition to it; certainly, this was how the communists perceived religion. On the other hand, the churches were obliged to live with and within the communist system and to that extent were constrained to evolve various compromises with it. Essentially, the churches largely accepted the power of the state over organisation in this world, but contested that power when it sought to encroach on the care of souls. Inevitably the possibility of friction and conflict was endless, over religious education for example, but a modus vivendi was reached. The Latin churches applied the principle of rendering unto Caesar what they thought was appropriate and insisted on what was due to God. In the case of Poland, the church's definition of what was due to God increased steadily with the years.[10] To that extent, it undermined the power of the communist system.

On the other hand, there were also areas where a tacit intellectual overlap between church and state existed, notably in the matter of the acceptance of dogma and the arguments used to sustain it. In this respect, the static, conformist attitudes promoted by communism after the initial revolutionary period were wittingly or not sustained by the church and to that extent weakened individual responsibility and choice. A good illustration of this came, again from Poland in the 1980s, by which time the party-state had largely retreated from some areas of social-cultural provision, leaving this to the Roman Catholic church. The church did not in any sense use this space to promote subversive doctrines, but in effect stabilised the situation for the state by meeting various demands and thereby defused possible dissatisfaction.

However, in addition to conserving patterns, there were other aspects of religion that have come to function as sources of conservatism in the present. First there is the traditional conflict between religion as a natural, unchanging order and the claims of modernity. By anchoring itself in a transcendental vision and proclaiming salvation in the next world, Christian religion—Orthodoxy more than Latinity—promotes a degree of passivity, acceptance of the present and weakens individual achievement. The second has already been mentioned, viz. the role of hierarchy and obedience. It is evident that hierarchy is in direct conflict with the equality of opportunity proclaimed by democracy and hierarchical thinking seriously constricts the political-juridical order supposedly based on the equality of all before the law.

Orthodoxy

Third, there is the particular difficulty of Orthodoxy. Put simply, whereas Latin Christianity seeks to integrate behaviour and belief, Orthodoxy and the cultures derived from it deemphasise belief in favour of conformity to externally imposed norms sanctioned not by conscience but by communal pressure. This pattern is known as externalisation or orthopraxy. It follows logically that such cultures are in a doubly difficult position in attempting to wrestle with the demands of democracy, in as much as they have the legacy of two, to some extent mutually reinforcing, closed systems to live with. Orthodoxy is as much a closed system as communism, except that its offer of a utopia pertains to the next world rather than this one.[11]

The saliency of form over content, the emphasis on contemplation rather than action and the perception of action as futile, the long periods of inactivity punctuated by outbursts of purposeless bouts of action, the prominence of the community over the individual, the weakness of futurity and the consequent tendency to dismiss anything related to future performance (agreements, contracts, treaties) as meaningless, soulless and empty are all characteristic of these cultures. Understandably it is difficult, to put it at its lowest, to establish the bonds and structures needed for democracy when building on cultures such as these. None of the foregoing should be understood in a deterministic way, however. Cultures are not set in concrete, they can be transformed though only over a long time. The problem for South-East Europe is that the Europeanised élites that might have set this transformation in train have either been eviscerated (Romania) or too closely linked with communism and swept away with its collapse (Serbia) or divided and contending for power (Bulgaria). The last 15 years in Greece suggest that change in Orthodox societies is possible, though difficult.

The Family

In some respects the use of the family and its ramifications can also act as a factor of conservatism. The essence of the argument is that family relations in the post-communist countries are far more tradition-bound than is the case with their counterparts in the West. In part, this is the result of the role that the family was obliged to play under communism, when it was one of the few authentic social spaces, in which the individual was relatively free of state interference. This inevitably endowed the family with political functions that it could not easily meet. At the same time, economic circumstances—a very severe housing shortage—has given rise to great problems in household formation, in that it proved extremely difficult for young persons to establish their own, separate existence. Several generations were obliged to live together in the same household, with the result that the authority of the older generations could not be challenged in the same way as in the West and parental power has remained much stronger. This has allowed the evolution of political currents under post-communism that have looked to an ideal-typical family as a source of positive values, ignoring the proposition that individual choice is significantly curtailed as a result and hierarchical, anti-innovative values have been conserved.

Intellectuals

The way in which intellectuals occupy certain positions and exercise certain functions can equally give rise to form of conservatism. Some of these have already been discussed in the section on thought-worlds above, but these structures and functions can and do pose problems for free choice and opportunity. The argument in this section is based in the first place on Bauman's identification of intellectuals as messianic legislators claiming a monopoly of rationality.[12] When secular intellectuals first entered the European scene with the Enlightenment, they found themselves in the West in a fairly complex social matrix, competing for power, status and influence with the declining neo-feudal élites and the rising bourgeoisie.

In Central and Eastern Europe, on the other hand, they encountered no such resistance, given the weakness of society and the remoteness of the ruling élites. Hence they were able to establish a preeminent position for themselves as surrogates with a wide range of functions that had no parallel in Western Europe. Crucially, they were able largely to seize the agenda of nationhood and attempted to arrogate to themselves the definition of moral, political and cultural universes. By the current period, this claim has acquired near traditional legitimation and has become very difficult to challenge, not least because their role was repeatedly reinforced by the communist experience of oppression and their preeminence in the collapse of communism.

Intellectuals and Power

However, the transformation has seen something new, in that considerable numbers of intellectuals have come closer to political power than ever and, indeed, they are actively determining the shape and content of the new political systems. There are a number of problems associated with this and these require further study. In the first place, there is a clear conflict between the role of intellectual and the role of politician.[13] Whereas the intellectual is supposed to clarify situations through his critiques of the present and to formulate alternative variants of the future, the politician's role is to integrate conflicting interests by establishing the least unacceptable compromise, i.e. to blur boundaries and avoid clarity. The expertise of the politician is politics, rather than technical knowledge. However, in post-communist systems these definitions are not widely understood and the intellectuals now in power seem loath to elaborate them, not least because that would undermine their own status and power.

To this may be added the intellectuals' tutelage over society, the intellectual élitism of the Central and East European tradition, which has generally been suspicious of demotic inputs into politics, regarding at best as a vulgar, populist irrelevance and at worst as an unmitigated evil deeply threatening to the "progress" claimed as the heritage of the enlightened intellectual. To some extent this assessment is stereotypical, but these stereotypes continue to play a role—notably in

Poland, where the conflict between Mazowiecki and Walesa could at least in part be interpreted in these categories. Analogous currents are visible in Czecho-Slovakia and Hungary.

Thirdly, the control of the language of public discourse by intellectuals and their insistence on using a high-flown, abstract form of expression unquestionably hinders democratic development, above all because it detaches the individual from politics and makes it very difficult for the individual to become a citizen in the strict sense. The language of public discourse, instead of aiding comprehension and political communication, acts as an obstacle to transparency and at the same time, of course, also as a source of power for intellectuals, by legitimating their control and power.

Information Flows

Finally, there is the problem of information and modernity. In these societies, there is clear evidence of inexperience with the handling of information, of how information is to be interpreted, weighed and acted on. In part, this is the legacy of the intellectual paternalism just discussed and in part of the highly restrictive information policy practised by the communists. The monopoly of information of the communist system of rule and the way in which it was used as a source of power and blackmail has served to infantilise the population and to encourage it regard information as something untrustworthy and to be treated with suspicion. This has bred habits of interpretation that are clearly inimical to easy communication, because they tend to read between the lines and to overinterpret what is presented. The way in which ideas are understood, as noted above in the section on thought-worlds, is unhelpful in this regard, in that black-and-white world views and conspiracy-mindedness make it difficult for institutions to be seen as real.

There is inexperience, too, with the sudden rush of incoming information. Presumably, it will only be a matter of time until new modes of absorbing, assessing and digesting information are mastered, but for the time being, there is a suspicion that public opinion in Central and Eastern Europe is non-plussed by the information overload that it is encountering and that it is responding to it with passivity.

Finally, there is a strong current of personalising information, of regarding it as reliable only if it has some kind of individual's imprimatur on it, i.e. it is to be trusted because X says so. Here one can clearly see the weakness of institutions against persons. This is, as in other matters, attributable to pre-communist and to communist patterns. Pre-modern societies greatly prefer face-to-face communication and, indeed, are distrustful of and hostile to the impersonal modes of exchanging information developed under modernity. In the communist system, everything official was deeply distrusted, hence the preference for what could be personally assessed. The legacy of this is the continuing personalisation of information, where commentaries and interviews take the place of reportage and analysis. The detachment, emotionally value free nature of the latter are not fully trusted.

Nationalism

Nationalism in Central and Eastern Europe is a further source of conservative thought. Among some nationalists, there is a strong adherence to rigid definitions of acceptable and unacceptable behaviour in politics and it is relatively straightforward to seek to delegitimise one's opponents by accusing them of "unpatriotic" behaviour, with some expectation of a receptive audience from among a relatively untutored population. Nationalism feeds into rather static modes of thought, which perceive the nation as an unchanging category, usually inherent or immanent, and reject any suggestion that there nationhood is subject to political influences like other activities and that the content of the national ideology may be influenced by debate. There is, in any case, more than a hint of organic ideas of society at the deeper levels of nationalism, in as much as it looks to a future in which all members of the nation will have equal access to the state and power and do not need intermediate institutions. In moments of crisis, in particular, the invocation of nationhood can be potentially effective in excluding all other arguments, given that one of the functions of nationhood is to make provision for the affective dimension of politics and as a result, the outpouring of collective emotion severely curtails the possible options open to politics. The backward-looking aspects of nationalism in Central and Eastern Europe, the stress on the ethnic elements of nationhood—history, descent, symbols and rituals—can likewise contribute to introversion and hostility to change and choice.

In conclusion, one can see under post-communism a variety of interlocking and interacting features, which are sources of conservatism, in as much as they impede the impersonal judgements and free interchanges that are characteristic of modern liberal democracy. The inclination to resort to absolute value systems is a serious obstacle to tolerance and compromise, without which no democracy can function. And there is effectively no modern party of the right that can begin the process of modernising conservatism.

Notes

1. Leszek Kolakowski, "Nach dem Tod des historischen Menschen", *Frankfurter Allgemeine Zeitung,* 14 April 1991.
2. Giuseppe de Lampedusa, *The Leopard,* (London, 1970), p. 22.
3. I have explored this in greater detail in George Schöpflin, "Der unterentwickelte Konservativismus in Ungarn", *Europäische Rundschau,* Vol. 19, No. 1 (Winter 1991), pp. 51–58.
4. Havel's ideas are set out in *The Power of the Powerless,* (London, 1985) and *Disturbing the Peace,* (London, 1990). On Masaryk, see Eva Schmidt-Hartmann, *Thomas Masaryk's Realism: the Origins of a Czech Political Concept,* (Munich, 1984).
5. On thought-worlds, see Mary Douglas, *How Institutions Think,* (Syracuse, NY, 1986).
6. On closed systems, see István Bibó, "A politikai hisztériák természetrajza", *Az európai egyensúlyról és békéröl,* in *Válogatott Tanulmányok, 1935–1944,* Vol. 1, (Budapest, 1986), especially pp. 376–380.
7. Witold Wirpsza, *Pole wer bist du?,* (Luzern, 1971) analyses this phenomenon in Poland, but it can be found elsewhere.
8. László Bogár, *A fejlödés ára,* (Budapest, 1983).
9. János Kornai, *A hiány,* (Budapest, 1982) discusses this in the context of the "soft-budget constraint", a concept that has become associated with his name.
10. Józef Tischner, *The Spirit of Solidarity,* (London, 1984).
11. Mózes P. Gábor, "A bizánci paradigma", *Valóság,* Vol. 28, No. 12, (December 1985), pp. 95–104.
12. Zygmunt Bauman, "Intellectuals in East-Central Europe: Continuity and Change", *Eastern European Politics and Societies,* Vol. 1, No. 2 (Spring 1987), pp. 162–186.
13. On the role of the politician, see Max Weber, "Politik als Beruf", *Gesammelte Politische Schriften,* 2. Auflage, (Tübingen, 1958), pp. 534 et seq. Weber emphasised "Leidenschaft im Sinn von Sachlichkeit", responsibility and detachment (Distanz) as the necessary qualities that a politician must possess and warned against vanity (Eitelkeit) as something that undermined distance and responsibility; given the role of violence in politics, an ethically based use of power was paramount, he insisted. (English edition, "Politics as a Vocation", in (eds.) H.H. Gerth and C. Wright Mills, *From Max Weber,* (London, 1948), pp. 115ff.)

III

From Civil Society to Civil Disobedience? On the Sociology of Transformation

11

The Forgotten Legacy of Marginal Intellectuals

Ivan Bernik

The discussions of the role of intellectuals in Central and East-European socialist societies were strongly influenced by the thesis that the "maturation" of these societies led to the gradual acquisition of political power by intellectuals (see Konrád and Szelényi, 1979; Gouldner, 1979; Szelényi, 1986–87). From this point of view, the collapse of socialist regimes can be seen as the final step of intellectuals to the dominant political positions. In this paper I would like to show that the role of the intellectuals in the transition from authoritarian to democratic regimes should be looked at in a much more differentiated way. The problem will be addressed on relatively abstract level, but some illustrations, related to the developments in Slovenia, will be also given.

Although the thesis on the rise of intellectuals to "class power" in socialist societies focused almost exclusively—as argued by some critics (Schlesinger, 1982)—on the role of technocracy as the supposed avantgarde of the knowledge stratum, the thesis could not entirely overlook internal differentiation of intellectuals. Konrád and Szelányi paid some attention to a sub-group of intellectuals, whose growing importance should accompany the rise of technocrats to political power positions. They called this group the marginal intelligentsia. The term indicates the basic characteristics of this sub-group; it is marginal in the sense that it has no direct access to political power. But this enables the group to keep a reflective and critical distance not only vis-à vis the political authorities, but also to social reality at large. Regarding this, Konrád and Szelányi drew on M. Rakovski who, in the analysis of the intellectual stratum in Eastern Europe, stressed that this sub-group of intellectuals was capable of creating its own ideology and culture and even its own counter-culture and the embryo of counter-institutions. The basis of this creativity is communication among the members of the marginal intellectuals, which manages to escape the control of the Communist Party. This communication "forms, in the framework of science and culture, a public sphere which serves as functional equivalent of political discussion and organization of the participants" (Rakovski, 1986: 64). At least for this group of intellectuals, we could freely use Gouldner's term "speech community", which, according to him, refers to the whole knowledge stratum. Of special interest, in the ranks of marginal intellectuals, is the sub-group whose endeavors to preserve its autonomy from official ideology lead it into open conflict with the "official" cultural and political standards. Rakovski called the members of this sub-group "marginalized nonconformist intellectuals" (1986: 77).

An attempt at a more detailed definition of the marginal intellectuals reveals that they have, as a sub-stratum, only few common denominators. Its members were active in different functional fields within the framework of different formal organizations. Their primary shelter was—without special mention of the self-employed—the university and other research and cultural organizations. However, it should be borne in mind that these organizations did not "host" only nonconformist intellectuals, and that tolerance towards intellectual nonconformism was highly variable in time. From this point of view, intellectual nonconformism was highly mobile: it managed to establish itself and survive in niches inside different organizational settings. The church, as one of the rare organizations, which in socialist societies to a large degree escaped the control of the political elite, played an important role in countries where the marginal intelligentsia had very little room to manoeuvre (Pollack, 1990).

On the basis of this characterisation of marginal intellectuals, it cannot be hypothesised that they could play an active role in transforming the socialist societies. It seems much more probable that their role was limited to the critical reflection of reality, but they had no effective means to influence the course of change. At best, they could act as ideologues of the "real" social forces, such as technocracy, as suggested by Konrád and Szelányi. In the next section we will try to question this proposition, arguing that this sub-group of intellectuals played a much more important role than the term "marginal" suggests.

An attempt to account for the role of marginal intellectuals in "mature" socialist societies presupposes at least a passing discussion of the basic systemic characteristics of socialist societies, especially of the obstacles which prevented a successful "reformation" of these societies within their own systemic borders.

We shall proceed from the thesis that the key characteristic of all the socialist systems was the difference between the rulers and the ruled. This difference did not determine only the political system; due to the low level of separation between politics, economics, law, science, etc., the functioning of the whole societal system was dependent on this difference as well. The deepening crisis of the legitimacy of political authority in socialist societies in the 1980s (see Fehér et al., 1983; Pakulski, 1986; Rychard, 1989) implied that the reproduction of the difference was increasingly endangered. In spite of the fact that more and more resources (from economic to ideological ones) were "invested" on the part of the rulers to assure stable communication between them and the ruled, the number of disruptions in this communication grew. The sporadic reform attempts from above in countries like Yugoslavia, Hungary and Poland generated only limited change; they increased divisions between "ideologists" and "pragmatists" within the ruling elite, but left the dichotomous power structure unchanged. A no less important, though less visible, indicator of control was the broadening of the "second society", i.e. of self-organised activities, more or less independent of intervention by the political authorities (see Hankiss, 1988; Bernik, 1990).

The ability of marginal intellectuals to create a relatively autonomous sphere of communication can be seen in this context as an important phenomenon of "second society". Cultural capital, the resource at the disposal of the intellectuals, cannot be entirely controlled politically. Marginal intellectuals use this fact to create a highly autonomous and specific communication area. In other words, all who wish to participate in creating and maintaining this area belong to marginal intellectuals.

The first signs of the resurgence of intellectual nonconformism appeared in Slovenia in the early eighties. The attempts of the political elite to eliminate any form of dissent, which characterised the political life in the seventies, were losing momentum. The repressive measures had not been directed only to political dissent; even the "deviations" in culture, especially in social sciences, were also enclosed in small enclaves and thus marginalised. The first change was felt just in this field: "The transition between 'alternative culture' and 'generally acceptable' or 'official' one became soft (in the eighties, I.B.), . . . whereas the situation in the forties, seventies and also the sixties was much harder, exclusivistic and conflict ridden" (Rupel, 1987: 243). The growing autonomy of cultural activities created possibilities for relatively free and public discussion in which also themes which were not strictly "cultural", were addressed. It was not surprising that the first forms of political dissent, such as the criticism of dominant ideology and of certain political decisions, were couched in "cultural" terms.

An important sign of growing autonomy of cultural activities was also the ability of some forms of youth subculture to withstand the repression. This subculture opened the room for an "autonomous social action" which was, in the middle of the eighties, filled up by new social movements, especially by peace, ecological, feminist and gay movements (see Mastnak, 1990: 440–2). In these movements younger intellectuals played an important role. These intellectuals gradually took over the weekly "*Mladina*" (The Youth) which in the mid-eighties became an influential place for alternative ideas and bitter social criticism.

Although perceived by their protagonists as non-political or as "anti-political", these ideas and activities exerted far-reaching political influence. They brought new themes and problems in discussion, thus gradually changing the political discourse. A good example of such an influence was the initiative for alternative service for conscientious objectors, initiated by the Slovenian peace movement in the mid-eighties (see Tomc, 1987). Although the initiative was rejected on the part of the official organisations (the rejection by the federal authorities and the Yugoslav army was sharper than by the Slovenian authorities), the topic could not be banned from the political scene. At the same time, the rejection has demonstrated the sterility of the political elite and the inability of the official political system to generate innovations or to absorb them.

These experiences directed the activities of the mainstream political nonconformists towards more active—or more "political"—stance. This development can be well illustrated by the case of "*Nova revija*" (New Review), a monthly founded by a group of intellectuals in 1982. The foundation of the journal was approved by political authorities after long hesitation. The founders defined the main aim of the journal as fostering autonomous cultural production, and the emphasis on autonomy left the selection of topics wide open. Among the many topics which emerged in the first two volumes, special attention deserves the one related to the "Slovenian national question". The mainstream approach to this question was determined by the thesis that there existed no Slovenian national program (S. Hribar, 1983: 2044). This thesis, which was initially meant as a critique addressed to the political elite, gradually stimulated the collaborators of the journal to accept a more active approach to the "national question". These endeavours culminated in the publication of an issue (1987) which was exclusively devoted to this topic.

The publication provoked a sharp reaction on the side of political authorities in Slovenia and Yugoslavia. Nevertheless, the attempts to discipline the journal failed, showing the decreasing effect of repression. At the same time the failure encouraged the collaborators of "*Nova revija*" to formulate their political dissent more openly. This course was most clearly manifested in a publication in 1988 of "Theses For a New Slovenian Constitution" and in 1990 of an issue on Slovenia as an independent state. These two publications have clearly indicated the gradual transformation of a set of diffuse alternative ideas to a more consistent nationalistic political programme.

The gradual transformation of political dissent to organised political opposition cannot be understood without taking into account the changes in attitudes of the Slovenian political elite and its political organisations. Since the beginning of the eighties the elite gradually adopted more reconciliatory attitude towards political nonconformism. In 1985 the concept of civil society, which was the hallmark of dissent ideologies, found its way into the Party ideology (see Mastnak, 1990: 444). During the following years the political elite tried on the one hand to "make contacts" with some groups and personalities of the alternative scene, and on the other hand to use limited repression to control some other alternative activities. This strategy did not lead to the pacification of dissent, it nevertheless accentuated some differences in the ranks of the alternatives (see Rupel, 1988: 279). But the repercussions on the political elite and their organisations were much more profound. The ability to learn from some of their critics did not strengthen the position of the Communist Party; moreover, it leads to its transformation to a social-democratic type organisation. In this process the Party also lost control over its allies; moreover, one of them—the Communist Youth Organisation—established itself relatively early as one of the alternative political centres. In 1988 the Party declared its readiness to "retreat from power".

The transformation of *the* Party to *a* party was one of the main preconditions for the Slovenian "Velvet Evolution", which culminated in the parliamentary elections in spring 1990. This transformation made possible a gradual transformation of the political alternative to organised political opposition and a differentiation in the ranks of opposition. It should not, of course, be forgotten that the process of democratisation was not induced by the Party, but by the political alternative. The protagonists of political dissent, or at least some of them, had good reasons to celebrate—they did not only "arrange" the great political transformation, they also proved that they were right. Or, as one of the founders of "*Nova revija*" put it at the tenth anniversary of the journal: "The events in Slovenia took the course, which was in accordance with our wishes and foreseen by many of our analyses. We tried to foster this development by every issue (of the review, I.B.) . . . " (T. Hribar, 1990: 1098). The "Velvet Evolution" in Slovenia was not just a result of many convergent decisions of different political actors. This process was strongly influenced by the political and cultural context in which Slovenian society as a small and ethnically relatively homogeneous society was/is located. As in the eighties the tensions in Yugoslavia grew and the effectiveness of the federal state to deal with mounting problems declined, it was not surprising that the Slovenian "national question" became one of the most exciting political issues. It included a demand to redefine Slovenia's relation both to Yugoslavia (looser ties) and to West Europe (intensification of contacts). The issue was met by broad public response and was one of the main topics in the election campaign later.

The growth of political dissent indicated the falling legitimacy of the elite and its political organisations. To regain some public support, the internal reform of the Party and other organisations was not enough; the elite had to dissociate itself from other Yugoslav political elites, especially from the Serbian one whose actions were increasingly marked by aggressive nationalism. The transformation of the old elite was exemplified by its contacts with the Committee for Defence of Human Rights, an umbrella organisation founded in 1988 to coordinate activities against the open repression by the federal authorities of four Slovenian citizens accused of "subversive" activities. One year later the opposition and the "official" political institutions jointly organised protests against the Serbian and federal repression of Albanian inhabitants in Kosovo (see Mastnak, 1990: 447–8). Through these activities a necessary consensus between the political alternative and the representatives of the old regime was established which enabled a relatively smooth transition to democracy.

On a rather general level, two typical strategies on the part of the political elite to neutralize the effects of political nonconformism on the political system could be observed. The Slovenian case fits into a strategy which was marked at the beginning by certain permissiveness towards political nonconformism and later even by selective "domestication" of nonconformist ideas and practices. Apart from Slovenia, this strategy was followed also in Hungary (see Bruszt and Stark, 1991) and, in a very specific form, in Poland. In contrast to the first one, the second strategy was based on systematic repression of political nonconformism. This strategy was practised, in different forms, in the former East Germany, Czechoslovakia and Yugoslavia, with the exception of Slovenia.

Since it tended to establish some links between the political elite and the marginal intelligentsia, the strategy of selective "domestication" deserves particular attention. Its most important effect was the reduction of rigidity of the political elite. But the selective innovations changed the political elite's cohesion, leading to growing differences between its factions, especially between "hardliners" and "reformers". These processes allowed for nonconformist intellectuals to enter the political scene as a semi-institutionalised political force.

The effects of the second strategy were diametrically opposed to this. The strategy of repression strengthened the rigidity of the political elite and minimized the production of new political ideas. Nonconformism was contained within the borders of dissident politics.

Despite their radical differences, both strategies implied at least a tacit recognition of the importance of political nonconformism by the political elite. The influence of political nonconformism was therefore more far-reaching than could be judged from the number of its proponents or their position in (or better: exclusion from) the political system.

The increase in the marginal intellectuals' political influence strongly affected their self-perception and thus, the content of their political ideology. In the centre of their self-perception was the notion that they voice the interests of society at large, instead of representing a particular political interest, as did the political elite. In other words, the marginal intellectuals did not see themselves as "organic intellectuals" of only one class, stratum or professional group but as representatives of the whole society or the nation. Due to the notion of universal interests, the marginal intellectuals' political ideology contained pronounced moral undertones. Political nonconformism was not perceived as a means to achieve certain pragmatic aims, but as a value in itself; it was not seen as a means in a struggle for political power.

From an evolutionary point of view, political democratization can be seen as radical intensification of the internal differentiation of the political system. The forming of a number of new structures and functions in monocentric political systems is a primary condition for their democratization. Thus, democratization inevitably implies a considerable increase in the number of organised political actors. This increase in "moral density" also demands a change in the norms and rules, which regulate the complex processes of a political system. In comparison to a monocentric political system, the democratic political system is able to select and process much more information and therefore to respond adequately to the needs of its environment.

The appearance of nonconformism in socialist societies is a first step towards the differentiation of the political system. In the long run it led to a snowball effect; it paved the way for the emergence of new organised political actors. If the initial phase of the political system transformation was characterized by the difference between political conformism and nonconformism, the "final" phase is characterized by the newly established difference between government and opposition (see Luhmann, 1989). Democratization therefore does not mean just a "quantitative" increase of organised political actors, but a change in their roles.

Why did the various socialist societies undergo dissimilar paths of democratization? Some variations in the democratization process can be explained by the political elite's reactions to political nonconformism.

In societies where the political elite adopted the strategy of selective domestication of nonconformist political innovations, the changes of the political system were gradual, without any spectacular discontinuities. Both the "internal" changes of the political elite and the strengthening of political nonconformism's presence on the political scene cleared the space for other new political actors. These actors gradually constituted themselves as political parties. The gradual changes and their containment to the organised political actors minimized the direct role of the "masses" in the process of democratization. In retrospect, it appears that the turning point was not the parliamentary elections but, rather, the possibility of forming political parties.

The Slovenian case proved the relative unsuccessfulness of nonconformist intellectuals, in comparison to political late-comers, in establishing firmly organised political parties. It was not due just to the fact that they lacked the necessary resources; in this respect their position did not differ much from the position of the other new political actors. The main problem for marginal intellectuals was that party formation represented a decisive step from "anti-politics" to *Realpolitik.* This also included the acknowledgement of deep divisions in their own ranks. The results of the parliamentary elections in Slovenia in 1990 showed that the "veterans" of the democratisation process were relatively unsuccessful in gaining the support of the voters. This was evidenced by the fact that in the winning coalition the Christian Democrats, and not the Slovenian Democratic Alliance, which represented the dominant part of nonconformist tradition, established themselves as the strongest party. The voters' support for new social movements, which entered the election as an independent political group, was insignificant.

The second parliamentary elections in 1992 showed even more drastically that the merits of nonconformist intellectuals in democratizing Slovenia and making it independent were almost forgotten by the voters. This fact was illustrated by the repeated electoral failure of the Slovenian Democratic Alliance which has become one of the smallest parties represented in parliament. This failure was parallelled by the unexpected rise of strongly nationalistic parties, which unscrupulously profaned the ideas which stimulated and guided the democratization process. It means that both the political ideas and the actors which had initiated far-reaching changes in Slovenian society were adversely affected by these changes (see Rupel, 1992: 1114).

Despite many differences between individual socialist societies, it could be argued that the transition to democracy most intensively affected the relative position of both the former political elite and nonconformist marginal intellectuals. It seems that not only the political elite was in the final result negatively affected. Moreover, the stronger was the role of nonconformist marginal intellectuals, the more obvious their "defeat" seemed. The claim that the nonconformist intellectuals, who played a heroic role in the democratisation process belong to the losers, certainly needs some explanation. The transition from an authoritarian to a democratic political system implies "wiping out" the difference between political conformism and nonconformism. This change is reflected, among others, in the fact that the nonconformist intellectuals cannot any longer claim to be representatives of the society or the nation versus the authoritarian state, but they are only one of the many organised political actors on the new political scene.

The "negative impact" of democratization on the political influence of marginal intellectuals went even further. Nonconformism never represented a homogenous political orientation. Its common denominator was, as already shown, its relationship to "official" politics. In other words, in the light of the difference between political conformism and nonconformism, the existing differences and divisions within the ranks of marginal intellectuals were of minor importance. This was exemplified by the broad, but short-lived, umbrella organizations of practically all nonconformist forces, such as the Opposition Roundtable in Hungary (see Bruszt and Stark, 1991: 22) and the Committee for Defence of Human Rights in Slovenia.

Under the growing openness of the political system, the heterogeneity of former nonconformism became obvious and all-encompassing organisations were not viable any more. This actually signalled the disintegration of marginal intellectuals as a distinctive political grouping. Thus, the political force which had played a significant catalytic role in the process of the democratization of former socialist societies was gradually disappearing from the political scene. Some of their heritage, both "staff" and ideas, has been appropriated by the different political parties, but most of it has gradually fallen in oblivion.

The claim that the nonconformist intellectuals belong to the losers of the democratisation process by no means implies that some of them have not managed to attain influential positions in the new political system. The above description refers above all to the fate of the political project of marginal intellectuals. The core of this project was the radical remaking, by arousing the potentials of "civil society", of the relationship between politics and society. But in the course of democratisation those parts of the civil society were also mobilised, which "can be described as politically and democratically undeveloped" (Mastnak, 1990: 449). These "undeveloped" forces have, according to the marginal intellectuals, influenced the outcomes of the democratisation process. The "veterans" were confronted with only two unattractive options—they have had to adapt to the rules of the new political game or to accept a new sort of political marginality (see Siklova, 1990). It is not surprising that those, who have chosen the second option look at the democratisation process with a lot of disenchantment. For them "really existing democracy" is not what democracy should be.

Bibliography

Bernik, I. (1990): "Dual Society. On Some Systemic Properties of the Socialist Societies"; Revista Internacional de Sistemas, 2, 3.

Bruszt, L. and Stark, D. (1991): "Remaking the Political Field in Hungary: From the Politics of Confrontation to the Politics of Competition"; in Banac, I. (ed.): Eastern Europe in Revolution, Ithaca, New York: Cornell University Press. 1992.

Fehér, F. et al. (1983): Dictatorship Over Needs, Oxford: Blackwell.

Gouldner, A.W. (1979): The Future of Intellectuals and the Rise of New Class, London: Macmillan Press.

Hankiss, E. (1988): "The 'Second Society': Is there an Alternative Social Model Emerging in Contemporary Hungary"; Social Research, 55, 1–2.

Hribar, S. (1983): "Tihe gro`nje"; Nova revija, 2, 19–20.

Hribar, T. (1990): "Nova revija v novi dobi"; Nova revija, 9, 101–102.

Konrád, G., Szelényi, I. (1979): The Intellectuals on the Road to Class Power, Brighton: Harvester Press.

Luhmann, N. (1989): "Theorie der politischen Opposition"; Zeitschrift für Politik, 36, 1.

Mastnak, T. (1991): "Civilno drustvo u Sloveniji: od opozicije do vlasti"; Sociologija, XXXII, 4.

Pakulski, J. (1986): "Legitimacy and Mass Compliance: Reflections on Max Weber and Soviet-Type Societies"; British Journal of Political Science, 16.

Pollack, D. (1990): "Das Ende einer Organisationsgesellschaft"; Zeitschrift für Soziologie, 19, 4.

Rakovski, M. (1986): Vzhodno-evropskemu marksizmu naproti, Ljubljana: Komunist.

Rupel, D. (1987): "Alternativna gibanja v kulturi"; in: Neformalne dejavnosti v

slovenski dru`bi, Ljubljana: SSD.
Rupel, D. (1988): "Nekaj malega iz zgodovine in iz prihodnosti"; Nova revija, 7, 69–70.
Rupel, D. (1992): "Kultura in politika v casu razocaranja"; Teorija in praksa, 29, 11–12.
Schlesinger, P. (1982): "In Search for the Intellectuals: Some Comments on Recent Theory"; Media, Culture and Society, 4.
Szelényi, I. (1986/87): "The Prospects and Limits of the East European New Class Project: An Auto-Critical Reflection on The Intellectuals on the Road to the Class Power"; Politics & Society, 15, 2.
Siklova, J. (1990): "The 'Gray Zone' and the Future of Dissent in Czechoslovakia"; Social Research, 57, 2.
Tomc, G. (1987): "Alternativna politika"; in: Neformalne dejavnosti v slovenski druzbi, Ljubljana: SSD.

12

St. Peter and John Stuart Mill

Marcin Król

I should like to begin with the role of the *Advocatus Angeli*. The dramatic conflicts and misunderstandings between the Catholic church and the liberal, "enlightened" section of Polish society, which largely, perhaps even overwhelmingly, professes the Catholic faith, stem from many causes. There are misunderstandings on both sides, in fact, for while the Church takes certain negative manifestations of liberalism to constitute its true nature, the Church's critics appear to have forgotten the essence of its mission.

Apostleship and the Truth

The truth has been revealed. The truth is not known to us in full. God is a secret, but the existence of the truth is beyond dispute. Bloody battle has been waged between theologians, prophets, and ordinary believers since the dawn of the Church's history over the extent to which that truth is accessible to us men, over what the miracles, the Holy Places, and biblical history have to tell us, and finally over how far the Pope embodies that truth and holds it in charge. Within the Church, however, there is one thing that nobody contests, and that is the existence and unalterability of the truth. The history of heresy is as old as the Church itself, of course. The Church has learned much from heresies and even borrowed heavily from them, but the truth, particularly the dogmatic core of the truth, was never allowed to be shaken.

Heretics who failed to understand that were banished from the Church for ever.

It is not my intention, in what follows, to add a further interpretation of the truth to those already in existence, although I should like to stress that acknowledgement of the truth is incompatible with relativism of any kind. Belief in the revealed truth is not a psychological phenomenon. At the same time, it must not be forgotten that the revealed truth does not encompass everything and that many of its elements have been variously interpreted down the centuries, inevitably giving rise to the impression that the Church is dependent upon trends or (even worse) that it occasionally allows itself to be guided by opportunism. That impression is false. The Church is, after all, an institution in the world, and its priests have no other access to the truth than any other believers.

How, then, is the fifth commandment to be interpreted from the standpoint of the truth and from that of the Church as an institution? Is any qualification of that commandment possible? Self-defence in war, capital punishment, and protecting the life of the woman in labour constitute exceptions in so far as, in them, one life is weighed against another. All three exceptions are capable of various interpretations, of course, and there is no reason why the Church should impose one interpretation in particular. Two possibilities present themselves. The first is to appeal to the human conscience. However, society is governed by laws and institutions that operate according to definite rules and only exceptionally admit the conscience of individual members as an overriding principle. The second possibility consists in seeing the Church as an institution that plays a part in public life in that it exerts a positive influence on social and moral practice. In neither case, however, does the Church or its representatives have the authority to pronounce a final judgement with regard to the correct interpretation of the fifth commandment in public life.

At a time when there is so much discussion of the Church's stand on abortion and when its negative attitude comes in for such criticism, it should not be forgotten that the Church has the right, perhaps even the duty, to call for a ban on the practice of abortion. At the same time, however, it is no more competent than the other institutions of public life to decide at what moment a human being becomes a human being. Were the Church to lay claim to sole rights of representation in this sphere, it would quickly find itself in difficulties because it would then also have to administer justice. Much the same is true with regard to the question of capital punishment as well as with regard to the ethical questions thrown up by war. It is against this background that the Pope's attitude during the Gulf War must be viewed. The Church cannot do the job of the United Nations, nor is it able, nowadays, to state with authority whether or not a particular war is just.

"You shall not kill"—a straightforward command, yet exceptions would seem to be unavoidable. Granting them can and must be a burden on the individual conscience. Determining and above all controlling such exceptions cannot become the public function of the Church unless the latter were prepared to assume full responsibility for the entire life of the community. That would be possible only in a theocracy. It does not look as if the Church wishes to assume any such responsibility.

On the other hand, it would be a misunderstanding to expect the Church to confine itself simply to proclaiming the revealed truth. The task of the Catholic church is proselytism. Even if the apostolic mission has been variously fulfilled in the history of the Church, its motivation has always been the same. And since forced proselytism is obsolete today, the Church employs various other methods to perform its mission—not just simple persuasion.

Apostleship and Politics

In this connection I should like to consider a contention that is often put forward, namely that the Church ought not to meddle in politics. The Church, it is argued, should not publicly support any specific political groups or parties; indeed, it should avoid intervening in public life altogether, even though its fundamental apostolic mission includes just that.

If we regard the Church as an important part of society, pursuing its legitimate interests like any other part, it would be sheer hypocrisy to refuse to allow it to play an active part in public life.

Rather more problematical is the role of the Church in the political struggle. A particular party would of course capitalise enormously on support from the Church. However, regardless of the sympathies of individual bishops or members of the clergy, canon law forbids any taking of sides politically and any public expression of support for parties or individuals. Yet, critics will argue, did not priests call upon people to vote for Walesa at the time of the 1990 presidential campaign? True, they did, although those representatives of the Church were departing from the rules. What else can one do in a free country but expose such things? Yet this did not happen. How are we to explain the fact that even those politicians and political groups hostile to any involvement by the Church in public life showed little courage when it came to calling a spade a spade and taking a public stand?

In Poland the Church (or rather, many of its representatives) shows little finesse in its public words and actions. At the same time, actors in the public arena are the victims of real or (as I tend to think) imagined pressure from the Church. The upshot is that the Church, straying beyond its apostolic mission, ventures into areas of life where it has no business, and in the long run this does it harm. Naturally, the Church derives a good deal of its intimidating authority from the part it played in the fight against Communism. In the years when there was still some hope of reforming Communism, this role played by the Church was underestimated by a great many Polish intellectuals. Following the events of March 1968, when people had ceased to believe in the reformability of Communism, the role of the Church did receive some recognition, but it was misunderstood. A classic instance of this was Adam Michnik's book, "Church, Left, Dialogue", published in Polish in Paris in 1977.

It is probable that nearly all sensible and honest people at the time shared the view of the author, who must of course have been aware of the artificial nature of his position. I am not concerned with condemning either the book or its author but simply with that fundamental illusion on the part of the Polish opposition at the time, the painful consequences of which are today being suffered by so many.

The illusion is based on an identification of the anti-totalitarian front with a liberal world view. When it became apparent, in the wake of the collapse of the Communist regime, that the Church did not share that world view, its allies manifested disappointment, even outrage. So long as there was a deep and unbridgeable gulf between the Communist authorities and the non-Communist opposition, the Church was the ideal mediator. Clearly, those who welcomed such mediation at the time are anything but enthusiastic in the light of the fact that the Church still lays claim to the role of arbitrator today. To outsiders who do not understand the nature of the Church's mission, this appears to constitute a surprising change. The Western press furnishes proof of this often enough. But those who have always been critical of the political influence of the Church, or who on the other hand welcomed it, are not aware of any radical turnaround. The circumstances have altered, not the Church.

What is the function of the arbitrator? In the day-to-day life of a democracy there are many situations and many problems that throw up ethical questions. The Church cannot be expected to be silent here; its basic mission, after all, is to proclaim the truth. For instance, the Church cannot adopt an uncritical attitude towards the idea of a permissive society. We know from history that it is prepared to use the most diverse methods to realise its mission. Some of those methods turn out to be wrong or even, with regard to the target aimed at, positively harmful. Often, however, this does not become apparent until after the event. What is important is that the Church will be able to take up only so much room as society allows it. And if a certain disproportion is in evidence here, the responsibility lies with *civil society*, which is not capable of calling a halt to the ambitions of the Church.

So long as this situation continues, fear of the Church is going to distort public life. Fear, firstly, that a person will be accused of being left-wing, an advocate of moral relativism, if he does not stress his connection with the Church or if his political views fail to take account of God. Such a fear does not in fact spring from the hostility of the Church; it arises spontaneously among liberals themselves, who once fell in so uncritically with an alliance with the Church that now the least criticism is seen as heresy. No one who was pleased to exhibit work on church premises and showed a predilection for painting crosses and graveyards should say today that the Church limits his artistic freedom. That was the way we wanted it.

Secondly, there is no convincing alternative to the Catholic faith. Spiritual life was so devastated by Communism that Christian belief was seen as man's only place of refuge. Now, with the possibility of choice, religion is no longer a comfortable haven. It has become problematical, yet there are no spiritual alternatives available, and that paralyses the critical faculties. The candidacy of Stanislav Tyminski showed in exemplary fashion how political capital may be made out of the current lack of a sense of direction. Polish liberalism is still too weak to provide a moral and spiritual lead. Concentrating mainly on economics, which is not unusual for the beginning, it is quite simply not capable, in this form, of meeting the challenges of society.

The greatest fear, finally, is fear of the Pope. I am convinced that worry lest the Holy Father should one day indicate his sympathy for (or disapproval of) one or another political group in Poland is having a paralysing effect on the political life of our country. Here again we are dealing with a major error. The Pope scarcely meddles in Polish public life at all. A far more powerful factor is that the profound breakdown of all authority and the fast-waning attraction of the heroes and martyrs of the opposition have led to a situation where no one in Poland today feels called to provide spiritual and political leadership. There is a general dearth of authority. John Paul II could supply that kind of authority. He says nothing, though, because it is not his job to organise Poland's political affairs. Not the least of the things we must learn to do is to say goodbye to an excessively romantic view of politics. We in Poland are just beginning to understand that elements of cynicism and opportunism are unavoidable in the democratic system, and that people in public life are only rarely distinguished by virtue and strength of character.

Apostleship and Liberalism

There remains the fundamental illusion of a "liberalisation of Catholicism", coupled with a simultaneous "catholicisation of liberalism". Hopes of a "liberalisation of the Church" are as old as the Church itself. They spring from an understandable desire to adapt the faith to a modernised society. The clash for which we have, for our purposes, selected as protagonists St. Peter and John Stuart Mill goes back to the beginning of the modern period.

Of all the achievements of the modern period, the freedom of the individual is the most significant. Indeed, present-day civilisation has become unthinkable without it. Anyone who neglects, curtails, or questions that freedom is an enemy of democratic liberal thinking. Although our understanding of freedom and its limits is constantly changing, and despite all the appalling experiences of the twentieth century, John Stuart Mill's dictum that every assault on individual liberty is wholly evil still holds good today. Looked at in this way, the Catholic faith (not the private kind but faith as a factor in public life) does restrict and even threaten the freedom of the individual.

Hopes of a liberalisation of Catholicism are usually associated with the demand for a privatisation of belief. Private belief, unaffected by apostolic interests, stands in no contradiction to individual liberty. On the other hand, the faith that aspires to a public function does represent a potential threat. Private belief, moreover, though absolute in itself, does not impose any kind of world view on society. That is above all the fear of those who, having succumbed to a secular totalitarian temptation, attribute something similar to the Church.

For the Church, however, faith always has two aspects. In history and doctrine the private, mystical element prevails, although occasionally this seeks to invade public life in the form of sects. But there has also always been a strong tendency for religious belief to be seen as having a public role to play as well. Basically, the Church has always preferred Thomas Aquinas to Augustine; the faith of the Crusaders has been dearer to it than that of the mystics, the idea of active dissemination closer than that of private election.

How, though, are the moral and political restrictions arising out of belief to be reconciled with the absolute primacy of individual liberty? For instance, may a member of parliament accept the party whip when his party's decision conflicts with his belief? The question is exacerbated by the fact that the Catholic faith differs radically from all other Christian confessions in saying that St. Peter's successor is here among us, that the head of the Church is not merely its elected representative but that with his election certain qualities are bestowed upon him that no other person on earth possesses. A Catholic cannot remain true to the Church's teaching without according the Pope this special status.

This being so, some restriction of the liberty of the Catholic individual, together with the conflicts arising therefrom, is indispensable and unavoidable. That leaves only an argument that is frequently put forward, namely that no one forces us to be Catholics and that ultimately these conflicts spring from our own free decision.

The argument is a false one because, whereas in a free society no one forces us to go to the cinema or to vote for a particular political party, the choice between belief and non-belief is, from the Church's point of view, a choice between salvation and destruction.

A reconciliation between St. Peter and John Stuart Mill is therefore not possible. On the other hand, life and its trivial demands impose alliances and compromises. An important alliance in Poland, for instance, is that formed by the anti-totalitarian forces, while the round-table agreements constitute a historically momentous compromise. The provisions governing the separation of Church and state are another example. It is in the nature of things that all these attempts to find a *modus vivendi* touch the surface only; they are not to be confused with permanent solutions of principle.

Things are rather different in the realm of economics. Here the Church's separation of the private sphere and the state seems much clearer. Granted, despite all the disappointing experiences of our century, the Church is looking with undiminished determination for new and more equitable economic models. But in the new social encyclical, *Centesimus Annus*, the Pope for the first time takes up a position on economic life without at the same time putting forward alternatives of his own (for example, an economic model committed to the myth of a "third road" between socialism and capitalism).

The Pope is here seeking to answer the question whether the failure of Communism implies the victory of capitalism: "If by 'capitalism' is meant an economic system which recognises the fundamental and positive role of business . . . as well as free human creativity in the economic sector, then the answer is certainly in the affirmative. . . . But if by 'capitalism' is meant a system in which freedom in the economic sector is not circumscribed within a strong juridical framework which places it at the service of human freedom in its totality, and which sees it as a particular aspect of that freedom, the core of which is ethical and religious, then the reply is certainly negative" (*Centesimus Annus*, paragraph 42).

No liberal can object to that. The Pope, after all, is concerned not with creating a new economic system (as was the case with his predecessors) but only with the relationship, which for centuries has been criticised both by conservatives and by people on the left, between the economy and human freedom. Here the Church could provide an extremely important ally for all those who are working to improve the moral and psychological foundations of the free-market economy.

Apostleship and Europe

Criticism voiced by the Church regarding the state of European civilisation and the European spirit is of course nothing new. Even outside the Church there is no shortage of critics of Europe, and as we know the capacity for self-criticism is a central feature of European culture. This time, however, it is a matter of answering the question expressed most forcefully by Francis Fukuyama and since taken up and attacked from many quarters: the question, namely, of whether history has reached its culmination, now that with the victory of liberalism the dreams of men have found fulfilment and Utopias become reality. It is conceded that many ideals remain unrealised; the project itself, however, has purportedly succeeded, to all intents and purposes.

Speaking in Warsaw on 9 June 1991, the Pope subjected this view to an indirect yet devastating critique. That critique recalled the ideas of Zygmunt Krasinski, whose writings inspired many papal speeches. Take two fragments from Krasinski's Memorandum to Pius IX, written in 1848: "Europe presents a picture of grim and pathetic horror such as has not been seen since the collapse of heathendom and the Roman Empire. The similarity is striking. It arises from the fact that few souls are living true lives in faith and love. The majority are eaten up by doubt, depravity, or destitution. And countless numbers are waking from a long lethargy, uncertain of which way they should go and with no goal that they wish to attain. . . . And here I may be permitted to ask whether it is not one of the holiest duties of the Holy See to mobilise all forces and endeavours to avert such appalling disasters. Is the Holy See not there to save mankind, to strengthen it, and to guide it to the right end? When thunderstorms gather in the distance, is not its task to see them coming and stay them off? We have endeavoured to show that this storm will not move away except under one condition, and if that condition is a thoroughly Christian matter, can there be any hesitation?"

We know that Krasinski's Memorandum failed in its objective. The Vatican was unable to react in the appropriate way to the dangers that Krasinski predicted. The Church of the day was not prepared for a European mission. Europe itself, drawn along by its own industrial and civilisatory momentum, looked to be in good fettle. There was a further reason, too, why the Memorandum remained without effect. The Polish spiritual elite was made up of deeply religious people who at the time were in constant conflict with the institutional Church. The strength and patriotism of the Polish church and the extent of its actual influence on society in the nineteenth and early twentieth centuries were very much less significant than is often asserted today. It was only the years after 1948 that brought an unprecedented increase in the religiousness and hence also in the social influence of the Church as an institution.

The re-evangelisation of Europe, which undoubtedly started with

John Paul II's speech in Warsaw, has a double significance. Firstly, Poland came to be seen as a country to be missionised, a country, in other words, that must be won or reconquered for the Church. Interestingly, Polish Catholics have scarcely reacted to the Pope's call. It would seem that our general complacency, coupled with our conviction that we are exemplary Catholics, has not exactly made us receptive to so tart a message. Secondly, the Pope, like the romantic Krasinski before him, recognised that Poland is a good starting-point for the evangelisation of Europe. I do not know whether this plan will succeed, but the foregoing considerations make it sufficiently clear that the Church must win the old continent back for itself if it is not to become so eroded by liberalisation as to lose its identity.

Reproaches were immediately levelled at this kind of crusade. Above all the Church is charged with entertaining an anti-modernist attitude and the Pope with conservatism and a contempt for democratic institutions. The Church has always been anti-modernist, since the ideal of civilisatory progress remains outside its interests. The existence or non-existence of computers has not the slightest importance so far as our salvation is concerned. It is not the Church that has claimed to see the devil in machinery; such imaginings have always been the work of ideologists. The reproach of anti-modernism is absurd, in fact, since the Church has always taken its stand on conservatism. But it is a conservatism of a rather special kind, one that springs from fidelity to a truth rather than to custom. As the most recent encyclical shows, the Church's attitude towards democratic institutions is neither dismissive nor derogatory. The views of John Paul II cannot be compared with classic anti-occidentalism, particularly not of the Russian variety. This is not an attack on Europe with its democratic, parliamentary system but an attempt at a renewal of what Europe itself regards as its roots.

Apostleship and Private and Public Life

In his last book but one, "If God Did Not Exist . . . ", Leszek Kolakowski put forward two possible versions of the relationship to the hidden order of reality. Belief in the existence of God anchors the sense of order and meaning and enables the believer to distinguish evil from good. Rejection of any kind of transcendental authority, on the other hand, necessarily leads to an acceptance of the state of chaos. Such a description is quite adequate for the requirements of the individual and his private life. It depends entirely and exclusively on himself and on God whether he is accorded the state of grace and hence what perception he forms of the world order. It would be nice if things were so simple. The Church, and particularly the Catholic church, (some non-Christian religions are equally exigent in this regard), demands of us that we bear witness to our faith.

This means for one thing that we obey the Christian commandments, that for example we help old people across the road, that as employers we treat our employees fairly, that we conduct our private lives in a disciplined manner, or that we attend Sunday mass. On top of all this, however, there are the duties of active apostleship. This is where, in the modern world, we run into problems that we cannot handle, and inevitably our problems are also those of the Church. The world, for believers, is built around a hierarchy of values, with the Christian revelation at the top, but at the same time there is no escaping the fact that it is a world of liberal permissiveness.

A consistent approach to behaviour would inevitably lead to a rejection of virtually everything that modern, liberal civilisation has given mankind in terms of freedom (a freedom that civilisation has good reasons for defending against the advocates of moral crusades). But say a person is unwilling to forfeit that freedom and at the same time wishes to be a good Christian: does that mean he must live in a state of unresolvable tension? And is he not thereby qualifying the values bound up with belief, and does not any kind of qualification mean the end of belief?

There is in fact no clear and simple answer. However, we are moving in the direction of a solution when we recognise that the spiritual plane takes precedence of the material plane. The opportunity of reaching this view used to lie and may still lie in the exceptional situation of Poland, where social mobilisation has been almost exclusively fuelled by spiritual impulses. After Romanticism, for the second time in the history of Poland there is evidence today of a "vertical" vision restoring spiritual values to their proper place. If the Church proves incapable of welcoming and absorbing that vision, we must openly rebel. It would be a rebellion not against the Church but against a levelling world view that seeks either to reduce us to a prosaic existence or to compel us to seek refuge from modern civilisation. But if we know what we believe in and what we think, we ought not to lack the courage to resist. We all need that kind of courage today, because a prosaic, political, or liberalised Church would signify not only the failure of our private lives but that of European civilisation, with Poland becoming a country without a soul, a veritable no-man's-land.

The parliamentary elections in September 1993 produced a majority of post-communist parties in the Parliament which proved that the political influence of the Church is not so strong as it has been feared. One might think that it was a victory of John Stuart Mill. But I believe this would be a wrong conclusion. Church has only started to adapt to the new democratic situation and committed all possible mistakes. Now it is going to learn from the past errors and probably look for completely new ways of promoting its teaching. John Paul II's *Veritatis Splendor* seems to me a proof of that.

13

From Velvet Revolution to Velvet Divorce? (Reflections on Slovakia's Independence)

Martin Bútora, Zora Bútorová & Olga Gyárfásová

One Month Before: At the Crossroads

Bratislava, the capital of the Slovak Republic, May 1992, one month before the second post-communist parliamentary elections.

"The common state is the best road for us," says Martin Porubjak, Deputy Prime Minister of the Slovak Republic and President of the Civic Democratic Union (ODU). "We must not stop halfway," smiles the Vice President of the ODU and Minister for Privatization Ivan Miklos, encouraging the people to continue the radical economic reform. The ODU is the successor of Public Against Violence (VPN), the winner of the parliamentary elections in 1990 and the most frequent target of criticism by the opposition.

"People"—this only word is to be found on the poster of the coalition formed by the strongest Czech political subject, the Civic Democratic Party (ODS) and by the rather weak Democratic Party (DS) operating in Slovakia. The program of the coalition is clear; its leader is minister of the Federal Government Václav Klaus, the author of the Czecho-Slovak economic reform.

Both the ODU and the DS are pro-reform and pro-federal. Both point out the geopolitical risks of the disintegration of Czecho-Slovakia: growing tensions in the relations with the neighboring countries, problems with national minorities, especially with Hungarians, the danger of Slovakia falling into an unstable, unpredictable sphere of influence of Ukraine and other parts of the former Soviet empire, and the lack of interest of foreign investors to invest in a politically unstable region. Both parties may pay a high price for the negative impacts of the economic reform in Slovakia. One can only wonder why these parties do not create a coalition. The fragmentation of the pro-reform and pro-federal forces appears as too high risk.

By contrast, the Slovak National Party (SNS) approaches the voters by sending them a paper imitation of a new "Slovak crown"—the currency of a future independent Slovak state. The SNS is the third strongest party in Slovakia, so far the only parliamentary representative of Slovak secessionism.

"The time has matured, Slovakia!" declares the Slovak Christian Democratic Movement (SKDH). Only two months ago, the SKDH split from the Christian Democratic Movement (KDH) whose leader is Ján Carnogursky, the Slovak Prime Minister. The representatives of the SKDH believe in the sovereignty—prosperity equation. They combine the idea of Slovak independence with an economic program of state paternalism.

At the same time, Carnogursky's KDH is inclined to support the radical economic reform, as well as the preservation of the common state. Paradoxically, however, Carnogursky has contributed to undermining Czech-Slovak statehood: it was he who proposed the idea that Slovakia should remain in the common state only until the year 2000 when it would get its own seat in the European Parliament and its "own star" on the European firmament.

"A chance for the capable—security for the hard-working," says an uncompromising critic of the current economic reform, the popular Slovak politician Peter Weiss, the Chairman of the opposition Party of the Democratic Left (SDL). Since the last elections the image of this party has substantially improved; the former communist party has become the second strongest political group in Slovakia. In the controversy about Czech and Slovak coexistence, the SDL shows a wait-and-see attitude. In general, the leaders of the SDL express support for a common state of two equal republics. But at the same time, their social and class rhetorics contains national elements when criticizing the "unitarian" approach of federal and Czech bodies which, allegedly, do not respect the interests of Slovakia.

"The whole world believes Dubcek. What about you?" asks the

extraparliamentary Social Democratic Party in Slovakia (SDSS), which was recently strengthened by Alexander Dubcek, the second most popular Slovak politician, star of the Prague Spring in 1968 and President of the Federal Parliament since 1989. Dubcek has joined the SDSS after a long hesitation, despite his inclination to the Movement for a Democratic Slovakia (HZDS). The SDSS is supporting the preservation of a common state which would respect the sovereignty of the Czech and the Slovak Republics. However, the credibility of these proclamations is decreased by the affinity of Dubcek to the HZDS.

The favorite in the elections is the Movement for a Democratic Slovakia, the party of the first Prime Minister of Slovakia after the 1990 elections, Vladimír Meciar. The HZDS was formed after the split of Public Against Violence in Spring 1991, when Meciar with some other ministers were recalled from the government of the Slovak Republic.

Immediately after its formation in 1990, Meciar's government initiated negotiations about a redistribution of power between the federal bodies and the republics. This resulted in the so-called Law of Competencies issued by the Federal Parliament in December 1990. The vigor with which Meciar pushed through the cause of equal partnership of both republics carried him to the very top of political popularity in Slovakia.

When radical economic reform started in 1991, Meciar began to stress the necessity of preserving social security, even at the expense of slowing down the reform. He increased his popularity by defending "the interests of the man in the street" and by sharp attacks against "federal bureaucracy".

The transfer of HZDS to the opposition led to an essential transformation of Slovak political configuration. The HZDS soon became the strongest political party, and formed an *ad hoc* alliance with the Slovak National Party and the Party of the Democratic Left in the Slovak and the Federal Parliaments. They blocked the adoption of several laws, mainly of those on the constitutional structure of the state. Meciar turned his back to the concept of an authentic federation favoring a confederative arrangement.

Meciar's opponents point out his populism, inclination to authoritarian leadership, unprincipled manipulation with the truth for the sake of his own power interests. They see in him a politician of national-and-socialist orientation.

The HZDS is a typical umbrella movement [29]. Its supporters are united by their devotion to Meciar's charismatic image. People disappointed or threatened by the economic reform associate very optimistic expectations with Meciar's comeback [29]. The days before the elections he smilingly embraces his voters from the big posters all over Slovakia.

As to the top leadership of the HZDS, it includes besides confederalists and advocates of Slovak sovereignty also politicians inclined to accept a federation; besides reform-communists also populistic anti-communists, social democrats and Christian socialists. Anyhow, they share two main principles: state interventionism and a stronger position of Slovakia.

While some corrections of the reform course can probably be negotiated with the future Czech political partners, Meciar's vision of the constitutional structure of the state raises a greater concern: he would hardly find partners on the Czech side and could lead to the disintegration of the common state.

The split of the CSFR and the disadvantaged position of minorities in independent Slovakia raises worries among the Hungarians living mainly in the southern part of the Republic. With elections approaching, the tension between the Slovaks and the Hungarians slightly increases. The Hungarians will probably vote for the coalition of the Coexistence, and the Hungarian Christian Movement (MKDH) which present themselves as defenders of the minorities' rights. Weaker are the chances of the liberal Hungarian Civic Party (MOS).

The walkers and the drivers passing the posters are approaching the crossroad: in one month's time they will decide about their future. Which direction will they choose? Will it be the road toward state sovereignty, which has been followed during recent years by dozens of millions? Or will they preserve the common state?

Winners and Losers

The euphoria of the "Velvet Revolution" has faded away. The downfall of communism paved the way for democratic development. At the same time, however, it lifted the lid off serious social problems. In many faces a "post-communist panic" (Belohradsky) is reflected [5]. The rapid changes come into conflict with the value orientations and norms of behavior carried over from "real socialism", as well as from the more distant past.

For an impartial observer, Czecho-Slovakia has successfully mastered the first two years of post-communism—with the exception of the constitutional set-up of the state. The legislative foundations of the rule of law and a market economy have been laid. The Federal Parliament alone adopted within the last two years 170 new laws. The economic reform has rapidly progressed and prominent international institutions have appreciated its basic elements: the liberalization of prices, a low rate of inflation, a relatively stable currency. The "small" privatization has been carried out and the "large" privatization is in full swing.[1] More than 80% of adult population have participated in voucher privatization. A new middle class is coming into existence.

The last two years have been characterized by a relative political stability, at least on the federal level. The federal government formed by the coalition of the Civic Forum, Public against Violence and the Christian Democratic Movement has been a firm safeguard of the economic reform. Even in Slovakia no anti-reform convulsion has taken place.

Obviously, every political and economic reform has its winners and losers. Since November 1989, the number of those feeling disadvantaged by the recent developments has increased in the CSFR, especially in Slovakia.[2] Repeated surveys [1,2,3,28,29] show the alienation of the "new power elite" from the everyday needs of the people. Trust in parliamentary democracy is low, and the disillusionment with the performance of the democratic regime leads to authoritarian nostalgias [8]. Political frustration is combined with a fear from the come-back of ruthless capitalism and merciless competition leading to social inequality. Strong is also the fear from the negative economic, political and cultural consequences of opening up the country.

These feelings are more frequent in the Slovak society than in the Czech one, a fact to which the harsher impact of the economic reform on the Slovak population (an approximately three times higher rate of unemployment, problems with the conversion of the military industry, loss of the Eastern market, etc.) has greatly contributed. A substantial part of the Slovak population finds that the economic transformation threatens the national interests of Slovakia.

The level of national and ethnic tensions is relatively high in Slovakia [12,14,26]. There is a broad spectrum of friction points. Besides the Czech-Slovak relations [14] which are the subject of our study, one should mention the Roma question [5], the problem of the coexistence of Slovaks and Hungarians in the southern regions of Slovakia [26], and the increased wariness of Slovak population toward the Jews [12,32].

The Divided Slovakia

The new political class has not succeeded in fulfilling one important promise: in spite of very intensive negotiations, the Federal Parliament has not been able to adopt a federal constitution. Although Slovakia has stimulated constitutional change and has had more initiatives in the transformation of the common state than Bohemia, the Slovak politicians have not so far formed any "united front for independence", as it was the case in many newly independent post-communist states. Plainly expressed, Slovakia is not Slovenia or Croatia. Slovakia is characterized by a wide plurality of citizens' attitudes towards the problem of national revival, national identity, and the constitutional structure of the state.

On the one hand there is a critical attitude towards the Slovak national movement, which is perceived as nationalist, representing a new kind of collectivistic ideology [4]. The re-awakened nationalism is here understood as a disintegration trend: the formation of an independent national state would reduce the volume of the market and would counteract the European integration trends. "Let us not return to the 19th century!" warn the critics of nationalism who prefer "the citizen" and "the civic principle" to "the nation". Correspondingly, they advocate either a united state, or a federation of regions (similar to that of the *Bundesländer* in Austria and Germany).

The opposite opinion pole is occupied by people who see in the increasing national self-awareness a healthy and desirable process and, moreover, a final break with the internationalist principles of communism. These people stress the authenticity of national rights and aspirations, the value of cultural individuality. The search for national identity, they say, need not be in contradiction with the integration processes in Europe. Quite on the contrary, the united Europe has to respect, and even to protect the national specificities: otherwise it will not be an integration of the member states with equal rights, but only a new version of superiority and inequality. This argument often refers to the national and regional changes in Western democracies, quoting the examples of Scotland, Catalonia, the Basques, Quebec, and the Flemish question.

This approach has two versions. According to the moderate one, independence has to be achieved in the long run, while respecting the constitutional character of each and every step taken on the road toward national emancipation, i.e., the right to self-determination (e.g., the principle of a referendum), and an agreement with the Czech partners. This would be a peaceful way toward independence, toward a Slovak "star on the European heaven". It is our wish that Slovakia would enter Europe in a respectable way, using the main entrance, and not the backstairs which are for the servants only,—say the protagonists of this line. In contrast to them, the radical advocates of state sovereignty speak about a "national revolution" and stress their demand to reach the independence of Slovakia here and now. In fact, what many of them have in their minds, is the Slovak "nation-state".

The representatives of a third solution aim at combining the civic and the national principle, considering them not as incompatible, but as complementary and mutually enriching. The civic and national anchorage are two means by which man comprehends the world: both of them help to create the feeling of home, as Václav Havel writes in his "Summer Reflections" [17]. From a political point of view, this solution relies on the principle of federalism, emphasizing at the same time the necessity of decentralization and local self-government.

Soon after November 1989, the Slovak political scene was shaped by the controversy between these different intellectual streams. Those proclaiming the priority of the civic principle to the national one, or the complementarity of them, are raising the question: Will the Velvet Revolution not result in a new form of totalitarian, or at least authoritarian regime, this time in national colors?

Radical secessionists formulate the problem in a different way: Will the Slovak nation continue to be the younger brother only, going for the left-overs and doing some patchwork in the shadow of Prague's fame?

Mutual labelling has become a typical feature of political discussion. For secessionists, the federalists are cosmopolitans similar to the communist internationalists, traitors of their own nation, lackeys of foreign masters. The federalists, on the other hand, see the secessionists as nationalists who, in their greed for power, strive for replacing one kind of totalitarianism by another one, pushing Slovakia towards the Balkan, into the sphere of political instability and chaos. The latter indulgently smile at such "ghost stories"; being inspired by the Yugoslav developments, they presume a possibility "to part in a civilized way", on the basis of some agreement.

The supporters of the sovereignty and/or state independence of the Slovak Republic are attracted by the following arguments. The first of them accentuates the plebeian character of the Slovaks, their poverty and the injustice that has been done to them. The second one suggests the vision of the Slovak nation as a community of deeply religious people, practically unaffected by the long decades of communism, who must be protected from tricky Western liberalism infiltrating Slovakia also through the Czech Republic. The third argument refers to the historical continuity of the efforts by the Slovaks to create an independent state of their own and stresses the achievement of this goal in Tiso's totalitarian Slovak State during World War II (see later). The fourth argument overlaps with the previous one, stressing the legitimacy of Slovak aspirations and considering an independent state the *conditio sine qua non* of a healthy political, economic and cultural development of any nation: "we are the last unliberated nation in the post-Communist realm—let's finally make an end with the federal Brontosaurus". And, last but not least, according to the fifth argument, the Slovaks need an independent state for being able to find the "third road" between socialism and capitalism.

All these different types of argumentation stress the historical and cultural difference between Slovak and Czech society, absolutize them and draw conclusions about the irreversible divergence between Czech and Slovak society.

Why are these arguments so convincing? Like in other Eastern European countries, we must go back to history. After 1989, the past suddenly entered the present, and its interpretation became part and parcel of the political struggle.

The Shadows of the Past

Legacy 1: Dilemma of the Young Czechoslovakia: Unitarism Versus Federalism

Unlike the Czechs, the Slovaks have never had—with the only exception of World War II—a state of their own. For 1000 years, the Slovak people was seeking a consensus with the Hungarians within the framework of the Hungarian state and later within the Austro-

Hungarian Monarchy. The coexistence of Slovaks, Hungarians, and other nations had been more or less satisfactory for a long time. It went wrong only in the 19th century when the concept of a Hungarian state was reinterpreted as a dominance of the Hungarian nation over all neighboring nations. The struggle of the Slovak nation for its survival reached its peak at the end of the 19th century and the beginning of the 20th century when it had to resist a very strong pressure for Hungarianization.

The foundation of the first Czechoslovak Republic in 1918 was an optimal solution for both Slavic nations. The Czechs regained a state of their own, built on democratic principles; the Slovaks found their national and cultural salvation. However, despite the fairly common language, the new state included rather different national entities: here the lower economic and educational level as well as the strong Catholicism of the Slovaks are to be mentioned.

Nevertheless, the official concept of a *single* Czechoslovak nation with two branches and languages meant that the existence of separate—Czech and Slovak—nations was not recognized. This concept was asserted by the founding fathers of Czechoslovakia mainly for pragmatic reasons. They assumed that the position of Slovakia would improve in the future. Czechoslovakism met with a considerable resistance in Slovakia [19], it was accepted only by the smaller part of Slovak politicians. The theory of Czechoslovakism was not accepted by the Slovak emigrants in the USA either, whose representatives had discussed the future shape of the state with the later founders of the Czechoslovak state, including its first president, Tomás Masaryk during World War I. In the Cleveland Agreement (1915) and in the Pittsburgh Agreement (1918) the Slovaks reached an accord with Masaryk that Slovakia would be granted autonomy within the new state. At the time when the new state came into existence it was necessary, however, to act quickly and pragmatically. For this reason all the leading Slovak politicians professed the idea of a "Czechoslovak nation" in their declaration in the city of Turciansky Sv. Martin on 30th October 1918 (the so-called Martin Declaration). The new common state affected the Slovak nation favorably. A modern political structure emerged, the educational and cultural level of the country was raised. Czechoslovakia made it possible for Slovakia to become a part of democratic Europe.

What was good for the Slovaks in October 1918, became unsatisfactory a bit later. The Czechs have outnumbered the Slovaks two to one, and they staffed most of the administration also in Slovakia. As a result, the Slovaks could not with full responsibility take their destiny into their own hands. While the country as a whole was between the two wars one of the most developed countries in Europe, this did not apply to its Eastern part: the living standard remained lower, unemployment higher, and emigration was substantial. The industry in Slovakia became even weaker than under Hungarians. The Slovaks were often injured by a paternalistic approach on the part of the more advanced Czechs. Gradually, Czechoslovakism became an anachronism, and in Slovakia it was increasingly identified with Czech nationalism. While the Czechs quickly identified themselves with the new state and interpreted it as the extension of Czech statehood, the Slovaks wanted to see the common state as an alliance of two sovereign subjects.

Although these two different conceptions of the common state had been manifested immediately after the foundation of Czechoslovakia, they started to clash only during the second decade of its existence. In the beginning the Czech and Slovak politicians fully realised that only a strong state had a chance to survive in this region. The ideas about such a strong state, however, were different. The Czechs understood this strong state to be unitarian, centralized; while according to the Slovaks the common state should have been strengthened by the autonomy of Slovakia. Thus, Slovak political thinking was, in principle, autonomistic and federalistic. The Slovaks had been demanding autonomy from the Hungarians, and gradually this demand was pushed through in the first Czechoslovak Republic, too [24].

Since the foundation of the Czechoslovak Republic there was a tension between Slovak Catholicism and secularized Czech culture and politics. The Catholics, although constituting the majority of the Slovak nation, did not feel to be politically represented, in contrast to the Slovak Protestants who traditionally felt a higher affinity to Czech culture. At the same time, an insensitive approach of some secularized Czechs towards Slovak Catholicism which hurt common Slovak people provoked a negative stereotype of Czech liberalism [29]. Catholic autonomism was confirmed by the foundation of the Slovak People's Party under the leadership of the charismatic Catholic priest Andrej Hlinka in 1918.

The Czech-Slovak relationship was, in principle, not deadlocked: it would only have needed political imagination and goodwill on both sides. However, these lacked. In the 1935 elections the Slovak People's Party won 30% of the votes and became the strongest political power in Slovakia.

Legacy 2: The Slovak State in a Tragical Context

After the humiliating Munich Agreement in 1938, the events developed precipitously. Czechoslovakia ceded its borderland to its neighbors (Hungary and—to a lesser extent—Poland). Slovakia lost a considerable part of its territory, at the same time it was granted autonomy within the framework of the Czechoslovak Republic.

The Republic gradually abandoned the principles of democracy which had been built up in the course of twenty years. While in Bohemia a feeling of defeat prevailed, in Slovakia a euphoria of autonomy was dominant. The divided Czechoslovakia was prepared for total capitulation to Hitler.

In March 1939, Bohemia and Moravia were changed into a Protectorate, while Slovakia was constituted as an independent state. However, the sovereignty of this state was a pure illusion.

Due to the war, Slovakia was economically prosperous. Its political regime, closely connected with Catholicism, had many totalitarian features, such as the monopoly of one party of nationalist, clerical and populist orientation, with fascist groups operating in it.

The totalitarian character of Tiso's regime found its most conspicuous expression in the adoption of cruel anti-Semitic laws and the deportation of almost sixty thousand Jews [23]. All these features, and the fighting aside Nazi Germany in the war, earned the Slovaks a bad reputation. It was a tragical paradox that Slovakia obtained its state independence in such a form. The Slovaks' fame was only partly restored by the Slovak National Uprising in August 1944.

Legacy 3: The Communist "Solution"

The Slovak National Uprising had among its aims the restoration of the Czechoslovak state, but with a truly federal structure, based on the principle of equal partnership.

Following the agreements with the Allies, pre-war Czechoslovakia, with the exception of Ruthenia, was reinstated. The Czechoslovak government adopted a program granting the Slovaks a somewhat ill-defined degree of self-determination within the common state. But neither President Benes, nor the communist regime installed in 1948 have accepted the principle of Czech-Slovak partnership demanded by the Slovak National Uprising. On the contrary, the communists introduced a tightly controlled unitary state.

After 1948, the Catholics were object of hard political persecution [20]. The period of the Slovak State became a taboo, its representatives were condemned, first of all for their clericalism and anti-communism. The totalitarian character of this regime was not mentioned by the communists. Anti-Semitism was not formulated as a moral problem of the whole society. As a consequence, a loss of historical memory has taken place. The tendency to idealize the Slovak state and some of its representatives, especially its President Tiso, is a typical case. According to the results of repeated surveys on the historical conscience of Slovak population after November 1989, only one third of respondents assumes a negative attitude towards the Slovak state. In the opinion of another one third the virtues of the Slovak state prevailed over its vices; the last third is unable to adopt any evaluating attitude at all [1,2,3].

During the next twenty years the communists introduced a policy of forced homogenization. They claimed that the national question is of secondary importance and can be resolved by the development of communism, which will first assert the primacy of the working class and ultimately eliminate all classes and national differences. Shortly after the Communist takeover, "Slovak policy" as an independent articulation of the Slovaks' interests began to disappear: instead, "the policy in Slovakia" was implemented [23,p. 296]. By September 1948, the Communist Party of Slovakia became subordinated to the Communist Party of Czechoslovakia. "The socialist industrialization of Slovakia" was declared and presented as a principal key for solving "the Slovak question". In 1960, the competences of Slovak authorities and institutions were drastically restricted.

A sad chapter of Czechoslovak history was the fight against so-called "bourgeois nationalists", which led to the trials of those, first of all Communists, who were involved in the Slovak National Uprising. The trials were an integral part of the Stalinist purges of the representatives of national resistance and followed the same scenario as those in Hungary, Bulgaria and Poland. But in Slovakia this campaign organized by the Prague Stalinists was regarded as an attack against

Slovakia. In the mid-sixties, after the "bourgeois nationalists" had been released from prison, they joined the wide stream of "anti-dogmatic" intellectuals, who participated in the preparation of the political thaw in 1968.

Legacy 4: Potemkin Village of the Normalized Federation

During the "Prague Spring" in 1968, the Slovak issue erupted again. One of the central planks of the Action Program, an official document of the reforming Communist Party, was a truly federal state in which the two republics would have been the primary repositories of governmental power and the central government would have had largely derivative and carefully enumerated limited powers. Similar to the past, it was again the Slovak politicians and intellectuals who came up with the demand of an equitable model of Czech and Slovak coexistence. In Slovakia the national dimension of the ongoing reform was much more widely discussed. And although the concept of "socialism with a human face" was inseparably connected with the name of Alexander Dubcek, who was Slovak, many leading Czech intellectuals and politicians remained insensitive towards the Slovak demands [26].

Like in other moments of history, the Slovak political and intellectual elite was divided into two main streams: into those who stressed the necessity of democratization, while interpreting the federalization issue as its integral part, and those who defined the solution of the Slovak problem as the prerequisite for democratization. Some Slovak intellectuals coined the phrase "federalization first, democratization afterwards" without understanding that no real federation can exist without democracy. And in fact, as Václav Havel said, "this was followed by federalized totalitarianism." [22,p. 16].

The group preferring federalization was headed by the Slovak Gustáv Husák who later became General Secretary of the Central Committee of the Communist Party of Czechoslovakia and, at the same time, President of Czechoslovakia; the same man who had been condemned and jailed as a "bourgeois nationalist" in the 1950s. He was surrounded by politicians who reappeared as advocates of Slovak independence after 1989.

Two months after the Warsaw Pact intervention, in October 1968, the constitutional amendments were adopted. However, in the following period of normalization, under the conditions of hypocrisy and social schizophrenia, centralization was restored in a particularly harsh and repressive form. The federal institutions created by the constitutional amendments turned out to be nothing more than a Potemkin village. Everything was being decided in fact by the Communist Party center. Once again, the problems of Czech and Slovak coexistence and partnership were put in the "refrigerator" (Rupnik [33]).

Legacy 5: Jobs and Bread of Socialism

Among the historical burdens complicating the Czech and Slovak relations, the asynchronous nature of the processes of industrialization and urbanization in Slovakia and Bohemia must be mentioned, too. While these processes had started in Bohemia before the foundation of Czechoslovakia, in Slovakia they only took place after 1948 in large scale.

Slovak society, of course, could not avoid the typical social effects of rapid industrialization, with the destruction of traditional bonds, the release of social control, social pathology and an abrupt deterioration of the environment. Moreover, industrialization resulted in a low proportion of final products, a strong dependence of Slovak industry upon the import of raw materials and energy, and a large arms industry. That is why currently Slovak economy has to cope with a heavier package of economic and social problems than the Czech one. Nevertheless, the experience of rapid industrialization is still broadly used in communist propaganda: "We have given the people jobs and bread".

Legacy 6: The Soft Normalization in Slovakia

As compared to the Czechs, the Slovaks have to a lesser degree perceived the communist era as a period of civilization decline and loss of human dignity.

Also, in the period of "normalization" following the Prague Spring, Slovakia was a more pacified part of humiliated Czechoslovakia.

When the Charter '77 movement was founded, there was only one Slovak (the writer Dominik Tatarka) among the 242 signatories of its first declaration. The number of the signatories of the Charter '77 remained much lower in Slovakia all the time.[3] While "perestroika" in the USSR brought a revival of the Czech dissident movement, and various informal initiatives, associations and movements were founded in Bohemia, in Slovakia the attempts to oppose the communist regime were reluctant. This was also partly caused by an insufficient communication between Bohemia and Slovakia. The Czech dissidents underestimated the importance of including their potential Slovak partners in the opposition activities.

In Slovakia "consolidation" was not so dramatic as in Bohemia, where normalization marginalized hundreds of people, first of all intellectuals and artists and made them potential dissidents. The polarization of the Slovak society was not so deep; the dividing line between the official and alternative structures was not so sharp. Like many times in the past, Slovak intellectuals adapted themselves to the new political power. The difference between the Czech and the Slovak responses to the period of normalization has been characterized by the Slovak writer Milan Simecka jun.: "While in Bohemia the gap between those in power and the population became wider, in Slovakia the erosion of the totalitarian system continued by its humanization" [38,p. 3].

"Centers of Positive Deviation", November 1989 and the National Issue

The resistance to the communist regime in Slovakia was weaker and less visible than in Poland, Hungary and in the Czech lands. It was dispersed among several centers which have not been strictly defined, many of them overlapping each other. The intense networking among them started later than in Bohemia.

The small group of signatories of Charter '77 had an intensive contact with the Czech dissenters and liberal intellectuals abroad. In contrast to Bohemia, where many prominent representatives of the Prague Spring signed Charter '77, in Slovakia A. Dubcek and his associates retreated into the background and for almost twenty years refused open opposition. Only at the end of the 1980s, they joined the club of reform communists "Regeneration" (Obroda). The active dissent was up to November 1989 practically limited to a rather isolated enclave of writers or social scientists (first of all M. Simecka and M. Kusy). Very near to them was a circle of people who were younger by a whole generation and who grew up in the moral marasmus of the "normalization". This group developed a many-sided alternative artistic and publishing activity.

The most numerous group striving for religious freedom was formed inside the Catholic community. It was these circles which in spring 1988 became the initiators of the broadest so far public protest event in Czechoslovakia, the so-called "Candlelight Manifestation" in Bratislava.

Independently thinking artists, scientists, intellectuals were the clearest example of the overlapping of official and unofficial structures in the period of "normalization" in Slovakia. While being employed in well-known scientific, educational or cultural institutions, they extended the borders of "what was allowed" and showed that it was possible to overcome "learned helplessness". These "positive deviants" (Bútora [6]) or "small quantities" (Szomolányiová [30]) have contributed to the dynamization of Slovak society in the second half of the eighties.

In this period the ecological movement became a common platform for the above mentioned circles. The Slovak ecological movement was far from being a single-issue movement. Quite on the contrary, at the end of the 1980s, it became a typical umbrella movement. The critique of the environmental conditions in Slovakia, especially in Bratislava, extended far beyond the boundaries of ecology and reflected the fact that ecological anomalies are only resulting from a sick political system.

It was mainly these groups who became the driving forces of the revolutionary events in Slovakia. As November 1989 approached, a more intensive communication took place among them. The events in Prague in November 1989 abolished their isolation and contributed to a rapid unification of these groups within the framework of the movement Public against Violence (VPN), the sister organization of the Civic Forum in Bohemia. The platform of the VPN was joined also by a group of liberal Hungarian intellectuals of the younger generation who had expressed their discontent with the Communist regime already earlier.

In general, there was no visible nationalist orientation in the opposition circles of Slovakia. However, certain differences could already be seen at that time. The civic wing of the opposition which was predominant at that time emphasized the universal values of freedom, democracy and humanity. It did not mean, however, that this wing was anti-national or insensitive to the specific problems of Slovak society.

This orientation was incorporated into the Public against Violence's election platform, entitled “A Chance for Slovakia”. “Our aim”, the program said, “is to build a new house for the Slovaks and Slovakia, based on political democracy, the sovereignty of Slovakia within our common Federation, a market economy, the re-establishment of civil society, the protection of the rights of all minorities, the restoration of morality, responsibility and conscience, social policies and social sensitivity . . . Our aim is a new quality of life for the individual, the family, village, city, region and society. Our aim is rehabilitation of the family, protection of health, promotion of education, science and culture . . . [37]”.

The religious wing of the opposition concentrated upon the defence of the freedom of conscience. As it has been shown above, in the Slovak Catholic tradition there has been a firm link between religious and national matters embodied in the old slogan “For God and Our Nation!”. After the revolution, increasing national sensitivity became typical for one part of the Catholic community and Church.

However, in the domestic opposition there was no radical nationalist stream. Nationalism has been supported by some Slovak emigrants, especially those who left the country after World War II or after 1948. Characteristic of their attitude is an idealization of the Slovak State, rejection of the post-war changes in Czechoslovakia, a strong anti-Czech and separatist orientation.

The majority of those who emerged after November 1989 as the “tribunes of the Slovak interests” did *not* take part in the anticommunist movement. They served as functionaries or active members of the Communist party, and paid lip service to the ancien régime.

The Slovak Issue and the Refrigerator Effect: Three Stages of Defrosting

Stage 1: “The Hyphen-War” or Bringing the Slovak Issue on the Public Agenda

The first indication of Slovaks’ sensitivity towards national problems after November 1989 came during the discussions about the election of the new Czechoslovak president in December 1989. VPN supported Václav Havel, but a considerable part of the Slovak public was in favor of Alexander Dubcek. It was not only Dubcek’s historical merits and his continuing reform communist orientation that were often mentioned in his defence, but also the need to express the interests of the Slovak nation.

The tensions between Czechs and Slovaks erupted in the quarrel over the official name of the state—the so-called "hyphen war"—following President Havel's recommendation that the country should no longer be referred to as the Czechoslovak Socialist Republic. In this controversy the frustrating experience of both nations concerning a highly centralized system was reflected in which neither of them had control over its own affairs, and in which the Slovaks were less "visible" to the outside world. The discussions finally resulted in the adoption of a rather esoteric series of names for the common state. It included the official full name "Czech and Slovak Federal Republic" (CSFR), as well as two versions of writing the traditional name, "Czechoslovakia": in Bohemia without the hyphen and in Slovakia with the hyphen ("Czecho-Slovakia").

During the "hyphen war" the Slovak National Party (SNS) entered the political scene with its first public demonstrations. Its leaders cast doubt on the legitimacy of the federative arrangements of Czecho-Slovakia, although only some of them supported the idea of total independence of Slovakia before the first free parliamentary elections in June 1990.

Quite opposite was the style of argumentation of the VPN whose representatives took the stand of adherents of the Czech-Slovak coexistence. They underestimated, however, the necessity of repeatedly assuring the Slovak public that they will with full vehemence assert the demand for "just" Czech-Slovak relations. Very soon VPN was accused of "Czechoslovakism" and of indifference to national interests. A considerable part of the public condemned the cooperation of the VPN with the Hungarian Independent Initiative and with the Roma Civic Initiative, two political parties representing the most important national and ethnic minorities in Slovakia.[4]

By depicting the history of Slovakia as a series of wrong deeds and tricks by neighboring nations on the oppressed Slovaks, the Slovak National Party characterized the Czechs and the Hungarians as the greatest enemies of the Slovak nation. The search for the external enemy has been connected with a glorification of the merits of the Slovak nation, with a pathetic appeal for national pride, with an almost totalitarian emphasis on the need for national unity. The meetings of the SNS were characterized by a hostile atmosphere.

In playing the role of a defender of the common people, the SNS turned to social demagogy and focused on the feeling of social insecurity aroused by economic reform. The economic program of the SNS was fragmentary but very attractive: it promised social security and Slovak sovereignty.

The Slovak National Party did not criticize those former communists who converted to form a new economic mafia, nor the activity of the secret police. At the same time, they attacked, in a populist manner, the new "power elite", i.e., mainly the leaders of Public against Violence. All this brought the SNS good results in the 1990 elections.

Stage 2: The Language Issue

After the elections in June 1990 the confrontation between the civic and the nationalist attitudes continued, the former represented in the first place by the VPN, the latter by the so-called National Bloc, an *ad hoc* coalition of nationalistic parties. Among them the SNS and the *Matica Slovenská*, a cultural and educational organization, were the most influential.

In the SNS propaganda was oriented to the relations between Czechs and Slovaks. But after the elections, when the new Slovak government began to push through the redistribution of power between the republics and the federation, the SNS started to concentrate on the problems of coexistence between Slovaks and Hungarians in southern Slovakia. The instigation of anti-Hungarian attitudes fell on a fertile soil: a considerable part of the Slovak population, mainly those living in purely Slovak regions without everyday contact with Hungarians, accepted the idea that the interests of the Slovak nation were threatened [26].

A fresh wave of nationalism emerged in fall 1990 when preparations were under way for a Slovak language law regulating the official use of minority languages. SNS gained acceptance from the public by a vigorous support of barring any language but Slovak for official communication.

The government coalition responded with a bill which was in accordance with Czechoslovakia's international commitments concerning minority rights. Under the law as adopted, ethnic minorities may use their languages in those areas where the minority constitutes at least 20 per cent of the population. The decision of the Slovak National Council (the Slovak Parliament) in favor of this bill provoked a strong public protest.

Stage 3: Radical Economic Reform and Disintegration

Since the very beginning of the economic transformation in January 1991, it turned out that it would be more difficult in Slovakia to overcome the communist heritage than it had been expected during the first months after November 1989. The heavier impact of the reform upon the Slovak economy was combined with problems in the value orientation and behavioral patterns of the Slovak population. According to sociological surveys [2,3] defensive life strategies and state-paternalistic attitudes are more frequent in Slovakia than in Bohemia.

As a response to the difficulties of economic transformation, a new national wave emerged, this time with a clear-cut social accent. Social demagogy has been mixed with the interpretation of the economic transformation as Prague's instrument of exploiting and impoverishing Slovakia, and suppressing Slovak national interests. The program of loosening the link between the Slovak and the Czech republics could thus be supported by a most convincing social policy argumentation: the opinion polls show that it is precisely unemployment and the threat of social insecurity that worry the Slovak population most [2,3,17,34,35].

This program found its expression as early as Spring 1991 in the first attempt to declare the sovereignty of the Slovak Republic. The last attempt took place in May 1992, one month before the parliamentary elections. All these attempts failed, so it was possible to keep the constitutional order of the Federation for the whole period of two years. The major political parties in Bohemia, as well as the representatives of the Slovak Government coalition responded with a strong rejection. According to their argument, the sovereignty of the Slovak Republic was, in fact, included in the constitution of the CSFR. The adoption of the proclamation of sovereignty would mean the first step towards a dual legal status, chaos and disintegration of the common state. The only legitimate way was the referendum.

The position of the advocates of Slovak sovereignty was too weak in the Slovak Parliament to force through its adoption, nevertheless strong enough to prevent the agreement on the referendum in the Federal Assembly, that could give a chance to both nations and other nationalities in the CSFR to express their genuine will, whether to keep or to abolish the common state.

Typically, the main opponents of the referendum were those political parties which were rejecting the common state and supporting the confederative or secessionistic model. This seemingly paradoxical attitude was based on a realistic calculation: public opinion polls were showing that they would not get a sufficient support of the population. At the same time they believed that the time was on their side. Therefore they preferred the tactics of blocking irreversible decisions. The negotiations on the constitutional structure of the state eventually led to a deadlock. It is beyond any doubt that the obstinacy on the part of Czech politicians had its share in it as well.

The 1992 Elections: A "Yes" to the Dissolution of the CSFR?

Most of the future scenarios in both republics stressed the advantages of the common Czechoslovak state with its good international position and radical economic reform and, on the contrary, the economic disadvantages and geopolitical risks of the division of Czechoslovakia. During the whole post-communist period, support for a common state was stronger than rejection. The champions of an independent Slovak state and of the confederation constituted less than one third of the population [3,29].

At the same time, the signs of potential disintegration became more and more visible. Firstly, helplessness and misperceptions concerning the future constitutional set-up persisted among the Slovak population. Only a small number of people had a coherent idea about the alternative forms of the state [3,19,35]. Secondly, as a result of anti-federal brainwashing in which practically the entire political opposition (except for the Hungarian parties) took part, an increasingly large number of people in Slovakia came to believe that the Slovaks would lose and the Czechs win as a result of the reform. The attitude of the Slovaks towards the Czechs was characterized by a growing distrust, by the frustration of "the younger brother" [14]. The Czech side reacted in a similar way: while the feeling of Czech-Slovak belonging still prevailed, there was an increasing conviction about the Czechs who pay for the Slovaks, and about the Slovak ingratitude and national egoism [14].

The image of individual parties increasingly depended on how far they were able to take advantage of the combination of social and national arguments. The most successful program was proposed by Meciar who campaigned for a vaguely defined confederation, one that would allow Slovakia to enact milder measures of economic reform and gain Slovakia international sovereignty, yet preserving a loose form of a common state. The voter supported this obscure constitutional hybrid, despite strong criticism levelled against it by the federal media.

The elections caused a political polarization between the Slovak and the Czech Republics. In Slovakia they brought a crushing defeat for the supporters of federalism and radical economic reform: the Civic Democratic Union, the coalition of the Civic Democratic Party and the Democratic Party, the Hungarian Civic Party fell short of the five per cent threshold required for entering the Parliament. They paid for their failure to unite before the elections.

In the new government of Vladimír Meciar the Movement for a Democratic Slovakia held all but two ministerial posts. They relied on the support of the Slovak National Party, the third strongest party, and the Party of the Democratic Left which took the second place in the elections. A rather weak parliamentary opposition was formed by the Christian Democrats and Hungarian minority parties.

The absolute winner in the Czech Republic was the Civic Democratic Party (ODS) which in coalition with two smaller right-wing parties formed the government headed by Václav Klaus.

Immediately after the elections, the coalition talks between the ODS and the HZDS proved how irreconcilable were the views of the two parties in constitutional issues. Both of them agreed on the division of the CSFR into two separate states.

The citizens of Slovakia thus learned that they might be given their own state, although the majority of them wished to preserve Czechoslovakia. They responded passively to what had until then seemed an improbable outcome. The negative feelings which accompanied the gradual dissolution of the federation during the second half of 1992 did not result in effective political protest. Although the majority of the Slovaks regarded a referendum as the legitimate way to decide the future of the state, their wish remained unfulfilled. Thus the road to the formation of two independent states was paved with insufficient civic participation. The dissolution of Czechoslovakia had simply taken place before the inhabitants of both republics became real citizens.

One Year After: Post-Independence Hangover in Slovakia

Three years after a "velvet" start to execute deep systemic changes, Slovakia does not have a relatively stable spectrum of political parties.

Regional and local governments are too weak to become a respected partner of central administration and the non-governmental sector. The interest groups are still in *statu nascendi*.

Although the constitution of the Slovak Republic adopted in September 1992 invokes the thousand-year yearning of the Slovak people for independence, Slovakia as a sovereign state actually started its calendar from zero. The new constitution proclaims adherence to the principles of pluralist democracy and the rule of law. However, it is not free from ambiguities as regards "checks and balances" and the distribution of power [40]. Even more seriously, Slovakia lacks a tradition of constitutionalism in the sense of legal consciousness and culture.

The political climate in the first months of independence was full of tension and paradoxes. Although political pluralism was preserved, those involved in active politics have revealed little capacity for mutual respect and cooperation. What prevailed in practice was closer to raw majoritarianism with little attention paid to the rights of minorities. This has been reflected in the so-called "liquidation syndrome" vis-à-vis the opposition. "Federalists" and Hungarians have been accused of acting against the interests of the new state, of damaging its image abroad. Appointments—a new "cadre policy"—were often based on purges in the state administration, as well as in education, health service and other areas.

Considerable political pressure was exerted on the media labelled "un-national" or "anti-Slovak". Journalists were officially requested to submit to "ethical self-regulation" in the interest of national unity. Nevertheless, despite the precarious financial position of some critically-oriented papers, the 1989 revolution had sown its seed in this profession. There seems to be less chance for a repetition of the "normalization scenario" of the 1970s than was expected immediately after the 1992 elections.

The Price of Unfulfilled Promises

The majority of the Slovaks have not accepted the official interpretation which views the division of the CSFR as a culmination of Slovak national emancipation. In March 1993, less than one third of respondents of a representative survey indicated that if a referendum had been held, they would have voted for the dissolution of the CSFR.

The legitimacy of the new states is questioned also by the conviction that the country was divided in a non-democratic way, without a referendum [17].

Nevertheless, there is no political party in Slovakia, even among the former pro-federal parties of liberal-conservative orientation, which would campaign for reunification. The political struggle does not revolve around the Slovak statehood, but around the state's ability to continue the transition toward market economy and democracy.

Today Slovak independence is viewed in the context of the country's aggravated economic and social situation. Compared to some pre-election euphoria, the post-independence climate is palpably more pessimistic [35,17]. The dreams of the advocates of separation about the "national energy" which would emerge from the very fact of Slovak independence, proved to be mere illusions. Most people have come to understand that the disintegration of the CSFR only exacerbates the problems of transition.

The HZDS leaders were subjected to severe criticism for their failure to formulate a clear and consistent economic program which would further the transformation process. However, the rapid disillusionment has not been accompanied by a shift in the economic orientation of the population. State-paternalist attitudes are still shared by a substantial portion (40 per cent) of the population. About half of the inhabitants favor the "social market"; liberal-conservative ideas are accepted by the smallest group of people in Slovakia (10 per cent) [17].

The Process of Crystallization

The growing disenchantment brought a visible change in the political scene of the country. First of all, Meciar's popularity, and consequently support for the HZDS and the government, has decreased. His confrontational style, aggressive tendencies, and inclination to improvisation—factors which had worked in his favor in opposition—have started to evoke the opposite reaction.

During the first months of independence, the Movement remained an "umbrella organization" with anti-Communists and reform Communists of 1968 vintage, with proponents of a market economy and advocates of state interventionism, with former federalists and separatists, pro-Westerners and Slavophiles, European integrationists and xenophobic nationalists. All these people were kept under one roof by

Meciar's forceful personality and firm party discipline. However, the first signs of division appeared soon. The dispute involved supporters of Meciar's autocratic line and those who saw a need to introduce internal democracy and to cooperate with other political groups. A key figure among the rebels was Milan Knazko, the minister of foreign affairs, a former star of Public Against Violence.

Knazko's dismissal from the cabinet and from the ranks of the HZDS weakened the latter's position in Parliament. Since the Slovak National Party also left the coalition, Meciar found himself in the position of heading a minority government. The former communists within the HZDS have strengthened their hand in the top political institutions. Ex-Communists, now members of Meciar's ruling movement, hold all key positions, including those of the President, the Prime Minister, the Defense, Interior and Foreign Ministers, the Chairman of the Parliament, the Chairman of the Constitutional Court, and the General Procurator. Of the 150 deputies in the Slovak Parliament, three-fifths were members of the Communist Party.

To increase the potential of Slovakia for coping with the economic transformation, a further crystallization of the Slovak political scene is necessary, especially the emergence of a more effective right-left axis, defined in terms of support for a market economy at one pole and in terms of state intervention at the other. Changes in that direction have occurred in 1993. From among the parties represented in Parliament, the Slovak National Party has to find a new *raison d'être*. Its campaign goals were fulfilled by the creation of an independent Slovak state. Within its ranks a 'liberal' wing emerged which pledges allegiance to a free-market program and criticizes the government's privatization slow-down. This wing tries to become a representative of private entrepreneurs and thus to occupy the space on the right of the political spectrum which had been left vacant following the electoral defeat of the liberal parties.

The extra-parliamentary parties of liberal and conservative orientation have been trying hard to stop further fragmentation. The Civic Democratic Union was disbanded at the end of 1992, as some of its leaders joined forces with members of the Democratic Party and the Civic Democratic Party in Slovakia to create a new Conservative Democratic Party. At the same time, a Party of Businessmen also emerged and aspired to represent the interests of the private sector. Paradoxically, the closer these initiatives are to each other, the harder it is for them to find a common language or approach. As a result, one year after the elections, Slovakia's proclivity to the left seems unchallenged.

The prospect of a political and economic crisis in spring 1993 led parliamentary parties to find a common approach to limit the HZDS's autocratic tendencies and the risk of authoritarian rule. Some degree of cooperation seems likely despite the complexities of bridging the gulf between the anti-communist KDH and the post-communist SDL, as well as between the SNS and Hungarian parties.

The limits of the HZDS's ability to cope with the task of one-party government were made clear after the first round of presidential elections in February 1993, when Meciar's first candidate failed to obtain the required three-fifths support. The opposition parties also failed to agree on a joint candidate, and the post went to Michal Kovac, a former Communist and nationally oriented Catholic, who, as a leading functionary of the HZDS, was one of the key actors of the dissolution of Czechoslovakia. Nevertheless, his first steps indicate that the Bratislava Castle could become an alternative power center to the Prime Minister's office. This possibility has evoked two reactions. Some observers believe that any tempering of Meciar's harsh style by the President could only postpone a rejection of Meciar's policies by the public. According to others, it could provide an opportunity to follow the "Spanish model" in which the President would help establish a broader consensus across the political spectrum and facilitate the formation of a broadly-based coalition government.

Prospects for Power Sharing

The drop of public support for the HZDS was not accompanied by an increased support for other parliamentary or extra-parliamentary parties. The disappointed people remained in the category of undecided voters or non-voters who do not trust any party. Three months after the independence, the parliamentary parties represent only one half of the population [17]. This indicates a crisis of legitimacy. In such a situation, political leaders should invite other parties to cooperate in an attempt to create a nation-wide consensus in favor of the reform. However, the HZDS, and especially Meciar have shown little capacity for a policy of negotiation and power sharing. The prospects for a negotiated democracy in Slovakia are more and more often discussed in the context of early elections.

Notes

1. Within small privatization shops and smaller enterprises are sold. Large privatization concerns big state enterprises. The so-called "voucher privatization" is only one form of large privatization.
2. In May 1990, one month before the first free elections, only 24% of the citizens in Slovakia were dissatisfied with the changes after November 1989; in January it was already 72%. In April 1992, only one third of the adult people in Slovakia were persuaded that the present regime has more advantages than the communist one [2,3,29].
3. At the end of the 1980s there were 1,900 signatories of Charter '77 in the Czech Republic, whereas in the Slovak Republic there were only 19.
4. According to the March 1991 census among the 5.3 million inhabitants of Slovakia almost 11 per cent are Hungarians. The Roma community is recorded at only 1.5 per cent in the census, but according to more realistic estimates, it is around seven per cent of Slovakia's population [25].

Literature

1. "Aktuálne problémy Cesko-Slovenska"—november 1990. Správa zo sociologického vyskumu. (Topical Problems of Czecho-Slovakia—November 1990. A Report on a Sociological Survey). Bratislava, CVSP 1990.
2. "Aktuálne problémy slovenskej spolocnosti"—máj 1991. (Topical Problems of Slovakia—May 1991. A Report on a Sociological Survey). Bratislava, CSA UK 1991.
3. "Aktuálne problémy Cesko-Slovenska"—január 1992. (Topical Problems of Czecho-Slovakia—January 1992. A Report on a Sociological Survey). Bratislava, Centre for Social Analysis 1992.
4. Alan, J.: "Cesko-slovenské vztahy po pádu komunistického panství." In: Gál, F. a kol.: *Dnesní krize Cesko-slovenskych vztahu.* (Czecho-Slovak Relations Following the Fall of the Communist Rule. In: Gál, F. et al: The Contemporary Crisis in Czecho-Slovak Relations.) Praha, SLON 1992.
5. Bacová, V.: "Rómska minorita na Slovensku v súcasnosti." (The Roma minority in Slovakia.) In: *Etnické mensiny na Slovensku.* Kosice, SAV 1991.
6. Belohradsky, V.: "Postkomunizmus jako panika" (Post-Communism as a Panic). *Mladá fronta dnes,* 12.6.1991.
7. Bútora, M.: "Vyvzdorúvanie alebo kazdodennost pozitívnych deviantov." In: *Lesk a bieda kazdodenosti.* (Defiance or the Everyday Nature of Positive Deviants. In: The Glamour and the Misery of Everyday Life). Bratislava, Smena 1990.
8. Bútora, M., Bútorová, Z., and Rosová, T.: "The Hard Birth of Democracy in

Slovakia: The Eighteen Months Following the 'Tender Revolution'." In: *The Journal of Communist Studies,* Vol.7, December 1991, N.4.

9. Bútora, M.: "The Delayed Return of Prodigal Sons: Reflections on the Emerging Democracies in Central and Eastern Europe." In: *Politics in Transition: The American University Journal of International Law and Policy,* June 1992.
10. Bútora, M., and Bútorová, Z.: "Slovakia after the Split." In: *Journal of Democracy,* Vol. 4, No. 2, April 1993.
11. Bútorová, Z., Fric, P., Rosová, T., and Dobrovodsky, M.: "Rok po: Vyvoj politickej scény na Slovensku vo svetle vyskumu." (One Year After: The Development of the Political Scene in Slovakia in the Mirror of Research). In: *Sociológia* 1991/5-6.
12. Bútorová, Z.: "Two Years After November 17, 1989: The Hard Birth of Democracy in Slovakia." In: Gerlich, P., and Glass, K. (Hrsg.): *Zwischen den Zeiten.* Wien, VWGÖ 1992.
13. Bútorová, Z.: "The Hard Birth of Democracy in Slovakia." *East European Reporter,* January-February 1992, N.1.
14. Bútorová, Z., and Bútora, M.: "Wariness Towards the Jews as an Expression of Post-Communist Panic." Proceedings from the International Seminar on Anti-Semitism in Post-Totalitarian Europe. Prague, May 1992.
15. Bútorová, Z.: "A Deliberate 'Yes' to the Dissolution of the CSFR?" In: *Czech Sociological Review,* 1993, No. 2.
16. Bútorová, Z., and Bútora, M.: "A Democratic Road for Slovakia?" In: *Uncaptive Minds,* Vol. 6, No. 2.
17. "Current Problems of Slovakia after the Split of the CSFR"—March 1993. Report of the Sociological Survey. Bratislava, Center for Social Analysis 1993.
18. Cutler, L., and Schwarz, H.: "Constitutional Reform In Czechoslovakia: E Duobus Unum?" In: *The University of Chicago Law Review,* Spring 1991.
19. Fric, P., Bútorová, Z., and Rosová, T.: "Cesko-slovenské vztahy v zrkadle vyskumu." (Czech-Slovak Relations in Public Opinion). In: *Sociológia* 1992/1-2.
20. Gál, F.: *Z prvej ruky.* (First-Hand Experiences). Bratislava, Archa 1991.
21. Gyárfásová, O., and Ritomsky, A.: "Aktivita politickych strán na miestnej úrovni." (The Activity of Political Parties at a Local Level). In: *Sociológia* 1991/ 5-6.
22. Havel, V.: *Letní premítaní.* (Summer Meditations). Praha, Odeon 1991.
23. Kamenec, I.: *Po stopách tragédie.* (On the Track of a Tragedy). Bratislava, Archa 1991.
24. Kovác, D.: "Slováci a Cesi: pohlad v spätnom zrkadle." (Slovaks and the Czechs: a Retrospective View). In: *Kultúrny zivot,* 1992/5.
25. Krejcí, J.: *Czechoslovakia at the Crossroads of European History.* Published by I.B. Tauris & Co Ltd, 1990.
26. Kusy, M.: *Slovensky fenomén.* (The Slovak Phenomenon). Fragment 1990/3.
27. Lipták, L.: *Slovensko v 20. storocí.* (Slovakia in the 20th century). Bratislava, VPL 1969.

28. Miklosko, F.: *Nebudete ich môct rozvrátit.* (You Will Not Be Able to Eradicate Them). Bratislava, Archa 1991.
29. Peroutka, F.: *Budovaní státu. I.* (Building Up Our State. I.) Lidové noviny, 1991.
30. Pithart, P.: *Sedesáty osmy.* (1968) Praha 1990.
31. Preliminary Results of the March Census. In: *Lidové noviny,* 4 July 1991.
32. Rosová, T., and Bútorová, Z.: "Madarsko-slovenské vztahy vo svetle vyskumu." Hungarian-Slovak Relations in Public Opinion Polls. In: *Sociológia* 1992/1-2.
33. Rupnik, J.: *Eisschrank oder Fegefeuer. Das Ende des Kommunismus und das Wiedererwachen der Nationalismen.* Transit, 1990, No. 1.
34. Slovensko—Marec 1991. *Sociologická momentka.* (Slovakia—March 1991. A Sociological Snapshot.) Bratislava, CSA UK 1991.
35. *Slovensko pred volbami*—apríl 1992. (Slovakia before the Elections—April 1992). Bratislava, CSA 1992.
36. Szomolányiová, S.: "The Repolitization of Slovak Society." Paper at the 4th World Congress of Soviet and East European Studies. Harrogate, July 1990.
37. *Sanca pre Slovensko.* (A Chance for Slovakia). Volebny program Verejnosti proti násiliu, Bratislava 1990.
38. Siklová, J.: "Nacionalismus jako kompenzace." (Nationalism as a Compensation). In: *Prítomnost,* 1991, No. 10.
39. Simecka, M.: "Spytovanie." (Asking Questions) In: *Slovenské pohlady,* 1992, No. 2.
40. Valko, E.: "Poznámky na margo ústavy Slovenskej republiky." In: *Konstitucionalizmus na Slovensku.* Zborník z konferencie konanej pod zástitou Pew Charitable Trusts v januári 1993 v Bratislave.

14

Social Change, Political Beliefs, and Everyday Expectations in Hungarian Society: A Comparative View

Antal Örkény and György Csepeli

The Main Characteristics of the Transition Process in Hungary

In 1989, expectations about the advent of a perfect liberal society were very high in Eastern Europe. From Warsaw to Bucharest state socialism has been so rapidly destroyed that in the flush of victory no one could really foresee the coming troubles of the future. Apparently, the goals were absolutely clear during the political revolution: to introduce a multi-party system with modern democratic institutions and to bring to life a well-working market economy. On the other hand there was much less consensus concerning the means to achieve these goals. After having performed the enthusiastic rituals of free elections and forming of new democratic governments, some time should have passed in order to realize that in Hungary (and to some extent in all Eastern European countries) the major question to be answered is the following one: *How* can the transition to a market economy, a multi-party system and a full-fledged class society be achieved?

It became soon evident that it is much easier to be tempted by an idealized Western model of social organization than to implement it in a field which is historically so different. The Western values (property, liberty, equality) were not unknown in this area but their impact on society was limited by the traditional social structure. The social institutions stemming from modern Western values (market, democracy, nation-state, class society) remained underdeveloped.

As a result of Soviet dominance there was a widespread perception in the West that the similarities of the individual Eastern European countries will dominate over their economic and social uniqueness, and national individuality. As soon as the imposed external oppression disappeared the special features became apparent.

Narrowing our scope to Hungary we can state that at least two special factors motivated the way in which the Hungarian "silent revolution" was performed.

a. Following the repression of the Hungarian revolution in 1956, the post-Stalinist government was not able to maintain the rigid centralized redistributive system. From the mid 60's the redistributive model gradually underwent a major change that resulted from the incorporation of certain elements of market economy. This gave a room for limited autonomy of economic action on behalf of individual citizens as producers, sellers and buyers.[1] The emerging alternative economic system was called *second economy* as opposed to the official system of redistribution which was called *first economy*. The two economic systems, however, were not separated. Most frequently, the dividing line between the first and second economies was drawn in families and even in economic actors themselves. The dominant pattern of participation was twofold: the same family or the same person participated in workplaces maintained by the state and, at the same time, produced on small scale commodities for the market.[2]

b. From the mid 80's this process was paralleled by deep changes in the political-ideological field and in the civil society. There emerged a great number of pluralist structures and procedures substituting the earlier monolithic pattern of political-ideological integration.[3]

The dualism of redistribution and market gradually reached a breaking point. The latter was unable to perform its earlier function of compensating for the bureaucratic failures of the former. A major social and economic crisis seemed inevitable. As a result, a classical revolutionary situation emerged: the rulers lost their willingness to rule and the ruled lost their willingness to be ruled. The "revolution" came not only from above, as a consequence of the radicalization of the disillusioned reform-minded communist intellectuals but from below as well.

The centralized, monolithic, redistributive structures disappeared and were immediately replaced by the political institutions of democracy (multi-party system, parliamentarism, separation of the executive, legislative and judiciary powers, free press, observance of human rights). Unfortunately, the sudden shift made many observers forget about the lack of change in the system of state ownership, and of the emergence of civil society and strong communal autonomies.

As a result of the discrepancy between the success of political-ideological transition from state-socialism to democracy and the failure of change in the economic and social spheres there was no chance to develop a transparent political-ideological field in the society. Divergent economic, social, and cultural interests could not find their adequate channels of communication and the parties claiming to represent these interests were actually lacking clear ideological profile.

Instead of discussing the major problems (namely: what social groups exist in the society and what kind of social interests and aspirations work among them) the only question raised was how the process of political transition went wrong. Public opinion turned against parties and politicians mutually accusing each other for the frustration experienced as a consequence of postponing radical economic and social change. On the other hand, the political elite clashed and got involved in a futile ideological discussion about Hungarian national character, national loyalty and Christian morality.

Liberalism and Anti-Liberalism

This chapter is based on data provided by a survey carried out by the authors in 1989 and by some other more recent public opinion polls. In the survey[4] carried out in spring 1989 we attempted to measure the political-ideological mood of Hungary. We tried to get an insight into the characteristic belief systems in Hungary just before the decisive moment of the political transition (June 16, 1989, funeral of the martyrs of 1956).

Our sample consisted of approximately 700 respondents who were selected on the basis of their socio-economic position (market vs redistribution).[5] We didn't attempt to make a representative survey but tried the model by sampling quasi-experimentally the major structures of the economy and society. The aim of the study was to identify the causal links between the nature of political-ideological views (beliefs of *liberalism, socialism and nationalism*) and the fundamental factors of social existence (social descent, cultural capital, position in the market or in redistribution, political participation).

In spring 1989, the majority of the respondents accepted the basic principles of political liberalism. Surprisingly enough, the dominant trend was to reject not only any ideological manifestation of state-socialism but the stock of social-democratic values as well. This trend remained continuous. When in 1990 and 1991, people were asked about their judgement of the different democratic institutions, more than 90 percent emphasized the importance of the modern and democratic parliamentary system, free press, the multi-party system, separation of powers, etc.[6] Nevertheless, we must take into account four important limitations:

a. This extremely high rate of agreement with the principles of political democracy came from the strong rejection of the former state-socialist system. But from 1989 on, as time passed, more and more inconsistencies and ambiguities have weakened this overall liberal attitude.

b. The positive public support of liberal political changes was not accompanied by intense social participation. Since the second turn of the parliamentary elections, a constant tendency of voters' absenteeism has characterized Hungarian society.

c. In a comparative study Hungarians were found most rejective toward forms of open activities of political protests such as public meeting, demonstration, occupation of office building or strike. The only exception to this tendency was the taxi drivers' blockade and its nation-wide support in October 1990. On the other hand, we suggest that this blockade was a symptom of general public dissatisfaction with the government rather than an attempt to achieve social emancipation. (Cf. Sik's paper in this collection.)

d. We found that intolerance against minorities remained prevalent especially in disguised forms. The reasons to disguise intolerance and prejudice against minorities (especially against the Jews) root in sheer conformity. A tolerant, non-discriminatory attitude towards minorities is part and parcel of the general liberal attitude but subtle methods of investigation reveal the presence of intolerance against Gypsies and some neighbouring nations as well.

Against the background of an overwhelming rejection of the state-socialist past, there are differences of liberalism which should be explained in terms of social structure.

In 1989 we tried to model the causal linkage between social position and peoples' cognitive structure. In the case of liberal affiliation we found that access to cultural benefits was a crucial factor underlying liberalism. Economic and political liberalism, that is preference for market economy and free political institutions was likely to occur among intellectuals having high cultural capital measured by the number of books possessed, frequency of attendance of cultural events, foreign languages spoken, etc. Cultural capital, however, in itself was not able to cause liberalism unless it was coupled with opposition political activity.

Surprisingly enough, embedment in the market did not have a direct influence on political attitudes and certainly did not produce liberal values. For example, a firm approval of privatization, which is the heart of the liberal economic belief system, was not at all the consequence of the respondent's involvement in market transactions. Positive attitude toward privatization was likely only if the respondent had high cultural capital and participated intensively in opposition political activities against the one-party system.

The years of 1990 and 1991 brought about the decline of political involvement of any kind. As a consequence an important component of the liberal attitude disappeared. The slow process of privatization and the stagnation of the number of entrepreneurs (most of them coming from an anti-liberal social environment) are also not favourable for the prospects for liberal values.

Paradoxically enough, the former elite was found to be prone to participate in market activities. Although the managers, officials and bureaucrats of the collapsed state-socialist system did have cultural capital, they have never had strong attraction toward liberal ideological and political attitudes. Those sizable groups of first generational intellectuals whose parents were peasants or workers are also very easily excluded from the liberal trend because they were socialized under state-socialism and had no place in the "semi-market" of the second economy. Liberalism is accepted whole-heartedly only by a minority: i.e., by second or third generational intellectuals with a platonic attraction to the market.

Thereby in 1989 we could already predict that the introduction of market economy with all of its economic, political and social consequences will make the transition an extremely difficult and complex process. The problem of this process, we argued, would not be solved only by means of political action. Ideological devotion, liberal creed, sense of mission on behalf of politicians cannot be sufficient for making such a complete change. On a pragmatic level, people prefer the values of security, order and the idea of slow economic transition to the economic program of risky and painful shock therapy. Consequently more and more people are ready to give up the basic, and quite theoretical, liberal values of a market economy for their safety.[7]

The Sleeping Beauty of Socialist Values

Although there is consensus among Hungarians that the ideological heritage of state-socialism should be rejected, the hard conditions of social life necessarily lead to the re-emergence of socialist values such as social justice in terms of equality, social security, strong state intervention, limitations imposed on individual economic incentives and profit orientation. Ironically, people adhering themselves to these values would reject that doing so they can be considered as socialists.

In a recent survey[8] one third of the respondents of a national representative sample judged the Hungarian society as overwhelmingly poor. 90% of the respondents were extremely pessimistic concerning their future economic situation. 50% of the respondents felt uneasy thinking about their everyday survival. In defining the causes of poverty, the majority thought that the lack of institutions of social policy, growing unemployment and low quality of education were the major causes. Richness was attributed to good connections, ambition, and family inheritance.

Increased social expectations of state intervention, the praising of redistributive social policy, commitment to social equality stem from the permanent social deprivation which has been experienced ever since the transition period started. According to a public opinion poll in 1990, 78% of the respondents supported the idea that the state must provide general basic income to everyone, 90% of the respondents claimed that the state must provide job for every people and 77% of the respondents would accept income regulations by the state in order to reduce social inequalities.[9]

A cluster analysis showed[10] that 66% of the respondents belonged to the cluster of people who adhere themselves to socialist values without expressing any beliefs of liberalism. The rest can be characterized as liberal but half of them still insisted on the advantages of strong state intervention in social policy, education and the economy.

National Attitudes

Surveys of national identity indicate that on the basis of spontaneous identification two—liberal and ethnocentric—versions of national identity can be distinguished. As we gradually move away from the common plane of national identification, significant differences emerge among people according to their liberal, conservative or socialist attitudes. Thus, national identity hinders the crystallization of individual ideological and political beliefs and makes political clairvoyance and ideological orientation almost impossible.

On the other hand, any of these beliefs may claim immediate and extensive acceptance if it wraps its message in slogans of national ideology. To be sure, whatever a given political orientation gains in terms of its ability to get national consensus, it loses in terms of its ability to regard the social, political and economic issues as problems to be solved. (Unfortunately, the governing coalition in Hungary gave preference to national consensus instead of assuming clear positions with regard to the painful therapy of social, political, economic malaises.)

This peculiar prominence of national affiliation in Hungary and elsewhere in Eastern Europe cannot be explained only by historical circumstances, special political aspirations, motivations or ideologies.[11] There can be found important social background effects as well. In 1989 when we analyzed the background components of ethnocentric spirit in Hungary there was a reverse causal relationship between the level of cultural capital and ethnocentric components of national identity. The higher was the cultural capital, the less was the inclination of the given person to identify himself with ethnocentric nationalism. Ethnocentric nationalism consequently is caused by low social descent coupled with a low level of cultural capital. This is the social base of any kind of political aspiration which uses the tools of national affiliation.

Investigating clusters[12] of respondents we found recently that those who believe in state intervention and redistribution, and reject social democracy or socialism tended to prefer as voters the governing nationalist and conservative parties. Voters of the liberal opposition parties were more likely to occur among the liberal clusters favouring fast privatization. Voters of the Socialist Party were split along the three clusters which means that the constituency of this party cannot be considered as a pool of adherence to genuine social democratic values.

The 1990 success of the governing nationalist and conservative parties in Hungary could be attributed to the strategy of postponement of a radical transformation of the redistributive economy. Believers of redistribution and state intervention, however, dominate among non-voters whose numbers are increasing. It is up to the future to decide whether this silent majority turn back to nationalism or think that there is a need for a genuine social-democratic political force. Should neither of these options occur there is a danger that a radical right wing political party will occur which will not hesitate to resort to social demagogy.

Inconsistencies

"The political intellectual, the man of ideas, is nowhere very interested in defending inconsistencies, and every status quo is full of inconsistencies. Only by attacking the limitations of his political and social order can he feel he is playing a fruitful creative role. In Europe, he has been able to do this either by supporting a reformist utopia—an image of the good society of the future—or by advocating a conservative utopia, usually in the image of a society with traditional values an establishment and a creative aristocratic elite uninhibited by the need to flatter the uncreative masses. In either case he can criticize the present from the vantage point of an image of one or the other of these "good" societies. And quite often, both reformers and traditionalists dislike the same features of the present, like the nature of popular culture, which the leftist blames on the institutions of a business society, and the conservative sees as the necessary outcomes of democracy's giving the masses power over taste."[13]

This character of the intellectuals' thinking and role was not only very typical among Hungarian intellectuals, but led them into a pitfall on the road to obtain political power. While earlier their whole story had been about a permanent fight against a false and dishonest ideological consistency suggested by the former political leadership, now sitting in the seats of the new Parliament they had to give up this tradition. They found themselves in a double role: they run for new consistencies while they permanently oppose them from an intellectual position. Meanwhile they are unable to perceive those real inconsistencies which enmesh the whole society from the top to the bottom.

One of these real inconsistencies is reflected by the conflicting views of privatization. As we have indicated above, the popularity of market economy was high in the last days of the old regime. For example in 1989 it reached 75% among our respondents who strongly supported the idea of the market. Nevertheless, people become confused if they feel that the theoretically approved principles of market economy start to interfere with their everyday life and work. Recent public opinion polls showed that people who, in principle, are strong believers of privatization are much less prone to believe in its advantages if privatization involves their own workplace. (According to the result of a survey carried out in 1990 on a national sample, the rate of acceptance of privatization decreased from 77% to 54%.[14])

Another manifestation of inconsistency is connected with the acceptance of the conflicting values of differentiation and equality. In our survey carried out in 1991 we found that in forming their judgements on social justice people *simultaneously* accept the principle of achievement (high income, positive economic effects of making profit, inheritance) and the principle of equality (regulated income and limited profit-making, high taxation of inheritance).

A kind of political inconsistency can be revealed if respondents are asked about their beliefs concerning basic freedoms (protest, civil disobedience, strikes, demonstrations, freedom of press and speech, sexuality, etc.) and concrete activities. Faced with the prospects of various forms of social movements and protests their theoretical liberalism vanishes and a strong support for law and order emerges.

Conclusions

Public opinion polls have regularly shown disillusionment, frustration and even anger connected with the experience of transition not only in Hungary, but throughout Eastern Europe. A year after the collapse of the communist systems we carried out an international survey in twelve countries on popular perceptions of social justice.[15]

We have investigated variables such as satisfaction with own life, family life, community life, income level, job conditions, standard of living and finally satisfaction with the political system. Three tendencies were explored which dramatically anticipated the political developments to follow much later in Lithuania, Poland, and in Hungary. These developments reflect popular frustration and anger connected with the transition process, and kiss to life the "Sleeping Beauty" of socialism.

The first tendency shows a definite East-West slope which clearly demonstrates that following the demolition of the Berlin Wall and the iron curtain a "cognitive wall" has been erected between post-communist and advanced capitalist countries.[16] Graph 14.1 shows that the more we move from West to East the bigger is the personal dissatisfaction concerning income.[17]

Graph 14.2 demonstrates the satisfaction trends related to the political system of each country. The same slope appears again. This tendency also reveals a differentiation among post-communist countries. People of Poland, Slovenia, former Czechoslovakia and former East Germany seem to be more satisfied with their political systems than people in the rest of Eastern Europe.

We have also investigated the perceptions of poverty and wealth. Variable PMORALS indicates the tendency to blame the poor themselves, accusing them of moral and psychological defaults. Variable PECONS represents a reverse type of attribution emphasizing dysfunctional aspects of the economic system resulting in mass poverty. Graph 14.3 shows that the more we move toward East the more frequent is the occurrence of the individualistic moral and psychological attribution pattern. This is an important result indicating the strength of conservative tradition, the representatives of which are always prone to blame the victims of social inequalities.[18] In Graph 14.4 two variables represent the attribution patterns of wealth. Variable WDHORK indicates an emphasis on hard work and effort in understanding the causes of wealth. Variable WDISHON demonstrates the belief that wealth comes from social anomy and is a result of dishonesty.

The slope of WHDWORK points in the direction of the West demonstrating the increasing importance of this meritocratic principle of justice in advanced capitalist systems. In the case of WDISHON a reverse slope can be observed. These two slopes dramatically demonstrate the survival of egalitarianism in post-communist societies and prove that the change in values has not yet taken place.

Graph 14.5 reveals again a striking difference between post-com-

GRAPH 14.1
Income Satisfaction by Country

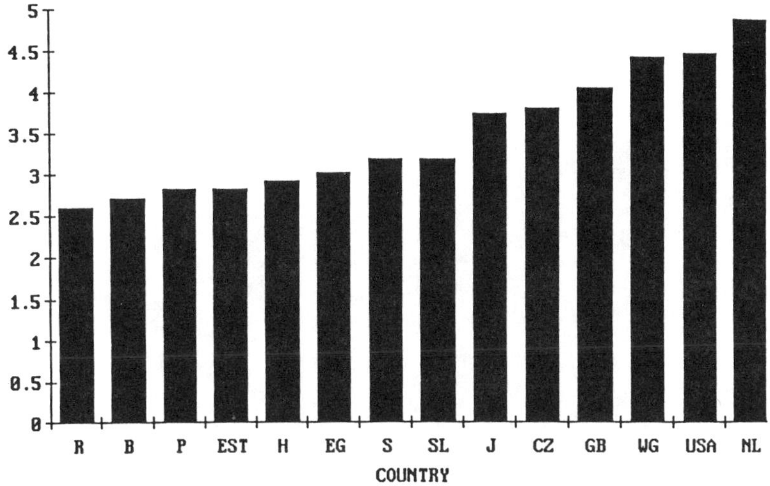

munist and advanced capitalist countries. People in Eastern Europe are more inclined to perceive society in terms of polar class differences than people living in the West who tend to perceive middle class as a dominant component of society.

Graph 14.6 shows the prevalence of the belief in post-communist

GRAPH 14.2
Satisfaction with Political System by Country

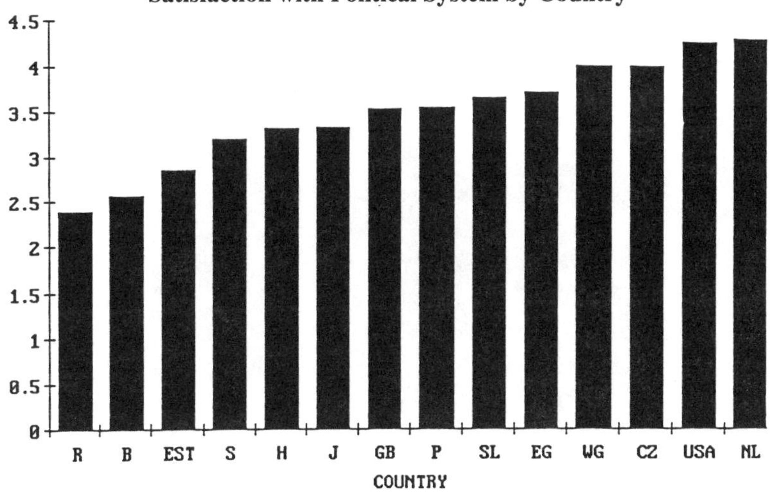

GRAPH 14.3
Explanation of Poverty by Countries

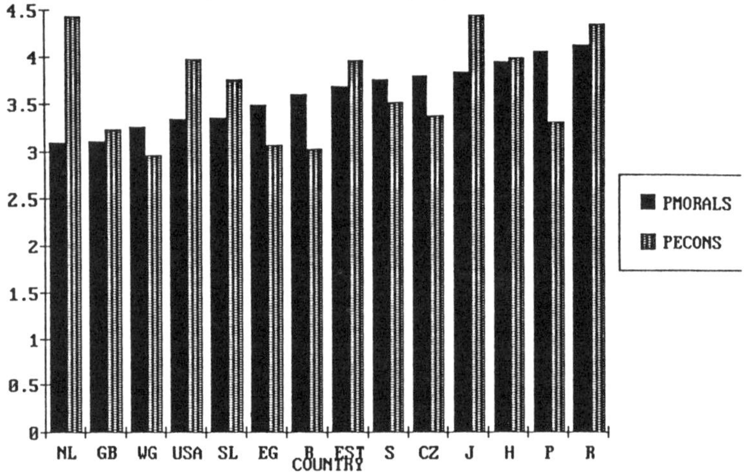

countries that it is the task of the state to ensure employment (GVTJOB). The disapproval of the idea of state intervention is especially strong among the Dutch and American people. Limiting the maximum of incomes by the state (GVTLIMIT) turned to be unacceptable to people living in market-economies. Tendencies of approval showed only a

GRAPH 14.4
Explanation of Wealth by Countries

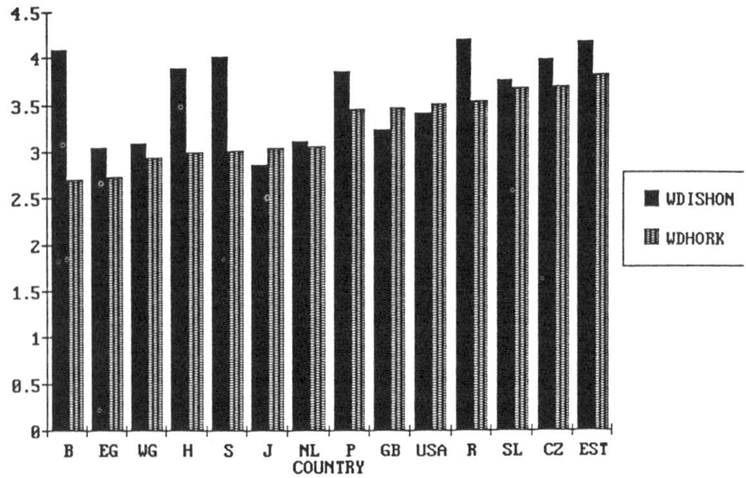

GRAPH 14.5
Perceived Percentage Poor, Middle Class, Rich by Country

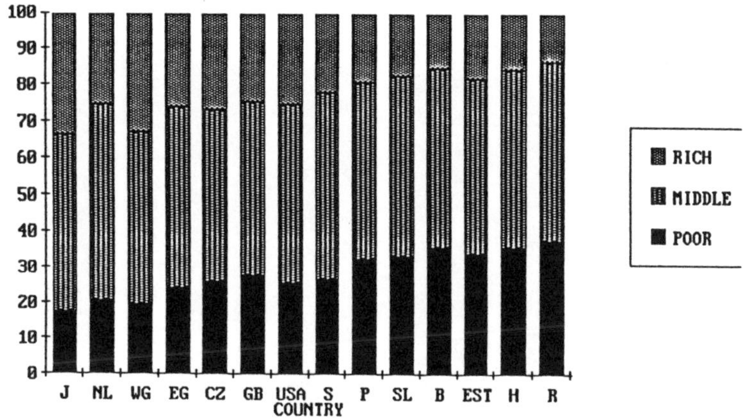

partial correlation (e.g., the Russians and the Czechs reject that idea).

Finally, according to Graph 14.7, members of post-communist societies are shockingly lacking any confidence in social justice. Negative experiences of the shortage economy under the old regime and the distorted legitimacy of the new political system have destroyed the

GRAPH 14.6
Approval of Government Intervention by Countries

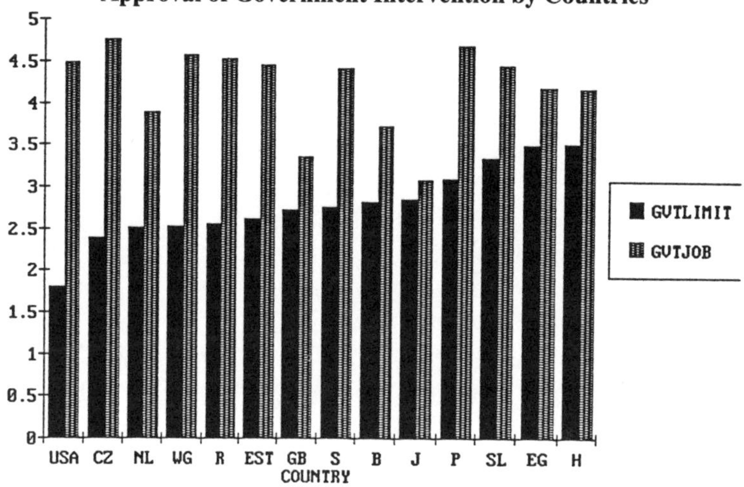

GRAPH 14.7
Skepticism Toward Social Justice by Countries

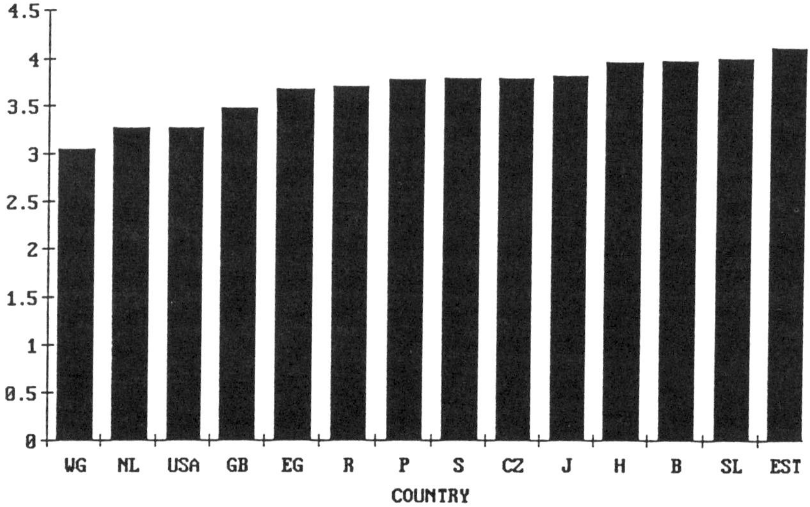

trust in justice and just institutions in these societies.

Pessimism and apathy became the major words of interpretation of the data provided by the surveys. It can hardly be otherwise unless research into the nature of the transition process undergoes radical changes. Concentrating on solely political issues, public opinion polls supply plenty of negative elements. There is, however, a deeper level of analysis which also shows optimistic expectations of the transition in the long run. People relentlessly believe in economic revival, in values of free society and in the importance of the overall transition. Differences in terms of social structure, income, family status, education, gender and age, etc., are influencing the expectations and attitudes related to the transition process. For instance, the prototypical liberal political belief system and the concomitant positive evaluation of market economy can be found in a narrow but very important group of the society: the educated, young, urban people.

Economic transition needs a flexible political discourse which is sensitive to the needs of progress. As a result a transformation of the social structure can be expected which provides social mobility and equality of opportunities. A kind of mental transition is also needed which would free the citizens of the new democracies from the psychological burden of state-socialism: helplessness, everyday aggression, disorganization, etc.

The successful introduction of full-fledged market economy and liberal political society cannot be conceived of without a development of new skills and motivations. The consistency of skills, resources and beliefs is a clue to the success of economic and social transition in Eastern Europe.[19]

This time the chances for catching up with the West are higher than ever and if they are missed, then the usual justification strategies such as scapegoating, blaming the enemy, etc. will be of little use. Consequently, now it is more than ever before up to the Eastern European actors themselves whether they will succeed or fail.

Notes

1. Kolosi, T. [1988]: "Stratification and Social Structure in Hungary." *Annual Review of Sociology* 14: 405–419.
2. Gábor, I. [1985]: "The Major Domains of the Second Economy." pp. 133–179 in *Market and Second Economy in Hungary.* (eds) Peter Galasi and György Sziráczki. Frankfurt: Campus Verlag.
3. Hankiss, E. [1990]: *Eastern European Alternatives,* Clarendon Press, Oxford.
4. Csepeli, Gy., and Örkény, A. 1992 *The Twilight of State Socialism. The Political Belief System in Hungary in the Year of the Peaceful Revolution.* London: Pinter Publishers; The Hungarian version of our book: 1990 *Az Alkony. A mai magyar értelmiség ideológiai-politikai optikája az 1980-as évek végén.* Budapest: ELTE.
5. Szelényi, I. [1983]: *Urban Inequalities under State Socialism.* New York Oxford Univ. Press.
6. Bruszt, L., and Simon, J. 1991 "A választások éve a közvéleménykutatások tükrében" (The Year of Elections Reflected by the Polls) in *Magyarország politikai évkönyve 1991.* (ed) Kurtán, S.-Sándor, P.-Vass, L. Budapest: Economix RT. pp. 607–646.
7. "Hol tart a szabadgondolat?" (Where is now the liberal thought?) 1991, Budapest: *Politikai Tanulmányok Intézete Alapítvány,* pp. 44–47.
8. Örkény, A., and Csepeli, Gy. 1992 Coexistence of Hidden Cognitive Representation of Socialism and capitalism in Hungarian Society, Working Papers #3 International Survey on Social Justice, Indianapolis: Butler University.
9. Kolosi, T. 1990. "Egyenlöségtudat nemzetközi összehasonlításban" (Perception of Inequality in Comparative Approach) in *Társadalmi Riport 1990.* (ed) Andorka, R., Kolosi, T., Vukovich, Gy. Budapest: Tárki pp. 373–401.
10. Örkény, A., and Csepeli, Gy. 1991 "Politikai-Ideológiai nézetek a társadalmi rendszerváltás folyamatában" (Ideological-Political Beliefs during the Social Transition in Hungary). Paper presented at a conference in Budapest, June 6, 1991.
11. Csepeli, Gy. [1989]: *Structures and Contents of Hungarian National Identity. Results of Political Socialization and Cultivation.* Frankfurt/New York: Peter Lange.

12. Örkény, A., and Csepeli, Gy. 1991 "Politikai-Ideológiai nézetek a társadalmi rendszerváltás folyamatában" (Ideological-Political Beliefs during the Social Transition in Hungary). Paper presented at a conference in Budapest, June 6, 1991.
13. Lipset, S.M. 1963 *Political Man; The Social Bases of Politics.* Garden City, New York pp. 345.
14. Szántó, J., and Tóka, G. 1990 *Vélemények az államról, politikáról és a privatizációról* (Public Opinions about State, Policy and Privatization). Budapest: Tárki.
15. The International Social Justice Project, a collaborative international survey, was supported in whole or in part by the following organizations: National Council for Soviet and East European Research (USA); National Science Foundation (USA); Institute for Social Research, University of Michigan; OTKA [National Scientific Research Fund] (Hungary); Economic and Social Research Council (UK); Deutsche Forschungsgemeinschaft (Germany); Institute of Social Science, Chuo University (Japan); Dutch Ministry of Social Affairs; Bulgarian Academy of Sciences; Grant Agency of the Czechoslovak Academy of Sciences; Saar Poll, Limited (Estonia); Ministry of Science and Technology of the Republic of Slovenia; State Committee for Scientific Research (Poland).

    For further details see Örkény, A. (1993) "Az igazságossági felfogások mindennapi percepciója a nemzetközi összehasonlítás tükrében" (Everyday Perception of Injustice Theories from the Perspective of International Comparison), Ph.d. Dissertation, Institute of Sociology, ELTE, Budapest.
16. The participating countries in our survey were the following: Bulgaria=B, East Germany=EG, West Germany=WG, Hungary=H, Slovakia=S, Japan=J, Netherlands=NL, Poland=P, Great Britain=GB, USA=USA, Russia=R, Slovenia=SL, Czech Republic=CZ, Estonia=EST.
17. For the measurement of income and political satisfaction (Graph 14.1 and Graph 14.2) we used a seven point scale where higher score meant higher satisfaction.
18. In Graph 14.3, Graph 14.4, Graph 14.6 and Graph 14.7 we used a five point scale for the measurement of the attitudes. Higher scores meant higher level positive acceptance of the attitude statements.
19. Angelusz, R., and Tardos, R. 1990 "Pártpolitikai mélyré tegek" (The Background of Parties) in *Magyarország politikai évkönyve* 1991 (ed.) Kurtán, S., Sándor, P., and Vass, L. Budapest: Economix RT. pp. 647–670.

15

The Vulture and the Calamity (Or, Why Were Hungarian Taxi Drivers Able to Rebel?)

Endre Sik

On October 25, 1990 the Hungarian Government raised the gasoline prices by 76%. In the afternoon thousands of angry taxi drivers protested before the building of the Parliament, and in the evening they blocked all the bridges across the Danube. Within hours the taxi drivers controlled the main streets in and out of Budapest.

On the next day (it was Friday) schools and offices, industrial plants and the international airport were practically paralyzed. The border between Austria and Hungary was closed to motorists to both directions.

By Saturday basic foodstuffs began to run low and the air became fresh, some people got afraid of the future, while others had a picnic on the middle of the empty bridges. In every hour the tension increased. The Government either deliberately or as a result of their confusion hesitated between police (or even military) attack and negotiations. The taxi drivers sometimes opened the blockades and closed down again. New actors appeared on the scene: trade unions offered their participation in a "round-table" discussion; the Hungarian Democratic Forum (the dominant party in the government coalition) organized a demonstration against the blockade; the Free Democrats (the biggest party of opposition) issued a plea for peaceful solution and supported the taxi drivers; other drivers joined the blockades all over the country, etc.

On Sunday, finally, the Government and the representatives of the employees and the employers engaged in a "round-table" discussion. The whole country watched the live show on the TV all day long. The result was a compromise i.e., the Government did not withdraw its decree but the rate of price increase was reduced and the Government promised pardon for those who participated in the action. The blockades were demolished in hours and an ordinary Monday followed the "long weekend of rebellion".

Why Vulture?

The purpose of this study is twofold; first, to prove that taxi drivers[1] were able to rebel against increased gasoline prices because of their vulture character; second, to suggest that they chose rebellion as a form of protest because they had long been in trouble and had been afraid that the calamity of the gasoline price increase would turn their trouble into a crisis.[2]

Why do I use the degrading analogy of a vulture to describe taxi drivers? I borrowed the term from the British socio-anthropologist G. Mars (1983) who in an analysis of occupational crime distinguished four categories symbolizing them with animal names.[3]

In his model the *hawk* is the symbol of the independent and individualistic entrepreneur whose goal is to maximize profits, who is free to decide what to embark on, how much to invest, how much and in what ways to cheat and to the prejudice of whom. Hawks are, for example, university professors, street peddlers, managers or hotel receptionists.

The *donkey* is just the opposite of the hawk. It represents a subordinated and isolated wage earner working in a fixed job who sometimes cheats his superior, and sometimes the customer but both in a piecemeal fashion and on a small scale. In doing so the donkey takes great risks because he is easy to check and replace. Donkeys include shop assistants or cashiers.

The *wolf* works in a pack which is held together by strong solidarity and long-standing personal ties and earns invisible income in a team effort. The team spirit is manifested to the outside world as a seclusive subculture united by the collective identity. Developed internal division of labour leads to distinct roles and hierarchy which are known to and recognized by all members and which hardly change. Such occupations include dustmen or dock workers.

The central figure in my story, the taxi driver, can be classified into Mars's fourth category—that of the *vulture*. The vulture is similar to the hawk insofar as both prey individually, i.e., there is neither specialization nor unequal hierarchical standing among them but is close to the wolf because there exists a loose network behind their actions that can quickly be activated as an efficient tool if needed. Under normal circumstances such a network is useful for coordinating, training and disciplining vultures but it has an equally important function of spotting danger immediately and giving increased efficiency of protection. Since the network is informal, there is no defined hierarchy among vultures although there are a few elected representatives who maintain the "inter-vulture" network. Mars's favourite examples for the vulture are insurance brokers, real estate agents and car dealers.

The Vulture Character of Taxi Drivers

Let us first look at the *socio-demographic composition* of taxi drivers. I would describe the typical taxi driver as a young to middle aged male living in the city, with professional driving skills. As to his *working patterns*, this occupation implies mobility in terms of area and time, and hardly resembles the two typical work places of our times—the factory and the office. Here, the place of work itself is on the move; there is no difference between day and night, only between good periods and bad ones; when other people enjoy leisure, it is the best time for the taxi driver to work. The taxi drivers are in full control of their working hours and enjoy enormous flexibility.

In this respect, taxi driving compares with household work where chores never end but can be interrupted at any time. This kind of unsystematic work schedule and constant mobility also makes it possible for the taxi driver to make himself scarce both for the family and the tax authorities. It takes a wife on her guard to know where her taxi driver husband can be. The high level of freedom from all kinds of control, and independent decision making play a great role in giving a sort of a "macho" image to the taxi drivers' *subculture*. The socio-demographic characteristics (young males) and the dense and widespread personal networks among the taxi drivers,[4] also add to the "macho" image.

Taxi drivers must be very good in communicating with strangers. They must be able to strike up and conduct a conversation, bear with all sorts of passengers and find the most effective technique to earn maximum tips. Moreover, they must also be able to tell when it is opportune to earn more than the ordinary fare plus tip (by cheating with the taximeter, giving wrong change, offering extra deals, etc.).

A very important factor in their lifestyle and also a further element of their "macho" image, taxi driving is a hazardous occupation. In return for the higher income from night hires, taxi drivers often have to pay a high price not only with their health and family life but sometimes also with their own lives. Though taxi drivers are not part of the underworld they mix with it every day.

It is not by chance that the public deals so extensively with taxi drivers and is so ambivalent about them: envying their entrepreneurial and illegal incomes but appreciating their entrepreneurial spirit; hating their driving style but admiring their professionalism; condemning them for beating up passengers but thinking highly of them when they take a woman in labour to the hospital and help catch criminals.

The *work organization* of taxi drivers is determined by the ways they can get customers. There are two forms of getting in touch with the client, either they pick him up on the street or are ordered to the client's address. It is this latter form which generates a centralized but very loose network among the taxi drivers. There is a cellular radio system to allocate the hires. But the cellular radio system is much more than that. In emergency, the network may be the key to survival. In addition, the cellular radio is a tool of social contacts, a communication channel for sending messages to one another, calling the family, setting up dates, searching for rare commodities, reporting on traffic jams, etc.

As to the *social position* of taxi drivers, it is not difficult to become a taxi driver. It practically requires no school expenses to get a professional driving licence in Hungary. Due to the fact that the overwhelming proportion of males below 40 have a driving licence, this licence does not give social prestige. On the one hand, you are still "only" a taxi driver even if you hold a university degree, and on the other hand, you can be a taxi driver without any education.

But in the past years the taxi drivers often should have also invested a car. From the mid-1980s self-employment became widespread in this occupation. This job was the first one in which the state tried to transform the widely existing hidden-illegal second economic activity into a visible-legal one. Without any restriction, everybody with a driving licence could get access to a driving permission i.e., one could become a taxi driver without any bribe or entrance fee. The number of these small-entrepreneur taxi drivers nowadays is greater than that of the other occupational form, the "double-dipper" wage earner. In the latter case the taxi driver is employed by a state firm for a fixed monthly salary but earns his income mainly from the tips.

Does the ownership of a car increase social standing? Not really because motor car is no longer an unattainable desire of the typical Hungarian household, and because the taxi driver's cab is not entirely an investment since it is used for household purposes, too.

Turning our attention to the *labour market strategy* of taxi drivers, there is hardly any difference between a "double-dipper" and a small-entrepreneur taxi driver. To increase the amount of tips one should apply the same methods with which the small-entrepreneur maximizes his profit. One possible strategy implies overwork, i.e., taxi drivers often extend the working hours to the physiological maximum. Secondly, both types of taxi drivers apply the same techniques to increase the likelihood to get tips.

Both types do other business during working hours in order to supplement their incomes. Such activities include various sorts of second economy activities, e.g., dealing in foreign exchange[5] or prostitutes.[6]

Finally, both groups have the same practices to reduce the driving costs: they combine passengers going in the same direction, jump the queue to avoid idle periods (and save gasoline), turn off the engine on slope, combining work and household chores (shopping, taking children to school, etc.).

Income maximization is thoroughly organized. First of all, there is a smoothly functioning price cartel, secondly there are strong groups which monopolize certain segments of the business (airport, hotels, furniture transport, etc.). The extensive personal contacts intertwining the entire subculture of taxi drivers provide a firm basis for these organizational forms.

It is fair to assume that the total income of both types of taxi drivers is largely similar, and that the income in both categories exceeds the average wages in Hungary,[7] although there are also substantial costs incurred and great monthly (and even weekly) variations.

In sum taxi drivers are of vulture character, on the one hand, because their work is of independent and of individualistic nature, and their business strategy is entrepreneurial. There is neither hierarchical difference nor specialization among them. On the other hand, a taxi driver is not entirely isolated from his colleagues. There is a strong communication system among them, and they have well developed cooperation patterns in the labour market. Finally, there is also the Taxi-Driver-Image, a subcultural phenomenon which maintains a common self-identity, and supports cooperation without any formal organization. Neither the wolf nor the donkey organization would fit in with the independent and mobile work pattern of the taxi driver. Also, due to the hazardous nature of the job and to the central communication system the total isolation of the hawk would have been also disadvantageous.

In addition to the organizational reasons there were also socio-historical ones which made possible the emergence of the vultures. It was relatively cheap to install the cellular radio system; the newly born small entrepreneurs in the early 1980s were ready for modernization both in cultural sense and financially; there was no pressure from the authorities to set up a more formal bureaucracy, etc.

Resentment among Taxi Drivers

The reason for resentment among taxi drivers was purely financial. For quite some time, due to the decreasing demand and increasing costs, their profits have been falling. I consider the increasing difficulties of taxi drivers only a trouble and not a crisis because they were able to cope with raising prices by self-exploitation and by the cartel system. Undoubtedly, they are worse-off now than in the early 1980s, but they are by no means different in this sense from the general trend in Hungary. Their number has not dropped significantly. In Budapest it is about 20000, according to some expert estimation five times more than in Vienna and four times more than in New York.

The taxi drivers were troubled by the diminishing number of customers, worrying about the rumours about increasing automobile and spare part prices[8] when they were slapped in the face by a sudden and drastic rise of gasoline prices. The Government presented them a calamity.

Of course, it was not the fact of the price increase itself that caught them by surprise. Although the Government tried its best to hide its plans from the public, Hungarians tend to have such sophisticated networks and sensors that everybody was certain about the upcoming price increase despite (or just because of) the staunch denial on the part of the Government. What was too much to bear was the rate of the increase. This rate was so steep that taxi drivers would have been unable to shift such a high rate of gasoline price increase on to their customers by simply raising their fares. The risk of losing their daily bread was high, and they could not cope with this problem using their regular defense means (a cartel price increase, extending their working time, pressing the customer to give bigger tips, developing new informal activities in the "black" economy).

Vultures on the Defensive

It does not follow, however, that they had to resort to rebellion. As possible alternatives, they

- could have followed standard economic textbooks and silently go bust, as the Government might have expected on the basis of the simple economic theories of market adjustment;
- could have been engaged in internal fights so that a minority would have redistributed the reduced cake and seized control over the new market;
- could have sought assistance or deferral from the Government through appointed representatives, and reduced the impact of the calamity through bargaining;
- and finally, could have gone on strike.

Why none of these alternatives was chosen can be explained on the grounds of the features I have discussed so far.

Individual reactions (from quiet acceptance of bankruptcy to innovative adaptation) would be typical of isolated hawks. The redistribution of the labour market would fit to wolves more than to vultures who are thwarted by the principle of solidarity and by the inertia of a successful cooperative strategy and also of a wide network. And perhaps more importantly, since the calamity hit many victims simultaneously, the "we are in the same boat" principle increased the likelihood of cooperation. Moreover, in a calamity there is no time to either desert solidarity or start redistributing the labour market.

Bargaining would have been equally time-consuming. Moreover, taxi drivers could not rely on the Government's willingness or ability to bargain. As one radical rebel put it:

> If we accept the 20 percent (gasoline price increase S.E.) now, they would top it with another 40 percent in two weeks. No, thanks. I am determined to stay here with this twenty-ton truck. The people are with us...All revolutions failed because those who controlled the events failed to persist. They were content with promises and gave up their positions without guarantees. Let's not do so this time.[9]

All the former protests, demonstrations and petitions of the taxi drivers had been ignored. Even on Friday, the second day of the rebellion, the Government refused to sit down with the taxi drivers. The incapacity of the taxi drivers' "chiefs of staff" for negotiations should also be noted as another argument against the bargaining strategy.

As to the strike, its impact would have been far less shocking on the public and thereby on the Government since not many people and not too often use taxis. In addition, taxi drivers did not have an effective union-like organization that could have ensured the success of a sustained action (or insurance funds to compensate for wage losses, a staff to keep the media alert, leaders to coordinate the action for a longer time, etc.).

What were the factors that made taxi drivers able to rebel? The fundamental reason for choosing rebellion lies in the "macho" nature of the subculture and in the vulture character of the organization of the taxi drivers.

"Macho" subcultures are always ready for immediate and violent reaction. However, personal grievances do not give rise to rebellion. Another important condition is that such grievances add up and be manifested in an effective concerted action. All this, however, requires solidarity and organization. The former condition is provided by the common subculture, the latter by the "inter-vulture" network.

The operation could be so effective because this network is a very sophisticated tool. The cellular radio system is technically more developed than all the communication systems the Government has.

This had a paramount importance when it came to large scale rebellion, i.e., simultaneous actions at different places. Solidarity means more than a taxi driver turning on his radio—he must believe that others feel the same way and will act the way he himself is instructed by the radio. The "elite squad" of taxi drivers, their mobility, logistic knowledge and their skills to organize actions largely influenced the form of the rebellion. They had already shown signs of their ability to block traffic (they had staged a demonstration a few weeks before) and had previously threatened with blocking the bridges.

Obviously, taxi drivers would not have embarked on such actions if they had not been certain of success. This extreme self-confidence was also due to the awareness that they were fighting for the interests of the "People" even though at the outset their action was free from political claims.

In the beginning, taxi drivers stood up for their own and purely economic interests. So much so that they claimed compensation for themselves rather than demanding the restoration of gasoline prices in the public interest.

The argument that taxi drivers fought first of all for the interests of the "People" appeared only at a later phase. But even in the very end in an "official" communique—released by the Hungarian Press Agency—the taxi drivers' organizing committee announced that "... our claims have been and will remain purely technical, free from political considerations."[10]

Nevertheless, the heroic stand-up for public interest fits in very well with the "elite squad" image of taxi drivers. It is a bit different from the macho culture I have described. It essentially depicts taxi drivers as the most active and entrepreneurial members of Hungarian society. There are several examples when taxi drivers offered their help voluntarily to the public, e.g., in great calamities (in snowdrifts), in accidents, and "passenger transporters and freight carriers were the first to offer assistance to the revolution in Romania. . . . "[11]

This image of the "elite squad" was jeopardized as the public grew increasingly hostile to the taxi drivers' rebellion over time while negotiations seemed nowhere near an end. And as the following report from a major Hungarian city suggests it was likely to happen as Monday crept closer:

> The man in the street still supported taxi drivers for the most part (it is about Friday morning—E.S.). Some people even got a kick out of it. . . . Early enthusiasm was only to increase when it was found out that a group of Yugoslav tourists on their way for shopping could not get through the blockade (the city is close to the Yugoslavian border E.S.) . . . Public feeling started to turn on Saturday when taxi drivers having cleared the streets again blocked downtown streets. There were fewer and fewer people willing to accept that total strangers required them to present stamped slips of paper or else a bunch of flowers to pass through.[12]

Therefore, taxi drivers had to change the justification of their rebellion. Little by little, the focusing on public interest became the main motivation for the rebellion in hindsight. All this was possible among else because political parties and trade unions were also inclined to adopt this kind of reinterpretation.

The Vulture Wins

Taxi drivers have undoubtedly come out as winners. As a summary, let us consider what they gained with the rebellion—in the short run.

They gained pardon. The loser (the Government) forgave the winner of the rebellion. The President of the Hungarian Republic proposed the Parliament to pardon the taxi drivers for their rebellion under the pretext that they had been unaware of what they were doing. And the vulture is ready for peaceful coexistence. In its communique, the "operative committee enjoying the confidence of all participants in the blockade" wished to thank everybody for everything. And as for the future, the communique read:

> . . . The only possible way we see is within the boundaries of law and the constitution. We consider our already existing and future professional forums for safeguarding and representing our interests to be legitimate for the purpose. We wish to avoid any further discussions, arguments and debates. With this communique we wish to contribute to social consensus in the days still burdened with tension and bringing further economic hardships after the present agreement.[13]

They gained time. Since after all gasoline prices did increase, the number of passengers continued to fall. Although taxi drivers averted the calamity, their position has not improved. But in contemporary Hungary it is an achievement if the rate of decline is a tiny bit slower. By the end of June 1991 the fuel price reached almost the level originally planned by the authorities before the blockade,[14] i.e., the rebellion postponed the calamity by 8-10 months at least.

They gained lower gasoline prices. In the short run their successful action enabled them even to increase their profits. In November, taxi companies not only raised or were about to raise their tariffs but two of them increased their fares from HUF 14 to as high as HUF 20 per km. This 43% rise was higher than the rate of gasoline price increase and much higher than the 13-15% which were estimated to offset the cost effects of increased gasoline prices.[15]

They gained organization. The rebellion proved the old premise of labour movements—unity is power. Looseness does not necessarily mean weak organization. Taxi drivers will obviously maintain this form of organization which turned out to be quite useful in coping with a calamity. In other words, taxi drivers should remain vultures.

However, there are certain functions that would require a more formal and stable organization that could concentrate technical expertise more effectively, i.e., a bureaucracy. Perhaps this is the reason for the formation of the Budapest Chamber of Taxi Drivers almost immediately after the successful end of the rebellion. But "external politics" will not be the only function of the taxi drivers' chamber. The Chamber has already been involved in reorganizing the price cartel, in a way institutionalizing an informal practice. The Chamber will also have functions which the "inter-vulture" network is unable to perform effectively:

> An internal charter will be prepared, setting forth strict conditions for obtaining licence for passenger transport . . . it will define the taxi drivers' code of work ethics and will monitor compliance. The committee overseeing work ethics will rule on passenger complaints and may decide to withdraw the defaulting taxi driver's licence in qualified cases pursuant to the Code.[16]

The objective is clearly to control the supply of taxi drivers. This process can be seen as the closure of the labour market by the "insiders" setting up guild barriers. The resulting labour market segment is the best form to safeguard high profits.

They gained a strengthened "macho" and "elite squad" image and a reinforced "inter-vulture" network. The institutionalized organization leading to labour market closure does not preclude the subcultural spirit or the informal network among taxi drivers. On the contrary, all this is absolutely essential for the management and control of the Chamber. Their victory, just as the subsequent Government pardon and public glory have rightfully boosted the taxi drivers' ego (machismo, solidarity and representative excellence), and their commitment to the inter-vulture network.

Some Conclusions

Being the first violent action of masses in Hungary after 1989 there are a great deal of possibilities of interpreting the events.

Just to mention a few:

- For journalists and mass media experts the rebellion offered an excellent case study to analyze the operation of the current communication system.
- For legal experts the basic problem was to define the events from a constitutional point of view. Was it a special form of strike or a public disobedience movement?
- For political scientists the role different political actors played in the events was the central issue (to what extent is the Government responsible for the whole rebellion and whether the Government could have done differently, whether the whole topic is about the growing disappointment of the citizens from party politics, whether the corporatist "round-table" was only a temporary solution or could be an institutionalized forum to negotiate fundamental issues in the future, etc.).

Obviously the rebellion offers several challenging starting points also for me, a sociologist interested in institutional economics and economic anthropology.

The taxi drivers' story is a perfect example of the vulnerability of modern society. It is sufficient to clot the arteries at a few points, and the thrombosis will block all communication channels necessary for everyday life overnight. Even the sequence of the paralysis can be simulated; the bridges and the main roads fail first only to be followed by the airport and the border crosspoints and later the overloaded telephone network collapse.

Transportation jobs, including that of the taxi drivers, have the power in every modern society to assert their interests by rebellion. Just a few examples: in Chile transporters and drivers were the Praetorean Guards in destroying Allende's regime; in Bratislava some weeks ago taxi drivers blockaded the Parliament to give emphasis to a nationalistic parade; some years ago peasants in Burgenland blockaded the roads between Hungary and Austria; lately Italian truck drivers blocked the Brenner Pass to criticize Austrian environmental policy; in Ottawa truck drivers blockaded the main streets close to the Parliament to demonstrate against the rising licence fees, etc. Perhaps modern societies are on their way to be at the mercy of small "key" occupations (e.g., nuclear plant engineers!), more than to political parties, the police or the army.

From a network analysis point of view, the taxi drivers' rebellion proves that "weak ties" can be very powerful tools in an emergency, that non-hierarchical organization can be the best solution in special contexts, that personal networks are not separated but very much intertwined with policy networks, that—unlike its textbook version—the market is far from being an anonymous institution.

For a dedicated follower of A.O. Hirschman this story is the first voice of the vulture. There have been attempts to describe the second economy of the East European socialist countries as the "soft" exit for those who did not want to remain loyal to the first economy or to raise their voice (or exit once and for all, i.e., to emigrate). Granted that there was some truth in this interpretation, the taxi drivers' rebellion is the first attempt to use voice instead of exit or loyalty to cope with the new Government. Moreover, this case study also shows that cooperative action can become more successful than "normal" societal solutions (e.g., individual adaptive reaction, monopolization of the market, corporative negotiations or etatist-bureaucratic action).

Finally, the taxi drivers' blockade is a lucid example of how a submarket of the former informal (second) economy can influence the transition towards a new formal economy. In this respect I would emphasize the multifacedness of this influence. The "positive" legacy of alternative culture can have negative and positive impacts on the transition, simultaneously.

No question, the second economy used to be a characteristic feature of the "Hungarian experiment". As coping means both for the masses and for the policy makers, the second economy should be counted as one of the most important "positive legacy" in Hungary. For example, illegal transportation for some decades used to be the only market in this segment of the economy. The existence of this "hidden but visible" market socialized both the buyers and the sellers to the market transactions (bargaining, calculation of costs and benefits, etc.). The sellers got accustomed to a kind of distorted entrepreneurial behaviour, i.e., profit seeking in a shortage economy, lacking modern fiscal (banking, taxation, credit, etc.) systems. Under the perpetual surveillance of the police one cannot expect the birth of an entrepreneurial stratum interested in long-term investment. Then in the 1980s, as perhaps the last effort to use second economy as a tool of reforming the first economy, the appearance of the taxi drivers as small entrepreneurs added further characteristics to their socialization: self-organization, cartel building and maintenance ability, quasi-corporate networking practice, etc.

Obviously, these features did not disappear in the course of political changes in and after 1989. Why would they? Just because the political regime changes in the short run, the institutional structure and the operation of the "lower economy" (i.e., those segments of the economy which produce low-tech goods services, and cheap or non-monetarized consumption goods) hardly change. Therefore all the practices, networks, whealings-and-dealings developed as coping means remain valuable assets. Furthermore, the growing uncertainty and the severing economic conditions urge the economic actors to stick to already developed trouble-shooting mechanisms.

But the distorted entrepreneurial socialization and the barter-corruption-cartel-ridden organization mean both an advantage and a disadvantage for the society. For developing a market economy it is perhaps better to have entrepreneurs around than only wage labourers, bureaucrats, cadres and unskilled workers. But, at least in the case of the transportation market this market will be lastingly distorted by the behavioural features of the vultures and the great inertia of their networks and organizations.

Notes

1. In the course of analysis I made two simplifications. First, apart from taxi drivers other private, cooperative and state-owned transporters and carriers also took part in the rebellion, especially by the end of it. Second, the analysis of taxi drivers is mostly limited to those operating in Budapest.
2. I would define crisis as a slowly emerging, not unexpected event which often has been fermenting for a long time. Trouble is less severe than a crisis and therefore its negative effects are easier to remedy. Difficulty and calamity are unexpected, shocking events, the former less, the latter more severely threatening social actors. (Sik, E.: Trouble, crisis, difficulty and calamity—on households' coping behaviour Budapest 1991 manuscript).
3. In his book the author gives an excellent socio-anthropological analysis of cheats, thefts, frauds, abuses, misappropriations and other illegal activities (Mars, G.: 'Cheats at Work', Allen and Unwin Pr. London, 1983).
4. Even the recruitment process involves the operation of personal networks. Very often newcomers are recruited by other taxi drivers or former school- and workmates, friends and neighbours decide jointly to become taxi-driver.
5. There was a short text in the Budapest Week (April 1991) with the following title "Banking Black: The Rate and Risk of Street Changing". According to this expert treatise, "Dealing with cab drivers is relatively safe (i.e., less safe than dealing with personal acquaintances but much safer than dealing with street hawkers—S.E.)...Mention that you have no local currency and he will offer to change your dollars. The exchange is made in the safety and privacy of the cab, giving you sufficient time to make sure the money is kosher."

6. Recently and for a minority, a new source of huge extras is to offer their services to international (mainly Turkish and Romanian) organizations which smuggle immigrants through Hungary to Germany.
7. At the time of the blockade the average gross income of a Hungarian employee was about 13000 HUF per month. According to some estimations, a taxi driver should earn around 20000 HUF per month.
8. Due to the collapse of COMECON, the price of automobiles from former socialist countries doubled and the price of their spare parts increased even more drastically (500-600%).
9. "Common sense has prevailed?", *Népszabadság,* 29 October 1990.
10. *Népszabadság,* 31 October 1990.
11. *Népszabadság,* 12 November 1990.
12. Havasi, J.: "The taximeter strikes", *HVG,* 3 November 1990.
13. *Népszabadság,* 31 October 1990.
14. Before the blockade state authorities aimed to raise the gasoline price up to 62 HUF but had to accept 50 HUF. Today (in June 1991) the price of one litre gasoline is 59 HUF.
15. Since then there were two more fuel price increases and a small and temporary decrease. But the taxi drivers made no attempt to organize another blockade. But just for the sake of safety during the latest fuel price increase there were police cars at the feet of the bridges in Budapest.
16. *Népszabadság,* 10 November 1990.

IV

Comparative Perspectives

16

Observations on the Transition in East-Central Europe

Peter L. Berger

Social science thrives on comparison. Any social scientist looking at the cataclysmic transformation that has been going on in the societies of "real socialism" will instinctively grope for a comparative perspective. In the event this is difficult, given the unique character of these developments. Except for rather minor adumbrations here and there, there has never occurred previously a massive change from socialism to capitalism. All comparisons, of necessity, will have an approximate, even metaphorical character. Still, some general observations may be attempted, with due modesty and tentativeness.

The common problematic underlying this collection of papers is subtle but nonetheless clear: It hinges on the question as to whether and how the forces of resistance to the old socialist order have become, or failed to become, forces for building up the new post-socialist order. In that sense, the question is not new. It occurs in the wake of all revolutionary changes, of whatever nature, and it occurred indeed in the wake of the revolution that produced Soviet-style socialism in the first place. Every revolution tends to devour its own children. The devouring, to be sure, need not take the monstrous form it took in the "first socialist society" in the 1920s and 1930s. But even if the Russian revolution of 1917 had resulted in a less homicidal regime than the one that was in fact established, it is doubtful whether the individuals, the social groupings and the ideas that had been instrumental in effecting the revolution would have been equally effective in constructing the post-revolutionary society. The virtues of resistance and rebellion, and the individuals embodying these virtues, are typically ill-suited to animate the efforts required when resistance and rebellion have succeeded. They run the risk of soon seeming to be irrelevant. Alternatively, what was deemed virtue in the old situation now appears as vice in the new. This was the key insight in Vilfredo Pareto's theory of elites, and while it is hardly the general law that he thought it to be, it tends to hold across a wide spectrum of empirical cases.

The question is particularly dramatic in East-Central Europe (and, it now appears, in the former Soviet Union itself) because of the uniquely repressive character of Soviet-style totalitarianism, which imposed what then seemed like a glacial uniformity. Resistance was pushed into a deep, rarely visible underground, mostly expressing itself *sotto voce* in intimate settings of the private sphere or at best in certain institutional "niches" that served as precarious refuges from the totalitarian structures. As *glasnost* loosened the latter structures, these subterranean or marginalized phenomena were suddenly catapulted into public view, with frequently surprising and even shocking results. Needless to say, the situation was different in different countries. Thus the repression was less severe, for a good many years, in Hungary and Poland than in Czechoslovakia and East Germany. But in all these societies, as the transformation occurred, it was as if people who had spent a long time in a dark cellar suddenly found themselves outdoors in bright sunlight. They blinked, and so did those who watched them emerge.

There can be no doubt that the triumph of the forces of resistance bestowed legitimacy on the new regimes. The figures of Václav Havel and Lech Walesa heading their respective republics powerfully symbolize this legitimacy. Human memories are typically short and the human capacity to reinterpret the past nostalgically is very great. Barring immense catastrophes (they would most likely be centered in the economy), it is probable all the same that this legitimating power of the symbols of resistance will persist for a while. But already, in at least four cases, one can observe how virtues come to be perceived, if not necessarily as vices, as potentially dangerous tendencies. The cases are nationalism, the church, intellectuals and the "second economy".

The case of nationalism, of course, is the most visible at the moment. Nationalist sentiments and the movements upholding them were a powerful, perhaps the singlemost powerful, force of resistance against the "socialist internationalism" imposed by the Soviet empire. One glance at any newspaper today indicates clearly enough that nationalism in the post-imperial era is capable of unleashing forces and events with profoundly disruptive consequences, in some countries putting in question the very possibility of economic and political reconstruction. The "Yugoslav specter", if one may call it that, looms over a large area of the region. Organized religion had been one of the toughest kernels of resistance to the totalitarian embrace, but in several countries its emergence from its "niche" brought to light features of fanaticism and power-hunger that had been "frozen" during the socialist period. Current debates over state-church relations in Poland are the clearest case of this at the moment, though the religious legitimation of ancient ethnic hatreds and irredentisms can be observed in several other countries. Intellectuals played a prominent role in the resistance and, initially, in the establishment of most of the new regimes. But intellectuals are always better at dissent than at governing, and many of them are now embittered by what they perceive as a betrayal of "their" revolution. The fate of the *Neues Forum* in East Germany is a prototypical example. The situation is aggravated by the fact that much of the intellectual opposition, however anti-Communist, retained strong *gauchiste* leanings and a lingering hope for a somehow better socialism. What is happening in these countries now is both disappointing and puzzling to these people (as indeed it is to a sizable body of their colleagues in the West). It is the bewilderment of someone who spent years in the dark clutching to his breast the ideas of Antonio Gramsci or Ernst Bloch, emerging into the daylight of a country in which, metaphorically, a statue to Adam Smith seems to have been erected in every public square. Finally, the illegal or semi-legal market economy, which to a large extent made the socialist reality tolerably livable, looks very different under conditions of a fully legal capitalism under construction. The character who before was seen as a heroic entrepreneur running circles around stupid bureaucrats is now perceived as an unscrupulous gangster, whose profits and whose role in the new economy are deeply resented.

The problematic becomes more complicated if one notes that the post-socialist order under construction actually involves two distinct processes of transition: The transiton from dictatorship to democracy *as well as* the transition from socialism to capitalism. In East-Central Europe, for historical reasons that contain no mystery, these two transitions have been experienced as one single, all-embracing transformation. While this perception is perfectly correct in terms of what has been happening in this region, it is severely distortive if it is linked to the assumption that these two transitions are intrinsically and necessarily one and the same. Emphatically, they are not. The empirical relationship between democracy and capitalism is complex, and it would be quite impossible to discuss it in detail in this space. It is possible, though, to describe the relationship succinctly as an *asymmetrical* one. But simply, the empirical evidence cross-nationally suggests that capitalism is the necessary though insufficient condition to democracy, but that democracy is neither a necessary nor a sufficient condition of capitalism. In other words, one cannot have democracy without capitalism, but one *can* have capitalism without democracy (at least for a certain period of time, after which, *if* capitalism is successfully established, certain democratizing pressures build up). If one accepts this formulation, the problematic must be further differentiated: It is possible that certain forces of resistance surviving into the post-socialist era are functional for the transition to democracy but *not* for the transition to capitalism, and vice versa. Hypothetically, take two cases: Intellectuals and their institutions may be a strongly pro-democratic force, but their persistent anti-capitalist animus may be an obstacle to the successful establishment of a capitalist economy. Conversely, entrepreneurs of the "second economy" and managers of formerly socialist enterprises may have precisely the skills and the capital (however illicitly gained) that are needed in the new capitalism, but their resented success may serve to undermine the legitimacy of the new democratic regime.

Finally, there is a very important and morally troubling matter, which is the *sequence* of the two processes of transition. At least in this century, the typical sequence has been that the transition to capitalism preceded the transition to democracy. In other words, most successful transitions to capitalism occurred under the auspices of dictatorial regimes. This was eminently the case in the "economic miracle stories" of East Asia, beginning with Meiji Japan and continuing in the post-World-War-II emergence of the so-called "Four Little Dragons" (South Korea, Taiwan, Hongkong and Singapore). Japan, of course, subsequently became a full-fleged democracy and there developed powerful; pressures toward democratization in the other East Asian success societies, but that is another matter. Two dramatic economic success stories in other parts of the world, those of Spain and

Chile, show a similar sequence. Most troubling, perhaps, is the case of China. The regime of Deng-Xiao-ping deliberately embarked on a policy of (admittedly limited) marketization *without* any concomitant moves of democratization. The economic and (especially in the countryside) social success of this policy was remarkable. The regime subsequently moved to squelch the democratizing pressures that nonetheless surfaced and, possibly in panic, also tried to put brakes on marketization. In the meantime, though, a capitalist "economic miracle" has been in the making in vast areas of southern China, especially in Guangdong province (which, let it be noted, has some sixty million inhabitants), effectively ignoring the economic decrees handed down by the central government. One is tempted to predict with some assurance that, as these economic developments continue, the democratizing pressures will resurface, this time around with different consequences than those that followed the events on Tienanmen Square. By contrast, an argument can be made (and, incidentally, has been made by Deng Xiao-ping) that democracy has been an important factor inhibiting the economic development of India.

This is *not* to say that dictatorship is a necessary condition for successful capitalist development in its early phases. Leave aside the very complicated question of the origins of capitalism in Europe. (Was England in the eighteenth century a democracy in our present sense? To what extent and until when did property qualification for the suffrage contain the anti-capitalist resentments in all Western countries?) There are notable exceptions in the post-World-War-II period as well—such as Pakistan in the 1960s, Sri Lanka and Malaysia more recently, and now, possibly, a number of Latin American countries. But enough has been said to make the point that the two transitions must be distinguished from one another.

The case of East-Central Europe, then, is distinctive in that transition from socialism to capitalism is occurring *simultaneously* with the transition to democracy. Morally speaking, this is a thoroughly appealing fact. Moral approval, though, must not blind one to the fact that this simultaneity creates its own difficulties and risks. There is no way by which the economic transition can occur without pain. Democracy creates the conditions by which those who suffer the pain may organize to seek relief, and in the process may delay or even abort the necessary economic transformation. Minimally, one may observe that the successful management of these difficulties will require both a high degree of legitimacy and extremely capable political leadership in the new democracies of the region. One may further speculate that the old forces of resistance will be of only limited usefulness in bringing this about. New people, new groupings and new ideas would seem to be called for.

17

Watching Eastern Europe, Thinking about Latin America

Barry B. Levine

The self-unmasking of socialist ideology, the collapse of Soviet control in the Eastern bloc and the demise of communism in the Soviet Union are perhaps the most important events of the late 20th century, certainly as important as the maturation of totalitarianism in the first half of the century. These are happenings that have come to pass in specific places but their implications are global. It is rather obvious then that what has happened in the Soviet Union will have an effect on the future of Cuba. But it is also obvious that what happened since 1989 in the ex-Marxist countries—once referred to as a second world of development—will have effects on the purported first and third worlds as well. When I watch events in Eastern Europe I think about their import for this hemisphere as well.

The thought that there could legitimately be alternative goals of development, equivalent in merit though different in kind (i.e., socialist versus capitalist development) was a strange result of the disaggregation of the concept of development itself, reinforced by the social science etiquette that grew out of the Cold War, and by what I like to consider the Weberian paradox.

The disaggregation of the concept of "development" began with the rejection of evolution as a valid model to describe social change. The fragmentation of the concept proceeded as analyses divided the concept into economic, political, and social aspects. It didn't take long, however, for social science to realize that these various aspects of development were not marching lockstep with each other. Societies started from different bases, chose to engage in development attempts at different moments in history, and sought to borrow different institutions. Even having said all this, there was yet less that could be confidently anticipated. Serendipity lurked, what I like to call Levine's Law ruled: "What is transferred is transformed." As it turns out, institutions borrowed by different societies produced results not only different from the initiator society but different from one another.

Development thus referred to something inter-national and not something intra-national, not something simply internal to particular societies. When social scientists today focus on development, they pay close attention to culture contact, the reality that societies learn from each other. All societies feign sovereignty when in fact they beg, borrow and steal whatever ideas and institutions they can from other societies that they may find of value. Interdependence not independence is the reality. Coming to terms with the international nature of attempts at development has revealed several things: (1) first, development is not assured. It is simply not the case that all economically backward countries will develop, and, in fact, few have. Second, modernity does not simply replace tradition but is often added to the traditions that a society may retain: there is no such thing as a "fully modern" society. Third, modernity in one sphere of social life does not guarantee modernity in others. Fourth, should change proceed, there is no pre-set order to any pattern of change. Thus, e.g., "industrialization" might precede "modernization" in some cases; whereas the reverse may result in others. (2) As a consequence of recognizing all this multiplicity, most sociologists now accept the assertion that there are many paths to development, including paths not yet tried.

This point—that there can be many paths to development—has been tricky. It has led to a kind of theoretical leniency and a belief that qualitatively different goals could somehow be equated. One might even say that sociology has been too generous, too sensitive to the very diversity of cultures that it was supposed to celebrate. Studying development strategies has required a sensitivity to differences among the social structures of nations seeking to modernize. But these same attempts were often conceptualized in terms of the etiquette of the day. Thus, during the height of the Cold War, the apparent military parity between the free world and the Soviet bloc led many to conclude that there was, in turn, a parity in development achievements. After all, a scientist who was "value free" was supposed to be neutral and, in a spirit of fairness, would have to declare the two opposing sides to be equally developed. This etiquette was enlarged to include a purported "Third World," embracing its members in the distorting if self-comforting concept, "developing nations." (3) It may have already been forgotten but until quite recently the tit-for-tat regarding empires was to equate the Soviet Union's relationship to Eastern Europe with the United States' relationship to Central America, a parallel that simply could not stand up against events (witness the February 1990 Nicaraguan elections).

Even as sophisticated and subtle a social scientist as Reinhard Bendix fell into the etiquette trap when he spoke of the "manifest success of Soviet industrialization." (4) He wrote that the Soviet system of domination "achieved rapid economic growth" and "produced a built-in ethic of work performance which . . . [was] 'rational' in the sense of being adapted to the bureaucratic fits and starts of forced industrialization." His argument, as we now know, was overwhelmed first with Mikhail Gorbachev's revelations in perestroika and then with the events that have dominated the news ever since. (5) What happened in the Soviet bloc turned out not to be a different kind of development than was claimed but to have been a kind of misdevelopment where "modern" obstacles to growth were substituted for more traditional ones.

Contributing to the etiquette trap was the Weberian paradox. Weber argued that a social order would best be guaranteed legitimacy (and in turn longevity) if people believed in it (more so than if they followed it by tradition, and certainly more so than if they merely followed it for aim-rational reasons). (6) Over the long haul, Weber's predilection for a necessary legitimacy proved to be accurate concerning events in the Soviet bloc.

But until those events occurred in fact, Weber's very preference made it difficult to gauge how legitimate the regimes were. The obverse of Weber's typological preference of ways to ensure validity of a social order is to assume that when a social order is followed for a long term there must be some significant degree of belief in its legitimacy. Forty-five years of domination by the Soviet Union seemed to many an outside observer to have stood for something. And this observation was guided by the same logic that ultimately demonstrated the validity of Weber's assumptions. It took a wire cutter splitting open the Hungarian-Austrian border, potentially emptying out the entire empire of its work force, to remind us of what Havel demonstrated so articulately in The Power of the Powerless (7) that compliance in Eastern Europe was based on a combination of aim-rational calculation and dull habit rather than on any acceptance of the system's claim to legitimacy. Weber proved to be accurate over the long run, even if paradoxical over the short run.

A common, although as it also turns out, misleading, way to describe this even-handed approach that had developed in sociology was to talk of Three Worlds of Development (8) a first world of capitalist development, a second world of socialist development and a third world attempting development within the shadows of the first two. Indeed, common parlance took up the terminology as its own. But the fall of communism has made clear the inadequacy of a notion of three worlds of development. There simply never was a second world of development. (9) This understood, all that remains left to contemplate when reflecting on comparative development experiences is a continuum of nations, from the least successful to the most successful, laid out along a single tape measure of economic growth. Development for social scientists now means economic success and its study is to isolate historical trails not divergent ends.

The New Academic Debate

The effect on scholarship concerning development will be to change the debate from one between Karl Marx and Max Weber to one between Max Weber and Adam Smith. The old debate was a somewhat arcane discussion of what some future socialism might look like in comparison to actually existing capitalism. The introduction of actually existing socialism into the debate made clear the weakness of the argument by the Left. The new debate is going to be about what kind of capitalism one will want and accept. Weberians will look to empirical examples for their data and vision whereas others of a more philosophically purist bent will look to Adam Smith for a source of inspiration.

For Weberians, modern capitalism is a historical institution, empirically observable. The institution came into being at a certain time and its existence is predicated on individuals mutually orienting their behavior to it. As with all human institutions, it is socially constructed.

There is nothing natural about it. There are examples where it has been successful and examples where it has not, but mainly, there are many examples. Two highly successful variations of modern capitalism are now recognized as that derived from the Protestant Ethic in Europe and that derived from a Confucian Ethic in the East Asia.

Students of the developing world (and this concept now includes the societies of the former Soviet bloc in addition to Latin America, etc.) watch carefully the events of the world to see whether other variations of successful capitalism are now coming forward. Concerning Eastern Europe, several issues have thus become quite critical sociologically: what are the new forms of economic institutions that are emerging; what relationship do they have with their society's past institutions; to what extent and by what means have they achieved legitimacy and what are the new roles of the state.

This book revolves around the thought that many of the social institutions that remain from the past, ironically including those that contributed to the end of the socialist regimes, may not prove productive in establishing the kind of new society that has been hoped for. While such caution may be wise, there is no necessary reason for it to turn officially pessimistic. On the one hand, development pessimism is not unique to Eastern Europe and thus has a certain gratuitous nature to it. (10) On the other hand, as sociologists, we must remember that the Devil himself added unintended consequences to the social mix, so much so, that it even affects our own theories: the best laid hypotheses of mice and social scientists often go astray. (11)

Jan T. Gross's paper points to one such irony. He argues that the 1989 Polish revolution which was undertaken to constitute liberty has been overtaken by technicians trying to repair a malfunctioning economy. Gross emphasizes that when a "rhetoric of expertise permeates political discourse in a republic it puts in jeopardy the very foundations of democratic process. . . . citizenship becomes meaningless." He argues that the very means to overcome the dictatorship—governed by a substantive rationality, outcome oriented, and by what Weber would add, an ethic of responsibility—is proving counter-productive towards creating a truly legitimate state—which needs to be governed by a formal rationality, procedure oriented, and with what Weber would call, an ethic of intentionality. Rebels don't always make good rulers.

Marcin Król warns that while the Catholic Church was a good ally during the fight with the Marxists their agenda differs markedly from that of liberal democrats. What was a good alliance before the revolution can not possibly last beyond it. The Church, believing in its dogma, will push its agenda to save souls. Liberals, in contrast, will have to stand firm against the Church if they hope to protect individual freedom and autonomy.

István R. Gábor tells us that the development of the second economy in the shadows of the socialist state-run shortage economy has trained a group of potential entrepreneurs unaccustomed to competition, who are accustomed to quick enrichment, bribery and "mute complicity", and who have become content in their marginality. He asks whether this group will be able to handle the liberalization of the economy, or rather won't oppose it and demand some kind of state protection especially against foreign competition—"entrepreneurs against the market." He himself worries that they will be so inefficient that Hungary might slip "into a new kind of economic duality"—efficient foreign capital and an inefficient domestic sector.

George Schöpflin recounts how among the legacies of communism is a worldview cluttered with all sorts of cultural tags: people are still statist and patronage oriented; conspiratorial and messianic rather than gradualistic and empirical; follow a dichotomous true-false black-white attitude as against a capacity for compromise, tolerance and ambiguity; surrender the faculty of choice and the responsibility that goes with it, and distrust all things official. "Inevitably, the opponents of Marxism-Leninism have come to resemble what they have opposed," he laments.

David Stark offers analyses of the constraints imposed on the processes of extrication from communism. The varying paths taken by Germany (reunification), Czechoslovakia (capitulation), Poland (compromise) and Hungary (electoral competition), in conjunction with their historically varying social structures have yielded different kinds of markets (as witnessed in their different attitudes towards attempts to privatize state enterprises) and different kinds of attitudes toward the state. Stark does well to remind us that East Europe is a pretty big concept, embracing much variability and detail, information worth focusing on. There's no *tabla raza* upon which to write the new history.

I am not sure that this is comforting, but many of these types of arguments are also heard when discussing Latin America. How often we have heard expressions re Chile or Mexico that an emphasis on economic progress was deflecting our vision from properly focusing on political liberties. Or to be told that once the economic problems were resolved, then the political ones could be dealt with more easily. And as to the role of the Catholic Church in the affairs of state, well that has been an issue since the days when the Liberal parties were founded all over the continent. The Church-State issue came to a head in Puerto Rico in 1960. The battle there reads like a preview to the battle that took place in Poland, three decades later. (12)

Latin Americans are also extremely interested in the economic potential of the second economy. And the issue is conceptualized in much the same way: can these people form the basis for a new entrepreneurial class once the state imposed restrictions that have weighted them down are removed. Their "liberation" has been taken up by liberals on the continent and was given impetus with the publication of *El otro sendero.* (13) The transmutation of language, the inversion of values and an unwillingness to shed old baggage is also of great concern to Latins. Mario Vargas Llosa, the world renowned writer and former candidate for the presidency of Peru, has argued about "a terrible propensity to denature what we say and do, to use words badly, to corrupt ideas and to fraudulently alter the meaning of the institutions that regulate our social life . . ." (14)

Nor does Latin America, or anywhere else for that matter, start from a clean slate. But that is not the issue, the issue is the region's capacity for transforming itself. Communist ideology has shrivelled up, there is no agricultural class to contend with, no Marxist intelligentsia to delegitimate hardwork and the accumulation of wealth. And there are hints that the transformation is possible. Chile went from dictatorship to democracy, the East German economy is beginning to take on life, and we do have examples of the "New Socialist Man" learning to work: discussions of the work ethic of Russians and East Germans sound much like discussions of the work ethic of the Marielito refugees that fled Cuba in 1980. It is important to note that, typically, the Marielitos adjusted to the fast Miami work pace with little difficulty and relative dispatch.

The East European examples have a special importance for those who follow development. There have been very few examples of successful development in the developing countries. And these examples have all been cases of top-down development. Japan is the most spectacular case history of catch-up directed by an elite deciding to attempt development. The Four Tigers of East Asia were examples of autocratic regimes that imposed development in the shadow of communist neighbors. Even the bright spots in Latin America have this top-down aspect: Puerto Rico in its heyday, Chile under the anti-communist dictatorship of General Augusto Pinochet, and today, Mexico, empirically a one-party state, is moving toward economic transformation with strong governmental direction.

In theory there should be nothing wrong with imposed development provided that it is successful and that one is willing to agree that economic success is more important than any restraints on liberty. But once having lived the communist nightmare, it is clear that it would be very difficult for East Europeans to agree with such a value judgment. (15) If Eastern Europe successfully negotiates development, willingly accepting the necessary austerity that the process calls for, without recourse to authoritarianism, then the implications for the rest of the globe will be enormous. Knowledge that economic success and political liberty can together grow from the otherwise unhappy condition of underdevelopment will be greeted with great acclaim. I, for one, am optimistic.

References

(1) Cf., Reinhard Bendix, Nation-Building and Citizenship: Studies of Our Changing Social Order (New York: John Wiley and Sons, Inc., 1964).

(2) "... we should recognize democratization and industrialization as two processes, each distinct from the other, however intimately they have been related on occasion." Bendix, Ibid., 62.

(3) Cf., Carlos Rangel, El tercermundismo (Caracas: Monte Avila Editores, 1982).

(4) Bendix, op. cit, pp. 146, 167–75. For another example of the etiquette trap, see Barry B. Levine and Ralph S. Clem, "Imperial Development: The Case of American Puerto Rico and Soviet Georgia," Comparative Studies in Sociology, Vol. 1 (1978): 319–336, where we postulated that economic success could buy off ethnic demands. Our hypothesis may still hold, although it is now clear that the Soviet instance was not a good example to demonstrate the positive case.

(5) Mikhail Gorbachev, Perestroika: New Thinking for Our Country and the World (New York: Harper & Row, 1987).

(6) Max Weber, Economy and Society: An Outline of Interpretative Sociology (New York: Bedminster Press, 1968 [1922]).

(7) Václav Havel, The Power of the Powerless (New York: M.E. Sharpe, 1990).

(8) Irving Louis Horowitz, Three Worlds of Development: The Theory and Prac-

tice of International Stratification (New York: Oxford University Press, 1966).

(9) If there never was a second world of development, then what was there? One world of development but three worlds of disenchantment, three worlds of disappointment and disillusionment with the hangover enlightenment optimism of the Marxist promise of a virile yet beneficent State. A first world of ideological embracement and then rejection, aware of a "God that Failed"; a second world of governmental policy and dissidence; and a third world of temptation and then repudiation that has self-consciously come to terms with the stark reality that there is one less actual alternative than was previously believed.

(10) The whole of the 1991 World Bank report, World Development Report 1991: The Challenge of Development (New York: Oxford University Press, 1991), is dedicated to fighting such pessimism.

(11) Witness Max Weber's prediction that "The Chinese in all probability would be . . . more capable than the Japanese . . . of assimilating capitalism." The Religion of China (1915), Émile Durkheim's preview of diverging gender roles: "[Woman's] role has become even more specialized. Today, among cultivated people, the woman leads a completely different existence from that of the man." The Division of Labor in Society (1893), Herbert Spencer's belief that "the advance of industrial society would render war impossible" Principles of Sociology (1876–96) [quotation by Don Martingdale, The Nature and Types of Sociological Theory], and, of course, Karl Marx's "Workers of the world unite, you have nothing to lose but your chains." Communist Manifesto (1848). Compare Marx's words with the outstretched sign paraded in an alternative May Day gathering in Moscow: "Workers of the world, we're sorry."

(12) "Their main objective seems to be the defeat of the Popular Democratic Party [the party of Puerto Rico's modernizing governor Luis Muñoz Marín], whom they attacked for having opposed religious education in the public schools and for supporting the dissemination of birth control advice. . . . " Henry Wells, The Modernization of Puerto Rico: A Political Study of Changing Values and Institutions (Cambridge: Harvard University Press, 1969), p. 272.

(13) Hernando de Soto, Enrique Ghersi and Mario Ghibellini, El otro sendero (Lima: Editorial El Barranco, 1986).

(14) Mario Vargas Llosa, "América Latina y la opción liberal," in Barry B. Levine (ed.), El desafío neoliberal: El fin del tercermundismo en América Latina (Bogotá: Editorial Norma, 1992). English translation mine.

(15) And not just East Europeans, Latin Americans, e.g., have no great desire to be tempted by a return to patrimonialism. See Barry B. Levine (ed.), El desafío neoliberal: El fin del tercermundismo en América Latina (Ibid.).

18

Cultural Legacies and Development: A View from East Asia

Robert P. Weller

The chapters in this book remind us that history never writes on a blank slate, even in revolutions as sudden and radical as East Europe saw in 1989. If sweeping away the old political systems opened a new world of opportunity, it also revealed the real depth of the economic, social and cultural legacies of earlier ways of life. The problems of the present transformations have thus begun to encourage an overarching pessimism where a naive euphoria once reigned. While the negative legacies of socialism have been clear all along, these articles bring even the apparently positive legacies into question, showing how closely even the resistance that finally brought down the regimes tied to the socialist system itself.

The entire picture seems very far indeed from the booming economies of capitalist East Asia. The four Little Dragons (Hong Kong, Singapore, South Korea, and Taiwan) already stand with the developed countries in many ways, having blossomed from poverty and destruction after World War II. Others, like Thailand and Indonesia, got off to a later start, but have apparently set off on the same road. Yet in spite of the obvious differences, East Asia after World War II shared with East Europe today an inheritance widely thought to constitute an enormous obstacle to development—a history of authoritarian rule, the economic deformations of living under colonial domination, and a culture judged inimical to capitalism. The Asian experience of the last few decades may yield few direct models for East Europe, but it does suggest some new ways of thinking about culture and economic transformation. At the very least, these cases show how "negative" legacies may have unexpected positive consequences, just as "positive" legacies may have negative ones.

A Legacy of Ironies

Communism claimed to have overcome the Marxist dialectic of contradiction and transformation that had shaped all earlier societies, bringing a kind of nirvana after millennia of miserable reincarnation. In reality, of course, it had created the seeds of its own destruction all along, as the sudden collapse of 1989 made clear. Yet as the articles collected here show, those seeds will not simply grow into a new system. Thriving in the gaps left by central planning and Party control, these areas of resistance were also thoroughly tied to the old structure. The end of the old systems revealed these internal dynamics in ways that their continuation never could. The results are especially important for our understanding of the People's Republic of China, which may in turn help to clarify features of the system elsewhere. Before turning back to capitalist East Asia, let me begin with those ironies typical of much real socialism—both the uncontrolled areas spawned at the edges of the totalitarian project and the limits on resistance stemming from its roots in the entire system.

All real socialisms have fostered second economies on some scale, and China followed (and has now far surpassed) Hungary in going very far down that road. While such arrangements incubate bits of capitalism, they are also thoroughly adapted to the margins of socialism, with serious implications for how people will behave during the transition to a new economic system. If the second economy suggested the sprouts of capitalism under the very nose of communism, Gábor's paper also ties it to bribery, the erosion of business morality, and new calls for protectionism. Sik similarly ties it to the "vulture" behavior of Hungarian taxi drivers in 1990. What initially appears as a positive legacy thus also creates serious problems for the long-term development of a market system. China has now taken this process much farther than any other country—less than half the economy is now under state control—but the Hungarian case injects a note of caution about easy and natural transitions to a truly capitalist economy.

Independent labor unions similarly appear to play an important role in reshaping socialism and eventually undermining it. China has clearly been at pains to stamp out the buds of such organizations that formed during the ill-fated demonstrations that ended on 4 June 1989. Yet they too are a mixed blessing at best during the transition, as both Osiatynski and Bruszt show. Countries with a history of strong unions find crucial managerial reforms like the ability to fire workers blocked. In China, too, attempts at comparable industrial reform in the state sector are being impeded by workers unwilling to lose their socialist rights.

Much the same holds true for the beginnings of civil society. Surviving at the margins of state power, and often resisting that power, the germ of change had existed for a long time. Antipathy to totalizing control went far beyond the dissident democratic organizations themselves, stemming from the quality of life itself. Yet even this legacy has a problematic realization. As Gross points out, knowing how to resist successfully is far different from knowing how to govern legally, democratically and well. The same ironic results recur across East Europe: a dedication to very open democracy stands alongside a tendency toward étatism and absolute values. This shows up in many of the core groups who promoted the transition—small entrepreneurs demanding protectionism (Gábor), the Church looking to impose its values (Król), and attitudes toward the natural authority and commanding role of intellectuals (Bernik, Kovács, and Schöpflin). China's June 4th leaders developed exactly the same dynamic. Student leaders in Tiananmen Square set themselves off as a miniature state apparatus, requiring personal connections for access to their little bureaucracy, creating a standing committee and a propaganda department, and surrounding their space with guards (Lubman 1989). They welcomed workers as supports, but not as leaders (Perry 1991). The exile dissident movement continues to show the same elitist tendencies (Chan and Kwong 1990: 560).

Even language itself has undergone the same process, as Schöpflin points out. The official insistence on the science of Marxism and the objectivity of its facts, along with the powerful control over alternative voices, led to a flowering of ambiguity, irony and other skills for avoiding control. Thus the system created too much meaning in a sense; something extra always seemed to lurk between the lines. Yet in another sense, there was too little meaning, as ambiguity and empty abstraction stood in the way of practical communication. The very abilities that undermined official control of meaning create new difficulties now that the old opponent has departed.

Not all of these phenomena are unique to post-socialist states. Authoritarian control elsewhere has often produced similar mechanisms of resistance, and the problems of language do not differ in kind from the post-structuralist critique of modernism in the West. Nevertheless, the particular combinations in East Europe (indeed in each country of the region) are unique, as is the post-socialist transformation itself. These papers contain both a promise and a warning for China. On the one hand, they clarify the inherent fault lines of socialist systems, and imply that Tiananmen Square in 1989 was only a first step, not a final chapter. They also suggest that if and when China begins its post-socialist transition, the current trend of production away from the state sector will ease the enormous privatization problems that face East Europe. On the other hand, however, they also dash the naive hope that even a strong dissident movement will make an easy transition to democracy, and that even a widespread private sector will guarantee the success of a full-fledged market system.

The East Asian Dragons went through a very different history to get where they are today. In spite of some similarities, colonial economies are not socialist. Just as crucially, East Asia is making a democratic transition only now, gradually, after many years of economic development. In East Europe, both the economic and political transitions must occur together in a tangibly more difficult process. Yet both regions inherited a set of apparently negative institutions and attitudes. The East Asians used theirs to turn social theory on its head, developing through the very means the experts said would block their success. While much in the general tone of these papers collected here warns of the negative consequences of the apparently positive legacy, East Asia reminds us that the apparently negative legacy can have very positive consequences, and suggests areas that might prove comparable in East Europe.

The Negative Turns Positive

All four of the Little Dragons had long colonial histories—primarily British for Hong Kong and Singapore, and primarily Japanese for Taiwan and Korea. It goes without saying that such experience limited political possibilities; Hong Kong held its first ever direct legislative election only in September 1991. Yet especially in Korea and Taiwan, the long occupation also had a decidedly mixed economic effect. In both cases, record-keeping was rationalized, education modernized and improved, and a new infrastructure built (only to be bombed out again during World War II). On the other hand, access to higher education was strictly limited, managerial responsibility lay almost entirely in Japanese hands, and the economy itself was dislocated into particular niches to benefit the homeland.

None of the regimes entered the 1950s with truly democratic states. If Britain was a benign overlord in Hong Kong, authoritarian control remained the rule elsewhere until the 1980s, with Taiwan changing fastest and Singapore slowest. Still worse, analysts in the 1950s saw little reason for confidence in these regimes. The Nationalist Party in Taiwan had the longest history of misrule, having established a reputation for corruption and incompetence on the Chinese mainland.

Much of the early pessimism about these economies looked at their loosely Confucian cultural roots. The personalism of Confucian morality was thought to encourage corruption and discourage the "rational" business ties needed for a modern economy. Coming from quite different roots, this nevertheless echoes the socialist legacy of relying on personal ties and back doors to accomplish everything. Absolute loyalty to the family allegedly created still more particularistic blocks in the way of East Asian modernity (e.g., Levy 1949: 354–9). The overbearing respect for authority generally would stifle individual initiative, creativity, and thus entrepreneurship in East Asia. The argument echoed claims that socialist bureaucracies snuffed the life out of individual incentive in another negative legacy of East Europe. In addition, China's "enchanted" religion, which failed to place humanity at fundamental odds with the world, would never provide the kind of Weberian motor for rationalization that Protestantism did in Europe (Bellah 1965). Even uses of language in East Asian cultures recall the developments under socialism. The importance of face in all social interactions, for example, led to both a personalization of meaning and a level of hidden meaning behind a ritualized politeness. Ambiguity thus became an art in East Europe for political reasons, and in East Asia for social reasons. In the eyes of many Western analysts (and consumers), this fatal combination appeared to damn East Asia to a future of impoverished piecework, making cheap tableware, plastic toys, and flimsy clothing.

The evidence against such a view is now so strong as not to bear repeating. The stunning success of these economies, while much of the rest of the developing world floundered, had many causes. Among other things, it has led to a full rethinking of that apparently negative legacy. Many authors, for example, now see great benefits in traditional Asian family morality. The family structure encouraged strategies of economic diversification and pooled resources. At the same time, traditional family values of filial piety, cooperation and long-term security fostered petty entrepreneurs by encouraging hard work, valuing independence from others, and cushioning the risks of private enterprise (Greenhalgh 1989, Harrell 1985, Hsieh 1989, Wong 1988). Webs of particularistic ties have also clearly remained important to large firm managers and owners (Numazaki 1991), and personalistic, paternalistic management styles prevail (Redding 1990:143-181). "Traditional" ties also form the basis for the informal credit networks that have invigorated small entrepreneurs in these economies.

Others have suggested that, in contrast to the older Weberian view, popular religion has in fact supported values appropriate to capitalist development. While some aspects of religion clearly tied to the imperial state structure, others seemed to encourage utilitarianism and to strengthen the informal social networks critical for raising credit and dealing with related enterprises in a market system (Gallin and Gallin 1982: 236–237, Li 1988, Yu 1987). Uses of paper spirit money in Chinese societies, for example, foreshadowed capitalist economic relations (Gates 1987), while the deities in general reinforced the idea of an imperial bureaucracy. Similarly, ghost worship emphasized an individualistic theme, while gods stressed community solidarity (Weller in press).

The clearly positive role of traditional attitudes and institutions has overthrown the initial judgment of modernization theorists that the old baggage was so much ballast that had to be jettisoned before the economy could take off. Good policy and the timing of their entry into the world system, of course, also played critical roles in the success of these countries. Yet clearly they also succeeded because they made positive use of supposedly negative cultural resources instead of throwing them away. East Asia is forcing changes in modernization theory, and not the other way around.

The roots of East Asian entrepreneurial success in family dynamics and interpersonal relations suggest areas where the apparently negative legacy of socialism may not be so bad. The thick networks of reciprocity ties, which characterize both East Asia and real socialism, can easily breed corruption; they certainly fit no Weberian ideal type of rational business behavior. In a half-reformed economy, these ties can let corruption blossom on an impressive scale, as both China and Russia now show. Yet they also clearly have the potential to form the base for long-term capitalist development, as they did in non-socialist East Asia. Family structures similarly deserve close attention, especially as the short-term crises of the transition give way to the long-term project of developing a dynamic economy.

Taking Opportunities

East Europe today faces a task more daunting than East Asia in the 1950s; it must build new political and economic systems, simultaneously, from the bottom up. The short-term problems exert a tremendous pressure, but one way or another, the transition will be completed. Privatization of the nationalized behemoth still stands as the most formidable obstacle, even after several years of pushing against it. Neither Ukrainian gradualism nor Polish shock therapy have yet fully solved the problem. Yet as Stark's essay shows, there is no lack of creative solutions. All will be difficult in the near term, and some are engendering strong reactions, but the problems will eventually be resolved.

East Asia has little to contribute to these most pressing problems of post-socialism, but the region does speak more clearly to the long term. After all, privatizing industry and setting up democratic institutions only create the possibility for capitalist growth; they do not guarantee it. In the long run, a successful economy will require an educated, disciplined and productive work force and a strong entrepreneurial spirit to take advantage of new opportunities. These are exactly the areas where the "negative" legacies of East Asian cultures have contributed most to their growth. The resources available in East Europe are quite different, but not necessarily less fertile. The challenge is to bring them to life effectively. Indeed, some evidence suggests that just these petty entrepreneurial areas are growing rapidly in much of East Europe, and that this smallest economic level is much healthier than national-level statistics imply.

East Asia also confirms what some of the papers here imply: at least in the short run, justice may not be served. In Taiwan, for example, the land reform program bought off large landlords with shares of government monopolies. Many landlords played this into enormous profits and business success, leaving their ex-tenants still at the bottom of the heap. Neither the perceived legitimacy of the state nor of the market was critical in East Asian development. In fact, evidence from around the world shows that capitalist markets regularly appear illegitimate, standing opposed to traditional values. Legitimacy and a questioning of the languages of legitimation stand as core problems of modernity. Small wonder that signs of reaction are evident in many of the former socialist countries, from the murderous ethnic nationalisms ranging from ex-Yugoslavia to ex-Soviet Central Asia, to the September 1993 electoral success of former Communist leaders in Poland. Yet in the end, in spite of initial inequalities, the fact of economic success for the mass of population in East Asia created a fundamental acceptance of the market system even as it promoted political democratization.

Bibliography

Bellah, Robert N. 1965. "Epilogue: Religion and Progress in Modern Asia." In *Religion and Progress in Modern Asia,* ed. Robert N. Bellah, 168–229. New York: Free Press.

Chan, Yuen Ying, and Peter Kwong. 1990. "Trashing the Hopes of Tiananmen." *The Nation,* 23 April: 545, 560–64.

Gallin, Bernard, and Rita Gallin. 1982. "Socioeconomic Life in Rural Taiwan: Twenty Years of Development and Change." *Modern China* 8: 205–46.

Gates, Hill. 1987. "Money for the Gods." *Modern China* 13: 259–77.

Greenhalgh, Susan. 1989. "Social Causes and Consequences of Taiwan's Postwar Economic Development." In *Anthropological Studies of the Taiwan Area: Accomplishments and Prospects,* ed. Kwang-chih Chang, Kuang-chou Li, Arthur P. Wolf, and Alexander Chien-chung Yin, 351–90. Taipei: National Taiwan University.

Harrell, Stevan. 1985. "Why Do the Chinese Work So Hard?" *Modern China* 11(2): 203–26.

Hsieh Jih-chang. 1989. "The Chinese Family Under the Impact of Modernization." In *Anthropological Studies of the Taiwan Area: Accomplishments and Prospects,* ed. Kwang-chih Chang, Kuang-chou Li, Arthur P. Wolf, and Alexander Chien-chung Yin, 273–84. Taipei: National Taiwan University.

Levy, Marion J., Jr. 1949. *The Family Revolution in Modern China.* Cambridge, MA: Harvard University Press.

Li Yih-yuan. 1988. "Taiwan Minjian Zongjiao de Xiandai Qushi: Dui Peter Berger

Jiaoshou Dongya Fazhan Wenhua Yinsu Lun de Huiying [The Modern Tendencies of Taiwan's Popular Religion: A Response to Professor Peter Berger's Theory of Cultural Factors in East Asian Development]." Unpublished Paper. Photocopy.

Lubman, Sarah. 1989. "The Myth of Tiananmen Square: The Students Talked Democracy But They Didn't Practice It." *Washington Post,* 30 July: C5.

Numazaki, Ichiro. 1991. "The Role of Personal Networks in the Making of Taiwan's guanxiqiye (`related Enterprises')." In *Business Networks and Economic Development in East and Southeast Asia,* ed. Gary G. Hamilton. Hong Kong: Centre of Asian Studies, University of Hong Kong.

Perry, Elizabeth J. 1991. "Intellectuals and Tiananmen: Historical Perspective on an Abortive Revolution." In *The Crisis of Leninism and the Decline of the Left: The Revolutions of 1989,* ed. Daniel Chirot: 129–46. Seattle: University of Washington.

Redding, S. Gordon. 1990. *The Spirit of Chinese Capitalism.* Berlin: Walter de Gruyter.

Weller, Robert P. In press. "Capitalism, Community, and the Rise of Amoral Cults in Taiwan." In *Asian Visions of Authority,* ed. Helen Hardacre, Laurel Kendall and Charles Keyes. Honolulu: University of Hawaii Press.

Wong, Siu-lun. 1988. "The Applicability of Asian Family Values to Other Sociocultural Settings." In *In Search of an East Asian Development Model,* ed. Peter L. Berger and Michael Hsin-Huang Hsiao. New Brunswick, NJ: Transaction.

Yu Yingshi. 1987. *Zhongguo Jinshi Zongjiao Lunli Yu Shangren Jingshen* [Modern Chinese Religious Ethics and Business Spirit]. Taipei: Lunjing.

Name Index

Subject Index